DYSLEXIA:
THEORY AND RESEARCH

DYSLEXIA:
THEORY AND RESEARCH

Frank R. Vellutino

The MIT Press
Cambridge, Massachusetts, and
London, England

This book was set in IBM Composer Baskerville by To the Lighthouse Press,
and printed and bound by The Alpine Press, Inc., in the United States of
America.

Library of Congress Cataloging in Publication Data

Vellutino, Frank R.
  Dyslexia.

  Bibliography: p.
  Includes index.
  1. Dyslexia. I. Title. [DNLM: 1. Dyslexia. WM475.3 V442d]
RC394.W6V44   616.8'553   79-14996
ISBN 0-262-22021-0

To my loved ones

CONTENTS

CONTENTS

PREFACE

A little over ten years ago, I became intrigued by accounts in the media of children with reading problems who supposedly perceive and write letters and words as their mirror images. This strange disorder—termed dyslexia—was said to be the result of neurological dysfunction uniquely affecting the perception of linguistic symbols. I have always been interested in perceptual phenomena and have for some time been fascinated by the ability of the human brain to generate analogues or facsimiles of physical events, as in the case of dreams, hallucinations, and perceptual illusions (for example, apparent motion). But the idea that deficient readers literally perceive letters in reverse seemed to me to be far-fetched, particularly since the dysfunction was said to occur in otherwise normal children and only when they are confronted with letters and words in print.

However, because I was involved in other pursuits at the time, I gave no more thought to the matter except to make note of the claim that a number of prominent people, such as Albert Einstein, Nelson Rockefeller, and Lee Harvey Oswald, suffered from dyslexia in early childhood. Disorders that afflict the famous and infamous are somehow accorded a degree of status and notoriety that inevitably breeds folklore and misconception, and my natural disdain of this fact made me even more skeptical of the existence of dyslexia as it was characterized in the media. It was therefore ironic that a university post I later accepted involved me in more formal study of developmental disorders in young children, as a result of which my interest in the problem was renewed.

My initial exposure to the literature concerned with dyslexia was disappointing. That is, a good deal of the evidence offered in support of the perceptual deficiencies ascribed to poor readers was clinical and anecdotal, and most of the laboratory studies available were found to be wanting from both a conceptual and methodological standpoint. And since the writings of even the most prominent theorists were no more enlightening to me than descriptions provided by the popular media, I decided to do the unorthodox thing and began tutoring some children with severe reading problems. My experience in this enterprise was invaluable, and the knowledge I acquired about the problems children encounter in learning to read led me to believe that even the most severely impaired readers do not suffer the visual anomalies attributed to them by perceptual deficit theorists. It also prompted an in-depth survey of the literature addressing the study of reading disability in young children, which involved a historical tracing of papers written on the topic from before the turn of the century up to the present. This effort brought me into contact with several other conceptualizations of dyslexia, certain ones emerging as plausible alternatives to the perceptual deficit theories available. One of these conceptualizations suggests that some poor readers may have difficulty integrating information coming into the various sensory systems. Another suggests that reading disability may be caused by dysfunction in processing serial information. The third is more generic and suggests that difficulties in learning to read may be occasioned by deficiencies or malfunction in one or more aspects of language. A closely related possibility is that some readers may be subject to a more circumscribed impairment in associating visual and verbal information.

My experience in working with deficient readers, the information gleaned from theoretical and research accounts, and some degree of intuition led me to doubt the logic behind the first two possibilities mentioned and seriously consider the latter two. I was especially impressed by the fact that so many of the children with whom I worked appeared to have difficulties not only in the decoding of printed words but also in word retrieval and expressive language in general, suggesting the possibility of specific language disorder as a basic factor contributing to dysfunction in learning to read. I was therefore prompted to design and conduct a series of studies evaluating these alternatives, and focused primarily upon contrasts of perceptual, intersensory, and verbal processing deficit explanations of dyslexia. This work has been

discussed in a number of published research papers, as a result
of which I was invited to summarize my findings and perspective
for publication.

Because recent findings in the study of dyslexia have generated
a number of controversial issues as well as a geometrically expanding number of studies concerned with these issues, what was
originally intended as a research monograph dealing primarily with
my own work turned out to be a full-length book critically analyzing traditional and contemporary theories of reading disability,
and relevant research evaluating those theories. Given its scope and
in-depth treatment of the topic from a historical, theoretical,
and methodological standpoint, this volume should be especially
useful for those conducting both basic and applied research in the
study of the reading process and children's reading problems, as
well as to those concerned with development in related areas such
as child language, language disorder, perception, memory, and
other cognitive functions. It should also be of interest to academi-
cians, students, and professionals (reading specialists, special educators, psychologists, speech and language therapists, physicans)
concerned primarily with applied problems, specifically those who
must necessarily be critical in the application of given points of
view to the assessment and treatment of reading difficulties.

Following a brief introduction, the book is divided into *three*
major sections. The first section is concerned with the definition
of dyslexia for research purposes and discusses the methodological
problems attendant upon the selection of a research population.
It also outlines the various theories of dyslexia that have appeared
in the literature over the past eighty-five years. The second section
constitutes the main body of the text and presents a detailed
review and critique of laboratory studies that have attempted to
validate the most prominent and influential theories. The third
and final section is essentially a general summary and integration
of points made throughout the text, with concluding remarks
highlighting the salient issues discussed in the main body. Concrete suggestions are made for future research, and general guidelines for remedial instruction are somewhat cautiously outlined.
The reader should be apprised that this chapter is sufficiently comprehensive to serve as an overview of the topics treated in greater
detail in the text proper; it may be useful to read this section
first.

ACKNOWLEDGMENTS

I wish to express my sincere gratitude and appreciation to a number of individuals who made significant contributions to much of the research discussed in this book and to those who assisted greatly in the preparation of the manuscript itself. First, I would like to thank Joseph Steger, my friend and colleague, who not only helped shape the conceptualizations and designs of several of the studies issuing from our laboratory but who also taught me how to do research. Second, I am extremely grateful to Esther Senning for her creative and untiring effort in helping me initiate a research program, in assisting in the construction and validation of many of the measures employed in our studies, and in coordinating data collection for the first five years of our program. Thanks in abundance is also due Rosemary Linsider and Donna Scanlon, who at different periods carried out their responsibilities with the same tradition of excellence established by Mrs. Senning; and to Sylvia Durban, Virginia Russum, and the many students who assisted in data collection and analysis. I would in addition like to acknowledge the cooperation of the public and parochial schools in Albany, Schenectady, Troy, and surrounding areas and express my appreciation to the principals and teachers at these schools for allowing us to employ their children as subjects for our studies.

With respect to the preparation of the manuscript itself, words cannot express the depth of my gratitude to my good friends and coworkers Melinda Tanzman, Veronica Carney, Melinda Taylor, and Florence Yanko for their tireless efforts in making this book a reality—Melinda Tanzman for reviewing and critiquing virtually every draft and revision of the manuscript and the others for their

assistance in typing and editing these revisions. I would also like
to thank Mary-Louise Kean of the University of California, Irvine,
for critically reviewing an early draft of the manuscript as well as
Grace Yeni-Komshian of the University of Maryland and Mary
Huba of Iowa State University for their constructive comments
on specific chapters.

Special recognition should be accorded the staff at the Schaffer
Library of Health Services of the Albany Medical College for their
excellent service in procuring needed references and for providing
me with a quiet place to work. I would also like to acknowledge
that the conduct of certain of the studies discussed in this text and
the preparation of the manuscript was supported in part by research and demonstration grants received from the National Institute of Child Health and Human Development (Grant No.
1R01HD0965901) and the Bureau of the Educationally Handicapped of the U.S. Office of Education (Grant No. G007604369).

Finally, I wish to extend my thanks to the following authors
and publishers for granting their permission to reproduce specific
figures: John L. Arnett; Lillian Belmont and the American Ortho-
psychiatric Association, Inc.; Robert C. Calfee and Lawrence
Erlbaum Associates; Paul A. Kolers, Mildred Mason, and the
American Psychological Association; Frederick J. Morrison and
The American Association for the Advancement of Science; Peggy
Pope Snyder, David Wechsler, and Perceptual and Motor Skills;
Gordon V. Stanley and The Society for Research in Child Develop-
ment, Inc.; The Canadian Psychological Association, Cortex,
The Journal Press, and Pergamon Press, Ltd.

DYSLEXIA:
THEORY AND RESEARCH

Chapter One INTRODUCTION

No disorder of childhood has generated more interest or prompted more controversy than severe and pervasive reading disorder in otherwise normal children, commonly referred to as developmental dyslexia or specific reading disability.[1] Indeed, in addition to concerned parents and other members of the lay public, reading disability has attracted the attention of researchers and practitioners alike, and much of the interest is due to the pioneering clinical studies of Samuel Torry Orton (1925, 1937). Orton, whose ideas are still influential, has imbued dyslexia with a certain exotic quality, manifested most prominently in the popular belief that children so afflicted literally perceive letters backward and frequently reverse them in their printing and writing, for instance, calling *b, d* or *was, saw.* Such inaccuracies, typically viewed as curious manifestations of brain malfunction, were said to be the result of spatial confusion caused by a maturational delay in hemispheric dominance for language. Letter reversals, in fact, occupied a central role in Orton's conceptualization of reading disability and have long been offered as the primary support for this and other perceptual deficit explanations.

Orton's theory of dyslexia is prototypical in that it exemplifies the basic process models that have been postulated in the literature concerned with the etiology of reading disability. The majority of those theories hold that the difficulty arises because of dysfunction in visual perception, presumably associated with neurological disorder. Maturation and lateral dominance problems are commonly inferred in such instances, although some accounts make reference to structural or functional deficits associated with brain lesions, genetic predispositions, and various other types of neuropathology.

Not all basic process theories indict the visual system, however. Three that have achieved prominence in recent years earmark inferred dysfunction in integrating information from the sensory systems, in remembering things in their correct order, and in processing verbal information. The intersensory deficit theory has gained in popularity since Birch's (1962) initial treatment of the subject; it is now second only to visual deficit explanations. And although practitioners have for some time assumed that poor readers may support a select deficiency in serial order recall, only in recent years have attempts been made to formalize this point of view (Bakker 1972) or to explore its parameters in laboratory study.

Theories that implicate dysfunction in verbal processing as a basic cause of reading disability have had less currency over the years. This is somewhat paradoxical, considering that reading, by definition, entails the coding of one's natural language and would therefore seem to require intact linguistic ability. Of late, however, a number of investigators have become adamant in their insistence that reading is primarily a linguistic skill (cf. Kavanagh and Mattingly 1972), a claim that in my opinion has considerable validity. This view has led to more active exploration of the possibility that specific reading disability is caused by deficiencies in one or more aspects of linguistic functioning, but studies investigating this possibility have appeared only within the past decade. Thus, research in this area is of a seminal nature.

Recognizing the likelihood that dysfunction in a process as complex as reading is caused by a variety of factors, several investigators have proposed that more than one type of basic process disorder may lie at the root of a reading disability (Birch 1962; Myklebust and Johnson 1962). Typical suggestions have included deficits in all the major subsystems involved in reading, but dysfunction in either the visual or the auditory modality has been implicated most often. This point of view issues largely from clinical observation and has not yet been well documented in laboratory study.

Although competent researchers have recently become more actively invested in the study of dyslexia in young children, most descriptions of the disorder are based either upon clinical studies and informal observations or upon loosely designed experimental contrasts that have typically yielded equivocal and conflicting results. Furthermore, most existing accounts have not meticulously defined the behavioral correlates of the basic process deficits advanced in explanation of dyslexia, nor has there been any comprehensive or systematic attempt to critically analyze research findings and the theories from which they emanate. Such analysis is necessary, not only to evaluate and integrate results in the literature but, more important, to facilitate the framing of coherent, better defined, and more plausible theories of reading disability than most currently available and to develop more effective educational programs for correction and prevention of the problem.

Accordingly, this volume constitutes a detailed review and critical evaluation of the major conceptualizations of the etiology of dyslexia that have appeared in the literature. It focuses primarily on the ones already mentioned, because they have either been the most influential of those available or are currently becoming more prominent. The primary purpose is to examine the theoretical foundations of these conceptualizations, closely scrutinizing their logical consistency, their empirical validity, their ability to account for and integrate conflicting results, and their overall productivity. A special effort is made to discuss the methodology and conclusions drawn from the studies reviewed, as well as to analyze and detail their conceptual bases.

Because descriptions and definitions of the behavioral components of given process disorders described in the literature have not always been clear-cut, primary emphasis is placed upon the immediate, or psychological, correlates of specific reading disability rather than on ultimate, or neurological, correlates. In all instances, the analyses and critiques of particular findings and theoretical positions rely exclusively upon contrasts of overt and measurable behaviors; inferences about underlying etiologies, such as brain dysfunction, genetic predispositions, and so on are minimized.

The reader should be forewarned, however, that the discussion of respective theories of dyslexia and of empirical findings extending from those theories is not without bias. That is, I have for some time been skeptical of traditional conceptualizations of reading disability, in particular, of the predominant view that the disorder is caused by deficiencies in visual perception. Indeed, much of my own research has directly evaluated this hypothesis, and I have come to the conclusion that most visual deficit theories of reading disability qualify as little more than pseudoproblems and might better be discarded. I have also found reason to doubt the intersensory and serial deficit theories. In these instances my concern has issued from theoretical, methodological, and interpretive contraindications and, in the case of the serial deficit theories, from lack of definition as well.

On the other hand, my own laboratory studies and practical experience, the research of independent investigators studying normal and abnormal reading and language abilities, and some degree of intuition strongly suggest that a most promising but relatively unexplored avenue for additional study inheres in the possibility that specific reading disability is caused either by dysfunction in verbal processing or by a specific deficit in visual-verbal integration. I am inclined to agree with those who contend that reading is primarily a language-based skill, as illustrated in the fact that three of the five types of featural information contained in a printed word (graphic, orthographic, semantic, syntactic, and phonological) correspond with the major components of language. Thus the ability to learn to read would appear to be especially vulnerable to deficiencies in one or more of these linguistinc functions, though perhaps not in equal measure.

The ideas presented here are thoroughly discussed in the pages that follow. Particular emphasis is placed on the alternative conceptualizations of dyslexia, with systematic review and evaluation of the evidence for each. Inasmuch as my colleagues and I have been actively involved in research on various aspects of the theories to be discussed, I will generously refer to results of several of our own studies, integrating our findings with the results of others when indicated.

Part One   **DEFINITION OF
                            THE PROBLEM**

Chapter Two

Dyslexia is a generic term typically used to refer to children who are severely impaired in reading. It is also known as *specific reading disability,* the two terms being used interchangeably. Many investigators believe that dyslexia is a developmental disorder associated with some form of neurological dysfunction, but it is *not* a well-defined entity and is not clearly identified with any specific neurological abnormalities. Indeed, reading problems in any given child can be caused by a number of interacting contingencies, including such extrinsic factors as environmental experiences, lack of attendance at school, poor motivation, and deficiencies in organismic variables that are prerequisite to learning in general, for example, sensory and intellectual functions.

Some children have difficulty in learning to read in spite of adequate environmental circumstances and normal development in other relevant areas. Such children theoretically sustain specific deficiencies in one or more of the basic processes that support the development of skill in reading. In order to investigate the nature and extensions of such deficiencies, or indeed their very existence, specific reading disability must tentatively be defined by holding constant the multitude of extrinsic factors that could lead to reading failure. It therefore follows that the study of this disorder is best undertaken in children who have average or above average intelligence, intact (or corrected) sensory acuity, no severe neurological damage or other debilitating physical disabilities, and who have not been hampered by serious emotional or social problems, socioeconomic disadvantage, or inadequate opportunity for learning.

Defining a research population in accord with these criteria does not rule out the possibility that children who are initially excluded from laboratory study of dyslexia can nevertheless support a specific developmental deficit that by itself could lead to reading difficulty. Children with low intelligence and those who are emotionally disturbed or socioeconomically disadvantaged may be deficient in many of the same functions that result in reading disability in children who are otherwise normal. However, the extreme difficulty of determining the basic or primary cause of reading problems in such children is particularly troublesome when the major research objective is to determine the etiology of reading difficulties associated with more circumscribed deficits. Given such research purposes, it would seem that employing exclusionary criteria for initial sample selection is justifiable.

An implicit assumption is that children identified by the criteria listed are most likely to sustain reading disorders because of factors intrinsically related to the reading process itself, rather than to factors that may be necessary but not sufficient conditions for learning to read. Yet reading problems caused by extrinsic factors are not easily distinguished from reading problems caused by deficiencies that uniquely affect the acquisition of this skill. For example, any poor reader may be observed to have extreme difficulty in identifying or analyzing printed words, in abstracting and generalizing their common constituents *(cat, rat, can→ran)*, and in correctly orienting and sequencing their component letters. In addition, all poor readers are poor spellers. However, not every child who spells inadequately should be classified as dyslexic.

Many of the reading errors said to occur only in dyslexics can be observed in normal readers at early stages of learning to read. For example, *letter reversals (b/d, p/q)* and *directional sequencing* errors *(was/saw)* in oral reading and written language have long been thought to be particularly significant indicators of specific or primary reading disability (Orton 1925, 1937; Hermann 1959), but there is no convincing evidence that these anomalies signify any qualitative difference between poor and normal readers.

Before discussing the hypothesized causes of dyslexia that will constitute the primary focus of this book, it seems useful to elaborate on the definitional problems associated with the study of this complex problem in order to address certain issues that appear to be sources of confusion, in both laboratory research and clinical practice.

First, it is important to reiterate that in research as well as in clinical work, attempts to "define" dyslexia have most often employed exclusionary criteria in order to rule out secondary factors that could result in deficient reading ability. This procedure carries with it all the weaknesses inherent in definitions by exclusion, the most obvious being the absence of any clear-cut differentiating criteria with respect to critical reading behaviors and related skills. Although the use of exclusionary criteria circumscribes a more narrowly defined group of poor readers whose reading problems are not ostensibly associated with extrinsic factors, we as yet have little to guide us in recognizing a positive instance of dyslexia. Therefore, identifying the disorder becomes a probabilistic venture, success in no small measure depending upon (1) the productivity of available theories of basic process dysfunction and (2) the validity of the instruments employed to assess the constructs that those theories generate. Indeed, given our current understanding of the problem, it must be acknowledged that dyslexia as a qualitatively distinguishable disorder is itself a construct whose validity is yet to be determined (Monroe 1932; Robinson 1946; Malmquist 1960; International Reading Association 1972).

A second factor bearing upon the problems associated with defining specific reading disability is the degree of stringency that may characterize the operational definition of the exclusionary criteria employed in any given study. There is some degree of consensus in the literature as to the general categories of exclusion, yet a review of studies employing these categories in sample selection will make it apparent that operational criteria are nowhere near uniform. Furthermore, those inclined to conceptualize reading disability broadly often include under this rubric reading problems resulting from a confusing admixture of both primary and secondary factors. As Benton has observed in his most recent review (1975), the literature is marked by the failure on the part of many investigators to distinguish specific reading disability from reading difficulties that are due to extrinsic causes.

As any researcher who has attempted to study developmental reading disorder would verify, the problem of operationalizing selection criteria is formidable. This is not only because of the measurement and logistical problems that are inevitably involved in conducting careful research but, more important, because the exclusionary categories themselves are not always well defined, particularly with regard to their relation to reading disability.

2.1 CATEGORIES OF EXCLUSION

2.1.1 Intelligence

There seems to be widespread agreement that children with sub-normal intelligence are best excluded from initial study of the etiology of dyslexia, given the difficulty of determining the respective contributions of general conceptual deficiency and specific developmental disorders. Yet there is not widespread agreement on how one operationally defines intelligence for purposes of excluding such ability as a source of reading difficulty. Perhaps the most prevalent reason for employing given measures of intelligence is expediency. We need not dwell on the problems associated with this rationale (traditional issues of reliability and validity notwithstanding); it becomes indefensible when one considers that given tests of intelligence have no absolute validity as measures of a well-defined construct; they have only empirical validity in their demonstrated relation to a variety of measures, including reading skill. Therefore, in selecting prospective dyslexics, the investigator's measure of intellectual ability is not an arbitrary choice but depends upon his conceptualizations of both intelligence and reading disability.

Concretely, if one's theory of dyslexia is that children so afflicted are characterized by basic deficiency in visual-spatial processing, it might be counterproductive to employ, for selection purposes, an intelligence test that is highly saturated with items requiring spatial reasoning and visualization. The reverse would hold for linguistically oriented theories. And in the case of those conceptualizations emphasizing both verbal and nonverbal factors as possible sources of reading difficulty (Johnson and Myklebust 1967; Ingram, Mason, and Blackburn 1970; Boder 1970, 1971; Mattis, French, and Rapin 1975), the difficulty would be compounded by the expeditious choice of a measure of intelligence that is not balanced with respect to its assessment of verbal and nonverbal functions.

That commonly employed tests of intelligence may yield differential results for poor and normal readers receives some support from a large number of studies relating reading achievement to performance on subtests of the Wechsler Intelligence Scale for Children (WISC) (Wechsler 1949). For example, Huelsman (1970) reviewed twenty of these studies and found that in approximately 60 percent of them poor readers performed better on the WISC Performance subtests than they did on the Verbal sub- tests. Another characteristic of these studies was a high incidence, among poor readers, of low performance on the Information, Arithmetic, Vocabulary, and Coding subtests. Lyle and Goyen (1969) also found this pattern and argued that the results could not be due only to performance in school work, since the mag- nitude of the differences between poor and normal readers on these tests did not increase with age—that is, as a cumulative result of a long history of school failure owing to reading disability. However, Huelsman (1970) found that although the subtest pat- terns in question discriminated groups of poor and normal readers, they were not always characteristic of individuals.

Vernon (1971), in reviewing a number of studies demonstrating the low Verbal–high Performance IQ discrepancy, concluded that "there is only a partial dichotomy between Verbal and Perfor- mance test ability, which can hardly be applied effectively to the abilities of large samples of backward readers" (p. 90). She also cited two other studies (Ingram and Reid 1956; Kinsbourne and Warrington 1963) demonstrating higher Verbal IQs than Per- formance IQs in some poor readers and the reverse pattern in others. In later investigations employing much larger samples than in either of these two studies poor readers were higher on the Per- formance than on the Verbal scale and comparable to the normals on the former (Belmont and Birch 1966; Warrington 1967). And in nine studies conducted in our own laboratory from 1972 to 1975, poor readers were found to be substantially below normal readers on Verbal IQ but not significantly different from the normals on the Performance IQ.

The results of these studies are conflicting and therefore incon- clusive. Yet the data are consistent with the possibility that given measures of intelligence may differentially assess specific abilities in deficient readers. They therefore underscore the importance of selecting an appropriate measure of intellectual ability for identi- fying a research sample: a measure that does not attenuate the chances of mounting a fair test of a given hypothesis by screening out the population of interest. Unfortunately, the results of a sizable number of studies in the literature are questionable because the investigators designing those studies ignored such dictates.

It would of course be highly desirable to assess the intelligence of reader groups, in accord with sound theories of intellectual development which generate assessment techniques that are minimally influenced by deficiencies in reading, specific aptitudes, and previous experience. Of interest in this regard is the work of a number of investigators who have begun to explore the relationship between reading ability and stages of concept development as postulated by Piaget and his associates (Piaget 1963; Inhelder and Piaget 1953).

Elkind (1976) has suggested that competence in many aspects of reading is partly dependent on the successful development of conceptual abilities characteristic of given periods of mental growth. He accords particular status to changes in perceptual organization that theoretically characterize the shift from *preoperational* thought (2 to 7 years) to *concrete operational* thought (7 to 11 years). During the peroperational period, the child's preception is said to be *static,* that is, dominated by the physical properties of specific stimuli. Perception in the concrete-operational child is described as more flexible and *dynamic,* characterized by greater ability to alter figure-ground relationships and determined less by given stimulus qualities. These perceptual attitudes have been respectively termed *centration* and *decentration* (Piaget and Morf 1958; Piaget 1961), and the developmental changes associated with these two constructs are believed to be attributable to significant alterations in mental structures characterized by the use of logical operations, which facilitate increased orientation to part-whole relationships.

Elkind further points out that in learning to decode printed symbols the child must frequently reorganize his perception in order to abstract different meanings from physically identical stimuli in changing contexts. For example, the word *father* contains two separate words (*fat* and *her*), which combine to form one word that sounds quite different from either of the components in isolation. It is the child's ability to decenter that presumably allows him to correctly perceive all three words apart from one another. In support of this contention Elkind and his associates have conducted a number of studies evaluating centration and decentration in preoperational and concrete-operational age children (Elkind and Scott 1962; Elkind, Koegler, and Go 1962, 1964; Elkind 1964; Briggs and Elkind 1973). Of particular interest in this context is a study by Elkind, Horn, and Schneider

(1965) that attempted to relate decentration to ability in reading. In this investigation decentration was operationally defined in terms of (1) ability to decipher word anagrams, (2) perception of embedded figures (Gottschalk 1926) and (3) judgments of size on a diamond illusion test; subjects were lower middle-class children in grades 2 through 6, estimated to be of average intelligence. It was found that reading achievement was significantly correlated with the nonverbal as well as the verbal measures of decentration employed. The authors were guarded in their interpretations of these results but suggested that their findings were consistent with the possibility that decentration, as conceptualized by Piaget, may be an important requisite for success in beginning reading.

Several other authors have made reference to the utility of Piagetian theories for evaluating cognitive development in relation to reading. For example, Almy (1966, 1974) has written extensively on the educational implications of Piaget's conceptualizations and has provided some support for a possible relation between ability to conserve and skill in reading. Specifically, it was found that kindergartners and first-graders who did not perform well on Piagetian measures of conservation also performed poorly on reading readiness tests and other measures of verbal and nonverbal ability (Almy 1974). Almy therefore suggested that the logical operations subsumed under the ability to conserve may well be important precursors of success in beginning reading.

Raven and Salzer (1974) adopted a similar position, postulating that the operations of reversibility and decentration are especially important in apprehending such relevant concepts as alphabetic coding, graphophonemic and orthographic invariance (as in *fat, cat, rat*), equivalence of upper- and lower-case letters, and other categorical relations involved in learning to read. Additional support for a possible relation between Piagetian constructs and reading achievement is provided by Lovell, Shapton, and Warren (1964), Briggs and Elkind (1973), Cox (1976), and several unpublished studies relating conservation to reading readiness (Roberts 1976).

On the negative side, Vernon (1965) found no significant correlations between a number of Piagetian tasks and reading achievement in a large factorial study assessing relationships between reading ability and a variety of verbal and nonverbal measures. It should nevertheless be apparent that work relating skill in reading to Piaget's developmental stages is gaining momentum and such research may eventually prove productive. The major premise of these studies is that conceptual ability at various periods of development is intrinsically related to reading ability; Piaget's stage theory of intelligence is considered a particularly useful paradigm for exploring relationships between these two sets of variables. However, conclusions drawn from the limited findings available can be questioned on both interpretive and methodological grounds.

For example, the suggestion made by Elkind, Horn, and Schneider (1965) that poor readers may be less decentered than normal readers seems tenuous, given the measures employed to evaluate this construct. It is not surprising that normal readers performed better than poor readers in deciphering word anagrams, considering their greater facility in spelling and word decoding. Reader group disparities on tests of embedded figures and size judgment are more difficult to explain. Nevertheless, it may be that such differences were due to experiential factors and not to differences in decentration in the Piagetian sense; it is possible that normal readers performed better than poor readers, in part because of perceptual skills acquired in school learning, especially in the area of reading. As a result of their experience in code acquisition, the normal readers may have developed a perceptual set to search for invariant and synthetic relationships, attitudes that would no doubt assist them in their encounters with embedded figures and like tasks. This possibility will be discussed in greater detail in section 5.3.3. Inasmuch as the evidence supporting the inferred relationship between reading ability and decentration is questionable, acceptance of its extensions is therefore premature.

A similar concern may be expressed in the case of studies relating conservation to measures of reading readiness. Neither conservation (Flavell and Wohlwill 1969; Bryant 1974) nor reading readiness are understood well enough to permit definitive conclusions as to the significance of findings relating these two variables. Reading readiness has been fraught with both measurement and definitional problems (Dykstra 1967; MacGinitie 1969; Calfee 1977) and is thus a questionable criterion against which to validate conservation as a means for predicting conceptual readiness for learning to read. Consequently the results of studies correlating the ability to conserve and reading readiness must be interpreted cautiously.

There is little doubt that currently available measures of intelligence are not ideal for evaluating conceptual development in poor readers, given the heavy emphasis those measures place upon previous experience and specific aptitudes. The construction of tests that may eventually overcome these limitations is certainly a worthwhile objective, regardless of the ultimate validity of their theoretical foundations. At very least, studies such as those mentioned provide preliminary correlates that could eventuate in the development of such instruments. Indeed several authors have already begun work on the construction of standardized versions of Piagetian conceptual tasks and initial results appear promising (Kofsky 1968; Pinard and Laurendeau 1970; Tuddenham 1970; Uzgiris and Hunt 1975).

In summary, many problems are associated with the measurement of intelligence in children who sustain reading difficulties, primarily because we lack both understanding of the nature of intellectual development and clear-cut criteria to distinguish so-called dyslexia from reading problems stemming from environmental causes. No intelligence test is completely devoid of the influence of experience, particularly as it might relate to success in reading and school achievement in general. The possibility that given tests of intelligence may be differentially related to skills and subskills requisite to reading achievement further compounds the problem. Thus it is incumbent upon the researcher to select his criterion measure in accord with the constraints of the theory he wishes to test and the limitations imposed by the unique contents of the instruments currently available. The reliability and validity of the intelligence test measure chosen should also be a basic consideration.

2.1.2 Sensory Functions

Most laboratory studies of specific reading disability exclude from their research samples poor readers with hearing loss or uncorrected visual acuity problems. There is a general consensus that sensory disorder that results in distortion of proximal stimuli is reason to question any inference of specific learning disability. Yet some professionals working in the field insist that oculomotor functions have a significant role in determining visual perception, even when visual acuity is adequate (Getman 1962; Anapolle 1967; Flax 1970; Rosner 1972). This is particularly true of members of the optometric profession, who along with others (among them, Kephart 1960; Frostig and Maslow 1973) claim that accurate perceptions presuppose proper integration of the perceptual-motor systems. The primary inference is that inability to effect such integration results in characteristic difficulty in establishing relations among visual, verbal, and kinesthetic stimuli involved in learning to read and write. Spatial orientation problems, dysfunction in eye-hand coordination, poor body image, deficient sensory integration, and poor attention span (among other things) have been related to dysfunction in binocular fusion and accommodation, exophoria, hyperopia, and like optical problems.

For a theoretical foundation, professionals in this field have relied heavily upon the studies of Renshaw (1939-1965) and Gesell (1924, 1945, 1952), both of whom emphasized the role of action systems in vision. Research conducted by Renshaw and Gesell became the basis for technical studies by Nichols (1947) and Brock (1966), who developed a series of visual training exercises designed to correct visual anomalies of the types mentioned. Such exercises were later employed in diagnostic and remedial work with children sustaining learning disabilities (Skeffington 1959; Getman 1962; Anapolle 1967) and currently enjoy widespread use.

Not all optometrists are in accord with this position however. In 1963, B. Flom voiced the opinion that there was insufficient evidence to support the purported relations between oculomotor functions and learning disorders, a suggestion that was reinforced in a later statement by M. Flom (1970). Carter (1970) also contended that the incidence of visual abnormalities may not be more frequent among academic underachievers than among those who are making satisfactory progress in school.

Support for this point of view is provided by Lawson (1968). In reviewing a large number of studies spanning a period of more than seventy-five years, this author observed that the incidence of visual difficulties was no greater in poor readers than in normal readers. He therefore concluded that specific reading disability is a symbolic learning disorder caused by central rather than peripheral dysfunction. That conclusion is supported by the results of a recent study conducted by Fox, Orr, and Rourke

(1975), who found that a standard optometric examination did not discriminate poor and normal readers.

Other authorities studying dyslexia are in agreement with Lawson's conclusion. For example, Critchley (1970) suggested that scanning and eye-movement difficulties are the result rather than the cause of reading problems. Similarly, Benton (1975), in discussing the relationship between dyslexia and oculomotor disorders, points out that congenital or acquired defects of the eyes (for instance, nystagmus) are not necessarily correlated with characteristic features of developmental reading disability.

Although there is little doubt that acuity problems and other ocular anomalies can create difficulties in learning to read, by virtue of discomfort or fatigue, these factors are of a secondary nature and cannot in and of themselves account for the severity of the reading problems of particular interest to anyone studying dyslexia. Nor can they account for the fact that many children with excellent vision are extremely poor readers. The etiology of specific reading disability will have to be found elsewhere.

2.1.3 Severe Neurological and Physical Disability

The use of neurological and physical disabilities as exclusionary criteria has created some confusion in our understanding of specific reading disability. It may seem a contradiction that investigators who hypothesize that dyslexia is a neurologically based disorder exclude children with severe neurological disability from research samples. Yet these two stipulations are not really incompatible. It is well known that gross brain damage may entail a variety of sequelae, not the least of which is deficiency in the ability to abstract and generalize. These skills are important (if not crucial) prerequisites to reading. Furthermore, as Rabinovitch (1959) has pointed out, a highly probable consequence of severe neurological disorder is limited ability to attend and concentrate. He considered such factors secondary causes of specific reading disability. Therefore, children with gross brain damage are typically not included in investigations studying dyslexia.

These considerations in no way deny the possibility that dyslexia is a developmental constitutional disorder associated with possible dysfunction in the central nervous system. The distinction I am making is a subtle one. It could be thought of as a contrast between definitive tissue damage with a high probability of multiple handicaps, on the one hand, and neurological disorder of unknown origin resulting in more circumscribed behavioral effects, on the other. Yet one may also include in this contrast children with inferred neurological disorder with no definitive tissue damage, such as those who sustain global developmental defects in capacities known to be important to reading achievement. A good example of one such capacity is spoken language. Researchers typically do not include in their research samples children with a well-defined history of major receptive and expressive language deficiencies who show obvious residuals of these disorders (Benton 1975). Here again a fine distinction is needed, since exclusion of children with pervasive and persistent defects in oral language does not necessarily rule out the possibility of uncovering more subtle language problems as possible factors contributing to reading disability.

A question similar to the one raised by the use of gross neurological disorder as a category of exclusion arises when one deliberately rules out subjects who are physically disabled. It may be argued that this criterion is far too broad to be useful, given that many physical disabilities should have no effect whatsoever on cognitive functioning. A cardinal example might be the loss of a limb, which should be unrelated to reading ability. Nevertheless, few people would disagree that there is a high probability that the environmental experiences of children with physical disabilities, particularly disabilities of a multiform nature, would be different in ways that might affect reading achievement. An example for which there is some research evidence (Schonell 1956) is the child with cerebral palsy who, in spite of adequate intellectual potential, may be provided with inadequate educational opportunities because of stereotyped impressions of such youngsters as limited in their ability to engage in a regular academic program. Yet it is common knowledge that many such children become quite literate in spite of their physical handicaps.

In view of the possibility that physical disability might introduce a bias in the types of environmental experiences to which a child is exposed, compared with school children at large, the more conservative course is to exclude such children from laboratory study of developmental reading disability. The same is true of those with gross neurological deficits. Thus the researcher who does not include neurologically or physically impaired children in investigations of dyslexia makes an arbitrary decision in the interest of reducing the probability of including as false positives some children whose reading problems may be of a secondary nature.

2.1.4 Emotional and Social Factors

There seems to be general agreement among those investigating reading disability that poor readers with significant emotional and social problems should be excluded from initial study of this disorder, primarily because of the attentional and motivational deficiencies typically associated with such problems. This criterion is one of the most difficult to implement because there are currently no adequate measures of emotional and social adjustment that can be reasonably employed as selection criteria. Consequently, the researcher is forced to use measures that are very gross at best. The impediments to learning that characterize the child with severe and long-standing emotional disorder (the psychotic child) are readily identified even by the layman, but the impeding attributes characteristic of the child with more subtle behavioral idiosyncracies are not so apparent, the basic integrity of the personality being maintained in such instances. The latter group might include children with limited incentive for achievement who have poor work habits as well as those who have developed subtle avoidance patterns as a result of some degree of anxiety issuing from personal problems. Furthermore, the child who has basic learning disability can be expected to have a significant degree of emotional and social difficulty in relationships with parents, siblings, teachers, and peers. This statement was amply documented by Bryan and Bryan (1975), who reviewed a sizable number of studies demonstrating a significant incidence of behavioral and adjustment problems in children sustaining various types of learning disability.

It appears, therefore, that there is no satisfactory way to disentangle subtle emotional and adjustment difficulties from primary learning disorder for purposes of studying reading disability that is not the result of secondary or extrinsic factors. This, of course, poses a dilemma for the researcher, who can do little more than exclude from his sample children with grossly debilitating emotional disorders. Consequently there is a high probability that given studies might include a significant proportion of children with less obvious but no less impeding adjustment problems, thereby rendering conclusions drawn from such studies tenuous at best.

2.1.5 Socioeconomic Disadvantage

There is increasing evidence that underachievement in reading and other school subjects is correlated significantly with cultural differences and socioeconomic disadvantage. McCarthy (1954) has provided a comprehensive review of a sizable number of studies demonstrating the adverse effects of minority status, socioeconomic disadvantage, and environmental deficits upon language development. Similarly, Templin (1957) found that deficiencies in speech articulation, "auditory functioning," vocabulary, and expressive language were less often observed in high- than in low-socioeconomic children (ages 3 to 8, chronologically). Deficits in such areas could, of course, adversely affect the development of reading skill.

A review similar to McCarthy's, undertaken by Bloom, Davis, and Hess (1965), related social class to educational factors. They assessed the role of environment and social class upon a large number of psychological variables, including language and other cognitive functions. Their major conclusion was that underachievement in the socioeconomically disadvantaged is the result of early experiences that do not adequately prepare such children for the types of learning that would characterize their experiences in the school setting and their environment at large.

Deutsch (1963) provided some evidence to support the hypothesis that socioeconomic disadvantage results in cumulative deficiency in language development and school learning. Elementary school children were found to differ (Deutsch 1963, 1964) on measures of language (phonological processing, word meanings, syntax, verbal fluency), reading, and related subject matter, as a function of social class, age, and grade, and the differences between children in upper and lower socioeconomic brackets increased with age. Deutsch (1965) subsequently attempted to document the effects of early "perceptual" experience on academic readiness, testing the hypothesis that lack of adequate stimulation in the home setting results in language, reading, and other cognitive disorders. The results of this study suggested that poor performance on visual, tactile, and auditory tasks was positively correlated with scarcity of manipulable objects and a high degree of competing noises in the child's environment. Coleman (1966) has provided additional evidence to support Deutsch's cumulative-deficit hypothesis.

Bereiter and Englemann (1966) also stressed the significance of below-par linguistic ability in low socioeconomic groups, indicating that "disadvantaged children of preschool age are typically at least a year behind in language development—in vocabulary size, sentence length, and use of grammatical structure . . . in practically every aspect of language development that has been evaluated quantitatively" (Bereiter and Engelmann 1966, 4). McGrady (1968) advanced a similar hypothesis.

Although the results of the above studies can be taken to mean that disadvantaged children are characterized by inferior language and cognitive development, other investigators—Goodman (1965), Labov (1967), and Venezky (1970), to name three—have adopted a different view. These authors argue that cultural influences resulting in significant variations in dialect and other linguistic patterns are *not* tantamount to inferior development in these areas, but that such differences may nevertheless cause reading problems. Gibson and Levin (1975) refer to this position as the linguistic interference hypothesis (Gibson and Levin 1975, 506); after reviewing several studies evaluating this conceptualization, they conclude that there is little evidence to substantiate it. They also reject the cultural-deficit hypothesis of Deutsch, Bereiter, and Engelmann (among others) as being based on misconception as well as unsound methodology. They acknowledge, however, that there *are* significant discrepancies in the reading abilities of children in different cultural and socioeconomic brackets. They suggest that the most critical differences in the experiences of such children probably occur in the school setting, where they are confronted with educational programs implemented by teachers who have insufficient knowledge and experience to circumvent cultural differences and motivate disadvantaged students to perform academically. Some evidence to support this suggestion was provided by Vellutino and Connolly (1971); they found that out of twenty-six disadvantaged second-graders who were severely impaired in reading, only two failed to read at or above their grade placement after one year of intensive individual remediation.

Finally, Birch and Gussow (1970) have provided evidence that in many disadvantaged children general development is significantly below that characteristic of their middle-class peers as a result of health and nutritional deficiencies; they suggest that such deficiencies may also adversely affect cognitive growth and achievement in this group.

These various findings amply justify socioeconomic disadvantage as a category of exclusion in the study of developmental reading disability. Although there is controversy over the causes for achievement differences in this group, the general consensus is that such differences do exist. This does not exclude the possibility that cultural and social factors may coexist with specific reading disability. Yet in view of the difficulty in separating these factors, the more productive course at present would seem to be to exclude such children from initial study of the disorder, except in contrasts where reading disorder in children from minority groups is employed as an experimental variable.

2.1.6 Opportunity for Learning

This criterion can be thought of as encompassing several of the prerequisites to successful learning already detailed. That is, a child who has undiagnosed sensory deficiencies can be said to have inadequate opportunity for learning, and so can children who have emotional problems, severe physical disability, or other limitations that intrinsically deny them access to a quality education. As the term is being used here, however, *opportunity for learning* directly refers to the adequacy of a child's school program and his participation in that program. These factors in turn are related to such complicated and involved issues as educational philosophy, resources, and personnel available in the educational setting and in the community, as well as to such factors as quality of instruction.

Unfortunately, the evaluation of educational programs has been fraught with difficulty. In their review of educational evaluation techniques of the 1960s, Worthen and Sanders (1973) cite a number of deficiencies. These include a less than adequate evaluation theory, uncertainty as to the information that is most critical in evaluating educational programs, and an insufficiency of appropriate instruments and designs. At the same time, there is a real lack of adequately trained personnel who might effectively organize, process, and report evaluative information. In response to these needs, a number of frameworks for educational evaluation have been proposed (Stake 1967; Scriven 1973; Stufflebeam 1973). However, despite wider acceptance of broadly based evaluation, the educational bureaucracy is slow to incorporate the type of dependable information that would lend reliability and validity to evaluations of teacher and program effectiveness. Furthermore, given so many complex interacting factors relating to the adequacy of educational programming—vis à vis individual and environmental variables unique to specific children—it is entirely possible that opportunity for learning can never be measured in any precise or satisfactory way. Thus, while the investigator may reasonably exclude from research samples those children residing in school districts with a high incidence of reading failure and children who are frequently absent from school, he is left with the need to devise indirect means to compensate for less obvious environmental factors impeding a child's opportunity for learning.

2.2 CORRELATED CHARACTERISTICS

A number of investigators, including Bryant (1965); Critchley (1970), and Benton (1975), have made note of other identifying characteristics that appear less frequently and perhaps sporadically in dyslexics, but that are said to occur often enough to be examined for their possible significance. Those most often mentioned are as follows:

1. Boys are observed to have reading problems more frequently than girls, the ratio generally exceeding 4:1 (Eisenberg 1966; Benton 1975).

2. The incidence of reading difficulties in the families of dyslexics has been found to be statistically significant (Hallgren 1950; Hermann 1959; Owen et al. 1971; Finucci et al. 1976).

3. Dyslexics have been observed to have difficulty in other forms of representational learning, such as telling time, naming the months and seasons of the year or the days of the week, and distinguishing left from right or up from down. A common inference is that such anomalies are reflective of the tendency in such children to be disoriented in perceiving temporal and spatial relations.

4. The appearance of neurological soft signs (abnormal reflexes, minor coordination problems, deviant EEG patterns, and so on)

has been reported in both clinical and laboratory study of dyslexics, reinforcing the suggestion that reading problems in some
children may be associated with neurological disorder (Rabinovitch 1959; Conners 1970; Bryant 1965; Owens et al. 1971;
Preston, Guthrie and Childs 1974).
5. Some evidence suggests that dyslexia is significantly correlated
with a history of developmental problems, particularly in one
or more aspects of language (Kawi and Pasamanick 1958; Lyle
1970).

2.3 OPERATIONAL DEFINITION

Operational definition of specific reading disability is a formidable
undertaking. Since available measures are imprecise, the identification of a representative research sample is probabilistic at best,
the utility of defining criteria being ultimately dependent upon
the validity of the theories one generates. In investigations conducted in our laboratory, my colleagues and I have evolved the
following general guidelines for identifying a population of severely impaired readers that may be the object of fruitful study.
We arbitrarily refer to such children as *probable dyslexics,* the
reference being to those whose reading problems are probably
due to primary rather than secondary factors.

First, the probable dyslexic typically has unusual deficiencies
at the level of individual word decoding and consequently has difficulty with all aspects of reading (see Calfee, Chapman, and
Venezky 1972; Frith 1972; Shankweiler and Liberman 1972).
Second, the probable dyslexic is not only extremely impaired in
his ability to identify whole words on sight, but has equal difficulty in analyzing their component sounds. In fact, unlike some
investigators (Myklebust and Johnson 1962; Boder 1970, 1971;
Mattis, French, and Rapin 1975), members of our laboratory are
inclined to consider the possibility of primary reading disorder—
that is, reading problems not caused by extrinsic factors—only
in those children who are deficient in both whole word learning
and word analysis. Our research samples do not typically include
children who have poor comprehension of what they read but
have adequate ability to identify words on sight, nor children who
are mildly to moderately impaired in word identification.

Therefore, for purposes of studying only the most severely
disabled readers, we have invariably employed tests of oral reading

administered individually for greater reliability. We prefer these measures to measures of silent reading because the latter yield no direct information about word decoding ability. Moreover, silent reading tests are too easily confounded by poor motivation, inattention, and deficient study skills, thereby attenuating the chances of identifying only the extremely deficient reader.

A convention in the literature has been to select for research study, only those children whose scores on standardized reading measures are two or more years below their grade placement. This criterion is presumably employed to insure the selection of the poorest readers. However, the use of reading tests employing grade equivalents as achievement criteria occasion the researcher some degree of risk, owing to certain measurement and interpretive problems associated with this scaling procedure. Several authors have discussed these problems in some detail (Gulliksen 1950; Beggs and Hieronymus 1968; Angoff 1971; Stanley and Hopkins 1972) and I will summarize their main points.

First, because of the unique way in which they are obtained, grade equivalents constitute rather coarse metrics and thus cannot be interpreted with any degree of precision.

To be specific, most grade equivalent scores are extrapolated indices derived from curve-fitting procedures (estimating the average performance at given grade levels from the actual performance of pupils at other grade levels); such procedures do not take into account variability in the relationship between test performance and grade level. Consequently, the same grade equivalent score may not signify identical rankings in different sampling distributions, depending upon such factors as the shapes of the distributions within grades and disparities between median scores at adjacent grade levels. If, for example, there are wide variations in the shapes of the distributions at each grade level or if there are sharp differences in median scores at adjacent grades, there will be low correspondence between the grade equivalents yielded by specific raw scores and the rank orders associated with those scores.

Unfortunately the latter circumstance typically characterizes the distributions of achievement test scores across grades. Stanley and Hopkins (1972) have demonstrated empirically that variability in these measures typically increases at each successive grade,

which has the general effect of increasing the overlap in distributions of raw scores from grade to grade. This means that grade
equivalents in the upper grades do not signify the degree of contrast between raw score medians (for adjacent grades) that are sig-
nified by grade equivalents in the lower grades. Thus a grade
equivalent of one year below grade placement in second grade
represents a greater deviation from the raw score average for that
grade than does a grade equivalent one year below placement in
sixth grade.

A closely related problem is the tendency for grade equivalents
to exaggerate small differences between test scores, owing to the
fact that they obscure (through curve fitting operations) large
variations within groups. It is entirely possible for a child who is
only moderately above or below the average for his grade on a
given achievement test to appear to be much farther removed
from this standard.

Grade equivalents derived from achievement tests may also fluc-
tuate in accord with the unique experiences of children at specific
grade levels in given educational settings. Gulliksen (1950) and
Angoff (1971) have pointed out that grade equivalent scaling is
greatly influenced by such things as instructional approaches
and emphasis, the nature of curricula, materials employed for
instruction, and promotional philosophies. Thus the implicit assumption that a grade equivalent score received by a child at a
specific age and grade has the same meaning as that particular
score obtained by a child at a different age and grade is clearly
in error, given the likelihood that the educational experiences of
these two children are vastly different. Moreover, some achievement tests incorporate different forms at different grade levels.
In such instances *no* comparisons across grades are possible since
children in grades that may be contrasted are exposed to different
content.

Another difficulty is that the use of grade equivalents assumes
a constant rate of growth throughout the school year. This has
been demonstrated to be an errant assumption in that the performance levels of children tested at different times during the
year have been found to vary greatly (Beggs and Hieronymus
1968; Stanley and Hopkins 1972). Consequently, there is the
danger of either overestimating or underestimating a given child's
standing in a particular reference group, depending upon when he

is tested. It would also be problematic to attempt to compute grade equivalents from test data obtained on subjects in a research sample if these children were tested at times different from those in the standardization sample, since the results derived from these two groups would not be directly comparable. Adding to the problem is the fact that not all test manuals provide the kind of information that would be needed to control for these difficulties.

It should be clear that the use of grade equivalents in sample selection is hazardous at best. In fact, there appears to be general agreement (Angoff 1971) that this scaling procedure is inferior to percentile ranking if the purpose is to compare an individual child's performance with that of other children or to determine that child's standing on several tests. Grade equivalents do have the advantage of simplicity and apparent ease of interpretation, but their difficulties may outweigh this advantage if the researcher is not thoroughly conversant with the risks occasioned by their use.

In spite of all these problems, those studying the etiology of dyslexia have typically adopted grade placement as the normative standard and have employed grade equivalents for sample selection. The primary justification appears to be the desire to compare subjects along a developmental continuum. This is an understandable rationale, considering the nature of the problem being studied, and is no doubt the reason that other scaling procedures (for instance, percentile ranks) have not enjoyed widespread use by these investigators. Yet even rough approximations to developmental comparisons are obviated by tests characterized by different content at different grade levels.

Many of the difficulties occasioned by the use of grade equivalents for sample selection can be circumvented (or attenuated) if the researcher employs certain safeguards in both selecting his samples and interpreting his results. First, investigators would do well to employ selection procedures that allow them access to the populations of major interest while providing sufficient margin to minimize sampling error. In relation to the present problem, sampling criteria should be stringent enough to insure selection of the most severely deficient readers, who by definition are those functioning normally in other areas, relative to their age and grade placements. Second, groups to be contrasted should be selected within the same time frame so as to guard against the problems resulting from different levels of competency in children tested at different times of the year. Third, researchers should avoid literal interpretation of grade equivalent scores, particularly when making comparisons across grade levels. For example, rather than claim that a second-grader who achieves a sixth-grade equivalency index performs at the level of a child in sixth grade, it would be more accurate to report that he performed successfully on material that was standardized on sixth graders, which itself is useful information. Conservative descriptions of this sort are especially important when differences in grade equivalents are of low magnitude.

Fourth, the populations sampled should be comparable with respect to demographic characteristics, particularly as these relate to academic and social experiences that might result in undue variations in performance levels. Fifth, because the variability in reading achievement scores characteristically increases from the lower to the upper grades, investigators would do well to adopt a more stringent criterion for selecting disabled readers in the upper grades: two or more years below grade level rather than one year below, a standard that has frequently appeared in the literature. Sixth, researchers should employ individually administered oral reading measures that facilitate developmental comparisons by allowing children at different grade levels to be tested on the same material. Finally, they should employ reading achievement measures with demonstrated reliability and validity.

2.3.1 Suggested Sampling Procedures

Achievement Criteria   In accord with these constraints, we have employed the following sampling procedures in our own investigations. Initial samples were selected by asking teachers in local school districts to refer for research study only their most severely impaired readers. We requested, however, that they rule out children whose learning problems appeared to be due to secondary or extrinsic causes and we provided them with written guidelines for making their selections. To each child referred to us we gave an individually administered test of oral reading ability (Gilmore 1968). Research subjects were then tentatively selected on the basis of grade equivalent scores, in keeping with the convention employed in the literature. We typically selected only those children whose scores were two or more years below their grade placement, with the exception of second graders (the lowest grade level sampled in our studies), who were chosen if they scored at least one full year below grade level. Such children were also administered a test of word analysis skills[1] employing pronounceable pseudowords, for purposes of comparison with normal readers, but initial sample selection was made on the basis of oral reading test scores. All poor readers tentatively selected as prospective research subjects were further screened in accord with certain exclusionary criteria, and we have consistently procured our samples from school districts with roughly comparable demographic characteristics, where we sampled on an annual or semiannual basis.

We have determined that these procedures consistently identified children whose scores on the oral reading test fell between the 4th and 10th percentiles, these indices being derived from the percentile rank tables reported in the test manual (Gilmore 1968). This has been true of children from second through sixth grade, the range we have most frequently sampled.

Table 2.1 presents descriptive statistics for the reading and IQ scores of a random sampling (N=20 each group) of poor and normal readers tested between 1971 and 1976. Results on the oral reading test are reported in grade equivalents; results on the phonic skills test are in raw scores (see note 1). The two groups are widely disparate on both measures ($p < .01$), the poor readers falling well below the performance levels characteristic of their peer groups. Thus the subjects we have typically included in our samples can reasonably be considered to be severely handicapped readers.

Of particular interest here is the rather large disparity between our poor and normal reader groups on the pseudoword test of word analysis ability. Since we did not employ this measure in selecting any of our samples, we may safely conclude that the subjects included in our studies were differentiated on the basis of their knowledge of grapheme–phoneme relations, as well as on their ability to identify whole words appearing in running text. This suggests that poor readers in these samples were impaired in all aspects of word identification.

Table 2.1
Means and standard deviations for intelligence and reading achievement criteria for randomly selected samples of poor and normal readers (N = 20 each group) employed in studies conducted by Vellutino et al between 1971 and 1976.

Grade	Reader Group	VIQ	PIQ	FSIQ	Oral Reading[a]	Phonic Skills[b]
2	Poor $\overline{X}$	105.50	105.90	106.15	.36	2.75
	S.D.	10.90	9.99	9.69	.65	3.04
	Normal $\overline{X}$	113.50	110.65	113.35	3.46	17.50
	S.D.	8.79	11.23	8.49	.56	6.50
3	Poor $\overline{X}$	100.10	100.75	100.50	1.77	4.85
	S.D.	11.72	9.63	9.81	.62	4.22
	Normal $\overline{X}$	101.55	105.15	103.50	4.32	19.05
	S.D.	10.44	11.44	9.41	.60	6.79
4	Poor $\overline{X}$	103.35	105.00	104.60	2.49	9.05
	S.D.	13.79	11.15	11.64	.76	3.94
	Normal $\overline{X}$	106.90	109.25	108.85	5.26	22.65
	S.D.	9.43	7.58	7.06	1.15	6.49
5	Poor $\overline{X}$	97.05	97.85	97.20	3.11	12.65
	S.D.	8.91	8.10	7.59	.70	4.48
	Normal $\overline{X}$	106.55	104.95	106.30	6.04	27.05
	S.D.	8.71	11.88	8.34	1.37	4.07
6	Poor $\overline{X}$	94.50	103.25	98.75	3.44	14.30
	S.D.	9.39	14.41	10.44	.90	5.25
	Normal $\overline{X}$	106.30	100.80	104.00	7.37	25.45
	S.D.	8.62	11.62	9.56	1.84	4.84

[a] Grade equivalents
[b] Raw scores (total possible=35)

Note: Intelligence was in all instances measured by the Wechsler Intelligence Scale for Children (Wechsler 1949); the table includes the Verbal (VIQ), Performance (PIQ), and Full Scale (FSIQ) quotients. Oral reading was measured by the Gilmore Oral Reading Test (Gilmore 1968). The test of phonic skills is an experimental measure and has no published norms.

Exclusion Criteria   Before turning to the operational definition of exclusion criteria, we might look briefly at the relative merits of employing a percentile rank scale for sample selection. This metric indicates the percentage of individuals in a particular distribution scoring below the midpoints of given scores or score intervals. It therefore constitutes a straightforward and comprehensible approach to rank ordering and is certainly defensible for simple comparisons of relative standing in particular distributions. Thus percentiles can be useful for sample selection if the researcher wishes to study only circumscribed proportions of a given distribution and has some a priori reasons for doing so.

However, if the researcher wishes to contrast the relative standing of subjects in different distributions, he is limited by the fact that percentiles constitute an ordinal rather than an interval scale and therefore permit no such comparisons. This would be problematic for anyone interested in rank ordering subjects along the same continuum (like comparing the performance of children at different grade levels on the same tests of reading ability). Since they are not points in a continuous distribution, percentiles would also be inappropriate in statistical computations that assume interval scaling. Because of these limitations, it is suggested that percentiles are less useful for the study of reading disability than grade equivalents, which (theoretically) conform to an equal-interval scale. However, depending upon the statistical properties of the particular samples contrasted, similar difficulties may be encountered with grade equivalents.

Perhaps it would not be unreasonable to suggest that either grade equivalents or percentiles may be employed for sample selection, the choice being determined initially by the interpretations and generalizations one wishes to ascribe to a given data set relative to the limitations of each of these metrics. The utility of either criterion for specific research objectives can only be determined empirically and the investigator must take into consideration the unique properties of his selection procedures and his measuring instruments. It is also obvious that the ultimate determinant of given sampling criteria is the reliability of differentiating attributes yielded by experimental contrasts employed with groups selected on the basis of those criteria. When placed in the latter context, the argument over the validity of one or the other scaling procedure for selection purposes becomes a needless one, since grade equivalents or percentiles may consistently be associated with specific experimental results, and the use of either in subject selection will yield samples with similar characteristics. When this situation obtains, the primary problem is the possibility of erroneous interpretation, a possibility the researcher should be keenly aware of and assiduously attempt to avoid.

One final note. The use of either grade equivalents or percentile ranks for research purposes should be clearly distinguished from their use in educational assessment and programming. Neither metric provides information that is very helpful for evaluating the presence or absence of specific skills and subskills or for planning differential remedial programs. The remarks made here apply only to the comparative utility of grade equivalents and percentile ranks for sample selection; they should not be taken as an endorsement of one or the other for practical purposes.

Operationalizing exclusion criteria is somewhat more problematic than defining achievement in reading. With respect to the first criterion, intellectual assessment, individually administered tests are preferable to group tests for a number of reasons, the first being their greater reliability. Second, most group tests require some reading, which, of course, obviates their use with poor readers. Third, certain of the individually administered tests available are more effective than group tests in circumventing the problem of screening out children who may have different levels of abilities in verbal and nonverbal areas. Although reader group differences in these skills is itself an empirical question, there is enough evidence to suggest that such differences can be a contaminating factor that needs to be controlled in some way.

In most of our studies we have employed the Wechsler Intelligence Scale for Children (WISC, Wechsler 1949) and have selected children with an IQ of 90 or above on *either* the Verbal or the Performance scale. Although it may be true that our initial results can be generalized only to children whose intelligence has been assessed on the WISC, we feel that employing the same selection device in several studies testing related hypotheses is a necessary control for error variance that may be occasioned by the use of different intelligence tests from one study to the next. The same logic applies to other selection criteria, the strategy being particularly important in the case of initial tests of a given hypothesis.

Table 2.1 presents means and standard deviations for the
Verbal, Performance, and Full Scale IQs of randomly selected
subgroups of poor and normal readers included in our research
samples. All subjects fall well within the average range of intelligence, and the groups are by and large comparable with respect
to intellectual ability, at least as measured by the WISC.

The researcher encounters more difficulty in operationalizing
the remaining exclusionary variables. Evaluation of sensory acuity
is the least troublesome; most school systems provide their own
screening programs and information from them is usually available. Similarly, parents and school officials can be expected to
provide information about a child's medical history to rule out
gross neurological and physical disabilities; the more severe emotional and behavior disorders are rather easily documented. We
have typically employed questionnaires to procure such information. In the case of subtle emotional and social disorders, however,
screening is not as readily accomplished and the researcher must
rely upon less direct methods of controlling these variables. We
have generally avoided laboratory study of clinic populations
because such children are frequently plagued by multiple handicaps that further complicate the definitional problem. But not
all investigators have adopted this strategy (Bender 1956, 1957;
de Hirsch, Jansky, and Langford 1966; Silver and Hagin 1960,
1970).

Socioeconomic disadvantage and cultural differences could
theoretically be assessed through standardized measures (Hollingshead and Redlich 1958) and statistics comparing achievement
levels in given school districts. However, such measures are not
always obtainable; furthermore, achievement test data may not be
comparable across different school districts, where the tests may
differ and factors influencing test scores can vary considerably.
In addition, educational evaluation is not yet a fruitful enterprise.
Thus to provide some degree of control over achievement levels
and the difficulties posed by socioeconomic disadvantage, we have
adopted the technique of studying only children attending schools
located in suburban and middle-class locales, which obviously
limits the generalizability of our results.

The only other recourse available to the researcher to compensate for the flaws in these exclusionary criteria is to cross-
validate given findings by (1) conducting replication studies with

independent samples, (2) varying methodological strategies in tests of the same hypotheses, and (3) employing identical sampling procedures in all follow-up studies. Our own research has been typically characterized by these strategies.

We have not attempted to employ, as criteria for sample selection, the correlated characteristics outlined in section 2.2, nor do we believe it is reasonable to do so. Each characteristic listed is of a hypothetical nature and explanations of their occurrence is open to question. To illustrate, the higher male-to-female ratios found in extremely poor readers has been well documented in the literature but the reasons for this finding are not evident. One suggestion is that it is related to genetic factors, another is that it may be the result of differential expectations of boys and girls in a given culture (Owen 1977). These of course are research questions, but the consistent finding of very high male-female ratios among extremely poor readers is an empirical fact that has prompted some researchers to include only males in their samples of poor and normal readers. We feel that this procedure unduly constrains the generalizability of one's results, especially since there is no evidence that the etiology of reading disability differs in boys and girls. In the absence of such evidence we have elected to control for possible sex differences in our own samples by allowing the male-female ratios to vary in accord with their natural incidence among poor readers. We then duplicate this proportion in comparably selected samples of normal readers at the same age and grade levels.

A similar constraint characterizes the observation of a significant incidence of reading disability in the families of dyslexics (Hallgren 1950; Hermann 1959; Owen et al. 1971; Owen 1977; Finucci et al. 1976). This finding along with other pertinent evidence, such as the twin studies of Hallgren (1950) and Hermann (1959), provides some support for the possibility that reading disability may be determined by genotypic deviations. Yet this too is a research question; genetic criteria that may unequivocally distinguish poor and normal readers have not yet been determined. Thus our sampling procedures have not included case history data that would provide information on the incidence of reading disability among the relatives of our subjects.

We have not employed as selection criteria other anomalies often associated with dyslexia, such as deficiencies in telling time;

naming the months, seasons, and days of the week; and so-called left-right discrimination. Although some investigators have thought that these problems reflect time and space disruptions in dyslexics and are thus of diagnostic significance, it is my opinion that such an interpretation is incorrect. Instead, difficulties of this description may be a consequence of basic naming and labeling problems in such children, a point to be discussed in greater detail.

The possibility that dyslexia may be related to early language deficits has some support in the literature. Yet the reliability of retrospective studies is so difficult to insure that we do not believe it would be profitable to employ such information for purposes of sample selection.

Finally, observations of neurological soft signs in some poor readers, though suggestive (see Owen et al. 1971), are highly tentative and do not justify the time and expense of performing medical examinations on every prospective subject.

2.4 SUMMARY AND CONCLUSIONS

In studying the etiology of specific reading disability, the probability of identifying an appropriate research population is increased if one selects only children with average or above average intelligence who are functioning well below age and grade expectancy on measures of oral reading and word analysis. It is necessary to determine that these children have no sensory, neurological, physical, or emotional disabilities. In considering the possible contribution of environmental disadvantage, objective measures of socioeconomic and cultural status are highly desirable. If such measures cannot be obtained, some control for these factors is provided by sampling only in schools located in middle-class or upper middle-class neighborhoods. In order to hold constant those factors for which there are no adequate selection criteria, certain other strategies must be adopted. Cross-validation studies become critical and the researcher should replicate his findings with independent samples and varying methodologies. At the same time, he should conduct these replications on groups chosen in accord with original sampling procedures and the focus of such studies should be to test the same or related hypotheses.

In selecting subjects for studies conducted in our laboratory, my colleagues and I relied initially upon referrals from teachers,

requesting that they provide us with the names of their most severely impaired readers. We then gave each child individually administered measures of oral reading ability, word analysis skills,
and intelligence. Except for second-graders, children were selected
for our poor reader groups only if their reading achievement scores
were two or more years below their grade placement and only if
they achieved an IQ of 90 or above on either the Performance or
the Verbal subscales of the WISC. Each child was also screened
for relevant exclusionary criteria and poor and normal reader
groups were equated for sex differences. An equal number of poor
and normal readers were selected from each school participating
in our research, and samples were taken only from schools located
in middle- to upper middle-class locales to control for socioeconomic and cultural factors. Subjects were typically in regular
classroom situations and none were clinic cases. Thus our sampling
procedures were rather stringent, typically including the most
severe cases of disabled readers, each of whom had extreme difficulty in all aspects of reading. Obviously our results can be
generalized only to populations of poor readers similar to those
sampled.

Developmental reading disability has been the subject of considerable interest since the initial descriptions of the disorder by Morgan (1896) and Kerr (1897). Professionals concerned with learning and child development have puzzled over the inability of some intellectually capable children to acquire skill in reading, and a number of hypotheses have been offered in explanation of such difficulty, some more detailed than others. We will examine several theories of dyslexia that have appeared in the literature during the past eighty years in the interest of historical perspective and to create an appropriate context within which to place current research and theorizing. Space permits discussion of only the major theoretical views, and special emphasis will be given to those that have been most influential. These theories fall into two groups, on the basis of their implicating one factor or more than one factor as causing reading disability; they will be discussed accordingly. Several of the theories have recurrent and overlapping themes, whereas others are quite disparate. The explanations of dyslexia converge upon specific types of process dysfunction, evidence for which will be discussed in subsequent sections.

3.1 SINGLE-FACTOR THEORIES

3.1.1 Developmental Theories
At the turn of the century two English physicians, W. Pringle Morgan and James Kerr, independently wrote about children they had examined who were unable to learn to read though apparently normal in all other respects. Morgan (1896) described a now-famous 14-year-old boy named Percy who had pronounced

reading and spelling difficulty in spite of having adequate intelligence. Finding no evience of definitive brain injury, Morgan inferred that the boy's reading problems were due to a congenital defect that resulted in difficulty in "storing the visual impressions of words." Following Kussmaul's (1877) use of the term *word blindness* (in reference to acquired reading disorder in adults), Morgan employed the term *congenital word blindness* to refer to specific reading disability in children. He further suggested that the difficulty might be caused by faulty development in the left angular gyrus of the brain, a suggestion he never documented in any systematic way.

The first extensive description of specific reading disability was written by another English physician, James Hinshelwood (1900, 1917). Hinshelwood's explanation of developmental reading disability was similar to Morgan's and he also referred to the disorder as congenital word blindness. Both Morgan and Hinshelwood theorized as to the possibility of deficiencies in local areas of the brain specifically responsible for storing visual images. This postulate was not only in keeping with the localization (of brain function) theories popular at the time but presaged subsequent theories of dyslexia that emphasized deficiencies in the storage of visual templates.

In a historical review of the problem, Thompson (1966) points out that for the first quarter of the twentieth century very little was written about the concept of specific reading disability except for a few scattered articles by physicians (for example, Claiborne 1906). The study of the normal reading process was of considerable interest to psychologists and educators during this period, beginning with Cattell before the turn of the century (Cattell 1885; Erdmann and Dodge 1898; Huey 1908; Gray 1917, 1921). Only after 1920, however, did they begin to show much interest in the study of reading disability, and only a few authors concerned themselves with the problem even then (for example, Fildes 1921; Dearborn 1931; Monroe 1932).

Not until the appearance of Orton's initial paper on the subject in 1925 was serious consideration given to the possibility that developmental reading disorder in some children may be qualitatively different from reading problems resulting primarily from environmental causes. Without doubt Orton's theory has been the most influential of any that has appeared in the literature. It is certainly among the more comprehensive and well articulated conceptualizations available and is one of the few that has generated testable hypotheses (Orton 1925, 1937). In contrast to earlier suggestions by Morgan and Hinshelwood that the disorder is caused by structural deficiency in the brain, Orton proposed that specific reading disability (which he called *strephosymbolia,* or "twisted symbols") is due to a developmental delay that defers the normal establishment of hemispheric dominance for language. He further suggested that the two halves of the brain, though alike in size and design, are reversed in pattern, so that the records or memory *engrams* of printed letters and words are normally stored symmetrically in the two hemispheres as mirror images of each other. As a result of the failure to establish lateral dominance, the disabled reader is presumably subject to distorted visual perception characterized by spatial confusion in oral reading, misperceiving *b* as *d* or *was* as *saw.* Such distortion was thought to be uniquely associated with deficient visual memory for the stored engram that corresponded to the distal stimulus. The essential features of Orton's theory are clearly articulated in the following passage:

The tendency common in young children to mirrored or reversed writing, as reported by Fildes, and as seen in our own cases, and the spontaneous production of a mirrored reversal of letters on first attempts at writing with the *right* hand, as recorded in the case of M. O., all point to the existence in the brain of a mnemonic record in mirrored form which serves as the pattern for these motor expressions. Further, the difficulty in our cases of reading disability in differentiating p from q and b from d and their tendency to confuse palindromic words like not and ton and on and no suggest that the mnemonic record exists in the brain in both orientations.

Letters are in themselves merely objects until they have come to acquire meaning through sound associations or through association in groups of sounds which constitute a word. We would therefore assume that in the process of early visual education, the storage of memory images of letters and words occurs in both hemispheres, and that with the first efforts at learning to read the external visual stimuli irradiate equally into the associative cortices of both hemispheres, and are there recorded in both dextrad and sinistrad orientation. Images of objects require no definite orientation for recognition or differentiation, but when we are dealing with letters, which have come by custom to be used in one orientation only, it is clear that the orientation of the recalled image must correspond with that of the presented symbol, or confusion will result. This suggests the hypothesis that the process of learning to read entails the elision from the focus of attention of the confusion memory images of the nondominant hemisphere which are in reversed form and order, and the selection of those which are correctly oriented and in correct sequence. (1925, 608)

Orton reinforced his contention by pointing out that many poor readers are able to copy letters and words (which they cannot read) when they do not have to rely upon memory (1937, 78). He further qualified his position by suggesting that spatial confusion would be manifested only in the dyslexic's encounter with symbolic material and would not be evident in visual-motor activities that did not require the deciphering of coded information. He was also of the opinion that confusion of letter forms within words would generally improve with maturity but that orientation and sequencing errors might persist because the printed word does not readily prompt the letter sounds in their proper sequence.

Orton suggested, in addition, that his theory could account for difficulty in skills closely related to reading, such as spelling and handwriting.[1] He attributed spelling disability to the failure to stabilize visual representations of letters and words (as in reading), fostering overreliance on phonetic coding of word constituents (Orton 1931). Children who sustained such disorder were viewed as deficient in their ability to develop an accurate impression of the "look" of a word and could therefore be expected to have particular difficulty in both oral and written spelling of nonphonetic or irregular words.

With respect to handwriting disorders, Orton distinguished four subgroups, but only two were explained by the failure to establish hemispheric dominance. Children in the largest of these subgroups were said to be characterized by poorly established lateral dominance and had, in addition to handwriting difficulties, reading and spelling problems, stuttering, congenital apraxia, or other manifestations of "lateral confusion." A second and closely related group consisted of children who manifested none of the accompanying disorders but nevertheless demonstrated no clear-cut dominance in handedness and eyedness. In the other two groups the difficulty was thought to be due either to damage to the motor system or to inappropriate training, particularly in the case of those normally left-handed (Orton and Gillingham 1933).

Orton placed special emphasis on those children who were observed to have similar difficulties in reading, spelling, and writing. These were the so-called mirror writers, whose written language was said to be characterized by a high incidence of errors in the orientation of single letters, especially those that are mirror images of one another, and frequent reversals in the directional sequencing of letters within words and the sequencing of the words within sentences. Orton believed that such errors constituted strong evidence that symmetrical engrams of symbolic stimuli are stored in each of the hemispheres.

Orton's theory, not unlike other earlier ones, is a template theory, in that it makes reference to the storage and retrieval of prototypes or memory engrams. According to such theories the inability to retrieve these engrams or prototypes presumably led to the characteristic misperceptions and directional errors commonly observed in the reading and writing of severely impaired readers.

Lauretta Bender (1956, 1957, 1975), in line with Orton, postulated that reading disability is attributable to developmental lag. Based on a curious admixture of Gestalt psychology, psychoanalytic theorizing and percepts issuing from the developmental studies of Schilder (1935, 1944, 1950) and Gesell (1924, 1952), she suggested that slow and uneven differentiation of neurological patterns results in such disorders as poorly established dominance, specific language difficulty, and dysfunction in reading and writing. Bender gave particular emphasis to inferred deficiencies in visual organization and pattern perception (figure-ground dysfunction), which she believed would be reflected in gross motor activities, postural reflexes, and the copying of graphic figures. She also noted similarities in the clinical manifestations of dyslexic, emotionally disturbed, and mentally defective children (in neurological soft signs, EEG patterns, general immaturity, and so on) and suggested that a basic deficiency that may be observed in all such youngsters is a disruption in the "gestalt function" (Bender 1938).

Bender's theory of reading disability is both amorphous and all-encompassing and does not readily lend itself to experimental verification. In this regard it is not unlike a number of others that appeared at about the same time, most notably the developmental theories of Eustis (1947) and Olson (1949).

Eustis considered reading disability to be one major constituent of a syndrome of associated characteristics, which included clumsiness, speech and language difficulties, ambidexterity, left handedness, and related anomalies. He attributed the syndrome to an inherited disposition toward "slow tempo of neuro-muscular maturation." The reading disability itself was believed to be directly caused by inadequate left-right orientation, presumably due to an involuntary tendency for the eyes to reverse their gaze at irregular intervals.

Olson (1949), in adopting what he referred to as an *organismic* view, suggested that reading disability was attributable to a general maturational lag and could be predicted by rate of achievement of such developmental milestones as motor functioning, language, and other aspects of physical and mental growth. The writings of both Eustis and Olson, like those of others of that period, strongly emphasized maturational factors. All were probably influenced by the work of Gesell (1952) who placed heavy emphasis upon the role of maturation in explanation of perceptual and cognitive development.

3.1.2 Other Single-Factor Theories

One of the better articulated conceptualizations of dyslexia, aside from Orton's, was that of Knud Hermann, who suggested that word blindness, as he too referred to it, is due to an inherited tendency toward inadequate development of the "directional function." Directional disturbance was said to be related to "a failure of lateral orientation with reference to the body-schema, such that the concepts of direction are either uncertain or abolished" (Hermann 1959, 146). Such difficulty was said to manifest itself in both two- and three-dimensional space, resulting in orientation problems in the object world as well as in learning to code symbols. Thus it theoretically accounts for confusion in the left-right identification as well as reversal, rotation, and sequencing errors observed in both the reading and the written language of dyslexics. Hermann also suggested that directional impairment would be evident in learning involving other graphic symbols such as numbers and musical notations.

Hermann was careful to point out that directional confusion of the type suggested occurs when the individual attempts to compare identically shaped configurations that differ only in spatial orientation, and is *not* characterized by perceptual distortion of the distal stimulus, as Orton and others had suggested. "It must be made clear," Hermann wrote, "that rotations are confusions between letters. It is not, as some seem to think, a case of the letter, in the process of perception in the brain, being turned round and seen as its mirror image. A d is perceived visually as d, even though it becomes called b; the d is perceived as a figure with its hook on the left but is named incorrectly" (p. 45).

The nature of the directional confusion postulated by Hermann is not clear-cut. He refers to the difficulties poor readers have in remembering a particular shape in a given orientation and thus in correctly associating the figure with its name. It would appear therefore that the disturbance occurs in the mental comparison of similar figures such as *b* and *d* or *p* and *q,* rather than in the perception of the figures individually. But such a distinction seems amorphous in that the child may readily generate a representation of one or another of these figures and even graphically reproduce it without being able to name it. The difficulty could therefore be in the correct labeling of the figure rather than in its visualization, an interpretation that might readily be inferred from the above quotation. Unfortunately, the author provided no clarification of this issue.

In support of his theory, Hermann drew a parallel between reading disability in children and the clinical signs associated with Gerstmann's syndrome (Gerstmann 1940), a neurological disorder that has been the source of considerable controversy (Benton 1962; Gardner 1975). The cluster of symptoms said to be characteristic of this disorder include left-right confusion, finger agnosia, reading and writing difficulties, calculation difficulties, and deficiency in symbolic learning generally. The parallel between Gerstmann's syndrome and developmental reading disability should be obvious, but its existence as an isolable syndrome has not been verified.

Hermann and an associate, Edith Norrie, produced some objective evidence for the possibility that dyslexia is inherited through a dominant gene (Hermann and Norrie 1958). In studying twin samples, they found that for uniovular twins reading disability occurred invariantly in both children and to a significant degree in biovular twins. Similar observations were made by Bertil Hallgren (1950), who found reading disability in three sets of uniovular twins as well as in 99 of 112 members of given families.

The hereditary aspects of dyslexia were more recently addressed in a symposium dealing with the definition and etiology of this disorder; research data were presented to support the possibility that reading disability is genetically determined (Childs, Finucci, and Preston 1978; McClearn 1978; Owen 1978). However the general consensus among these investigators was that available findings, although suggestive, are inconclusive. There was also agreement that a major impediment to studying the genetic correlates of reading disability is the lack of clarity in defining and measuring its behavioral parameters.

A single-factor explanation of reading disability quite different from those discussed thus far is that of D. J. Bakker (1970, 1972). Bakker postulates that deficient readers have particular difficulty in the perception of temporal order and conceives of sequential memory as a specialized ability distinct from gross memory. Furthermore, he contends that the poor reader's difficulties in temporal order occur only in the processing of *verbal* stimuli and that the temporal processing of such stimuli in most individuals is supported by the left or language hemisphere, whereas (temporal) processing of nonverbal stimuli is supported by the right hemisphere. Bakker specifically rejects the possibility that dysfunction in ordering verbal stimuli is due to generalized language disorder or deficiencies in such linguistic functions as labeling and naming, pointing out that poor readers may be able to name letters or numbers but may still find it difficult to remember ordered series of these items.

A number of other authors have also suggested that reading disability may be associated with dysfunction in temporal sequencing and have provided some research evidence that presumably supports this suggestion (Senf 1969; Zurif and Carson 1970; Bannatyne 1971; Bryden 1972; Corkin 1974). However, none of these authors have articulated a theory of reading disability in the strict sense.

Several other investigators have proposed tentative explanations of dyslexia that may be arbitrarily grouped under the heading of single-factor theories, but only a few can be mentioned in passing. Rabinovitch (1959, 1968) suggested that disabled readers are characterized by deficiencies in language and symbolic learning which he inferred lead to disturbances in acquiring abstract concepts related to orientation, time, size, number, and like variables. Rabinovitch was one of the first to consider the possibility that developmental reading disability may be associated with language disorder. He did not, however, attempt to evolve a comprehensive theory specifying possible relations between various aspects of linguistic functioning and components of reading.

Like Hermann, Drew (1956) paralleled reading disability and Gerstmann's syndrome, but suggested that maturational lag in the parietal and parietal-occipital areas is the probable cause of the disorder. He made particular note of disturbances in gestalt (figure-ground) functioning as the basic process disorder causing reading and spelling problems, in addition to disturbed spatial orientation, mixed dominance, motor problems, handwriting deficiencies, and inattention.

Elkonin (1973) and Downing (1973) have independently argued that there is an intrinsic relationship between reading disability and deficiencies in phonologic processing. Specifically, they suggest that some poor readers have little awareness of the phonemic constitution of spoken words and have not apprehended the symbol-to-sound mapping that characterizes words in print. Liberman and her associates (Shankweiler and Liberman 1972; Liberman et al. 1974) have adopted a similar position. These authors appear to be among the few who limit their descriptions of disabled readers to the behavioral manifestations of reading disability and refer very little to neurologic causes of the disorder.

Finally, Zangwill (1962) suggested that dyslexia could conceivably be due to poorly established dominance, resulting in speech and language problems as well as spatial defects and motor deficiencies. However, he also suggested that there may be another form of reading disorder (pure dyslexia) characterized by complete lateralization. Such cases, he believed, may be genetically determined. Zangwill was not specific about the behavioral manifestations of these two types of disorders nor about the distinction between them. It is therefore difficult to comment further on the validity of his observations.

It is convenient to summarize single-factor theories of dyslexia by highlighting their common features. First we might point out that most have a medical-organic foundation implying that some form of neurological dysfunction is the underlying cause of reading disability. Second, almost all of these theories implicate dysfunction in visual-spatial processing as a factor contributing to reading disorder and several place special emphasis upon deficiencies in visual memory and perception. Some stress the possibility of poorly established hemispheric dominance along with maturational lag. Still others emphasize congenital or genetic factors. Only a few authors (Rabinovitch 1959, 1968; Downing 1973; Elkonin 1973; Liberman et al. 1974; Perfetti and Lesgold 1978) have suggested that language disorder may be a significant cause of malfunction in reading, although many loosely refer to dyslexia as a specific language disability (Orton 1925, 1937; Bender 1956, 1957). Yet the possibility that poor readers are characterized by linguistic deficiencies has been strengthened by results of studies that have recently appeared in the literature.

3.2 MULTIFACTOR THEORIES

A number of investigators have suggested that the etiology of specific reading disability is heterogeneous in nature, there being presumably more than one type of basic process disorder causing reading problems. Theorists in this group are to be distinguished from those who suggest that reading disability is probably associated with a number of possible environmental factors interacting with individual differences in (reading) "aptitude" and intelligence (such as Monroe 1932; Robinson 1946; Malmquist 1960). Such individuals de-emphasize, if not deny, the possibility that some poor readers may support an intrinsic deficiency whose origin is qualitatively different from the multitude of environmental factors that cause most reading problems. Members of this group do not postulate theories of dyslexia nor make reference to organic or underlying causes of reading disability as do the multifactor theorists. For that matter, not all of the multifactor explanations to be examined qualify as substantive, well-integrated theories. Some are more accurately classified as descriptions that emphasize the likelihood of categories or subtypes of reading disability, rather than as etiological theories in the strict sense.

The most influential of the multifactor theorists is, without question, Herbert Birch. Synthesizing a great deal of work in both comparative and developmental psychology, Birch (1962) tentatively hypothesized that dyslexia is associated with three separate types of basic process disorder, each affecting somewhat different aspects of the reading process. Of these, the hypothesis that has received the most attention is that poor readers may be deficient in the ability to establish intersensory equivalences. In studies with normal children (Birch and Lefford 1963), Birch provided documentation that the ability to match and integrate intersensory information takes some time to develop. Relating his work with children to evidence from research conducted with subhuman species and adults (see Pavlov 1927; Lashley 1929), Birch suggested that "some individuals with reading disability are disabled precisely because they have nervous systems in which the development of equivalences between the sensory systems is impaired" (1962, 167). He further suggested that such impairment would not be limited to the visual and auditory systems but would appear in the learning of visual-tactual and kinesthetic relationships as well. The intersensory deficit hypothesis has proved to be one of the most provocative in the literature and has stimulated a great deal of research.

A second hypothesis advanced by Birch is that reading disability in some children may stem from inadequate development of appropriate hierarchical organization of sensory systems (1962, 164). He pointed out that normal development is characterized by increasingly greater dominance of the teleoreceptor systems (vision and audition), and that in older children and adults these systems take on the dominant role in processing environmental stimuli (see Renshaw 1930). He therefore suggested that reading is a process requiring visual dominance, and that failure to establish hierarchical dominance of the visual system may cause difficulty in learning to read. Such disorder appears to be similar to the figure-ground deficiencies presumed to be characteristic of poor readers, suggested by Bender and Drew, among others. It should be noted that sensory hierarchical dominance as an explanatory construct is central to *both* intersensory deficit and sensory dominance theories of dyslexia.

Birch's third hypothesis is that reading disability may be caused by dysfunction in visual analysis and synthesis. According to this theory, visual perception undergoes developmental changes over time, from gross discrimination of identities in the first stage, through a period of perceptual analysis (decomposing a figure into its component parts) at the second stage, and terminating in the ability to synthesize part-whole relationships. Thus visual perception appears to be defined as a *structural* as well as a *functional* entity, characterized by capacities that differentiate and expand during the course of development. Birch suggested that at least some poor readers are deficient in the ability to analyze and synthesize visual information.

Several other theorists have postulated that poor readers can be classified on the basis of deficiencies in one or another sensory mode. For example Myklebust and his associates suggested that there are two types of dyslexia, which they termed *visual dyslexia* and *auditory dyslexia* (Myklebust and Johnson 1962; Johnson and Myklebust 1967). Visual dyslexia is presumed to be characterized by deficiencies in visual perception and visual memory. Children who are described as having this disorder are said to be able to learn to read through the auditory modality if given proper remediation; the orientation and sequencing errors commonly observed in poor readers are thought to be characteristic of such children. Children believed to be afflicted with auditory dyslexia are said to have difficulty in such diverse areas as discrimination of speech sounds, sound blending, labeling and naming, and "auditory sequencing." The auditory dyslexic, like the visual dyslexic, may be able to learn to read in the alternative modality. Myklebust is of the opinion that these deficits are basic and suggests the term *psychoneurological learning disabilities* to distinguish such disorders from those that result from extrinsic factors.

Boder (1970, 1971) has proposed a classification schema similar to Myklebust's. Employing the analysis of spelling errors as a vehicle for classifying dyslexics, she claims to have isolated subtypes identified by primary difficulty in either visual or auditory learning, or by admixtures of both types of deficit. One group, which she calls *dysphonetic dyslexics,* is thought to have a basic deficiency in letter–sound integration and in learning phonetically. Individuals in this group are inclined to approach the tasks of word learning and spelling in a global manner. They may have a sizable repertoire of words recognizable on sight, but their spelling typically bears little resemblance to the words they attempt to read. A second group of deficient readers presumably have basic difficulty in "perceiving whole words as gestalts" (1970, 289). Such individuals, referred to as *dyseidetic dyslexics,* presumably read and spell phonetically, are inclined to be over analytic, and have great difficulty in building a sight vocabulary. The third group *(dysphonetic-dyseidetic)* are thought to be the most severely impaired of all; they appear to manifest difficulties in both whole word learning and phonetic analysis.

Ingram, Mason and Blackburn (1970) propose a classification that in essential features is almost identical to Myklebust's and Boder's. Children with audiophonic difficulties are said to have poor discrimination and blending skills and a general deficiency in phonetic analysis. Children with visuospatial difficulties manifest visual discrimination and orientation problems and have difficulty recognizing even simple words at sight.

Mattis, French, and Rapin (1975) claim to have identified at least three subgroups of dyslexics. The largest of these groups is said to consist of children with a variety of types of language impairments, which may include phonologic deficiencies, labeling and naming problems, and inadequate knowledge of syntax. A smaller proportion is presumed to be characterized by dysfunction in the motor system resulting in speech articulation problems and visual-motor (handwriting) deficits. The smallest subgroup consists of children who are thought to be impaired in visual-spatial functioning, as evidenced in visual discrimination and visual memory problems. With the exception of the role ascribed to speech articulation and visual-motor problems, these distinctions are similar to those outlined in other multifaceted explanations of reading disability.

One final theory of reading disability that may be reasonably grouped with the multifactor theories is that of Satz and his associates (Satz and Sparrow 1970; Sparrow and Satz 1970; Satz and Friel 1974; Satz, Friel, and Rudegeair 1974a, 1974b). These authors suggest that dyslexia is the result of a general lag in maturation, resulting in delayed lateral dominance. Developmental problems are believed to be associated with abnormality only in growth rate and *not* with specific structural defects in the central nervous system. In fact, the dyslexic is described as parallel in development to a normal child chronologically younger. According to this point of view, disabled readers at younger age levels (ages 6 to 8) should be significantly impaired, relative to their normal age-mates, on skills believed to develop at an early age: sensorimotor, perceptual, somatosensory, and nonlinguistic functions generally. In contrast, older children with reading difficulties (ages 9 to 12) should manifest deficiencies in those skills presumed to develop later, such as language and conceptual functions. Reading problems would consequently occur as a result of lack of readiness for acquiring certain abilities, but the poor reader's difficulties would be qualitatively different at different periods of development. Problems encountered by the beginning reader would occur primarily because of visual perceptual disorder. Between 9 and 12 years of age, however, visual-motor problems should attenuate; during that time language and conceptual difficulties should become evident and thereafter should constitute the major cause of reading deficiency.

Satz's theory is unlike other multifactor theories in that it postulates a single underlying factor—general maturation lag—as the ultimate cause of reading disability. However, inasmuch as it implicates qualitatively different types of disorders as contributing to reading difficulties at different periods of development, it may be viewed as essentially a multifactor theory.

To summarize, the multifactor theories of specific reading disability generally emphasize intramodal deficiencies that theoretically constitute qualitatively different types of process dysfunction. Some theorists have suggested that reading disability could also result from deficiency in *inter*modal integration, but only Birch (1962) has detailed such a theory. In fact, Birch has provided much more specificity with regard to testable hypotheses and greater documentation of his theories than any of the other multifactor theorists, most of whose explanations of dyslexia do not qualify as well-integrated theories or even taxonomies in the strict sense. They may be more accurately referred to as categories or subtypes of process disorder.

3.3 SUMMARY AND CONCLUSIONS

Single-factor and multifactor explanations of reading disability have similar and dissimilar elements. Most of these explanations are alike in that they emphasize dysfunction in perceptual processes, the largest proportion postulating deficiency in visual-spatial organization. There is also a considerable degree of support for the possibility that dyslexia is a constitutionally based developmental disorder that is qualitatively different from reading problems caused by extrinsic factors. The majority of authors make reference to some form of neurological deficit as the basic cause of reading disability; only a few have limited their descriptions to the behavioral manifestations of this anomaly. But very few of the explanations advanced have the characteristics that earmark a detailed, well-integrated, and productive theory.

The two views are dissimilar in the emphases they give to one or another type of process disorder. The multifactor group, for example, stresses auditory and linguistic factors more than the single-factor group does, but without ignoring the possibility of dysfunction in visual processes as well.

The individual theories in both categories are also dissimilar with respect to the degree of specificity they provide in regard to both behavioral and organic correlates of reading disability. Thus they differ in their heuristic value and in their ability to generate testable hypotheses.

The etiological constructs and explanations advanced in all theories discussed reduce to a variety of hypotheses that alternatively focus upon four basic areas of concern, deficiencies in which are believed to be central to the disorder: (1) *visual perception and visual memory,* (2) *intersensory integration,* (3) *serial order recall,* and (4) *verbal processing.* We will examine each of these possibilities and the relevant research findings either for or against theories that implicate them.

Part Two

**STUDIES OF BASIC
PROCESS DYSFUNCTION**

Chapter Four

INTRODUCTION:
BASIC PROCESS MODEL

In order to facilitate clarity and integration of the contrasts to be discussed, we will examine research results within the context of a synthesized model of the components of human memory, a model whose attributes enjoy some degree of consensus in the literature (see Neisser 1967; Craik and Lockhart 1972; Norman 1972; Massaro 1975).

As Simon (1972) has pointed out, any architectural structure designed to depict information processing in children, particularly as it relates to learning and development, should ideally accord prominence to both initial and short-term storage of information as well as to attentional mechanisms that determine what attributes of the sensory stimulus will be selected for central processing. The structure should also represent, in some functional way, the properties of long-term storage, since it is becoming increasingly more evident that one's permanent knowledge is highly influential in determining the types and levels of processing that take place at all stages of memory. Simon further suggests that consideration be given to the possibility of hemispheric specialization in processing information from different modalities, a suggestion that is particularly applicable in the present context (see Geschwind 1962; Gazzaniga 1970; Milner 1971; Posner, Lewis, and Conrad 1972). I would add that the model should be sufficiently general to accommodate an understanding of memory in children (see Hagen, Jongeward, and Kail 1975) since those models available are based primarily on work done with adults. And the model should be broad enough to facilitate an understanding of process differences in poor and normal readers, in both intrasensory and intersensory functions.

Figure 4.1 presents such a paradigm. The representations of memory stages are deliberately quite general; the schematics and notations relate only to broad features upon which there is considerable agreement.

The first stage—*sensory storage*—is the capacity that facilitates retention of the sensory image within specifiable limits (0 to 300 milliseconds) unless interrupted by subsequent (sensory) stimulation. For example, in reading connected text the duration of the image for a reasonably fluent reader is estimated to be approximately 250 milliseconds, or the average duration of fixations between saccadic eye movements. This stage of processing was the object of much research during the 1960s (Sperling 1960; Averbach and Coriell 1961; Haber 1969) and has more recently been discussed in reference to both normal and abnormal reading ability (Alwitt 1963; Stanley and Hall 1973; Stanley 1975a, 1975b; Massaro 1975). Its primary function is said to be the initial detection of the physical features of a given stimulus, the end result of which appears to be a literal copy of the sensory stimulus.

The second stage is commonly referred to as *short-term* (or primary) *memory* and is thought to be a limited capacity system of restricted duration (Waugh and Norman 1965; Norman 1972; Deutsch and Deutsch 1975). The number of units or *chunks* of information that can be stored in short-term memory is estimated to be four to seven for children 5 to 10 years old (Simon 1972) and five to nine for most adults (Miller 1956). Estimates of duration vary, but the longest period reported has been no more than 30 seconds, as measured by laboratory tasks (Glanzer and Cunitz 1966; Craik and Lockhart 1972). The presumed functions of short-term memory are to facilitate the recall of information to be retained for only brief periods, and to place new information into permanent storage. Both functions are said to rely heavily upon recoding and rehearsal processes, prompting some to refer to this system as the *working memory* (Kleiman 1975). Several authors cite deficiencies at this stage of processing as the basis for many of the differences observed between poor and normal readers.

A memory stage intermediate between sensory and short-term store has been deliberately omitted. That stage has been referred to as a precategorical store by Crowder (1972) and as synthesized memory by Massaro (1975), to describe a stage in which sensory information is synthesized and perceived at a

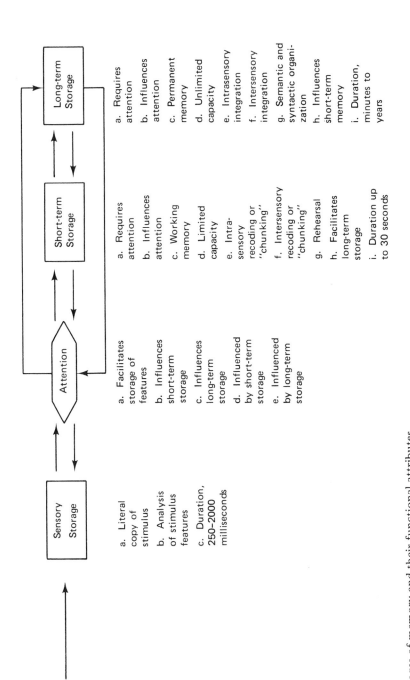

Figure 4.1 Stages of memory and their functional attributes

Sensory Stimulation

a. Visual
b. Auditory

Sensory Storage

a. Literal copy of stimulus
b. Analysis of stimulus features
c. Duration, 250–2000 milliseconds

Attention

a. Facilitates storage of features
b. Influences short-term storage
c. Influences long-term storage
d. Influenced by short-term storage
e. Influenced by long-term storage

Short-term Storage

a. Requires attention
b. Influences attention
c. Working memory
d. Limited capacity
e. Intra-sensory recoding or "chunking"
f. Intersensory recoding or "chunking"
g. Rehearsal
h. Facilitates long-term storage
i. Duration up to 30 seconds

Long-term Storage

a. Requires attention
b. Influences attention
c. Permanent memory
d. Unlimited capacity
e. Intrasensory integration
f. Intersensory integration
g. Semantic and syntactic organization
h. Influences short-term memory
i. Duration, minutes to years

level higher than that characterized by the feature detection that takes place during initial (sensory) storage. However, this level of perception is believed to be prior to the processing of such categorical information as semantic and syntactic meanings. Thus one may be able to recall and repeat a nonsense syllable or reproduce a novel design without associating such stimuli with higher-order relationships. Although these are useful distinctions, for the sake of simplicity, this intermediate stage is excluded from the model.

Certainly influencing the type and amount of material that is processed at all stages of memory is the degree to which *attention* is deployed to one aspect or another of a given array. Neisser (1967) points out that while the sensory or preattentive store is capable of synthesizing stimulus features into a cohesive figure or *icon*, it is *focal* attention that ultimately determines the fate of the sensory image and no doubt influences processing in permanent as well as short-term memory. Reciprocally, it is almost certain that activity taking place in short-term storage determines, in part, the selective aspects of focal attention, as does information of a given type programmed in long-term storage. The reciprocal and interactive relationships among the various components of memory are represented in the model with bidirectional pairs of arrows from one component to another.

The final stage in the model is long-term or permanent storage. This is thought to be an unlimited capacity system, which may hold information for an indefinite duration. Only in recent years have investigators begun active exploration of the organization and structure of long-term memory (Tulving and Donaldson 1972; Kintsch 1974; Massaro 1975); consequently, little is known about its basic properties. However, permanent memory is thought to contain knowledge that is categorized and integrated in ways that facilitate rapid and automatic comprehension of information entering the sense modalities in both natural and coded forms. This must include semantic and syntactic programs, to allow understanding and communication of spoken and printed language; and it must include permanent records of objects and events encountered in one's experience, to allow recognition and commerce with things and people unique to those experiences (Paivio 1971; Tulving 1972). Without doubt, long-term memory influences all other memorial processes and is in turn influenced by them.

In addition to this basic process model we will have occasion, in the following sections, to call upon a conceptualization of the normal reading process, the major tenets of which have particular relevance for research to be discussed. I refer to the developmental theory of word perception recently articulated by Gibson (Gibson 1971; Gibson and Levin 1975). Briefly, Gibson suggests that letters and words are perceived through the discovery of *distinctive features* and *higher-order invariants* as a function of acquired cognitive strategies that tend toward economical and selective ordering of stimulus input. She divides the distinctive features of words into five general classes of information: *graphic, orthographic, phonologic, semantic,* and *syntactic.* Information from all five featural classes is said to be processed sequentially and hierarchically; priorities in the perceptual ordering of stimuli within each class are determined by developmental changes associated with cognitive and linguistic growth as well as by experiences in reading. The beginning reader is presumably more sensitive to the semantic and syntactic features of the words he encounters than to their graphic and phonologic features. At an intermediate stage—when the reader is learning to "break the code"—graphic, orthographic, and phonologic features are probably in greater awareness. With greater fluency in reading, the child again becomes primarily sensitive to the semantic and syntactic characteristics of printed words, which then take precedence over graphic and phonologic characteristics. Gibson suggests further that the word features processed in a given instance will depend upon such factors as the reader's purpose (proofreading versus reading for meaning), the difficulty of the passage, momentary fluctuation in set, and general reading skill (Gibson 1971).

I will refer to the stages of memory or to certain aspects of Gibson's theory when they can be usefully employed as an aid to understanding; I will not attempt to relate research findings or theoretical views to either model in any systematic or exhaustive way.

Chapter Five

READER GROUP
CONTRASTS IN VISUAL
PERCEPTION AND
VISUAL MEMORY

5.1 VISUAL PERCEPTION

By far the most popular explanation of specific reading disability
is deficiency in visual perception and memory, presumably associated with some form of neurological disorder. Initially stated
by Morgan (1896) and Hinshelwood (1900, 1917), this explanation was given its primary impetus by Orton (1925, 1937), who
attached particular significance to the orientation and sequencing
problems observed in letter and word identification (*b/d, was/saw*).
Such disturbances were thought to be a manifestation of delayed
development of lateral dominance, resulting in the failure to sup-
press mirror images of visual representations, which Orton believed were stored in the two hemispheres. And as already mentioned, the variants of Orton's theory all have in common the view
that dyslexia is primarily the result of visual organization and
memory problems.

The perceptual deficit hypothesis has enjoyed a surprising
longevity in spite of the fact that research supporting it is at
best equivocal. Benton (1962), in an initial review, made note
of methodological weaknesses and conflicting results in most
of the studies that had appeared in the literature up to that time.
Critchley (1970) made similar observations. Since most of the
studies they reviewed were described in some detail, they will not
be discussed here. It should be pointed out, however, that they
were remarkable in the heterogeneity of the reader groups compared. Many studies included children of subnormal intelligence
(Fildes 1921); others included those with neurological defects
(Galifret-Granjon 1952) or emotional problems (Bender 1956
1957; Silver and Hagin 1960; Silver 1961). Furthermore, little

attempt was made to control for socioeconomic and cultural factors, and operational criteria for assessing reading ability often complied with no designated standard.

With respect to methodology, most of the investigations were descriptive or correlational (Gates 1922; Monroe 1932), and some would be better classified as clinical rather than laboratory studies (Bronner 1917; Orton 1925, 1937; Bender 1956, 1957; Silver and Hagin 1960). Commonly employed dependent variables were measures of visual-motor coordination, visual discrimination, visual memory, spatial orientation, and directional sequencing, these functions being most often assessed through match-to-standard and figure-drawing tests.

Benton concluded from his review that deficient form perception and impaired directional functioning are not significant correlates of reading disability. He allowed, however, for the possibility that perceptual problems may exist in children younger than those employed as subjects in the investigations reviewed (that is, children under 9 years). He also suggested the likelihood that reading problems in older children (9 years and above) are associated with dysfunction in some aspects of verbal mediation. In a later account he came to the same conclusion, stating that "the importance of visuoperceptive and visuomotor difficulties as determinants of reading failure has been overrated by some authors" (Benton 1975, 15).

I am in essential agreement with Benton but feel it necessary, in view of the popularity of the perceptual deficit hypothesis, to document my position in somewhat greater detail. I will place particular emphasis upon recent investigations comparing visual processing in poor and normal readers. A number of these studies were not reported by Benton (1975); they are presented here because their findings are central to the point of view I will progressively evolve.

Most of the perceptual deficit theories that have been advanced in the literature cite dysfunction in visual-spatial organization as the immediate cause of dyslexia. They may therefore be reasonably construed as implying some type of disorder at the very first stage of visual processing (*sensory storage,* in figure 4.1). However, all of the theorists in one sense or another infer basic deficiency in forming reliable sensory images. Thus, by extension, storage and retrieval at higher levels of cognitive functioning are impaired, thereby accounting theoretically for the poor reader's presumed inability to remember the shapes and orientations of the objects and symbols he encounters. Neisser's suggestion (1967) that initial (preattentive) perception involves an active synthesis of sensory stimuli is consistent with the possibility that deficient perception in poor readers is caused by (inferred) malfunction in the development of a cohesive sensory image at the first level of visual processing. Neisser essentially adopts a constructivist position; his theory, taken to its extreme, would allow for the possibility of the types of perceptual distortions said to occur when the disabled reader (presumably) "sees" *b* as *d* or *was* as *saw.*

Although the perceptual deficit hypothesis has many variants, the poor reader's unique difficulties are most often said to be manifested in *deficient form perception* or *dysfunction in visual analysis.* Deficient form perception is believed to be a manifestation of difficulty in organizing the constituents of a given figure into a cohesive whole or *gestalt.* Most theorists who have postulated such disorder (for example, Bender 1956, 1957) have drawn upon principles of perception associated with Gestalt theorizing (Wertheimer 1923; Kohler 1929; Koffka 1935), and constructs such as similarity, closure, proximity, and continuation have been employed as criteria against which to ascertain adequacy of perceptual functioning. Also influential are the positions held by developmental theorists who stress the importance of maturation and motor functioning in perception (Gesell 1924, 1952; Bender 1938, 1956, 1957; Schilder 1944, 1950; Werner and Strauss 1952; Piaget and Inhelder 1956). Figure drawings and matching tasks have been most often used to evaluate form perception, though a few more recent studies have directly assessed perception at the initial or feature detection stage of visual processing. We will therefore examine a representative sampling of studies employing each of these evaluative procedures.

Ability to analyze visual materials obviously implies adequacy of form perception. It also assumes the existence of perceptual attitudes that allow one to separate focal stimuli from extraneous background and to detect the critical and distinguishing features necessary for accurate recognition. Several studies have compared poor and normal readers on particular aspects of analytic skill:

spatial and directional orientation, figure-ground perception, and speed of perceptual processing. A number of these studies will also be reviewed and their results will be analyzed in relation to the perceptual deficit hypothesis.

5.2 FORM PERCEPTION

5.2.1 Visual-Motor Ability

Perhaps the most commonly employed technique for evaluating perceptual deficit theories of reading disability is to compare the performance of poor and normal readers on tests of visual-motor ability—most often the copying of geometric figures. Such instruments are frequently used in clinic and school settings for differential diagnosis of perceptual and perceptual-motor "deficiencies" (Koppitz 1964; Keogh and Becker 1975), being second only to the intelligence test in popularity among practitioners (Sundberg 1961). Many practitioners believe, in addition, that figure drawing tests have utility for assessing general level of maturation in the interest of detecting "developmental lags" that presumably hamper achievement (Ilg and Ames 1965). It therefore seems important to critically evaluate the theoretical and empirical rationales of those who have promulgated the use of visual-motor tests to determine the etiology of reading disability.

Figure-drawing tests have long been used for studying perceptual processes (Wertheimer 1923), but their prominence in evaluating disorders of childhood dates back to Bender's (1938) initial description of the well-known Visual-Motor Gestalt Test (see figure 5.1). Bender was influenced by the classical teachings of the Gestalt school (Wertheimer 1923; Kohler 1929; Koffka 1935) as well as by the developmental studies of Schilder (1944) and Gesell (1924, 1952). From the Gestalt psychologists, she adopted the notion of wholistic perception as an innate characteristic of the normal, well-integrated organism; the studies of Schilder and Gesell impressed her with the importance of motor factors, personal drives, and maturational changes as determinants of perception.

Bender theorized, in line with the works of these authors, that the individual (innately) perceives visual stimuli as gestalten, or whole figures that transcend specific relationships among their component parts. The ability to perceive such gestalten was

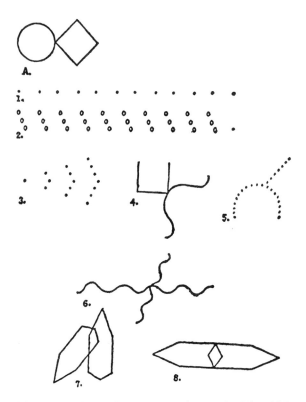

Figure 5.1 Figures included on the Bender Visual Motor Gestalt Test (Bender 1938). Subjects are presented with figures individually and asked to copy each. (Plate I on page 4 of *Instructions for the Use of Visual Motor Gestalt Test.* Reproduced by permission of the publisher, the American Orthopsychiatric Association.)

described as a dynamic process that is complexly determined by stimulation from the distal figure interacting with "sensory-motor action patterns," personal drives, attitudes, and other organismic factors. Perception was also viewed as constantly changing, and any given percept was said to be a "momentary point of equilibbrium" between biological and stimulus variables.

Bender further suggested that a variety of pathological states may disrupt the integrity of the organism and thereby impair perceptual and perceptual-motor functioning. This suggestion was made largely as a result of extensive analyses of the visual-motor productions of several hundred adults and children suffering from various neurologic and psychiatric disorders. A number of graphic deficiencies commonly observed in the protocols of these individuals eventually came to be employed as diagnostic signs, presumably reflecting disturbances in "organismic integration." These typically included such anomalies as size and shape distortions, "primitivization" (drawing loops for dots) perseveration, orientation difficulties, angulation problems, difficulty in closing or connecting figures, additions, and deletions.

Such deficiencies were typically observed in various organic and functional disorders, but Bender (1938, 1956) provided evidence for age differences in the quality of childrens' drawings. From this she inferred that normal maturation proceeds in stages characterized by qualitative changes in visual-motor functioning along the developmental continuum, especially between the ages of 3 and 11 years. She made note of similar findings in research conducted by Gesell and his associates (Gesell and Thompson 1934; Gesell and Amatruda 1947). Such results strengthened her view that many developmental disorders are attributable to neurological maturational lags and led her to suggest that visual-motor productions may be useful in identifying cognitive and personality deficits associated with delayed development.

Bender's theorizing provided the basic rationale for employing figure drawings to investigate the etiology of reading disability and other disorders of childhood. The utility of such instruments for assessing maturation was subsequently reinforced by Ilg and Ames (1965), who compiled age norms for the copying of geometric designs and human figures, and by Koppitz (1964), who standardized a scoring system for the Bender Gestalt Test (see also Keogh 1968).

In harmony with the views of Bender, Schilder, and Gesell, several other individuals have suggested that veridicality of perception is largely dependent upon the alignment and coordination of sensory and motor experiences, namely, Strauss (Strauss and Lehtinen 1947), Werner (1948), Kephart (1960), and Cruickshank (1968, 1972). Each of them has emphasized the role of maturation in their conceptualizations of perceptual disorder. Perceptual deficiencies were, in fact, viewed as major determinants of learning disabilities and were said to be the end result of disturbances in sensory-motor integration. They therefore inferred that such deficiencies could be diagnosed through the use of measures that evaluate the adequacy of visual-motor development. Several of these authors have even constructed perceptual and perceptual-motor tests for this purpose (Frostig 1961; Roach and Kephart 1966), and their work, along with that of Bender, has popularized the notion that children who sustain reading and other learning disabilities are characterzed by visual-motor and visual-perceptual deficits.

Studies Differentiating Poor and Normal Readers on Visual-Motor Ability   Empirical evidence in support of such points of view is both equivocal and tenuous. Studies comparing poor and normal readers on measures of visual-motor functioning have yielded conflicting results and those offering positive findings are typically characterized by methodological or interpretive difficulties.

Benton (1962) reported a study by Galifret-Granjon (1952) in which differences were found between poor and normal readers on the Bender Visual-Motor Gestalt Test (BVMGT) as well as on various other measures of visual-motor skill. The magnitudes of these differences were observed to be greater in younger children (7 to 10 years) than in older ones (11 to 13). However, as Benton noted, the poor readers in this investigation were a heterogeneous group, including mentally defective and brain-damaged children as well as those with adequate intelligence. Thus the results may not be applicable to children with specific reading disability.

Silver and Hagin (1960) administered a battery of neurological, perceptual, and perceptual-motor tasks to 150 children, all of whom were clinic cases referred for behavior disorder. Their ages ranged from 8 to 14 years, their IQs from 81 to 123. No other description of the sample was provided. There was no control group, although mention was made of a controlled study with subgroups of children selected from this sample (Hagin 1954).

Silver and Hagin reported evidence for a "syndrome" of deficiencies in 92 percent of their subjects, characterized typically by positive neurological indicators, visual-perceptual and visual-motor deficits, phonological difficulties, and tactual discrimination problems. Performance defects on the BVMGT that were reported as statistically significant were as follows: difficulty with angulation, tendency to verticalize diagonals, primitivization, and the use of cues to facilitate alignment of figures. Figure-ground problems were also observed, as manifested on the Marble Board test employed by Strauss and Lehtinen (1947). Silver and Hagin (1960) found, in addition, a significant incidence of auditory dysfunction, though visual-perceptual and visual-motor deficiencies were said to be far more prevalent. It was therefore concluded that reading disability is a generic disorder associated with incomplete lateralization and maturational lags affecting a variety of basic processes germane to the development of skill in reading.

The results of the Silver and Hagin study can be questioned on several counts. First, the failure to provide comparative statistics for normal readers makes it difficult to evaluate the conclusions, especially in relation to specific reading disability. Second, though reference is made to results that achieved statistical significance (results on BVMGT), no information is provided as to levels of significance, central tendencies, and variances associated with relevant findings, which again renders interpretation hazardous. Third, no data on the incidence of specific disorders in individuals or subgroups is presented; it is therefore unwarranted to suggest that reading disability constitutes either a syndrome of related disorders or subgroups of relatively homogeneous disorders. It may be, for example, that the performance of many of the children in the study was impaired on most tasks as a result of behavior disorder and not because of neurological or perceptual deficit. It is also possible that some children were afflicted with multiple handicaps, which would further increase the probability that performance deficits in such youngsters were due to factors that would result in general, rather than specific, learning disability. A fourth criticism is that the authors did not discuss the socioeconomic status of their subjects. One therefore cannot be certain that their results are representative of children with reading disorder associated with intrinsic or developmental factors as opposed to extrinsic or environmental factors.

Finally, Silver and Hagin's inference that the visual-motor defects observed in their subjects are due to perceptual integration problems is not very compelling, given the likelihood that tests of visual-motor functioning are measuring skills that are factorially more complex than those involved in simple form discrimination, a point to be discussed in greater detail.

Poor performance on a visual-motor test may be partly due to emotional and attitudinal factors rather then perceptual disorder. This possibility is provided some support in a study by Lachmann (1960), in which the BVMGT was administered to three groups of children at two different age levels. One group consisted of normal readers with no apparent emotional problems. A second group consisted of children referred to a clinic for emotional problems but who had no reading difficulties. The third group consisted of children referred to a reading clinic for remediation of reading difficulties. Subjects' ages ranged from 8 to 11 years, and the groups were equated for age, sex, and intelligence.

Two findings are worthy of note. First, though there was some tendency on the part of poor readers to perform less proficiently than normal readers on the BVMGT, the magnitude of the disparities was not impressive. This is reflected in the chi-square for over all differences, which did not achieve statistical significance. Second, there were no significant differences between poor readers who had no apparent emotional problems and emotionally impaired children who had no reading difficulties. However, the performance of both these groups was less proficient than that of the nonimpaired normal readers.

These findings cast doubt on the notion that poor performance on a test of figure drawing is caused by deficiencies in form perception. Tests such as the BVMGT require preplanning, effort, and concentration, as well as the disposition to self-correct; it would not be surprising to find limited enthusiasm for compliance with these requirements among either deficient readers or proficient readers experiencing emotional difficulties, perhaps because of the lack of motivation to attend to the type of detail in execution necessary for adequate performance. Consistent with this interpretation are the results of Wolfe (1941), who found that poor readers comparable to normal controls in age, intelligence, and socioeconomic status performed below the level of the controls on a variety of perceptual and cognitive tasks. However, they were also less well motivated and less attentive than the controls, as measured by a personality inventory and observations of test-taking behavior.

Lovell, Shapton, and Warren (1964) compared matched samples of poor and normal readers on design copying and various other tests of perceptual and cognitive functioning. The groups were equated for nonverbal reasoning ability, social class, age (mean chronological age = 9.8), sex, and school setting. Poor readers were less able than the normal readers on several measures involving spatial orientation, but they were comparable to the normal readers on a measure of expressive language. The authors concluded from these findings that reading disability may be a sympton of "brain dysfunction" resulting in perceptual deficiency, a conclusion that would seem to be unwarranted in that the poor readers' performance on the various tests was quite variable. For example, although these subjects differed from normal readers on some portions of a test of left-right discrimination, they performed as well as normal readers on other portions of this same test. Inconsistency was also noted on measures of spatial and verbal skill, the deficient readers functioning below the level of the normals on some of these measures (Block Design and Vocabulary subtests of WISC) but not on others (Object Assembly subtest of WISC and knowledge of syntax). Such variability casts doubt on the inference that reader group differences were due to perceptual or perceptual-motor disorder associated with neurological dysfunction.

The results of a second study were even more variable (Lovell, Gray, and Oliver 1964). The groups in this investigation were matched in accord with the criteria outlined for the first test, but the subjects were older (14 years). The tasks employed were quite similar to the tasks in the earlier study. Of five visual-spatial and visual-motor tests, only two differentiated between reader groups. There were also inconsistencies with respect to reader-group-by-sex interactions. In the case of boys, poor and normal readers differed on measures of both spatial and verbal ability; among the girls, poor and normal groups differed only on a measure of vocabulary. In spite of these disparities, Lovell, Gray, and Oliver concluded that reading disability may be associated with perceptual deficiency, essentially the same conclusion as that drawn in the study by Lovell, Shapton, and Warren.

The equivocal nature of the results obtained in these two studies vitiates the authors' interpretations. The reader group differences observed can just as easily be attributed to general learning impediments as to specific disorder in perceptual or perceptual-motor functions, since no consistent pattern emerged in either investigation. Of particular significance in this connection is a finding in one of these studies (Lovell, Gray, and Oliver 1964) that was not highlighted by the authors. On tests comparing poor and normal readers on the copying of sentences as opposed to writing them from dictation, letter reversals distinguished these groups only on writing from dictation. Similar results were found in scoring for additions and omissions. These findings suggest that poor readers may have had difficulties in relating the visual and verbal counterparts of the letters and words dictated rather than in processing their spatial characteristics. The rationale underlying this suggestion will be discussed in greater detail in subsequent sections. Suffice it to say at this point that the studies by Lovell and her associates do not provide impressive evidence for the contention that reading disability is caused by deficiencies in form perception or spatial orientation.

A number of investigations have reported predictive relationships between performance on measures of perceptual and perceptual-motor functioning and reading achievement in the early elementary grades. A study that has been widely cited as offering support for perceptual deficit explanations was conducted some time ago by Goins (1958).

Goins administered a battery of visual, nonverbal tests to beginning first-graders and correlated scores on these tests with scores on reading and intelligence tests—Stanford-Binet (S-B) and Kuhlmann-Anderson (K.A.)—given early and late in the school year. The battery of so-called "perceptual" tasks included pattern completion, copying of abstract designs, matching designs and pictures, attendance to orientation of designs and pictures, and tests of visual memory.

Most of the tests correlated significantly and positively with subsequent reading achievement, but correlations in general were of low magnitude (ranging from .02 to .51). Among the perceptual tasks, those that correlated best with reading were, in order, pattern copying, which assessed the ability to copy geometric patterns (r = .51, second testing only) and reversals, a match-to-standard task, which evaluated the ability to detect differences in orientation of pictures (r = .47 first testing; r = .49 second testing). Correlations between the perceptual tests and intelligence measures ranged from .08 to .47, the highest being with pattern copying (r = .47 for S-B and .33 for K.A.) and figures (r = .45 for S-B and .37 for K.A.), the latter requiring skill in detecting orientation differences among abstract designs. Correlations between the reading and intelligence tests were also significant (r = .32 for S-B and .39 for K.A.).

Factor analyses of the test battery (exclusive of intelligence scores) revealed the existence of two component factors, only one of which was significantly associated with reading ability. This factor included tests of pattern copying, pattern completion, orientation to pictures and designs, matching of pictures, and reading achievement. Goins concluded that reading ability is determined in part by a perceptual factor, termed strength of closure, which was defined as the "ability to keep in mind a configuration against distraction" (Goins 1958, 99).

Goins's conclusion is undermined by the fact that the perceptual measures that correlated best with reading also correlated with intelligence, which itself was significantly related to reading. Furthermore, several of the subtests that correlated with strength of closure (the critical factor) had no relation to reading ability. Therefore, while reading and other tasks loading on strength of closure may be related by virtue of a common or underlying factor, this factor may not be accurately described by "strength of closure" as defined by Goins. My guess would be that the underlying factor is a conceptual factor not fully measured by the intelligence tests employed. This suggestion is based upon the observation that many of the so-called perceptual tasks were quite complex and required considerable reasoning ability. They also required effort, concentration, and attention to subtle details, dispositions not always found in very young children, especially those experiencing significant difficulty in school learning.

Finally, it is somewhat puzzling that Goins's study has been so often cited in support of the view that reading disability is associated with perceptual disorder, inasmuch as the subjects in this study were not disabled readers. Indeed all children assessed were reading at least at grade level. Thus the results cannot readily be generalized to youngsters who are severely impaired in their ability to read.

Several other investigations have attempted to employ visual-motor tests and various other cognitive tasks to predict reading achievement. Certain of these investigations are notable for their emphasis upon maturation lag as the basic factor contributing to reading disability. For example, de Hirsch, Jansky, and Langford (1966) administered a large battery (N = 37) of developmental tests to 53 children of average intelligence who were primarily from low middle-class urban environments. The prediction instruments included measures of behavioral stability, ego strength, work attitude, gross and fine motor functioning, visual-motor ability, visual and auditory discrimination, receptive and expressive language, and various tests of reading readiness (letter naming, letter copying, letter and word matching, rhyming, and new word learning and recognition). Criterion measures were two tests of reading achievement and a test of spelling ability administered at the end of second grade. The scores on the reading measures were combined to form an overall reading achievement index.

As regards the relationship between reading ability and form perception, it should first be noted that scores on the Bender Gestalt Test administered in kindergarten correlated significantly with reading achievement in second grade (r = .44). From this it was inferred that poor readers were deficient in perceptual integration as a result of maturational immaturity. Yet there was no significant relationship between reading achievement and a test of figure-ground perception, which, according to the authors, also measures perceptual integration. This disparity therefore questions their interpretation of the correlation found between visual-motor functioning and subsequent reading achievement. Furthermore, significant correlations were found between the reading achievement index and the tests of intelligence (r = .35), behavioral stability (r = .46), "ego strength" (r = .48), and work attitude (r = .43). Thus it is likely that the relationship found between the Bender Gestalt Test and the reading index may

be attributable to factors other than deficient perceptual integration. This suggestion is given additional substance by the clinical
descriptions of the poorest readers in the sample (N = 11), which
made it clear that motivation and attitude in these children were
problematic.

Interestingly enough the highest correlation obtained in this
study was between reading achievement and letter naming (r = .55),
a skill that is more directly related to reading ability than most of
the skills assessed. There were also significant correlations between
achievement in reading and all measures of verbal functioning,
a finding consistent with the view that success in reading is significantly influenced by individual differences in verbal ability.

In a later investigation Jansky and de Hirsch (1972) tested a
much larger (N = 401) and more diverse sample than that in the
1966 study in that subjects came from differing ethnic, cultural,
and socioeconomic backgrounds. The prediction battery (N = 19)
was similar to that employed in the earlier study and contained
ten of the measures used in that investigation. Additional tests
included measures of visual perception, language, and reading
readiness, as well as tests of oral and silent reading ability administered at the end of second grade.

The findings in this study were essentially in accord with those
in the earlier study. Visual-motor functioning as measured by the
Bender Gestalt Test accounted for a small but significant amount
of variance in the overall reading achievement index (r = .41).
Letter naming again manifested the highest correlation with
reading, along with picture naming, the two yielding identical
indices (r = .54). Word matching and other tasks involving letters
and words also correlated significantly with subsequent reading
achievement, as did all measures of auditory and linguistic functioning. Stepwise regression analysis indicated that five measures
in combination accounted for the greatest amount of variance in
reading achievement (43 percent). These, in order of their contribution, were as follows: letter naming (LN) 13 percent, picture
naming (PN) 12 percent, word matching (WM) 7 percent, visual-
motor skill (VMS) 6 percent, and sentence memory (SM) 5 percent. It is significant that three of these tests (LN, PN, SM) measure skills that were found in factor analysis to load significantly
on an oral language factor, and two (LN and WM) measure subskills directly involved in learning to read. These results along with

similar findings in the study by de Hirsch et al. (1966), suggest that language factors may be more important determinants of reading skill than visual-motor ability as measured by instruments such as the Bender Gestalt Test. Considering the small amount of variance in reading achievement attributable to individual differences in visual-motor integration, we may question further the suggestion that reading disability is associated with basic deficiencies in form perception and perceptual-motor integration.

In perhaps the most extensive of all the predictive studies conducted to date, Satz and his associates tested a large number of kindergartners (N = 497), evaluating their achievement in reading annually from first through fifth grade (Satz and Friel 1974; Satz, Friel, and Redegeair 1974a, 1974b; Satz et al. 1977). They hypothesized that dyslexia is caused by a general maturation lag characterized by perceptual and perceptual-motor deficiencies early in development (5 to 8 years), and language and conceptual deficiencies at older ages (9 to 12 years) (Satz and Sparrow 1970). It was predicted that kindergartners who were impaired on tests of visual-motor integration, visual discrimination, and other somatosensory functions would be subsequently found to be impaired in reading.

Contrary to expectations, measures of visual discrimination and visual motor ability obtained in kindergarten correctly identified (as either good or poor readers) only one to two percent of the total number of children evaluated for reading achievement in subsequent years. This represents approximately three to eight children in respective samples of over three and four hundred members of the group originally evaluated. Such data do not constitute impressive evidence either for Satz' theory or for the suggestion that reading disability is attributable to deficiencies in form perception.[1]

It is apparent that the studies discussed (which incidentally represent those most often cited in support of visual-motor deficiency in poor readers) are characterized by methodological and interpretive difficulties that call their findings and generalizations into question. An additional problem with all but two of these investigations (Lovell, Shapton, and Warren 1964; Lovell, Oliver, and Gray 1964) is the failure to control specifically for the possibility of confounding by virtue of differences in socioeconomic status. A number of investigators (Koppitz et al. 1959;

Keogh 1968; Zach and Kaufman 1969) have demonstrated that performance on the Bender test can vary as a function of socioeconomic level and it may be that this variable contributed to the reader group differences observed in the studies in question.

A closely related difficulty, characteristic of most of these studies, is the absence of sufficient control for emotional and behavioral problems. Indeed in the Silver and Hagin (1960) study the results came exclusively from a clinic population, and de Hirsch, Jansky, and Langford (1966) explicitly say that the poorest readers in the sample were in general uncooperative, unmotivated, and emotionally impaired. Without information to the contrary, the results of all of these studies may be reasonably questioned on the grounds that deficient figure drawings could be the result of attitudinal and motivational factors rather than basic disorder in visual-motor integration.

Finally, in those studies comparing poor and normal readers on a large number of measures (which often included tests of verbal as well as perceptual and perceptual-motor skill) a typical finding was that these groups were differentiated on a variety of measures and not only on tests of perceptual and perceptual-motor ability. This finding calls into question the presumption that the reading difficulties of children in those studies were associated with specific deficits in perception.

Studies Finding No Differences between Poor and Normal Readers on Visual-Motor Ability The contention that reader group differences on figure-drawing tests may have been due to factors other than deficient visual-motor integration is supported by a number of other investigations employing more stringent sampling procedures than those discussed in the preceding section. For example, Nielsen and Ringe (1969) administered the BVMGT, the Draw-A-Person Test (Goodenough 1954) and the Frostig Test of Visual Perception (Frostig 1961) to poor and normal readers (N = 20 each group), 9 to 10 years of age who were average to above average in intelligence. Reader groups were matched for age, IQ, sex, and socioeconomic background. The Draw-A-Person Test requires freehand drawing of a human figure; the Frostig Test comprises several subtests that include measures of visual-motor skill, visual discrimination, spatial orientation, and figure-ground analysis.

Although poor readers received high error scores more often than normal readers on the BVMGT, over half of the poor readers (N = 13) performed within the normal range on this measure, and there were no differences between reader groups on either the Draw-A-Person or Frostig Tests. Nielsen and Ringe concluded from these findings that reading disability is not significantly correlated with dysfunction in visual perception or visual-motor coordination.

In another study Symmes and Rapoport (1972) examined 108 poor readers between the ages of 7 and 13 and systematically eliminated from the sample any children with suspicious medical or developmental histories, sensory impairments, primary emotional disturbance, or below average intelligence, as well as those from low socioeconomic groups. Fifty-four children remained in the study, all boys. Each child was then administered a large battery of psychological tests, among which were the WISC and three design copying tests, one requiring reproduction of a standard from memory.

Subjects were generally found to be average or above average on intelligence though significantly below average on a test of word recognition. However, the most important finding to emerge from this investigation is that none of the subjects were found to be impaired in visual-motor functioning; in fact they were observed to be generally above par on the tests employed to measure this skill. In view of these findings Symmes and Rapoport suggested that "the association of immaturity in visual-motor function that is frequently related to reading difficulty appears only in populations heavily biased in the direction of attendant neurological signs" (1972, 87). Coupling this finding with the fact that all subjects in the sample proved to be males, they further suggested that reading disability in some children may be a genetic, sex-linked disorder characterized by unusual facility in spatial visualization. Such facility was said to contribute to a dominant and interfering tendency to perceive written symbols on a three dimensional plane.

Symmes and Rapoport's suggestion that some disabled readers may have outstanding spatial ability which impairs symbolic learning is unique and interesting. However, it is difficult to imagine the correlates and extensions of the types of reading disorder to which they make reference. Without a more articulate description of the causal relationships that may exist between the exceptionalities in question, I for one, am inclined to question the plausibility of the explanation of reading disorder advanced by these authors. Nevertheless, their results provide additional support for the prediction that perceptual and perceptual-motor deficiencies will not be evident in a sample of poor readers carefully selected in accord with the exclusion criteria outlined in chapter 2, criteria that were apparently employed in this study.

The results of several other studies conducted more recently are consistent with these suggestions. In two separate investigations involving severely impaired and normal readers from second through sixth grade the impaired readers performed as well as the normal readers on measures of visual-motor integration, including the BVMGT, and on tests involving visual recall of printed letters and geometric designs (Vellutino et al. 1973; Vellutino, Smith, Steger, and Kaman 1975). In both these studies the subjects were children from middle- to upper middle-class backgrounds, comparable in intelligence (average or above average), matched for sex, and free from sensory problems, severe emotional disorder, and gross physical or neurological disability. Thus the findings add substance to the contention that reader group differences on measures of visual-motor functioning found in the studies discussed earlier may have been due to factors other than deficient form perception.

The results of a study by Koppitz (1975) are also of interest in this connection. Koppitz compared three groups of 8- and 9-year-old children: two groups of special class pupils with learning disabilities and a control group of children who were achieving normally. All three groups were composed of youngsters of average or above average intelligence matched for age and IQ; all were from middle-class backgrounds. The significant fact is that one group of learning disabled children had normal reading ability but were doing poorly in other academic subjects, whereas the other learning disabled children were quite impaired in reading. The results on the BVMGT did not differentiate these two learning disabled groups, but there were significant differences between these children and the normal achievers on this test. Koppitz concludes that though performance on the BVMGT may be related to overall school functioning and learning disabilities in general, it does not appear to be uniquely related to reading achievement.

Finally, in a longitudinal study similar to the prediction studies already discussed, Stevenson et al. (1976) tested middle-class kindergartners of average intelligence on a number of cognitive and psychometric tests and then correlated the children's performance on these tests with measures of their reading achievement in first, second, and third grade. Neither the BVMGT nor tests of visual memory and visual paired-associates learning had much ability to predict reading achievement. In contrast, tests of verbal skill, visual-verbal learning, and letter and word discrimination were more successful predictors of later reading achievement. And in three other prediction studies, visual-motor functioning was not highly correlated with reading achievement (Rosen 1966; Rosen and Ohnmacht 1968; Ferinden and Jacobson 1970).

Contraindications to Visual-Motor Deficits as Correlates of Reading Disability   Several important points need to be considered as regards the relationship between visual-motor deficits and reading disability. In the first place, it should be apparent that the evidence supporting the contention that reading problems are intrinsically related to visual-motor disorder is weak. Those investigations that found significant correlations between reading achievement and visual-motor functions were characterized by methodological, interpretive, or sampling problems, whereas those finding no reliable association between these variables were better controlled.   Significant correlations between visual-motor integration and reading have appeared often enough in the literature to lend credence to the suggestion that measures of these skills may co-vary, but such findings need not imply that the skills in question are causally related.   For one thing tests such as the Bender may confound a motor deficiency with a deficiency in perceptual functioning unless there is specific control for this possibility. It is not uncommon to find that children with impaired motor functioning at the preschool level are later observed to have reading problems that have no necessary relation to their motor deficiencies: children with speech and language difficulties as well as visual-motor problems represent one example. On the other hand, many children with serious motor deficiencies, even at birth, later experience no difficulties in learning to read. Indeed, Gibson and Levin (1975) have pointed out that children with cerebral palsy can become quite literate in spite of visual-motor impairment, provided that they are exposed to adequate educational programs, and given that they sustain no other developmental anomalies such as intellectual retardation or language disorder. Yet such children can be expected to perform poorly on tasks requiring visual-motor integration.

A second point is that visual-motor tests that require reconstruction of relatively complex spatial arrays may be measuring some aspect of problem-solving ability rather than perceptual functioning. It is my belief and the belief of my associates that a child's graphic reproduction of a given figure is not a direct reflection of his perception of that figure, as is commonly inferred. In fact, it has been known for some time that children can recognize simple figures long before they can draw them (Binet and Simon 1950; Piaget and Inhelder 1956). Piaget argues that this discrepancy is due to the child's immature reasoning processes; the child does not draw what he sees but rather what he knows. With conceptual development there is presumed to be increasingly greater ability to represent, in motor executions, the things that one perceives. Olson (1970) and Goodnow (1977) make a similar point. Olson in particular provides convincing evidence that a preschooler's ability to construct a diagonal is a manifestation of his cognitive development, and demonstrates that children at this age are able to discriminate diagonals from other graphic figures well before they can reproduce them. In addition he points out that young children vary greatly in their ability to construct a diagonal,[2] the implication being that such variation reflects individual differences in rates and levels of concept development—and, I would add, in reasoning and problem-solving skills.

If these inferences are correct, one may speculate that many children found to have low Bender scores at the preschool level may have less conceptual knowledge[3] than children who perform adequately on this and similar tests. The former group may indeed be expected to acquire skill in reading more slowly than the latter, but not because of a perceptual deficiency. This suggestion is consistent with results indicating that visual-motor tests do not reliably identify disabled readers (Keogh 1965a, 1965b, 1970): In all of these investigations good performance on the BVMGT was associated with good performance on reading measures, but poor performance on the BVMGT was not necessarily associated with deficient reading ability.

Additional support for this suggestion is provided by the results of a pilot study recently completed in our own laboratory. Sixty randomly selected beginning first-graders from a middle-class suburban school were given the BVMGT, the Slosson Test of Intelligence (primarily a test of verbal ability: Slosson 1963) and a visual-verbal paired-associates task designed to simulate sight word-learning in reading. These tests were later correlated with measures of oral reading and phonic skills at the end of the first, second, and third grades. Correlations between the reading tests and predictive measures were as follows: with BVMGT error scores r = -.19 to -.41; with Slosson r = .37 to .66; with visual-verbal learning r = .28 to .47. However, whereas the Slosson and the visual-verbal learning measures correlated moderately with each other (r = .46, p <.05) neither was significantly correlated with the BVMGT.

Since the children in this sample represented an essentially intact population, with respect to intellectual ability and reading achievement, one may reasonably conjecture that the significant correlations between the BVMGT and the reading measures were in some degree attributable to conceptual factors rather than perceptual deficiency; that is, it seems unlikely that variation in *normal* reading ability at the age and grade levels assessed would be attributed to variation in basic perceptual skills at the beginning of first grade. In view of the fact that the BVMGT did correlate with the reading tests in this study, it seems plausible to assume that the BVMGT, at the age level administered, is in part measuring individual differences in conceptual development not adequately sampled by the other measures employed in the study. Reinforcing this suggestion are the findings of several other investigations indicating that performance on the BVMGT is more closely associated with children's age and mental maturity than with reading ability (Werner, Simonian, and Smith 1967; Silberberg and Feldt 1968; Clark and Leslie 1971).

A third factor that must be considered when attempting to interpret correlations between visual-motor integration and reading achievement is experience. It will suffice to point out here that many children who do well in reading in the early elementary grades are also apt to have had greater exposure to certain visual-motor activities as preschoolers than many children who do not achieve in reading; it is quite likely that the normal readers, unlike the poor ones, have acquired many of the transfer skills[4] that would allow them to copy novel geometric designs with some degree of success. In other words, children who have the benefit of particular kinds of experience can be expected to develop competence in areas that would facilitate good performance in both reading and grapho-motor functions. Thus individual differences in acquiring such experience is probably one of the reasons that significant correlations have been found between figure drawing and reading tests in randomly selected samples as well as in those in which extraneous variables such as intelligence and socioeconomic status have not been adequately controlled. Again, however, correlations between these variables need not imply causal relationships between them. It may be therefore in error to infer that reading disorder is intrinsically related to deficient figure drawings produced by children manifesting both anomalies or that such difficulties are the result of developmental (neurological) disability.

Some recent research provides empirical support for the contention that experience is related to success on figure-drawing tests. Zach and Kaufman (1969) found that black kindergartners from an impoverished neighborhood school did not copy Bender figures as well as kindergartners from a white middle- to high-income suburban school. However, on a second administration three weeks later, differences between these two groups had disappeared. Similarly Keogh and Becker (1975) found that both "high-risk" and "low-risk" children significantly improved their performance on the copying of designs from the BVMGT when presented these designs under three separate conditions administered in succession: (1) copying from memory, (2) copying under standard conditions, and (3) copying after demonstration of the correct executions by the examiner. Very few who failed under the first two conditions also failed when shown how to copy the figures accurately.

Additional evidence for the role of experience in figure-drawing tests is provided by a study conducted by Pope and Snyder (1970). This study demonstrated that inaccuracies in first-graders' copying of Bender test designs often occurred as a function of the level of graphomotor skill required by certain of the designs on the test and not because of "immaturity in perception." The results also suggested that degree of success in reproducing modified facsimiles of BVMGT designs—facsimiles that retained essential features of those designs (see figure 5.2)—was determined in part by the degree to which these modifications approximated shapes the children were familiar with. This again suggests that a child's reproduction of a given figure is generally more in keeping with his conceptualization of the figure and the information he has already acquired about its constituents. In other words, his drawings represent a synthesis of what he sees and what he knows about what he sees, which implies processing that is far more complex than basic visual discrimination. Thus, it cannot be presumed that poor performance on a figure-drawing test is necessarily indicative of deficiencies in form perception, visual-motor coordination, or any particular aspect of neuromotor development.

Finally, one may question on theoretical grounds the notion that reading disability is attributable to perceptual dysfunction, as manifested in visual-motor problems. A basic assumption of advocates of this view is that impairment in both reading and perception is associated with developmental immaturity or neurological damage that delays or disrupts perceptual-motor integration. Such integration is believed to take place in stages, characterized by qualitative changes or discontinuity at each stage of development. It has also been assumed that developmental changes in perception occur roughly in accord with Gestalt principles of perceptual organization (Bender 1938; Werner 1948). By extension, children who manifest significant visual-motor deficiency are believed to be characterized by immaturities in perceptual organization. Because a number of children having difficulty in learning to read have also been found to be deficient in copying and drawing tasks, it has been inferred that reading disability is caused by perceptual-motor immaturity.

Aside from the arguments issuing from the central contention that measures of visual-motor skill do not necessarily reflect the perceptual organization of a given stimulus array, the most basic objection to the position in question is to the implication that perception is a developmental *entity* that matures much like any other organismic structure or function (body parts, language, motor ability). Perception can be considered a dynamic process that involves one's recognition and interpretation of given stimuli and varies in accord with such factors as previous experience, perceptual set, attention, and the unique properties of the stimulus; it does not have "thing" value. To suggest that perception is

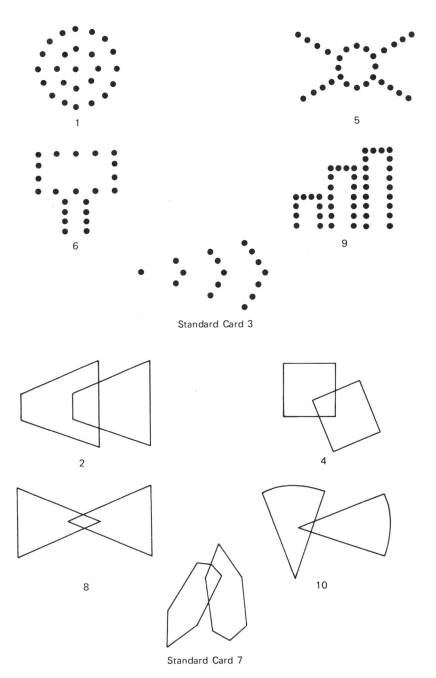

Figure 5.2 Modified facsimiles of stimuli employed on the Bender Test. (Reprinted with permission of author and publisher from: Pope, Peggy, and Snyder, Robert T. Modification of selected Bender designs and interpretation of the first graders' visual-perceptual maturation with implications for Gestalt theory. *Perceptual and Motor Skills*, 1970, 30, 263-267.)

an entity with its own maturation timetable is to give the concept excess meaning. Yet many of those who subscribe to perceptual deficit explanations of reading disability appear to make this error.

A closely related objection to the views of those who infer an intrinsic relationship between perceptual-motor functioning and reading disability is that undue emphasis is placed upon maturational factors in perceptual functioning to the exclusion or de-emphasis of learning. Gibson (1969) has provided extensive documentation for certain principles and mechanisms that may be involved in perceptual learning, which should serve to temper the views of those who overextend the role of maturation in perception. Particularly relevant in the present context is her discussion of the perceptual differentiation involved in reading (Gibson 1971; Gibson and Levin 1975). Briefly, she makes the point that discovery and functional use of the invariant relationships characterizing English orthography evolve over a protracted period, only after considerable interaction with the symbol system. Gibson cites evidence that normal readers do not become conversant with such relationships until approximately third or fourth grade, when they are presumed to be still acquiring the code (Rosinski and Wheeler 1972). This period of development encompasses age levels (8 to 10 years) at which maturation is said to be sufficient to effect adequate form perception, even in poor readers (Satz and Sparrow 1970). Yet fluency in reading—which obviously implies economical use of orthographic redundancies—is not accomplished until some time later. It may therefore be reasonably inferred that the visual-perceptual skills necessary for code acquisition and ultimate proficiency in reading are determined more by learning than by maturation, since the period during which the child is especially sensitive to the structural complexities of printed words is well beyond the stage at which form perception is thought to be tenuous.

A final contraindication to perceptual-deficit explanations of reading disability derived from reader group contrasts on figure-drawing tests is provided by the results of a recent study by Clark (1976). This author evaluated a variety of skills and abilities in a group of preschoolers who were precocious readers prior to any formal schooling. Many of these children were deficient on measures of visual-motor functioning, which obviously had no bearing on their ability to learn to read. Interestingly enough, all of these children were found to have excellent verbal abilities, capacities that the author suggested are especially important to success in reading (Clark 1976). In view of findings such as these and considering the equivocal nature of the results of many studies that have been discussed in this section, one may reasonably conclude that tests of visual-motor integration will in most instances tell us little of the etiology of reading disability.

5.2.2 Visual Matching

After figure drawing tests, the second most popular measure employed for evaluating form perception in poor readers is the match-to-standard test of visual discrimination. This technique, briefly described, requires simply that the child locate, among a number of distracter items, specific figures identical to a prototype or standard. The typical procedure is to present the standards and one or more distracters simultaneously, most often presenting the standard on the left and alternatives to its right. Such measures have been used to evaluate not only form perception but shape orientation, visual analysis, and speed of perceptual processing as well. A number of problems are associated with employing the match-to-standard technique for evaluating perceptual processing.

Reader Group Contrasts on Visual Matching Tests As noted by Barrett (1965) visual discrimination appears to have had widespread acceptance as a measure of reading readiness, no doubt because tests presumably measuring this skill have consistently been shown to have some merit as predictors of success in reading. Barrett reviewed a sizable number of studies conducted between 1928 and 1965 and found evidence that measures of visual discrimination employing both verbal and nonverbal stimuli frequently correlated significantly with reading achievement in first-graders. Most of the studies employed visual matching as the measure of discrimination, and the correlations reported were of low to moderate magnitude (.30 to .60). The finding of particular interest is that tests involving discrimination of letters and words were better predictors of success in reading than tests involving discrimination of pictures and geometric designs. There was also some suggestion that measures requiring both visual discrimination and knowledge of letter names are better predictors than tests that require only letter matching, an observation that has since been verified (Samuels 1972; Calfee 1977). A representative sampling of investigations reported by Barrett follows.

One of the earliest and most influential studies to employ visual matching to predict success in reading was that of Smith (1928). Beginning first-graders (N = 22) of three levels of intelligence (below average, average, and superior) were presented with lowercase letters from the entire alphabet, all twenty-six being placed in disarrayed order before each child. The children were then given an alphabetically arranged pack of identical letters and asked to find the correct match for each in turn, the amount of time allowed for each being two minutes. The total number of correct responses was correlated with scores on a word recognition test administered twelve weeks later. The resulting coefficient of correlation between these two variables was .87. Smith concluded from this and subsequent findings that letter and word matching would be useful measures of reading readiness. Perhaps as important, Smith's study became the primary impetus not only for a large number of studies assessing the relationship between visual discrimination and reading ability but also for the widespread use of visual matching tests to evaluate readiness for reading.

Three comments may be made about Smith's investigation. First, it is entirely possible that the high correlation between visual matching and word recognition was in some measure attributable to individual differences in experience and general intelligence, although this possibility was not adequately evaluated. Second, it is conceivable that many of the children in this group were previously acquainted with letters of the alphabet, which would certainly be advantageous in matching letters under the circumstances of testing. The degree of variability implied in such a high correlation would be consistent with this suggestion. Finally, the heavy demands upon memory imposed by Smith's procedure certainly belies a description of this matching task as a test of basic visual discrimination. Success on such a measure no doubt depends greatly on higher-level cognitive skill, and it may be erroneous to infer on the basis of her findings that achievement in reading can be reliably predicted by individual differences in perceptual skills.

An investigation by Goins (1958), which related nonverbal measures of visual discrimination to reading achievement in first-graders, has already been discussed. My conclusion was that the results supporting an inferred realtionship between perceptual functioning and reading ability were equivocal because of the failure to control for intelligence. I also took issue with Goins's interpretation of her results, particularly as they related to the factorial descriptions of her measures. Most of the tests employed in the Goins study were of the match-to-standard variety, involving either simultaneous presentations of standards and alternatives or memory for the standards. Although these measures yielded significant positive correlations with success in reading, the relationships were generally modest (r's ranged from .31 to .49). Furthermore, all of the tests required that subjects process considerable amounts of visual information, primarily because of the large number of alternative items that had to be systematically analyzed in order to arrive at a correct match. Thus in this investigation as in Smith's study memory may have been confounded with visual discrimination.

Another study relevant here is one by Gates, Bond, and Russell (1939), which contrasted letter and word matching with matching of nonverbal stimuli as predictors of success in reading. Ninety-seven students representing four first-grade classes were administered both types of measures; resulting scores were correlated with reading achievement at both the middle and end of first grade. Mean correlations between the visual-verbal and reading achievement tests ranged from .31 to .62. Mean correlations between two different groups of nonverbal tests and measures of reading achievement were .19 and .21. It is apparent that in this study, tests requiring visual discrimination of verbal stimuli (letters and words) were better predictors of reading achievement than were tests involving visual discrimination of nonverbal stimuli. This was true even in the case of nonsense words. Gates obtained similar results in two later studies (1939, 1940). Most of the measures in these studies employed the format for visual matching described earlier.

Of what significance are these findings? What do they tell us about the etiology of reading disability? It is quite likely that advocates of the perceptual deficit hypothesis would contend that such results support the view that disabled readers sustain basic perceptual impairment associated with neurological disorder. Those who suggest that malfunction in visual perception would be especially evident in very young children would no doubt be particularly inclined to so interpret these findings (for example, Satz and Sparrow 1970). However, there is reason to doubt the suggestion

that poor performance on the types of visual discrimination tasks
that have typically been employed in these and like studies is necessarily indicative of neurologically based disorder resulting in impaired visual discrimination. A more parsimonious interpretation
of the observed correlations is that some children are better
prepared for such tasks by virtue of knowledge they have previously acquired about the material the tasks typically include
(letters and words). It may also be true that performance on the
types of visual matching tests in question is determined more by
individual differences in cognitive functions such as memory and
coding ability than by differences in perceptual skill.

Calfee's Findings   Calfee (1977) has studied prereading skills
in kindergarten children and comes to a similar conclusion. In
commenting on the validity of the visual matching measures
typically employed in reading readiness tests, Calfee argues:

Suppose the student proceeds as follows: He first looks at the
target letter on the left, then moves his eye to the first test item
on the right, and compares his image of the target with the test
item. This takes about one-quarter to one-half second. Then the
eye is moved to the second test item to the right. By now, about a
second has passed, and the visual image of the target has decayed
to a tattered, ragged vestige. By the time the third test item is
examined, the student has only the faintest cues as to what he
is looking for. This model predicts that the further to the right
the test item is located, the higher should be the probability of
an error. (1977, 292)

In discussing the influence of previous knowledge of letters on
tests of visual discrimination he states:

Some first-graders can read when they enter school, or at least
they know the names of the letters. This gives them a distinct
advantage—they can recode the target into an auditory form,
which can be rehearsed in verbal short-term memory (Atkinson
and Shiffrin, 1968). In this form, the target can be retained for 30
seconds or so, more than enough time for the eye to move from
the left most test item to the right most item. In other words, a
reader is at a distinct advantage in performing this task, and hence
the correlation between this test and later reading achievement.
(1977, 293)

Calfee and his associates provided some empirical support for
these contentions. In a study specifically concerned with basic
prereading skills middle- and low-income kindergartners and

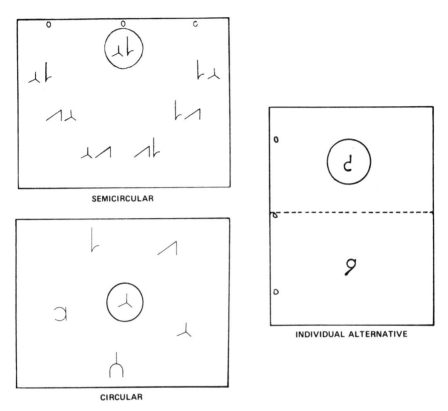

Figure 5.3 Examples of formats employed by Calfee in single- and double-letter matching tests. (From Calfee, Robert C. Assessment of independent reading skills: Basic research and practical applications. In A.S. Reber and D.L. Scarborough, eds., *Toward a Psychology of Reading. The Proceedings of the CUNY Conference.* Hillside, N. J.: Lawrence Erlbaum Associates, 1977. Reprinted by permission of author and publisher.)

first-graders performed letter-matching tasks that attenuated short-term memory problems by avoiding the left-right arrangement of standard and distracter items (Calfee et al. 1971). There were three different types of presentations. A single-alternative format and two multiple-alternative formats (see figure 5.3). The single-alternative condition was considered optimal; under these circumstances the standard remained in view at all times and matching stimuli appeared in a small aperture, one at a time. Subjects were asked each time whether the matching stimulus was the same as or different from the standard.

In the multiple-alternative formats the standard and the matching stimuli were presented simultaneously: in one condition the matching stimuli were displayed in a semicircular array, in the other they were presented in a circular array. There were frequently two correct matches among alternatives and some of the alternatives were reversals of the standards. Children were allowed to mark as many of the test stimuli as they wished and were told during a practice trial that "sometimes more then one is exactly the same"; feedback was not given on test trials. Synthetic letters were employed to control for previous exposure to letters of the alphabet (see figure 5.4).

The central finding in this study was that the percentage of correct responses in letter matching was extremely high (better than 96 percent in all groups) under all three matching conditions. Such a high degree of success using the procedures employed in this study implies considerably less variability in letter matching than has been (typically) found in studies employing the left-right matching format in children at comparable age and grade levels (Goins 1958; Barrett 1965). On the basis of Calfee's findings one may reasonably entertain the hypothesis that matching tasks employing the left-right format may be confounded by short-term memory problems or familiarity with standard and distracter stimuli. Calfee and his co-workers provide even more convincing evidence that tests of visual discrimination typically employed in the literature may be factorially more complex than has been generally surmised. Two additional studies are of interest here.

In a separate contrast employing the same subjects given the single-letter test children were presented with a word-matching task involving two-letter targets and six alternatives, again employing the synthetic alphabet shown in figure 5.3 (Calfee et al.

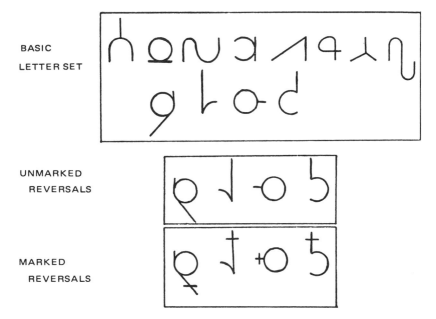

Figure 5.4 Synthetic orthography employed by Calfee in tests of letter-matching skill. (From Calfee, Robert C. Assessment of independent reading skills: Basic research and practical applications. In A. S. Reber and D. L. Scarborough, eds., *Toward a Psychology of Reading. The Proceedings of the CUNY Conference.* Hillside, N. J.: Lawrence Erlbaum Associates, 1977. Reprinted by permission of author and publisher.)

1971). The procedure was similar to that in the individual letter-matching tests in that the same formats (single and multiple alternatives) were employed. Again the child could select as many of the six alternative matching stimuli as he wanted and feedback was given only on the practice trial. The test matches included various combinations of given distracter letters and reversals of the target letters.

Discrimination accuracy was very high in this study, as in the earlier one. The mean correct for all conditions was 88 percent. There was also some effect of format. Performance was best with the single-alternative format (12 percent errors), second best with the semicircular format (19 percent errors), and worst with the circular format (19 percent errors. The largest number of errors were made on items reversing the order of the target. It is particularly striking that first-graders made twice as many such errors as kindergartners. Although this finding may seem somewhat anomalous, the explanation for it is clear-cut. Kindergartners were told in advance to be on the alert for alterations in the sequence of target letters among distracters and that these were considered incorrect responses. They were also given two to five minutes of practice on sample items. First-graders were given no clear instructions as to what constituted a correct or incorrect match and were simply told to mark an alternative "if it looks exactly the same" as the target. It is especially interesting that first-graders' scores on the word-matching test yielded a bimodal distribution whereas the distribution of scores for kindergartners was unimodal: Half of the first-graders marked the reversed order distracter on ten of the twelve items, the other half marked it on only two of the twelve alternatives. Calfee suggests that of those children (first-graders) who received no instructions, half assumed that *same* meant both letters present in any order and the other half assumed that order was to be taken into account.

The significance of these findings in relation to the issue in question should be obvious. They emphasize once again the hazard in ascribing perceptual deficiencies to children who perform poorly on discrimination tests that could be confounded by individual differences in experience, such differences possibly including perceptual and response sets that may be induced by the unique characteristics of the task. It should be pointed out that performance on word matching under the testing conditions employed in this study did not correlate significantly with reading performance. The same was true for scores on the earlier single-letter matching test.

Still further verification of these findings is provided by a later study conducted by Curry, Ross, and Calfee (1973). Sixty-four children, ages 4 and 5, were presented with a word-matching task employing essentially the same procedures as in the two previous studies. However, in this study the authors systematically manipulated materials (synthetic letters), task, and subject variables. Material variations included number of letters in a word, types of distracter, and spacing. The task variables were memory (target remaining in view or removed), instructions (informed or uninformed as to criteria for a correct match and practice versus no practice), and format (single-alternative or semicircular array). Subject variables were age (4 or 5 years), intelligence (above or below average) and sex.

The observation of particular significance in this study is that under optimal conditions (clear instructions, no memory involved, and single-alternative format) 5-year-olds made very few errors in word matching, even in the case of four-letter words. The 4-year-olds (especially those of low intelligence) had much more difficulty and seemed unable to understand what was expected of them.

When the matching task involved memory for the standard, there was much greater variability in performance than when memory was not involved. Under the former condition the differential effects of the length of letter strings became apparent in that there was a linear increase in errors as the number of letters in a word increased from two to four. It was also found that children with high intelligence were not affected by the absence of clear-cut instructions and appeared to have an implicit awareness that "sameness" had to account for such variables as order; children with low intelligence did not appear to have such awareness. The high-ability children also performed as well under the multiple-alternatives condition as under the single-alternative condition, provided that they did not have to match standards and alternatives from memory.

It should be clear that the results of a large number of studies employing visual matching tests to evaluate the relationship between visual discrimination and reading ability may be confounded by higher-order cognitive variables such as memory and the conceptual requirements of the tasks, as well as by previous exposure to the types of stimuli used on given measures. Such confounding is particularly apparent in studies employing letters and words as matching stimuli as clearly evidenced in Calfee's investigations, and in the discrepancies noted in other studies correlating verbal and nonverbal discrimination tasks with reading achievement (Barrett 1965).

Especially important to our discussion is Calfee's observation that controlling for memorial and experiential factors in letter and word matching resulted in minimal variability in performance on these tasks as well as greatly attenuated correlations between these measures and later success in reading. Aside from the fact that such findings dictate caution in interpreting the results of studies that do not control for such variables, they pointedly suggest that reading disability is not significantly associated with deficiencies in visual discrimination. With respect to the visual matching techniques at issue here, the case can be stated even more strongly: Any child with adequate visual acuity who has no difficulty with the conceptual aspects of the task will experience little or no difficulty in matching identical figures, provided that he is able to juxtapose target and matching stimuli so as to maximize the probability of processing visual features that distinguish the target from incorrect alternatives. Such a circumstance obviously implies minimal interference from perceptual and response sets, minimal interpretive bias, and minimal demands on short-term memory; corollary observation is that the child who discriminates effectively will no doubt have been sensitized to subtle but important criteria for establishing identity, such as positional and sequential constancy, invariance in size, and like factors. Such variables were not considered in the studies with kindergartners and first-graders reviewed by Barrett (1965), nor were they taken into account in studies, discussed in section 5.2.2, which employed matching tests to evaluate visual discrimination in elementary school children and kindergartners. This same problem arises repeatedly in studies to be discussed in subsequent sections.

5.2.3 Direct Assessment of Initial-Stage Processing
Most investigations that have provided support for perceptual deficit theories of reading disability have employed indirect methods of assessing adequacy of form perception in poor readers: figure drawings, traditional match-to-standard tests, and like measures. The results of such studies are equivocal because they confound perceptual functions with memorial or response variables. However, a few studies that have recently appeared in the literature have attempted to directly assess the possibility that reading problems are associated with dysfunction at the initial stage of visual processing. These investigations are unique in that they typically employ procedures that evaluate visual systhesis during the first 300 milliseconds following stimulus exposure. This time span represents the approximate duration of the visual afterimage; the brief existence of the afterimage in effect places a natural constraint on the amount of time available to determine adequacy of perceptual functioning. Since variability in performance on tasks involving short-term memory may be more accurately attributed to coding factors than to individual differences in perception, studies that have compared poor and

normal readers on measures of initial-stage processing have typically limited the duration of the afterimage so as to insure that
reported discriminations were based on direct analysis of the
stimulus rather than on coded representations of its properties.
Controlling the availability of the afterimage also facilitates
determination of the rate of transfer of visual information from
initial to short-term storage, which was of particular interest in
some of the studies. Procedures for assessing these functions
included selective reporting of given stimuli within the 300-msec
limit, systematic variation of the time interval between termination of an old stimulus and presentation of a new one, and backward masking.

Studies Evaluating Trace Duration Some of those investigators
who have more recently compared poor and normal readers on
initial storage of sensory information have been specifically concerned with the rate at which these groups process visual material.
A prototypical study conducted by Stanley and Hall (1973)
tested the hypothesis that poor readers take longer than normal
readers to transfer visual information from sensory to short-
term store. Of particular concern was the duration of the memory
trace or afterimage, which previous research has shown to persist
longer in children than in adults (Pollock 1965; Pollock, Ptashne,
and Carter 1969; Liss and Haith 1970; Gummerman and Gray
1972). An abnormally persistent sensory image could conceivably
interfere with incoming stimuli and thereby disrupt form perception. Stanley and Hall hypothesize that reading-disabled
children may experience such difficulty, the inference being that
visual functioning in this group is more like that of children at
younger age levels.

The subjects in this study were 33 dyslexics and 33 normal
readers between the ages of 8 and 12 (mean chronological age =
10.88 for dyslexics, 10.52 for controls). The dyslexics were
selected on the basis of teacher judgment and were reported to be
of average or above average intelligence and free from behavioral
problems and organic disorders. The normal readers also were
selected by teachers and in accord with the same criteria. However,
the only measure of intelligence employed was a Piagetian test
of conservation, on which the groups did not differ.

Two procedures were employed for measuring trace persistence.
The first was an adaptation of a perceptual integration task
devised by Erikson and Collins (1968), who found that sequential

presentations of separate components of a nonsense word was perceived as a composite if the interval between presentation of the different parts was very brief (20 msec). Increasing the duration of the interstimulus interval (ISI) up to some threshold level (which varied with the individual) had the effect of creating a break-up or separation of the component parts of the stimulus. Thus the magnitude of the ISI provided a measure of trace duration, ISIs of greater magnitude implying more persistent sensory traces.

Stanley and Hall essentially adopted this procedure in their perceptual integration study, except that the stimuli consisted of (1) the letters N and O, (2) two halves of a cross, and (3) a cross surrounded by a square (see figure 5.5). Each of these stimuli was presented for a series of trials in which the two halves of a given stimulus were presented sequentially for 20-msec exposure. Each series commenced at an ISI of 20 msec and increased gradually by increments of 20 msec until response criteria were achieved. The two response criteria were (1) the ISI at which the subject first perceived a given figure as two halves rather than as a single composite, and (2) the ISI at which the subject correctly identified the two halves of a figure on three successive presentations. Subjects identified stimuli either verbally or by drawing what they saw. The mean ISIs for initial detection of the separation of each of the figures was found to be 30 to 50 msec greater in poor than in normal readers, these results being essentially replicated in a subsequent study (Stanley 1975a). Similar findings obtained for the identification of each of the figures, although the proportional differences between reader groups was greater on the identification task than on the separation task.

In the second phase of this particular study, a backward masking paradigm was used in comparing poor and normal readers on the rate of transfer of visual information from sensory to short-term storage. The backward masking procedure superimposes a disruptive stimulus or mask (a random dot pattern) over a target stimulus at varying intervals of delay between presentations of the target and mask, thereby controlling the duration of the afterimage. The dependent variable in this condition was the interstimulus interval (ISI) at which single letters were identified. The same subjects employed in the first experiment were given 20-msec presentations of the upper-case letters H, J, R, M,

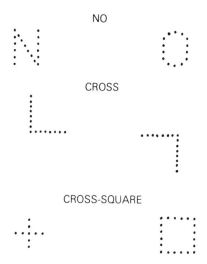

Figure 5.5 Two-part stimuli employed by Stanley and Hall to evaluate trace duration in poor and normal readers. The figures on the right coalesce with the figures on the left to produce the appearance of a composite when the interval between serial presentations of the two halves is very brief. (Reproduced by permission of author and publisher. © 1973 by the Society for Research in Child Development, Inc.)

K, S, F, C, followed by a masking stimulus consisting of a dot matrix. They were then presented either with the letter U or the letter O, each of which was again followed by the mask. In both instances the initial ISI between the target and masking stimulus was 20 msec and was increased on each trial until the criterion of three correct letter identifications was achieved.

Each of the letters could be identified by all subjects prior to the experiment proper. However, during experimental presentations, poor readers required a significantly longer interstimulus interval between target letter and mask to identify the same letters.

Stanley and Hall concluded from their findings that duration of the visual trace is greater in poor readers than in normal readers whereas the rate of transfer from sensory to short-term memory is slower. They therefore suggested (Stanley and Hall 1973; Stanley 1975b) that reading disability may be caused by visual interference resulting from the overlap of old and new visual material: "If VIS (visual information store) duration is not intrinsically related to eye movements, in dyslexics, then many of their

confusions may result from eye movements feeding new information into the visual system before the old information has been
processed or masked. Thus there may be some overlay of visual
information in storage" (Stanley 1975b, 192).

Stanley and Hall's results are interesting, but their interpretations of the findings are questionable. They themselves point out
that the use of the interstimulus interval to evaluate trace persistence is weak in that it is an indirect measure that depends too
heavily upon subjective judgments that may not always be reliable.
For example, it is entirely possible in the case of the perceptual
integration tasks employed in these studies (Stanley and Hall
1973; Stanley 1975a), that group differences in length of the ISIs
were due to the use of a more conservative response strategy on
the part of poor readers (attempting to be certain about what
they saw) rather than to differences in trace duration. This interpretation would seem to be plausible in view of the long history
of failure characteristic of impaired readers at the age and grade
levels involved. Furthermore, it is not surprising to find that poor
readers take longer than normal readers to identify letters, given
the uncertainty in letter and word identification characteristic of
this group even under optimal stimulus conditions. In brief tachistoscopic presentations of such stimuli poor readers can be expected
to be quite variable, and indecision or hesitation on the part of
even a few subjects could spuriously inflate the average interstimulus interval from trial to trial.

Evidence that runs counter to the claim that the visual trace is
sustained longer in poor than in normal readers is derived from
several other investigations, including two conducted later by
Stanley (Stanley and Molloy 1975; Stanley 1976). One of these
studies is of particular interest in that an attempt was made to
verify results obtained in initial tests of this hypothesis. To be
specific, Stanley and Molloy (1975) again evaluated trace duration in dyslexic and normal readers, but in this study they employed the *retinal painting* technique developed by Haber and
Standing (1969). This procedure involves the oscillation of a nar-
row slit so that only one or another portion of a specific figure (a
drawing of a common object) stimulates the retina at a given time.
If the rate of oscillation is too slow, the separate parts of the
stimulus are perceived intermittently, since the visual trace of one
segment will have decayed before the remaining segment is pre-

sented to the eye. However, at some threshold speed of oscillation (which varies with the individual) the stimulus figure is perceived as a whole. This is, of course, a spatial summation effect created by overlapping visual traces. The speed at which the oscillating slit facilitates perception of a whole figure therefore becomes the measure of trace duration.

Two separate experiments were conducted employing the above procedure. In one, 30 poor and 30 normal readers were selected in accord with the criteria outlined in the 1973 study by Stanley and Hall. Both groups were administered the retinal painting task, but no substantial differences were found between them. The authors acknowledged that this finding was unexpected in view of the results of the previous study but suggested that the two measures of trace duration may not be comparable.

In the other experiment employing the retinal painting procedure Stanley and Molloy compared randomly selected 9-year-olds (N = 32) and adults (N = 32) and found that the adults perceived the whole figure at a slower rate of oscillation than the 9-year-olds. The implication of this finding is that on the average the adults had *longer* trace durations than the children. This was an unexpected outcome and is contrary to previous results, which suggest that children have more persistent memory traces than adults. In an attempt to explain this disparity the authors suggested that the younger subjects in this study may have adopted a more conservative strategy than the older subjects. More specifically, it was thought to be possible that the children actually perceived the whole figure at slower oscillation rates but withheld their reports until they were sure of what they saw. The major effect of adopting this strategy would be to continue increasing the sweep rate until the criterion is definitively achieved, thereby accounting for the observed differences between the two groups. This explanation is similar to the one I offered for the disparities found between poor and normal readers on the perceptual integration tasks employed by Stanley in other experiments (Stanley and Hall 1973; Stanley 1975a).

The common factor in all of these investigations was use of the method of ascending limits, a procedure that may entail some degree of response bias and thus some degree of unreliability. It would therefore seem that an experimental method that did not rely so heavily upon subjective judgment would provide a more valid test of the hypothesis in question than the measures described thus far, particularly when employed with children.

One recently completed study adopted a forced-choice technique to evaluate trace persistence rather than the absolute-judgment format employed in the studies by Stanley and his associates. Arnett (1977) examined sensory persistence in poor and normal readers at four age levels: 7, 9, 11, and 13 years. There were 12 subjects at each level, half of whom were poor readers. All subjects were selected on the basis of relevant exclusionary criteria, although intelligence was measured by means of a picture vocabulary test, which is somewhat questionable as a measure of this variable. Reading ability was measured initially by teacher judgment and thereafter by scores on a reading comprehension test, which is not optimal for selecting the most severely impaired readers. In addition, the number of subjects in each cell was rather small and the reliability of the findings is questionable, so the results of this study must be considered tentative. Nevertheless, the methodology is unique and we shall therefore describe the procedures employed in some detail.

Two separate measures were employed to evaluate trace duration. The first was a modification of a perceptual integration task used by Hogben and DiLollo (1974). "Two horizontally adjacent 5 x 5 square dot matrix patterns were presented on a computer-driven oscilloscope by displaying a series of single dots *evenly* and *successively* over time [see figure 5.6]. The total temporal duration over which the dots were plotted on the oscilloscope on a single trial (plotting interval) was allowed to vary and on each trial a single dot from either the left or right matrix was not plotted. The experimental task was simply to specify the matrix from which the dot was missing" (Arnett 1977, 45).

At brief plotting intervals the dots forming the two matrices appeared clearly and simultaneously, making detection of the missing dot relatively easy. At long plotting intervals, however, the differential rates of trace decay yielded the impression that several dots were missing, rendering detection of the "missing" dot impossible. This is because the dots that were initially plotted had disappeared by the time the last few dots on each of the matrices were presented. Thus the measure of trace duration was the precise plotting interval at which the matrices were no longer perceived as wholes.

Figure 5.6 Example of a forced-choice dot matrix employed in the temporal integration task used by Arnett (1977). Subjects were asked to specify the matrix from which the dot was missing. (Reproduced by permission of the author.)

The dependent variable on the perceptual integration task was the temporal duration (in milliseconds) at which the dot matrices appeared fragmented, thereby precluding identification of the matrix containing the missing dot. This measure attenuated unreliability of judgment by requiring that subjects choose one of two stimuli to demonstrate discriminability. Additional control for subjective judgment was provided by automatically varying the plotting intervals presented to a given subject, using an adaptive psychophysical method developed by Taylor and Creelman (1967) known as parameter estimation by sequential testing (PEST). Briefly, this program randomly selects an initial plotting interval range of from 3 to 127 msec and adjusts each interval from trial to trial in accord with prespecified criteria of difficulty and prespecified increments of change. There was a series of eight presentations for each subject and the estimate of trace duration for each was the median plotting interval at which perceptual integration of the dot matrices was no longer achieved.

Subjects who were contrasted under these conditions were also compared in a backward masking condition evaluating rate of processing. The stimuli were essentially the same as those in the perceptual integration task except that the missing dot was randomly deleted only from the center of either the left or right matrix. In addition all dots were presented simultaneously rather than successively. The masking stimulus was a random dot pattern (see figure 5.6) superimposed upon the dot matrices at specified presentation intervals. Subjects were again asked to indicate which of the two matrices contained the missing dot.

The dependent variable in this study was the interstimulus interval (ISI) between display and masking stimulus, which was presumed to be a measure of the rate of transfer of visual information from sensory to short-term store. Longer ISIs were associated with slower rates of information transfer, shorter ISIs with more rapid rates of transfer. The stimulus presentations and the variations in ISIs were controlled by the computer in the manner described for the perceptual integration task. The quantification of the dependent variable was also similar in that the processing rate for each subject was the median ISI at which the subject performed at a 75-percent correct rate for eight consecutive runs.

The perceptual integration and backward masking tasks were presented in counterbalanced order for each age level and reader group. There was a 24-hour separation between presentation of the two stimulus conditions.

Two central findings are of note. The most important result for present purposes is that there were no significant differences between poor and normal readers at any of the age levels on either perceptual integration or rate of processing. These data are of course contrary to the results of the studies by Stanley (Stanley and Hall 1973; Stanley 1975a). However, because Arnett's procedures carefully controlled for unreliability that might be occasioned by response bias, they represent a distinct improvement over the procedures employed by Stanley and his co-workers. Thus Arnett's results might well constitute a more valid indication of perceptual functioning in dyslexic and normal readers.

The second important finding was clear-cut differences between subjects at successive age levels when rate of processing was the dependent variable. Age differences in both rate of processing and perceptual integration would be predicted by previous research (Pollock 1965; Pollock, Ptashne, and Carter 1969; Liss and Haith 1970; Gummerman and Gray 1972) and the results obtained for rate of processing were consistent with this expectation. However, no significant age differences were found on the perceptual integration task. Arnett offered no interpretation for this discrepancy, but one explanation seems plausible. The failure to find age-related disparities in the duration of trace persistence in Arnett's study may be attributable to the use of a forced-choice method of discrimination rather than an absolute-judgment task as in previous studies (Pollock, Ptashne, and Carter 1969; Gummerman and Gray 1972). As already noted, the use of a contrast stimulus may attenuate biased perceptual or response attitudes, whereas tasks involving absolute judgments may increase the probability that extraneous behaviors will confound test results. Simply because of uncertainty that might be normally associated with inexperience, young children might be expected to be more hesitant or conservative than adults in reporting qualitative changes in briefly presented stimuli when asked to make such judgments without a basis for comparison. A similar explanation was suggested by Stanley and Molloy (1975). There may, however, be no reliable differences between these two groups when such bias is controlled, as in forced-choice tasks of the type Arnett employed. The logical implication of this suggestion is that the results of other studies demonstrating age differences in visual trace duration may be artifactual, which of course necessitates further verification of such differences.

Nevertheless, the results obtained on the reader group contrasts in Arnett's study seem straightforward and support his conclusion that dyslexic and normal readers probably do not differ in their ability to process visual information at the first level of sensory functioning.

Interestingly enough, a later investigation by Stanley (1976) also employed a forced-choice method to evaluate rate of processing in poor and normal readers and yielded results that were in direct opposition to those reported earlier by Stanley and Hall (1973). The subjects in this investigation consisted of two groups of poor readers at different age levels (8 to 10 and 9 to 12 years) and one control group (9 to 12 years). Selection criteria were in accord with those in the earlier studies. A backward masking paradigm was employed to evaluate rate of processing of individually presented digits from 0 to 9. The masking stimulus was a dot matrix randomly displayed on an oscilloscope. Each digit was presented for 20 msec followed by a 20-msec mask presented at varying interstimulus intervals (8, 16, 24, 32, or 40 msec). Subjects were required to identify the digit that appeared on the oscilloscope by pressing one of ten response buttons labeled 0 to 9. Poor readers performed significantly better on this task than normal readers. Stanley suggested in explanation of the findings that poor readers may have employed a visual code in storing the stimulus information owing to the possibility of longer trace durations in such subjects. However, this interpretation would seem implausible in view of the fact that the masking procedure interrupted the memory trace at standard intervals allowing for no significant variability among subjects in trace duration. Furthermore, Stanley and Hall (1973) had employed a similar masking procedure in comparing poor and normal readers on recall of letters of the alphabet, and the poor readers were less proficient than the normal readers on this task. The disparities in the results of these two studies could be due to the fact that different materials were employed, although the data provided no apparent explanation for the fact that the poor readers in the later study recalled digits better than the normal readers; the finding could therefore be artifactual. The results are nonetheless contrary to the view that poor readers take longer than normal readers in transferring visual information from sensory to short-term storage, which was the interpretation offered to explain the group differences in recall of letters observed by Stanley and Hall. Such differences may be more simply attributed to poor readers' uncertainty with letter and word stimuli than to dysfunction in visual processing.

Another investigation evaluating trace duration in poor and normal readers further undermines the suggestion that poor readers are qualitatively different from normal readers in initial-stage processing. Fisher and Frankfurter (1977) assessed visual information storage as a function of age and reading ability, employing a backward masking paradigm. Subjects were compared under both mask and no-mask conditions, using a repeated-measures design.

There were three groups, one consisting of poor readers (age 10) and two consisting of normal readers. One of the normal reader groups was matched with the poor readers for age, the other was matched for reading level. Stimuli were upper-case letters (F, H, N, V, W, and Z), which varied in the number of letters presented randomly (two, four, or six) in a 4 x 4 cell matrix. The masking stimulus was a jumbled group of letter fragments. Each letter array was presented for 200 msec and the children were asked to reproduce the letters from memory directly after each presentation. The mask was presented immediately after the 200-msec stimulus exposure. The children wrote their responses on blank matrices; they were instructed to record the letters they saw as well as their exact location on each matrix. There were two sessions consisting of 72 trials, 24 for each of the three stimulus conditions (number of letters). The sessions were approximately one day apart, subjects receiving the mask and no-mask condition in counterbalanced order over the two-day period.

The dependent variables in this study were (1) number of letters correctly identified, (2) number of letters placed in their correct locations, and (3) number of letters both correctly identified and correctly located. The degree to which poor readers differed from normal readers in initial-stage processing was of particular concern. Also of interest was the possibility that poor readers are maturationally immature. It was conjectured that immaturity should be reflected (1) in similar performance on the part of poor readers and the younger subjects, with whom they were matched for reading level, and (2) in an extended trace duration in comparison with normal readers of the same age.

Contrary to expectations, the poor readers' overall performance on all the dependent measures was significantly better than that of the normal readers at both age levels. The only departure from this pattern was the poor readers' performance on the four- and six-letter arrays, which was not substantially different from their age-matched peers when the dependent measure was the number correct by location.

It should be apparent that these data do not support the suggestion that trace duration is longer for poor readers than normal readers, inasmuch as the backward masking condition did not affect the poor readers more adversely than the latter. The results are also contrary to the view that reading disability is associated with deficiency in form perception.

The data afford no ready explanation for the fact that the poor readers performed better than the normal readers in visual recall of the two letter arrays. Fisher and Frankfurter suggested that the disabled readers may have had a "task-training advantage" owing to the possibility that remedial programs in which they were involved may have provided them with a great deal of experience in simple graphemic identification. An alternative explanation is that the normal readers may have been more inclined than the poor readers to attend to a limited amount of visual information, consistent perhaps with an acquired tendency toward economy of processing in identifying words verbally. Such a strategy may not serve them well on a task requiring greater attention to visual detail, as in copying randomly arranged letters from memory in the Fisher and Frankfurter study. The poor readers, on the other hand, may have been more inclined to be overly attentive to the graphic features of individual letters because of their lack of success in learning higher-order orthographic units. Such difficulty would not seriously impair them when a limited amount of visual information must be retained and might even dispose them toward better discrimination than normal readers under these circumstances. This interpretation would account for the reader group differences observed and may, to some extent, explain the superior performance of the poor readers on identifying single digits in the study by Stanley (1976).

Other Studies of Initial Stage Processing   Two other studies may be discussed within the present context. Alwitt (1963) evaluated decay of immediate memory for visually presented digits in poor and normal readers matched for age, sex, and IQ. The age range was rather wide, involving subjects from 6 to 12 inclusive. Employing a paradigm devised by Sperling (1960), two rows of four-item digits were presented briefly (100 msec) for immediate recall under three separate conditions: (1) no cuing as to where to focus attention, (2) cuing to report one or the other row of digits, immediately before stimulus presentation (pre-cuing condition) and (3) cuing 500 msec after stimulus presentation (post-cuing condition). Stimuli were again presented under the first condition to evaluate the effects of practice. In accord with Sperling's findings, all subjects performed better under the pre-cuing condition than under the post-cuing condition. Normal readers generally recalled more digits than did poor readers, but the difference between pre- and post-cuing conditions was not proportionately greater for poor readers, contrary to expectations. From this finding Alwitt inferred that the rate of decay of the memory trace does not occur more rapidly for poor readers then for normal readers. It was also found that the differences in overall recall of digits increased monotonically with age. Possible interpretations of reader group differences included attentional problems, limited capacity in short-term memory, and deficiencies in verbal encoding of stimuli. Alwitt suggested that divergent age trends were related either to improved memory strategies in normal readers as a result of experience in reading or to basic deficiencies in poor readers, which place upper limits on their memory span. These possibilities were not thought to be mutually exclusive.

The results of Alwitt's study provide suggestive evidence that poor readers do not sustain any deficiency at the first level of visual processing—that is, in basic feature detection and organization. Although the poor readers were differentiated from normals in amount of information recalled, the apparent uniformity in the decay rates for the two groups provides indirect evidence that basic form perception in dyslexics is intact. In fact, aside from the possibility that poor readers might be limited with respect to storage capacity, the evidence could be taken as support for either attentional or recoding deficits in this group, as Alwitt suggested.

However, a qualification is indicated in that initial-stage processing may have been confounded with the second or short-term storage stage of visual processing (see figure 4.1). This qualification is necessary because no procedure was employed to terminate or mask the afterimage, as in the Sperling study. Thus the conclusion that Alwitt's findings were not due to reader group differences in initial-stage processing is necessarily inferential. Another reason for caution in interpreting the results of this study is that the sample was not stratified for age and grade and thereby included a wide range of developmental levels. Since the means were collapsed across groups, one cannot be certain that the results are not confounded by developmental changes affecting sensory storage. Finally, the study was conducted with clinic cases and the results may be biased accordingly. Thus Alwitt's conclusions as to the nature of reader group differences in visual information processing can be regarded as only tenuous.

The final study of interest is one recently reported by Morrison, Giordani, and Nagy (1977). They too were concerned with initial-stage processing in poor and normal readers and specifically contrasted perceptual and memorial functions in these two groups. The subjects were 12-year-old males in sixth grade, carefully selected to exclude children with below average intelligence, organic disorder, and emotional problems. Poor readers were reading at two or more years below grade placement, normal readers read at or above grade placement. All subjects were in regular class programs and none had received remedial instruction.

The procedure employed was a variant of the partial-report technique initially devised by Sperling (1960). Subjects were presented with circular arrays of three sets of eight visual forms for very brief durations; sets consisted of three different types of stimuli: upper-case letters, geometric forms, and abstract forms (see figure 5.7). Each array was exposed for 150 msec, followed by a teardrop indicator presented at varying delay intervals ranging from 0 to 2000 msec. The indicator appeared directly under the space in which a given form had been located and the subject's task was to report the form that had occupied that space. It was hypothesized that a perceptual deficiency would be associated with below par performance on presentations from 0 to 300 msec, which approximates the duration that visual information is held in initial storage. However, it was expected that an encoding or memory deficit would result in low performance only at delay intervals longer than 300 msec—that is, when information is believed to be processed in short-term memory.

It was found that the performance of poor readers was below that of normal readers only at delay intervals above 300 msec. The authors concluded that "poor readers were not deficient in the quantity or quality of information they initially perceived, or in the trace duration of that information in a raw perceptual form" (Morrison et al. 1977, 79). They therefore inferred that reading disability is probably associated with difficuty at later stages of information processing, perhaps involving encoding, organizational, or retrieval skills. They suggested in addition that such difficulty may not be limited to the processing of verbal stimuli since the groups differed in the recall of nonverbal as well as verbal materials.

Critique of Trace Persistence Theories of Reading Disability
It should be apparent that there is very little evidence to support the claim that poor and normal readers differ with respect to visual trace duration or rate of visual processing. The results of seminal studies demonstrating such differences are equivocal (Stanley and Hall 1973; Stanley 1975a), but negative findings are in greater abundance and issue from later investigations that appear to be methodologically better controlled (Arnett 1977; Fisher and Frankfurter 1977; Morrison, Giordoni, and Nagy 1977). It therefore remains for future research to further evaluate these hypotheses.

However, I must confess that I rather doubt the ultimate validity of the suggestion that visual perception in dyslexics may be impaired by lingering visual traces. In the first place, one may

Figure 5.7 Stimuli employed in the study by Morrison, Giordani, and Nagy, evaluating visual retention. (Reproduced by permission of author and publisher, from *Science* 1977, 196, 77-79. Copyright 1977 by the American Association for the Advancement of Science.)

reasonably question this suggestion on intuitive grounds. It would seem, for example, that a child who actually does sustain an atypically persistent memory trace would soon learn to adjust the volume of visual information he attempts to process as well as the rate at which he processes such information so as to insure clear vision and reliable perception. If such adaptation did not take place, one might expect that overlapping visual traces would give rise, not only to uncertain and unreliable perception but also to significant acuity problems. Yet there is no evidence that such dysfunction actually occurs in poor readers.

And though it may be argued in support of the hypothesis in question, that word decoding in these children is typically unreliable, there is no reason to believe that such unreliability is due to perceptual distortions caused by perseverative memory traces. Indeed, there is evidence that poor readers mislabel or mispronounce letters and words (*b/d, was/saw, lion/loin*) in spite of the fact that perception of these configurations is veridical (Vellutino, Steger, and Kandel 1972; Vellutino, Smith, Steger, and Kaman 1975). Such findings cannot readily be explained by a trace persistence theory of reading disability.

Unlike the stimulus presentations in studies such as those conducted by Stanley and his associates, the visual material with which the reader must contend is stationary and is therefore not subject to the constraints imposed by the brief stimulus presentations typical of research in the laboratory. This means that the masking effects that might be occasioned by trace persistence when the perceiver has only a fleeting glance at the stimulus would be far more troublesome than the masking effects created by the afterimages of printed letters and words, inasmuch as the reader has the option of adjusting the duration of his fixation pauses until he has a clear and reliable percept. Even if it were true that the poor reader is characterized by abnormally persistent memory traces, one would expect that in reading he could compensate for this anomaly, given that the letters and words that happen to be in focus can outlive the afterimages of those that may be momentarily perseverating.

One would also anticipate that trace persistence would eventuate in reader group differences *only* in the amount of time a reader fixates on letters and words and not in how accurately these stimuli are perceived. Indeed fixation time has been found to be greater in poor than in normal readers (Harris and Sipay 1975), but this finding need not necessarily be taken as support for a trace persistence theory of reading disability. Furthermore, there is increasing evidence that pause duration as well as many other differences that have been observed between dyslexic and normal readers in various aspects of reading are related more to dysfunction in processing the verbal components of printed words than to dysfunction in processing their visual components. This is a theme that will be evident throughout this text, but more immediately it brings us to yet another reason for questioning the view that dyslexia is attributable to lingering afterimages.

The major effect of a perseverating memory trace would be to degrade the letters and words upon which the reader happens to be fixated, thereby impairing perception of those configurations. Yet such difficulty could not in any way account for the majority of word decoding errors made by poor readers: the apparent inaccuracies in orientation and sequencing so commonly observed (*b/d, was/saw, ton/not*); semantic substitution errors in single-word presentations (saying /kitty/ for *cat* or /add/ for *plus*); and characteristic mispronunciations (saying /chip/ for *ship*). Such inaccuracies imply accurate form perception and would seem to be of linguistic origin. This conjecture derives support from the work of Goodman and his associates, who have shown that a sizable proportion of miscues made in oral reading are determined by linguistic response biases rather than the graphic features of the words read (see Goodman 1969). A trace persistence theory of reading disability would also be unable to account for the well-known fact that severely impaired readers have difficulty not only in decoding words and sentences but also in learning to name individual letters—an enterprise that should not be hampered by the lateral masking effects occasioned by trace persistence.

A closely related point is that the lateral masking effects that might be caused by a protracted memory trace in processing connected text would be minimal or nonexistent in single-word presentations, assuming that the graphic features of the letters in words are processed in parallel and not serially (Kolers 1970; Smith 1971; Brewer 1972). Yet the most severely impaired readers are primarily deficient at the level of single-word learning and spend a large proportion of their time in attempting to learn the names and pronunciations of words, which are most often presented in isolation. The trace persistence explanation of reading disability could not readily account for such difficulty.

But there are even more basic reasons for doubting the validity of a trace-persistence theory of reading disability. First, one may justifiably raise the question of why visual afterimages of letters and words do not disturb the normal reader as well as the poor reader. If such memory traces are normally from 200 to 300 msec in duration as is commonly believed (Sperling 1960), they should systematically infringe upon the word in focus, from one fixation to the next, even in mature readers. This effect would be predicted by virtue of the fact that the time taken for saccadic movements varies only from 10 msec to 48 msec (Tinker 1965, 67), neither of which is of sufficient duration to insure clearance of the sensory register. Yet no such difficulty is inferred in normal readers, whereas the opposite inference is applied to poor readers, primarily on the strength of trace durations that presumably last from 30 to 50 msec longer than those observed in children who read normally (Stanley and Hall 1973). This finding does not represent a very strong basis for the theory and certainly does not account for the normal readers' apparent lack of difficulty with visual afterimages.

That visual afterimages do *not* appear to be problematic for normal readers is perhaps the most compelling reason for doubting the validity of a trace persistence theory of reading disability. More explicitly, it suggests either that the visual system somehow manages to deactivate memory traces from one fixation to the next or that it reduces the effects of trace persistence to negligible proportions through some sort of adaptation process. Something analogous to either or both of these mechanisms would seem to be required not only to effect clear vision in reading but in visual functioning in general.

This question was originally raised in attempting to explain the absence of visual fusion effects during saccadic movement in reading and was thoroughly discussed by Huey (1908) shortly after the turn of the century. Huey underscored the well-known fact that discrete retinal stimulations presented in rapid succession at sufficient speeds will tend to fuse, yielding the effects of homogeneity and continuity. A simple demonstration of this phenomenon is provided by rotating a disc of black and white sectors which at speeds of 30 to 60 stimulations per second will coalesce to create a circular gray band. Other examples include apparent motion effects, such as the moving arrow illusion created by a series of neon lights illuminated in close succession. Fusion effects were also evident in many of the studies discussed earlier (Stanley and Hall 1973; Stanley 1975a; Arnett 1977), the common factor in all of these instances being the occurrence of perceptual integration in the case of temporally disparate retinal stimulation.

As pointed out by Huey, visual fusion is not apparent in reading, in spite of the fact that saccadic eye movements occur at rates much beyond those sufficient to create this effect. Furthermore, though we can readily blur the graphic features of letters and words by moving a line of print rapidly across our field of vision (provided that our fixation is stationary), no such difficulty occurs when the eyes are moving voluntarily, as in reading. This paradox is aptly reflected by Huey:

But why do we not see these gray bands as we read? Scarcely a trace of them has been reported by any experimenter, except that Professor Dodge believed that he could detect faint traces. I have found no reader who had any consciousness of them, and have none myself. We seem to see the letters and words as distinctly during the movements as at the pauses, and the visual field is unbroken to consciousness. (Huey 1908, 36)

Several explanations have been offered to account for this phenomenon. Cattell (1900) suggested that vision may actually be clear during eye movements and postulated in support of this hypothesis that the visual system may respond to changing retinal stimulations more rapidly when the eyes move than when the objects are in motion. Holt (1903), in contrast, suggested that the eyes are momentarily "anesthetic" during voluntary movement, as a result of central nervous system action that prohibits retinal responding. However, Woodworth (1906) found that an object projected onto the retina during the eye's movement is correctly localized in space. He pointed out further that objects that move with the eye (such as the particles of extraneous matter suspended in the vitreous humor) or that move at the same rate are seen clearly during the movement. These factors were offered as evidence that the eye is not anesthetized in any way when it moves voluntarily.

Dodge (1905) was in essential agreement with Woodworth but suggested that apparent imperception of a fused visual field during eye movements depends upon the interaction of three factors: (1) the positive afterimage of the previous stimulus, (2) the "inhibitive action" of the new stimulus, and (3) the tendency to "ignore" irrelevant stimulation in the interest of clear vision. In support of these conjectures Dodge specifically demonstrated that under the proper experimental conditions the masking effects of the afterimage during eye movements can be observed, but that such effects are unattended while the eyes are moving and are thereafter terminated by the inhibiting effects of the new stimulus.

These explanations of the absence of visual fusion in reading would seem to be instructive in relation to the trace persistence theory of reading disability at issue. One gleans from these disparate points of view a consensus that extraneous visual stimulation is not problematic in reading because of either inhibitive or adaptive mechanisms (or some combination thereof) that negate fusion effects. In other words, there seems to have been agreement that, in reading, the extraneous stimulation that may be caused by afterimages and visual fusion tends to be blocked from one fixation to the next, thus insuring clear vision. There was considerable disagreement as to the means by which the visual system manages to curb such disruptions, however, and the issue is yet unsettled.

Eriksen and Collins (1968) have recently addressed themselves to this issue and suggest that the visual system, being capable of integrating temporally discrete stimulations, must also be capable of detecting or responding to discontinuity in stimulation so as to permit discrete perception. In other words, clear vision may require mechanisms that terminate perceptual integration of temporal stimuli, although the nature of such mechanisms is not apparent. It is possible that the proper stimulus for triggering discontinuity detection is physical or psychological or some combination of the two. The stimulation occasioned by eye movements in reading could be categorized under the latter rubric. It is also possible that the ultimate response to such stimulation is either physiological (central inhibition) or psychological (inattention and adaptation), and these two are not mutually exclusive.

In any event I see no reason why such mechanisms would not be operative for poor readers as well as normal readers; if they were not, there would no doubt be a significantly greater incidence of visual acuity problems reported by poor readers. Yet there is ample evidence that this is not so (Lawson 1968). I therefore do not believe that a trace persistence theory of reading disability could be supported on the basis of the visual peculiarities the theory predicts, since there is good reason to believe that the visual system would naturally compensate for such anomalies.

Finally, a possible alternative to the arguments I have advanced is a recently articulated theory of visual memory that departs from more traditional conceptualizations of initial-stage processing (Sperling 1960; Neisser 1967), particularly in regard to the duration of the memory trace. That theory is DiLollo's (1977) two-stage model of visual short-term memory. Briefly, the model is based on the assumption that perception of form occurs in two separate stages, each involving qualitatively different coding operations: During the first stage visual features (edges, curves, angles) are abstracted in parallel from the stimulus display and encoded or synthesized into a cohesive form prior to identification; during the second stage, featural information is identified or categorized serially, the extremities of the display being processed before the middle portion. By the end of stage two the stimulus is presumed to be assigned to a meaning category where it can be further compared with categorical information stored in long-term memory. As described thus far, the model is quite similar to two-stage models such as Sperling's (1960) and Neisser's (1967). However, it differs from these and others in that sensory persistence is initiated at the onset of the stimulus display rather than at the termination of the display and that it continues for a given maximum duration of about 100 msec. Thus the stimulus trace would outlive the display *only* if the display is exposed for less than the maximum duration of the trace, measured from stimulus onset.

The implications of DiLollo's theory should be apparent. It predicts that neither the poor nor the normal reader should experience any difficulty whatsoever with trace persistence, because the amount of time necessary for saccadic movements, fixation, decoding, and comprehension (250 msec for normal readers, 250+ msec for poor readers) would result in pause durations considerably longer than the duration of the trace. The time differential would be even greater in oral reading, particularly for deficient readers. Indeed, Perfetti and Hogaboam (1975) found that the mean vocalization latencies for common words was 1180 msec and 1298 msec for third- and fifth-grade poor readers respectively, whereas the respective latencies for their normal reader counterparts was 916 msec and 949 msec. These values are much larger than the 100-msec trace duration estimated by DiLollo. Thus if the theory proves to be valid, one may safely infer that trace persistence as a source of reading disability is a pseudo-problem.

To conclude, there is no convincing evidence that reading disability is attributable to deficient form perception resulting from dysfunction in initial-stage processing. Only a few studies have employed procedures that directly evaluated this hypothesis and these have yielded conflicting results. Interpretations generated by investigations that reported positive findings were questionable owing to the possibility of response bias; in investigations that controlled for this difficulty the findings were negative. It is significant that studies that did *not* support the hypothesis outnumbered those that did. I am also inclined to doubt initial-stage theories on logical grounds. However, in view of the dearth of research evaluating such theories, continued study of the problem would be worthwhile, if only to clarify ambiguities in the studies contrasting poor and normal readers at this level of processing.

5.3 VISUAL ANALYSIS

That severely impaired readers may be characterized by deficient form perception has been one of the most commonly cited of the perceptual deficit explanations of reading disability, but as we have seen, the evidence supporting this idea is not very convincing. Several other variants of the perceptual deficit hypothesis have been proposed, each drawing on the possibility that dyslexics may have difficulty in some aspect of visual analysis. The most widely discussed disorders in this general category include confusion in *spatial and directional orientation,* malfunction in *figure-ground and pattern perception,* and deficiencies in the *speed of processing visual information.* A fourth (and recent) formulation implicates deficiencies in *perceiving spatial location* (Mason 1975). We will examine research relating to each of these possibilities.

5.3.1 Spatial and Directional Orientation
A common tendency among beginning readers is to mislabel and write incorrectly individual letters that are graphically identical except for their spatial orientation *(b, d, p, q)* and sequences of letters that are identical except for their order in words *(was/saw).* Such children also occasionally print or write words from right to left, even to the extent of reversing the orientation of the letters in a word as well as their order (as in ЯOЯЯIM). These response patterns are usually of a transitional nature and drop out in the case of children who make satisfactory progress in reading. However, in children who have difficulty in learning to read, they have been observed to persist well beyond the time at which they normally disappear, that is, somewhere between 7 and 8 years of age (Davidson 1935). This has led some authors (Orton 1925, 1937; Eustis 1947; Hermann 1959) to accord positional and directional errors special status in their conceptualizations of specific reading disability, the inference being that such errors are indicative of spatial and directional confusion associated with some type of neurological impairment. Indeed the dyslexic's tendency to make generalization errors in coding similar configurations such as *b/d, p/q, was/saw,* and like pairs has been traditionally viewed as compelling evidence in support of perceptual deficit explanations of reading disability. As we shall see, however, there is reason to doubt that this response tendency signifies perceptual deficiency in the literal sense.

The view that reading disability is associated with spatial and directional confusion is largely an outgrowth of the seminal work done by Orton, who suggested that such difficulties occur because of the failure to establish hemispheric dominance and can be observed in characteristic response patterns in reading and written expression. Orton specifically inferred that letter and word identification problems result from inconsistency in retrieving the stored engrams representing printed letters that are discriminable only by virtue of their spatial orientation and location in words. The ostensible consequences of such malfunction were said to be (1) misperception of the distal stimulus ("seeing" *b* as *d* or *was* as *saw*), (2) inability to establish a firm left-right set in reading, and (3) the tendency to make orientation and sequencing errors in writing *(mirror writing)*.

Another theory that incorporated the notion of spatial and directional confusion as a central theme is that advanced by Hermann (1959). Hermann differed with Orton in suggesting that developmental dyslexia is associated with an inherited disposition toward directional confusion rather than a maturational lag resulting from poorly established lateral dominance. This author was also of the opinion that the hypothesized anomaly created difficulties in perceiving all visual symbols, including numerals and musical notations, whereas Orton believed that spatial disorientation was uniquely associated with linguistic symbols. However, Orton's and Hermann's conceptualizations were harmonious in postulating spatial confusion as a basic cause of reading disability, a conjecture that has had considerable impact on the study of reading disorder as evidenced in the number of investigators who have been influenced by this point of view— for example, Davidson (1935), Harris (1957), Silver and Hagin (1960, 1970), Myklebust and Johnson (1962), Wechsler and Hagin (1964), Belmont and Birch (1965), and Money (1966).

Despite widespread acceptance of the notion that reading disability is associated with a specific defect in spatial and directional orientation, the idea has very little empirical support. Orton and Hermann based their theories largely on clinical and anecdotal evidence, and the research available has for the most part yielded equivocal and inconclusive results.

In his initial review of studies evaluating spatial confusion theories of reading disability, Benton (1962) expressed skepticism that the failure to establish a "directional sense" would account for most cases of developmental dyslexia:

The evidence that disturbed directional sense is a significant
determinant of developmental dyslexia, as distinguished from
mere relative backwardness in reading is very sparse indeed.
Whether continued investigation will strengthen the hypothesis
is an open question. I am personally inclined to doubt that it
will. For it seems to me that in order for a directional disability
to operate as the sole and sufficient cause of developmental
dyslexia, it would have to be quite severe and to extend into
diverse areas of behavior. The affected individual would not only
be dyslexic, but also would be expected to show spatial disorientation and praxic difficulties. A few dyslexics present this picture,
but most of them do not. (Benton 1962, 98)

Benton pointed out further that most of the earlier studies evaluating spatial deficit theories of dyslexia (Fildes 1921; Goins 1958;
Hermann and Norrie 1958; Silver and Hagin 1960) failed to control for such factors as intelligence, language ability, prior experience, and behavior disorder. He concluded that directional confusion may not be a significant correlate of reading disability,
except perhaps in very young children.

In a later review of studies testing this same hypothesis Benton
(1975) presented conflicting research findings, but came to no
definitive conclusion as to the relations between the variables in
question. Once again several of the investigations reviewed did not
adequately control for intelligence and interpretations of the
results of those that did attempt to account for this and other
exclusionary variables are open to question (Belmont and Birch
1965; Lyle 1969; Sparrow and Satz 1970). It will therefore be
useful to examine a selected sampling of studies comparing poor
and normal readers on various measures of spatial orientation in
an effort to reconcile disparate findings and conclusions. The
intent will be to demonstrate that spatial confusion, as it has been
conceptualized in the literature, is a pseudoproblem, not an actual
cause of reading disability, and that the orientation and directional
sequencing errors that seem to persist in the reading and writing
of disabled readers can be explained on grounds other than spatial
confusion.

It has been amply documented over the years that positional
and directional confusions produced by poor readers are in excess
of those produced by normal readers of comparable age and grade
levels (Jastak 1934; Krise 1949, 1952; Furness 1956; Lyle 1969;
Sidman and Kirk 1974); many authors have suggested that such

findings support directional confusion theories of reading disability. However, simply documenting a significant incidence of such errors among poor readers tells us little of their etiology, and to conclude that their occurrence affords confirmatory evidence that they are caused by spatial impairment is to be circular. Therefore, a few studies have attempted to provide evidence for the generality of spatial orientation difficulties in poor readers by employing procedures that did not involve letters and words.

We have already examined a widely circulated study by Goins (1958) that demonstrated, among other things, a significant correlation between discrimination of mirror-image forms and reading achievement among first graders. However, the results of the study were confounded by significant correlations between performance on this measure and a measure of intelligence; furthermore, these and other findings were not applicable to disabled readers because all of the children tested could read normally. A later study by Wechsler and Hagin (1964) also correlated reading achievement with nonverbal measures of spatial orientation; it too has been frequently cited as providing evidence for spatial confusion as a cause of reading disability. This investigation did make direct comparisons of children identified as progressing satisfactorily and unsatisfactorily in reading.

Wechsler and Hagin's specific intent was to evaluate the relation between axial rotations and measures of reading readiness and reading achievement. Subjects were first- and third-graders (N = 50 each group) whose median ages were 6.5 and 8.5 respectively. Good and poor readers were identified by teacher judgment in first grade and through a group test of reading achievement in third grade. No further description of the samples was provided. Axial rotation was measured by means of a matching test involving an asymmetric figure shaped like a lamb chop depicted in eight different orientations (see figure 5.8). Each item entailed matching a standard with one of six alternatives laid out in two rows of three figures each. The test itself was administered under two different conditions presented in invariant order. On the initial presentation, subjects were asked to match a standard stimulus with six alternatives in different orientations while the standard remained in view. The second presentation required that subjects match standards with alternatives from memory, after a 3-second exposure of each standard.

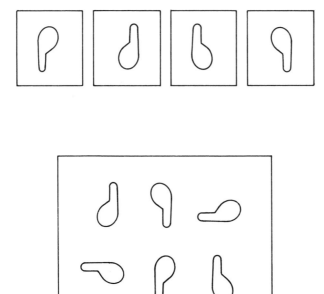

Figure 5.8 Sample stimuli from the "Lamb Chop Test" designed by Wechsler and Hagin for the study of spatial orientation in poor and normal readers. (Reprinted with permission of author and publisher from: Wechsler, David, and Hagin, Rosa. The problem of axial rotation in reading disability. *Perceptual and Motor Skills*, 1964, 19, 319–326.)

Aside from substantial improvement with age in accuracy of orientation, the most salient finding in this study was a significant relationship between reading ability and axial rotations. Group mean differences for number correct was greater for normal readers than for poor readers in both first and third grades under both the matching and recall conditions. Product moment correlations were also computed for measures of reading ability and axial rotations and were found to be statistically significant for only the first-grade comparisons (r = .39 for matching; r = .46 for recall). The magnitude of reader group differences on the matching task was greater under the memory condition than under the no-memory condition. There was no relationship between rotation errors and handedness, as might have been predicted by Orton's theory.

Wechsler and Hagin concluded from their results that the ability to perceive the lamb chop figures in correct orientation implies a high degree of reading readiness and that the child who has difficulty with axial rotations beyond age 6 will not make rapid progress in learning to read. The implication of these conclusions is that reading disorder is likely to be associated with deficient spatial ability. But there are several reasons for not accepting this interpretation of the findings too hastily.

First, there were no details about the characteristics of the subjects in this study, making it difficult to be certain that extraneous variables such as intelligence and socioeconomic factors were not significant contributors to observed group differences. Second, the criteria for reading achievement were entirely subjective (and therefore questionable) for first-graders and not adequately described for subjects in third grade. One cannot therefore be assured that the samples were representative of the population of interest here—that is, severely impaired readers of at least average intelligence whose reading difficulties are not attributable to environmental and experiential deficiencies.

A closely related problem is the failure to provide documentation that the reader groups actually differed with respect to the incidence of positional and directional confusions in reading and written expression. As observed in earlier research (Davidson 1935) orientation and sequencing errors are common among first-graders and may still be observed in second and third grade, even among normal readers. Since Wechsler and Hagin provided no comparison of reader groups on these error patterns, we have no way of knowing whether or not they were more prevalent in the poor readers. This, of course, limits the interpretation of results obtained on the measure of spatial orientation employed in their study.

One may also quarrel with the authors' conclusions on the strength of the possibility that their experimental task was measuring something other than ability to orient oneself in space. We have already examined problems inherent in employing match-to-standard tests with multiple alternatives, particularly those constructed in such a way as to tax the visual information processing devices of young children. Anyone not highly experienced or disposed to search systematically for distinguishing features of visual forms with many overlapping characteristics will have difficulty with such tasks, as will children who do not have the conceptual knowledge necessary for facilitating discrimination economically and efficiently. An implicit awareness that *same* and *different* can apply to stimulus dimensions other than shape is an example of the type of conceptual knowledge that can affect performance. The poor readers in the Wechsler and Hagin study may have had such difficulties, but this does not necessarily imply that they were spatially disordered in the sense in which these authors employed the concept.

Another plausible explanation of the findings is that satisfactory progress in reading may have provided the good readers with a decided performance advantage on the spatial task used, not only by virtue of sensitivity to orientation as an important discriminative cue but also as a function of experience in distinguishing identically shaped letters in different orientations. Indeed, one cannot help but be struck by the resemblance between most of the figures in the lamb chop test (figure 5.8) and the familiar letters *b, d, p,* and *q.* Thus one might argue that successful experience in discriminating these letters had transferred positively for the normal readers and perhaps negatively for the poor readers, thereby accounting for group differences.

In any event, it is entirely possible that factors such as those outlined may have been the primary determinants of the results observed in the Wechsler and Hagin study rather than disparities between poor and normal readers in spatial orientation ability. Without evidence to the contrary, one may reasonably suggest that the alternatives discussed constitute more parsimonious explanations of the findings than the interpretation offered by Wechsler and Hagin.

Several studies have assessed the spatial impairment explanation of reading disability by contrasting poor and normal readers on measures of lateral dominance and left-right identification. For example, Harris (1957) administered several tests of lateral preference (manual, eye, and foot dominance) along with a test of knowledge of left and right to 316 children with reading problems and 245 randomly selected controls. All of the poor readers were severely impaired in reading and all were clinic cases with IQs of at least 80 or above. The randomly selected group was presumed to represent a full range of reading abilities and was said to include a sizable proportion of children with reading difficulty

(10 to 15 percent). The subjects' ages were reported by the author to "have been consolidated into three groups, 7 and 8, 9 and 10, and 11 up." Most of the clinic cases were boys (87 percent); sex ratios in the control group were evenly balanced.

The most important finding in Harris's study was that the poor readers manifested greater difficulty in left-right identification and a greater tendency toward mixed lateral preferences than did children from the randomly selected sample. The author concluded from these results that both the ability to distinguish between right and left and a clear-cut manual preference develop slowly in children with reading disability, which, it was presumed, may be reflective of a maturation problem associated with neurological disorder.

Harris's interpretation is to be accepted with reservation, considering the possibility that the "reading disabled" sample may have contained a relatively high proportion of children of low intellectual ability who may have had difficulty with the conceptual aspects of some of the tasks employed. The use of clinic cases for the reading disabled group is also problematic in that the likelihood is great that the sample included a significant proportion of children with behavior disorders. Thus the reliability of the results may be questioned. Perhaps more important is the possibility that the test of left-right identification employed by Harris is measuring something other than spatial discrimination, a point to be elaborated further.

A subsequent study by Belmont and Birch (1965) also assessed lateral preferences for hand and eye along with knowledge of left-right identification. The sample in this study was much more carefully selected than that in the study by Harris. The subjects were all boys—150 very poor readers and 50 controls, matched for birth date and school placement. All subjects were between 9 and 10 years of age; intelligence test scores (WISC) were available for each subject; and the entire sample was representative of a broad range of socioeconomic levels.

Contrary to the findings of the Harris study, Belmont and Birch found no differences between poor and normal readers on the tests of lateral preference, though reader group differences were found on the tests of left-right identification. The authors suggested that there may be no significant relation between lateral preference and reading ability, but the group differences observed on left-right identification were interpreted as evidence for the "possibility of a defect in body schema and praxis."

One other study evaluated spatial confusion as a possible correlate of reading disability. Sparrow and Satz (1970) tested white middle-class boys (ages 9 to 12 years) who had WISC Performance IQs above 90 and found that at the younger age levels (9 to 10 years) the poor readers did not perform as well as the normal readers on a measure of left-right identification. The authors inferred from this finding that reading disability may be associated with delayed development of somatosensory functions.

It should be clear that there is no substantial evidence for the correlation between reading ability and handedness (that is, hemisphere dominance) that Orton's theory would predict. There is more consistent support for a possible relation between reading disability and the ability to identify left and right; yet I am inclined to disagree with those who infer from such findings that poor readers are hampered by spatial confusion and that that confusion causes their difficulties in learning to read. I tend to be more aligned with Benton's (1962) suggestion that left-right identification problems may be associated with verbal labeling deficits. Identifying the left or right sides of one's own body, or the left and right sides of another person's body not only requires spatial awareness but the coordination and integration of spatial, somatic, and linguistic referents. Difficulty in establishing these relationships could occur as a result of more basic impairment in verbal labeling, quite possibly associated with linguistic deficiencies. Evidence to support this suggestion was in fact provided by Benton and Kemble (1960). It is therefore conceivable that the problems experienced by poor readers in left-right identification, as described in the studies outlined, were actually the result of naming and labeling problems rather than spatial disorientation.

I should outline at this point the reasons for my belief that spatial confusion is an unlikely cause of reading disability. First, I see no justification for the assumption that children with specific reading disability are spatially disoriented in any sense of the word and am in complete accord with Benton's logical suggestion that such difficulty, should it exist, would be pervasive. Yet there is no evidence whatsoever that this is so. Furthermore, Orton's suggestion that spatial and directional confusion should only be apparent in learning that incorporates verbal symbols is highly implausible not only because it begs the question but, more important, because there are more parsimonious explanations of the types of difficulties encountered by poor readers in symbolic learning.

The second reason for doubting spatial confusion theories of reading disability is that the error patterns commonly observed in disabled readers may be due to malfunction in verbal rather than visual processing. It has already been suggested that observed deficiencies in poor readers' performance on left-right identification tasks may be attributable to verbal labeling problems rather than spatial impairment. A similar explanation may account for the spatial generalization errors commonly observed in the oral reading and writing of poor readers. It seems a reasonable conjecture that such inaccuracies are in fact linguistic intrusion errors caused by imprecision in verbal mediation rather than visual-perceptual distortions caused by spatial and directional confusion. Put more simply, I suggest that children who call *b, d* or *was, saw* do not perceive (literally see) these configurations differently from the way normal readers do, but because of deficiencies in one or more aspects of verbal processing, they have difficulty in remembering which verbal label is associated with which printed symbol.

The more general inference here is that the child who has normal ability to associate visual symbols with their verbal counterparts acquires, in time, an enriched network of verbal mnemonics that aid him in making the critical visual discriminations necessary for accurate decoding. More specifically, the child who has an implicit knowledge of the phonemic and articulatory differences in graphically similar letters and words (*b* and *d, p* and *q, was* and *saw, loin* and *lion*) and who, in the case of the words, knows the differences between their meanings and their uses in sentences has a variety of linguistic cues to aid him in programming the correct orientations and sequences characteristic of those configurations. Conversely, the child who has difficulty in acquiring such (linguistic) information is at a distinct disadvantage in making the fine-grained (visual) discriminations necessary for learning the code and for establishing visual-verbal equivalence generally. This is because of the negative learning that must inevitably accrue by virtue of the prolonged tendency toward making generalization errors caused by deficient visual-verbal integration. Thus he will continue to manifest positional and directional inaccuracies; these in turn promote the belief that he is spatially impaired.

Finally, it seems entirely unnecessary to suggest that poor readers are inherently deficient in their ability to establish a directional sense as suggested by Hermann, among others. Indeed, orientation in either two- or three-dimensional space is a relative rather than an absolute function and emerges largely because of learned relations, not because of inborn capacities specifically responsible for spatial and directional awareness. We store information to program proper orientation, and such information has functional value in direct relation to the unique properties of specific environmental and representational coordinates, most of which are quite arbitrary in nature. Successful arrival at and return from a particular locale depends upon our ability to store a series of directional maneuvers that completely reverse themselves in journeying to and from our destination. Under these circumstances, specific environmental landmarks or points of interest appear on our left or right depending upon our orientation and a successful journey is contingent upon the ability to shift direction in a relative rather than an absolute manner.[5] Analogously, written English proceeds from left to right whereas Hebrew and Arabic scripts proceed from right to left. In all of these instances directionality must be learned; it does not mature in the neurological sense (Orton, 1925, 1937), nor is it innate as suggested in directional "set" theories of reading disability (Hermann 1959).

Constitutional Versus Experiential Determinants of Spatial Orientation   The argument that the ability to orient oneself in space is acquired can be buttressed with recourse to research on the comparative importance of constitutional and experiential factors in determining spatial orientation in both subhuman species and normal children. A number of studies have employed a differential reinforcement paradigm in demonstrating that some animals and very young children (between 3 and 6 years) encounter little difficulty discriminating vertical and horizontal lines but manifest considerable difficulty in discriminating oblique lines oriented in opposite directions (/ \ ). Lashley (1938) observed this response pattern in the rat; Sutherland (1957) and Rudel and Teuber (1963) made similar observations in studying the octopus and normal children respectively.

Analogously, Rudel and Teuber found that children had more difficulty in discriminating mirror figures contrasted in a lateral or left-right plane— ⊏ versus ⊐ —than they did in discriminating mirror figures contrasted in a vertical or up-down plane— ⊔ ⊓ . Such findings stimulated considerable interest in and speculation about the possibility that the nervous systems of at least some species, including humans, are equipped with structurally and qualitatively different devices for discriminating and processing different types of spatial information. For example, Sutherland suggested that the octopus is endowed with a two-dimensional shape analyzing mechanism with receptors for processing only horizontal and vertical arrays. This notion leads to the prediction that visual stimuli that are laid out at 45° angles to a horizontal plane are not readily discriminated, presumably because they produce "equivalent" input.

Rudel and Teuber point out that Sutherland's model quite accurately predicts discrimination behavior in both the octopus and young children, the implication being that some phylogenetically different species may have analogous devices for effecting pattern perception. However in the octopus these perceptual devices can be construed as ontogenetically mature, whereas they can be construed as ontogenetically immature in children between the ages of 3 and 6, whose discrimination behaviors are apparently similar to those of the octopus.

In logically extending such findings to the present problem, it could be argued that the neurological underpinnings that presumably support the discrimination of orientation are qualitatively dissimilar in dyslexic and normal readers, perhaps by virtue of maturational differences between the two groups. However, notwithstanding the possibility that the maturation of neurological structures may ultimately prove to be a significant determinant of developmental changes in pattern perception (Teuber 1960), there is reason to question the assumption that the difficulties encountered by young children in discriminating mirror-image figures is attributable to the neurologically unique properties of their pattern analyzing devices. Specifically, Huttenlocher found in two separate investigations that discrimination of mirror-image figures depended not only upon the plane in which the figures were juxtaposed but also upon the relative positions of the figures

(1967a, 1967b). For example, discrimination of up-down mirror figures—□—was just as difficult for very young children (ages 4 and 5 years) as left-right open figures—⊆—but neither was as difficult as left-right mirror figures presented in lateral juxtaposition—⊏⊐. Similar results were obtained by Sekular and Rosenblith (1964) with first-graders and by Sekular and Houlihan (1968) with adults. These findings cast doubt on the notion that the nervous system is equipped with unique mechanisms for detecting orientation; instead they imply that the relation of one figure to another determines the difficulty encountered in discrimination. Indeed, experience would seem to be the important factor, as illustrated quite clearly in Rudel and Teuber's suggestion that left-right mirror figures may be particularly difficult to discriminate because ambulation changes the left-right features of the environment while leaving vertical dimensions unchanged.

Empirical support for the importance of experience in discriminating orientation is provided by a number of studies that have specifically addressed the issue. For example, Huttenlocher (1967b) found that children not only confused mirror images in copying designs but also in ordering an array of blocks laterally aligned. These errors were thought to be comparable in that both kinds appeared to be related to strategic factors rather than to spatial confusion:

Children tend to compare sample and copy starting at the point where these are closest to one another. Such strategy no doubt seems conservative to them. Note, however, that if one indeed begins his examination in this way and then compares outward in both directions from the mid-line, the copy would indeed be a mirror image of the original. (Huttenlocher 1967b, 1175)

Over and Over (1967) challenged the suggestion made by Sutherland and Rudel and Teuber that neurologically unique sensory receptors accounted for the difficulty encountered by young children in discriminating mirror-image obliques, suggesting instead that the failure to attend to or remember discriminating cues might explain such difficulty. Briefly, Over and Over presented vertical-horizontal (⊢) and oblique figures (/ \ ) to nursery-school children (ages 3 to 4 years), comparing the recognition method (differential reinforcement) used by Rudel and Teuber with a detection method whereby subjects were required to match a standard stimulus with one of two alternatives. They found that discrimination of obliques was often no better than chance under the recognition condition but improved dramatically under the detection condition. There was not much difference between these conditions in the case of vertical-horizontal discriminations. They concluded that the failure to discriminate obliques under the recognition condition was due to response variables rather than sensory input variables.

Additional support for the primary importance of learning in stabilizing orientation is provided in a series of studies conducted by Ghent, who questioned the widespread belief that very young children (3 to 5 years) are relatively insensitive to differences in spatial position. In two separate studies evaluating this hypothesis it was found that children between 3 and 7 years had difficulty in the tachistoscopic recognition of familiar figures and geometric forms presented in disoriented (upside down) positions, whereas older children manifested no such impairment (Ghent 1960; Ghent and Bernstein 1961). In a third investigation concerned with the same problem Ghent (1961) found that children between the ages of 4 and 8 showed distinct preferences for meaningless figures in given orientations when asked to choose the figure that was "upside down" or "wrong." The results of all three studies provide evidence that young children are indeed sensitive to the orientations of objects to which they are exposed and, further, that with experience a given figure comes to be recognized despite changes in its orientation. Following Hebb's (1949) theory of perceptual learning, Ghent suggested that children tend to scan figures starting from an acquired focal point that initiates a top-down scan terminating in recognition of the form:

The interpretation offered for the preferences for orientation suggests that the judgment of the orientation of a figure is not separable, for the young child, from the perception of its shape. That is, a figure is called right side up if its position facilitates the tendency to scan in a top to bottom direction and hence facilitates perception of the form. (Ghent 1961, 187)

Ghent's conceptualization of orientation in young children obviously places greater emphasis upon learning than upon species-specific mechanisms that program differential sensitivity to spatial position. Although her theory cannot readily account for age-related changes in form perception, it does offer a plausible alternative to Sutherland's and Rudel and Teuber's explanations for the response patterns manifested by young children in discriminating orientation of forms, in particular the differential levels of performance with left-right versus up-down transformations.

Wohlwill and Wiener (1964) specifically tested Ghent's downward scanning hypothesis with 3- and 4-year-old children, employing stimuli designed to attune subjects to differences in orientation, and found that they were proficient in detecting such differences when the task facilitated selective attention to spatial position as a discriminating cue. Recall that Calfee (1977) obtained similar results with kindergartners, employing synthetic figures specifically marked to facilitate attendance to orientation.

Thus the central component, if not all aspects, of Ghent's theory seems appealing, specifically the suggestion that young children are indeed sensitive to the orientation characteristic of given forms but do *not* discriminate the orientations of these figures apart from their shapes. In other words, the spatial position in which a particular form is typically encountered may be initially construed by a given child as an intrinsic component of its shape. The logical extension of this conjecture is that orientation differences not critical to the discrimination of a particular configuration will go unnoticed by that child until such a time as he is confronted with identical configurations having specific properties associated with variations in orientation, as in reading. This conjecture leads to the expectation that children will not only learn about the unique properties attached to specific figures in given orientations but will thereafter employ orientation as a distinguishing attribute in identifying identical figures. A corollary assumption is that a young child (beyond 3 years) has the ability to discriminate orientations of particular forms at a basic sensory level (given normal visual acuity), which can be readily demonstrated with appropriate experimental procedures, as illustrated in the studies by Wohlwill and Wiener and Over and Over. But the child's ability to respond appropriately to given forms in given orientations depends upon his ability to associate specific responses with each of those forms. And that depends upon learning, not upon maturation or inheritance of a "directional sense."

Additional evidence in support of this position comes from several other investigations. Gibson, Gibson, Pick, and Osser (1962) evaluated visual discrimination of letterlike forms in children from 4 to 8 years of age, using several types of transformations of standard figures. Performance in general improved with age. One transformation that yielded a comparatively high number of errors among the youngest age groups was change in orientation of given figures, as might be expected. Figures characterized by changes in linear perspective proved to be the most difficult to discriminate and performance on such measures did not improve much with age. The authors suggest that improvement in discrimination of letterlike forms is related to perceptual learning of the "features or dimensions of difference which are critical for differentiating letters": Discrimination of features such as orientation improves with experience because differences along this and like dimensions are important for distinguishing letters; changes in perspective, on the other hand, have no relevance in letter discrimination.

The results of this study and the authors' interpretation of the results are consonant with the premise that sensitivity to orientation of given forms is established in direct relation to the functional meanings attached to specific forms in particular spatial positions.

To illustrate further, Jeffrey (1958) attempted to teach 3- and 4-year-old children to attach the verbal labels *left* and *right* to the appropriate sides of a stick figure. He found that the children were unable to perform the task upon initial exposure but that with additional training in perceptual discrimination of the directional differences they readily attached the labels appropriately. Similar results were obtained by Hendrickson and Muehl (1962) with kindergarten children learning the correct names for the letters *b* and *d*. And Olson and Baker (1969) found that children between the ages of 3 and 5 could orient themselves accurately to the left or the right (pinning a tail on a donkey) even when deprived of visual cues and even when their own positions in space were systematically altered. Of particular interest in this study is the finding that some of these children could not verbally identify the left and right sides of their bodies, indicating that they lacked these semantic categories while possessing an adequate representation of the directional properties of space. This of course is consistent with our earlier suggestion that studies evaluating directionality, in both poor and normal readers, by asking a child to respond appropriately to verbal cues may misconstrue a verbal deficiency as a spatial deficiency (Harris 1957; Belmont and Birch 1965; Sparrow and Satz 1970).

One other study may be briefly mentioned here. Caldwell and Hall (1969) found that kindergarten children discriminated among the letters *b, d, p,* and *q* with more or less success depending upon whether exposure to pretraining conditions had attuned them to orientation differences, or to shape differences. The authors suggested that the child's conceptualization of *same* and *different* on such discrimination tasks is a more significant determinant of performance than are perceptual ability or attentional factors.

These results, taken together, provide considerable support for the basic premise that the functional attributes attached to particular orientations of given forms by preschool and school-age children are products of learning, not maturation or inheritance. At the same time, basic sensory discrimination of those orientations can be inferred in such children, assuming normal visual acuity. In applying these contentions to the present problem, I suggest that the normal reader responds appropriately to different orientations and sequences of identically shaped letters (both apart from and within the context of words) because he has attached the appropriate sounds and meanings to those stimuli. The poor reader, in contrast, does not readily learn these relations; he consequently has difficulty in stabilizing the positions and locations of letters in words and has particular difficulty in responding accurately to those with identical shapes. He may often appear to respond to such configurations as though they were spatially equivalent, but it is probably more accurate to infer that his basic difficulty is in learning the appropriate verbal responses to letter stimuli he has already learned to discriminate visually.

Some research carried out in our laboratory provides direct support for this inference (Vellutino, Steger, and Kandel 1972; Vellutino, Smith, Steger, and Kaman 1975). These studies demonstrated that poor readers (ages 7 to 12 years) had little difficulty in perceiving and graphically reproducing from visual memory words they were *unable* to pronounce and spell—even words that provided ample opportunity for spatial confusion errors of the types said to be characteristic of poor readers (*was, bin, loin, calm*).

These findings, of course, support the inference that inaccuracies in naming letters and words may actually be linguistic intrusion errors caused by verbal encoding deficiencies rather than perceptual distortions caused by spatial confusion. Additional support for the possibility is derived from a study by Liberman and her associates (1971) investigating the relationship between visual discrimination and oral reading errors in beginning readers, in particular, the problems of optical reversibility as initially postulated by Orton. Certain of their findings are particularly relevant here. First, in examining the relationship between reversals and other types of errors in this population, they found that *sequence reversals* and *orientation inaccuracies* accounted for only a small proportion (25 percent) of the total number of errors in word lists constructed to provide maximum opportunity for making such mistakes *(was/saw, bad/dad);* moreover, the error rates for such stimuli were unstable on test-retest comparisons. Second, sequencing and orientation errors in the same children were not correlated with one another as spatial confusion theories of reading disability would predict. Although there was some tendency for confusion among words containing reversible letters *(b/d),* as might be expected by virtue of their shape similarities, such errors were not as frequent when these letters were presented singly (tachistoscopically). This finding is inconsistent with a visual dysfunction interpretation of reading disability. Furthermore, errors on symmetrical letters were often not symmetrical (that is, confused with their "shape-mates," for example calling b /d/ or d /b/) and many of the errors could alternatively be interpreted as sound confusions *(b* and *p).* Therefore, the authors suggest that the orientation and sequencing errors commonly found in poor readers are more linguistic than visual in nature and may be an effect rather than a cause of reading disability. The results of several other studies we shall come to shortly are in accord with this inference.

Finally, the contention that poor readers are not spatially and directionally impaired is afforded additional support by two other investigations made in our laboratory (Vellutino et al. 1973; Vellutino, Steger, Kaman, and DeSetto 1975). In both studies poor readers (between 7 and 12 years) performed as well as normal readers in immediate visual recall of Hebrew words presented tachistoscopically (see figure 5.9), though neither group performed as well as children learning to speak, read, and write Hebrew. It is especially interesting that in both studies poor

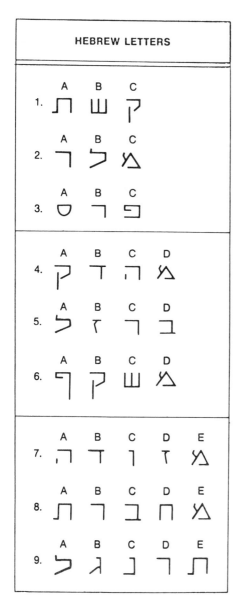

Figure 5.9 Hebrew letter stimuli presented to poor and normal readers in two studies. (Vellutino et al. 1973; Vellutino, Steger, Kaman, and DeSetto 1975. Reproduced by permission of the editor of *Cortex*.)

readers made no more errors in orienting and sequencing the letters in the words than did normal readers and were not different from the normals in scanning the material from left to right. These studies will be discussed in greater detail later (see section 5.4). Suffice it to say at this juncture that the results provide strong evidence that poor readers are not spatially and perceptually impaired; they thereby afford indirect evidence for alternative conceptualizations of reading disability.

In summary, the long-held belief that reading disability is attributable to spatial and directional confusion is questionable on empirical, theoretical, and logical grounds. The small number of studies providing evidence to support this hypothesis suffer from sampling, procedural, and interpretive problems, and their results are conflicting. Most of the measures employed in those studies compared poor and normal readers on lateral preference, left-right identification, or comparative frequency of orientation and directional errors in reading and writing. There was no convincing evidence that lateral preference is significantly correlated with reading ability; group differences in left-right identifications and reversal tendencies, however, seem to be reliable. Although some authors suggest that these differences are attributable to spatial and directional confusion, one can argue that they reflect basic deficiencies in verbal labeling and visual-verbal integration. The research that has been examined, as well as some yet to be discussed, provides strong support for this suggestion. One can argue further that sensitivity to the orientations and sequences of written symbols is a by-product of learning, rather than of maturation or inheritance; research evaluating the development of form perception in normal children appears to support this conjecture. I therefore conclude that spatial and directional confusion is *not* a significant cause of specific reading disability; indeed I question the very existence of this disorder as it has been discussed in the literature.

5.3.2 Mirror Writing

Directly extending from the spatial deficit theories of reading disability is the belief that dyslexics are subject to handwriting difficulties characterized by a tendency toward orienting and sequencing letters in reverse—an anomaly known as *mirror writing* or *reversed writing*. Poor reading and mirror writing have been closely linked in perceptual deficit theories of reading disability, the typical assumption being that these disorders emmanate from a common underlying cause—spatial and directional confusion.

The literature dealing with mirror writing is meager and no controlled studies evaluating this phenomenon could be found. All available accounts appear in the form of clinical anecdotes compiled primarily by physicians with a particular interest in the behavioral correlates of neurological disorders; thus available discussions of incidence, characteristics, and etiology of mirror writing are necessarily subjective.

The most comprehensive exposition available is a monograph written some time ago by Critchley (1928). Little has been added to our knowledge of the subject since then, but a more recent review by Trueman (1965) provides references to work done later.

According to both Critchley and Trueman complete mirror writing is very rare, but the tendency toward occasionally reversing letters and words is quite common among some groups: normal school-age children, disabled readers, mentally defective children, and right hemiplegic (right-side paralysis) adults following damage to the left hemisphere.

Estimates of the incidence of reversed writing among school children vary widely. Beeley (1918) reported that 1 out of every 2500 youngsters was found to be a mirror writer, whereas Gordon (1920) and Hecaen and DeAjuriaguerra (1964) reported figures of 0.45 percent and 0.50 percent respectively—or close to 5 out of every 1000. Critchley suggested that the right-to-left progression is more "natural" for left-handed persons, and that mirror writing should therefore be observed more often among children who are left-handed than among those who are right-handed. He indicated that his clinical experience verified this expectation, but he provided no independent support for his claim. By contrast, Hecaen and DeAjuriguerra (1964) found no significant difference in the tendency toward mirror writing in right- and left-handed individuals spanning a broad age range. However, the incidence of mirror writing has been found to be several times greater among mentally retarded than among normal children, the figures reported ranging from 8 percent (Gordon 1920) to 50 percent (Critchley 1928). Fildes (1923) provides additional support for the reliability of these observations.

Three possible explanations of mirror writing were discussed by both Critchley and Trueman. The most prominent is the visual-deficit hypothesis, which is similar to the theory of reading and writing disability advanced by Orton. The second theory is the "motor" hypothesis of Erlenmeyer (1879).

Put briefly and simply, Erlenmeyer hypothesized that "the most natural movements for one hand, are the mirrored replica of those of the opposite hand" and that the outward, abductive movements represent the "easiest, most coordinate and best controlled" (Critchley 1928, 22). For the right-handed person such movement proceeds from left to right; for the left-handed the natural progression is from right to left. The theory therefore predicts that by and large, mirror writers will be left-handed, but evidence for this prediction is scant and conflicting.

A third explanation assumed the possible existence of a "writing center" contralateral to the dominant hand. The writing center was believed to be both a structural and a functional entity, which presumably developed in the dominant hemisphere as a result of repeated movements of the fingers and hands. Memory for the movements of the preferred hand were supposedly stored in both hemispheres so that the engrams generated by one hand became, in effect, the mirror images of those generated by the other. Mirror writing would therefore occur, theoretically, when neither hemisphere emerged as dominant or when the influence of the dominant hemisphere had been disturbed, as in the case of brain injury.

This brief account should make it obvious that our understanding of mirror writing is extremely limited and virtually all explanations of the phenomenon are highly speculative. Indeed, from the available literature one may reasonably conclude that the very existence of mirror writing as a clinical entity is in doubt, a conclusion that is not without justification, as will be seen. I will therefore refrain from commenting further upon the relative merits of these three theories of mirror writing and will instead suggest an alternative explanation of the phenomenon.

According to Orton's theory of dyslexia, reading problems and mirror writing are two of a collection of disorders attributed to spatial confusion presumably associated with poorly established lateral dominance. Spelling disability was also included in this group, and the presence of orientation or sequencing difficulties in all three areas was viewed as confirmatory evidence to support a clinical diagnosis of specific developmental dyslexia. Orton further suggested that some dyslexics may be found to have an unusual facility in reading material written in the reversed direction while sustaining extreme difficulty in reading text arranged in conventional left-to-right order. He based these suggestions on impressions derived from work with clinic cases; no independent evidence to verify his observations was presented. The role of spatial confusion in accounting for the directional and orientational errors that can be observed in the handwriting of some poor readers has also been stressed by Hermann (1959) and others (Reinhold 1963; Silver and Hagin 1970). However, as already indicated, these authors do not necessarily agree as to the etiology of the symptom patterns that can be observed in disordered reading and spelling and, by extension, those that are apparent in dysfunctional handwriting.

The belief that reading disability and mirror writing are intrinsically related disorders has been widespread, not only among perceptual deficit theorists but among practitioners working with disabled readers as well as among the lay public. Indeed, as teachers of preschool and school-age children can verify, many parents become highly anxious when reversed letters appear in their child's written work, since they are frequently told that he may have spatial problems associated with neurological disorder. In attempting to allay their concerns, parents typically seek the advice of a physician, psychologist, or some other professional who they hope will provide them with definitive information about the basic cause of the disorder. Such a venture frequently results in a diagnosis of "dyslexia." which carries with it the implicit assumption that the child is indeed suffering from spatial disorder. Aside from the circularity involved in this exercise, the fact remains that there is virtually no well-documented objective evidence that the appearance of reversed writing in poor readers is a manifestation of anything more than lack of appropriate experience. Furthermore, it is well known that even some normal readers demonstrate a significant incidence of reversed writing when they begin to learn to read, casting doubt on the assumption that such behavior is caused by spatial deficiency associated with organic disorder. Maturationists may of course suggest that mirror writing in the latter group is an age-appropriate manifestation of incomplete development and may simply reflect a transitional period in the child's growth. However, this explanation appears to be contraindicated by the fact that the incidence of such reversals is far too variable to be considered a definitive milestone characteristic of a particular level of maturation. Furthermore, some children exhibit little of no tendency whatsoever toward mirror writing, whereas others show a marked inclination toward persistent reversal of at least some written letters. Yet proportionally few of the latter group ultimately fail in reading.

I therefore suggest that there is a more parsimonious explanation of the persistent tendencies toward letter reversals observed in poor readers. To illustrate, it is my belief that the appearance of reversed writing in preschool or beginning school age children is a predictable consequence of natural tendencies toward response generalization during a period when the visual-motor patterns and strategies of execution (such as always starting at the left) necessary for accurate formation of letters and words are still uncertain. It is probable that at this level of the child's experience he has stored preliminary motor programs (series of movements) involved in producing letters and words of varying shapes, but these programs do not yet include instructions that will effect positional and directional constancy. It is significant that the child's executions during this stage of learning are characterized by an implicit knowledge of specific topographical relationships that remain invariant over varying transformations in orientation and direction. Such relationships, in effect, constitute an internalized schema that he employs to both recognize and produce a particular combination. Thus the reversed R's in ЯOЯЯIM may typically incorporate a vertical line, a closed half circle conjoined with the top of the vertical, and a diagonal that angles the vertical line on the same side as the half circle and toward the bottom of that line. Occasionally the entire figure may be inverted so that the half circle is at the bottom of the vertical (ᖴ or ᖯ); but even if it is, the diagonal rarely angles the vertical on the side opposite to the half circle, either at the top (ᗡ or ᖾ) or at the bottom of the vertical (ᑯ or ᖯ). A motor program that would maintain the topographical invariance of the letter R in any given orientation of this figure might be as follows: (1) draw a straight line, (2) stop at the end of the line and turn outward, (3) curve around and come back and touch

the line in the middle, (4) stop and head out toward the other
end of the line on a slant. The child who stores such a program
will produce the correct shape of the letter R but will correctly
orient the figure only on a random basis, since the program does
not include instructions to effect either consistency or accuracy
of orientation.

The fledgling handwriter may also have acquired certain idiosyncratic modes of execution resulting in habitual response patterns that are unique. Consider, for example, the name ANNE.
This configuration may be described as involving three separate
programs (A, N, E), each consisting of a specific series of movements. The program for the letter N must also entail a repetition
command, and writing of the name as a whole implies a superordinate instruction by means of which spacing is effected. The
child first learning to write this name may be observed to consistently produce *one* reversed N, which, curiously, appears in
alternate locations: AͶNE   or   ANͶE . It could be argued in
this instance, that one execution of the letter N was impaired by
spatial dysfunction of the type suggested by Orton. However, it is
also possible that the mirror-image N's in this name are produced not as a result of confusion in executing a *three*-movement
program incorporating a repetition command but by means of a
six-movement program that instructs the child to perform a series
of up-down shifts, always making the second and fifth lines
diagonal to the verticals. With such a program, the name will
invariably contain one reversed letter and its location will depend
upon whether the program is initiated adjacent to the top or
bottom of the letter A. In other words, the mirror figures in the
middle of the name are not two separate letters, one of which is
reversed because of spatial confusion, but one figure consisting of
six separate movements, characterized by alternating changes in
direction and variable points of initiation.[6]

What I am suggesting is that the orientational and directional
inaccuracies apparent in the handwriting of beginning readers
are quite normal and need not imply spatial impairment of any
kind. This suggestion carries with it the assumption that such
children initially construe letters in various orientations and sequences as functionally equivalent. However, central to my
position is the additional assumption that satisfactory experience
in reading serves to alter this notion. The change in perceptual

attitude should be especially evident as children become more conversant with the critical differences in the sounds and meanings associated with given letters and words, this type of information ultimately expanding into a rich network of linguistic and other collateral cues that will serve as mnemonics to assist in establishing positional and directional constancy in both oral reading and writing.

In contrast, children who have significant and protracted difficulty in letter and word decoding will incorporate very few reliable cues to assist them in programming for accuracy in spatial orientation, and their efforts in both reading and handwriting will be hampered by considerable negative learning. To be more explicit, the child who cannot consistently remember which verbal label is associated with which member of potentially confusing pairs of configurations, such as *b* and *d* or *was* and *saw,* or who cannot readily employ letter sounds to assist in attaching the correct labels to these items may be expected to have prolonged difficulty in reproducing them in correct orientation and sequence. He will also be delayed in developing a set toward employing orientational and directional cues in word decoding and writing and will unavoidably engage in a good deal of negative practice. An implicit assumption here is that the reading problems such a child encounters are caused not by organically derived spatial confusion but by some other factors of unknown origin. Thus mirror writing and related anomalies can be reasonably viewed as secondary manifestations of reading disability rather than as a syndrome of symptoms that coexist with reading problems as a function of underlying spatial deficiency. I have expressed this view in previous contexts and will reaffirm it in later ones.

5.3.3 Figure-Ground and Pattern Perception
A number of investigators have suggested that disabled readers encounter significant difficulty in abstracting visual stimuli from complex backgrounds. An explicit assumption in most explanations of the problem is that poor readers are impaired in their ability to analyze and encode visual patterns because of basic dysfunction at the level of the nervous system. Unfortunately, there has been very little research to evaluate the suggestion that poor readers are basically impaired in processing figure-ground relationships.

Birch (1962,164ff) reported the results of studies evaluating his suggestion that some poor readers may be deficient in their ability to establish "visual hierarchical dominance." It is not clear from Birch's description whether this hypothesized dysfunction is supposed to occur at the level of attention (involving the limbic system and the arousal mechanisms: Malmo 1959) or within systems more directly related to cognitive processing. Nor are behavioral manifestations of deficient sensory dominance ever made explicit. Therefore testable hypotheses as to specific types of disorder that may have measurable effects upon skills related to reading cannot easily be derived from his conceptualization. Birch himself provided very little evidence to support this theory, although he made reference to two different research paradigms that provided initial verification of its validity.

One paradigm involved plotting separate curves for discrimination learning in each sensory system under mixed (alternating) modality presentations. The measure of sensory dominance in this instance was the comparative number of trials to learning in each modality. Birch reported results indicating that in poor readers discrimination learning was not as good in the visual modality as in other modalities, whereas the reverse was true in normal readers. The other paradigm was a conflict situation in which stimuli in two sensory modes were presented simultaneously, subsequent to criterion learning in both modalities. Differential tendencies toward emitting responses previously associated with given sensory stimuli were taken as measures of sensory dominance. Birch referred to a pilot study employing this procedure in which it was found that responses that had been associated with visual stimuli were preempted by responses that had been associated with various other sensory stimuli.

It is difficult to evaluate these preliminary investigations because, to my knowledge, no detailed account of further research findings are reported anywhere in the literature. Moreover, I know of no studies that have attempted systematically to vary sensory inputs in poor and normal readers in tests of Birch's theory. The longitudinal studies by Satz and associates (1974a, 1974b) mentioned earlier might be considered a close approximation in assessing the theory that somatosensory and verbal functions are dominant at different stages of development. However, Satz's findings provide, at best, tenuous evidence for this conjecture.

Similarly, Doehring (1968) found that poor readers performed better than normals on somesthetic activities but not as well on visual perceptual and verbal tasks. This discrepancy was taken as possible support for the theory in question. However, the evidence was not impressive owing to inconsistency in reader group comparisons on different measures of the same functions. Doehring's conclusions are therefore tenuous. Furthermore, Pick (1970) presented research evidence suggesting that sensory dominance is a relative phenomenon, determined by a biologically natural inclination to process a given type of sensory information in the modality that is best suited to the task. This, of course, is contrary to Birch's conceptualization of hierarchical dominance of the senses.

The chances of finding in dyslexics the type of deficit proposed by Birch would seem to be meager. Although I claim no expertise as to the neurophysiological bases of sensory development, it would seem that a deficiency in sensory dominance would be pervasive and should therefore manifest itself in most activities in daily living. Yet there is no evidence that this is the case. Indeed, I must confess that I have difficulty understanding what to look for in recognizing the disorder. Without greater explication as to the behavioral earmarks of deficient sensory dominance and their relationship to the reading process, Birch's theory has little value in explaining reading disability. Indeed, sensory dominance in humans seems highly task specific, varying functionally in accord with the individual's purpose in any given instance (listening to a symphony versus reading a novel). Thus, to suggest that there is an absolute ordering of sensory skills with vision occupying the prime position is counterintuitive. (Research evidence to support this contention is presented in chapter 6.)

Although Birch himself provided little evidence for his suggestion that poor readers are deficient in visual analysis, a few investigators have compared poor and normal readers on the ability to abstract simple figures embedded in complex arrays. Elkind, Horn, and Schneider (1965) found differences between poor and normal readers on an embedded figures test as well as on other measures of visual analysis designed to assess the relationship between reading ability and Piagetian decentration. A similar study conducted by Goetzinger, Dirks, and Baer (1960) found that poor readers, matched with normal readers for age

(10 to 12 years) and Stanford Binet IQ, had more difficulty than the normals in apprehending embedded figures on the more demanding portion (section B) of the Gottschaldt Embedded Figures Test (Gottschaldt 1926). They were also poorer than the normal readers on the Raven Progressive Matrices (Raven 1956), a nonverbal test of concept attainment that involves a considerable degree of visual analysis. The poor readers did *not* differ from their normal reading peers on another figure-ground measure, consisting of common objects embedded in homogeneous backgrounds of wavy lines and squares, each stimulus being presented tachistoscopically. It would seem from the latter finding that the poor readers' performance on the Raven and Gottschaldt tests may not have been due to deficient figure–ground perception, although the author made no attempt to reconcile the discrepancy in his measures of visual perception.

Lovell, Gray, and Oliver (1964) also found differences between poor and normal readers (ages 10 to 15) on the Gottschaldt test as well as on the Bender Gestalt Test (Bender 1938). Yet the two groups were equivalent on measures of nonverbal intelligence. The results in this study were conflicting in that comparisons of the boys in both groups yielded no differences between poor and normal readers on (1) WISC Block Designs, (2) a figure rotation test (Shapiro et al. 1962), and (3) a measure of spatial orientation (Semmes et al. 1955). Furthermore, comparisons of the girls in these groups yielded no differences on any of the measures. At the same time the poor readers, regardless of sex, were differentiated from the normals on WISC Vocabulary. Thus in this study as in the one by Goetzinger et al. (1960) the data are equivocal and the conclusion that poor readers are deficient in visual analysis is unwarranted.

Nevertheless, the question of why the Gottschaldt or other visually complex tasks may differentiate poor and normal readers remains to be answered (compare Elkind, Horn, and Schneider 1965; Silver and Hagin 1970; Blank, Berenzweig, and Bridger 1975). If not deficiencies in visual analysis and perception, then what? Aside from the possibility that poor readers may be generally less attentive than normals in dealing with any measure that requires effort and concentration, it may be that they are inclined to be inefficient rather than deficient (impaired neurologically) on complex visual tasks that require systematic analysis of stimu-

lus constituents. In order to perform successfully on such measures the perceiver must detect invariant and anchoring relations
that facilitate synthesis of visual information. That such skill takes
time to develop has been amply documented (Gibson, Osser, and
Pick 1963; Kerpelman and Pollack 1964; Elkind, Koegler, and Go
1964; Salapatek and Kessen 1966; Elkind and Weiss 1967; Gibson
1969; Pick and Frankel 1974). Of particular interest in this connection is the finding of Gottschalk, Bryden, and Rabinovitch
(1964) that the ability to systematically scan a complex visual
array, while not characteristic of 4-year-old children, did emerge
in 5- and 6-year-olds. Vurpuillot (1968) made similar observations,
as did Nodine (Nodine and Evans 1969; Nodine and Lang 1971)
and Olson (1970). Vernon (1971) points out that such scanning
does not develop until children begin to learn to read and conjectures that the acquisition of perceptual skills acquired in learning
to read might transfer to other (nonreading) tasks that also involve
analysis and synthesis of complex visual material. This seems an
attractive alternative to the widespread belief that low-level performance on a measure of visual analysis necessarily implies basic
perceptual deficiency that underlies reading disability. We also
agree with Vernon who suggests that "effective perceptual activity
is associated with intelligent understanding of the nature of the
material and hence appropriate direction of attention" (Vernon
1971, 20). It is probable that the child who makes satisfactory
progress in reading has, by virtue of his experiences in abstracting
the structural and invariant relations inherent in English orthography, acquired a number of general rules for efficient and economical perception that he may apply in processing visual stimuli
of other types. Thus the successful reader may have greater skill
than the poor reader in processing such complex symbols as letters, words, numbers, and musical notations in part because he
has developed the set to search for both invariant and distinctive
features to help discriminate these stimuli (Gibson 1969). He may
also have developed a disposition toward and a tolerance for engaging complex material and for searching the details for discriminating cues, all of these being general orienting attitudes
that classify as necessary but *not* sufficient conditions for successful perceptual learning (Gibson 1969).

   This is not to be taken as implying that the type of visual
processing involved in reading transfers directly to the processing

of nonlinguistic materials such as embedded figures. Although certain of the general orienting attitudes, such as those just mentioned, would seem to be necessary requisites for successful performance in both reading and abstracting embedded figures, the more fine-grained relationships that ultimately result in efficient perception are no doubt unique to those particular media. Such (specific) rules as positional and sequential constancy of letters, spelling to sound correspondences, invariances in orthographic structure, and semantic-syntactic redundancy would probably be of little use in learning to educe embedded figures. Conversely, analogous types of information acquired in abstracting embedded figures would probably be of little use in word perception. But the disposition to search for redundant patterns in a given array is a categorical skill that transcends both of these stimuli. Thus the inference we are making in explanation of reader group differences in studies employing embedded figures tests is that the poor readers in those studies are not perceptually deficient in the strict sense but are generally inefficient because they lacked the requisite orienting attitudes necessary for adequate performance. Considering the complexity of the structural relations that the child encounters in printed English, as well as the time and effort necessary to become a good reader, it is conceivable that success in reading could foster the development of these attitudes.

In relation to the memory model shown in figure 4.1, these orienting attitudes are subsumed under selective attention and (as the bidirectional arrows indicate) there is a reciprocal relation between all stages of memory and focal attention. Hence the competence of the good reader is reflected in part by his flexibility, enabling him to access information in any one of the storage bins (sensory store, short-term store, long-term store) as it becomes requisite for the task at hand.

More direct evidence to support this contention is provided by Gibson, Farber, and Shepela (1967), who demonstrated that first- and third-graders had developed a set to abstract common patterns in spelling clusters *(qu, ea, ng)* after training in detecting such relations. Furthermore, the tendency to search for invariance in letters apparently transferred to analogous problems employing color chips as stimulus elements. The reverse was also true; that is, training on problems employing color chips transferred to problems employing letter stimuli. Interestingly enough, kindergartners and several first-graders had extreme difficulty with these tasks. These findings are consistent with the view that sensitivity to structure in patterned information develops over a protracted period and, further, that such sensitivity may be partially determined by a child's experiences in school, particularly in reading.

One other study is relevant here: an investigation conducted by Kolers (1975b) comparing poor and normal readers on a pattern-analyzing task designed to evaluate memory for written sentences. The results of this study will be more meaningful if we first examine some background information.

Kolers (1968, 1974, 1975a, 1976a, 1976b) has developed a model of the reading process according to which the recognition of written sentences is determined largely by the pattern-analyzing operations that are active in encoding them. He disputes the more conventional view that the surface structure of a sentence is processed largely in short-term memory and thus retained only long enough to extract its meaning. He suggests instead that the strategies and techniques employed in analyzing the patterned relations contained in written words and sentences are part and parcel of their memorial representation. He suggests further that such operations are independent of the semantic and grammatical content of the material and that the meanings contained in printed text are derived from their graphic representations in long-term memory. This position is in sharp contrast to the view that meaning is stored in propositional form (Kintsch 1974) as a by-product of surface operations limited to processing in short-term memory.

Kolers and his associates have conducted a number of studies that presumably support his contentions (Kolers 1968; Kolers and Perkins 1969; Kolers 1974; Kolers and Ostry 1974; Kolers 1975a, 1976a, 1976b). Typically, these authors have presented adult subjects (usually college students) with sentence recognition tasks in which they must remember both normally oriented and geometrically transformed (inverted or reversed) typography (see figure 5.10). The usual procedure is to have subjects read aloud two decks of sentences, referred to as a read deck and a recognize deck. Both decks contain sentences in normal and transformed orientations presented in counterbalanced order. The recognize deck always consists of all the sentences in the read deck along with several new sentences that have not previously been

When Young Elephant was a few days old his mother took him

to the herd.

ƨɥɘ qɿɔʞɘb Ɉɥɘm wiɈɥ ɥɘɿ Ɉɿunʞ ɒnb ƨɈuɈɈɘb Ɉɥɘm in ɥɘɿ

mouɈɥ.

Figure 5.10 Illustration of normal and reversed typography used by Kolers in comparing pattern analyzing ability in poor and normal readers. (Reprinted by permission of author and publisher from: Kolers, Paul A. Pattern-analyzing disability in poor readers. *Developmental Psychology* 11, 3, 282–290. ©1975 by the American Psychological Association.)

presented. After reading aloud each sentence in the read deck, subjects are required to do the same with sentences in the recognition deck and then to classify them as previously read (old) or not read (new).

Three pertinent findings have emerged from these studies. First, it has consistently been found that sentences originally read in transformed typography were recognized better than sentences read initially in normal typography. Second, the graphic as well as the semantic content of the sentences presented in these studies were remembered more than a year later (Kolers 1976a, 1976b). Third, subjects generally improved their speed of reading transformed text on repeated presentations.

Kolers suggests that the disoriented sentences in these studies were remembered better than the sentences in normal orientation because they required more complex pattern-analyzing operations. He further suggests that information about these operations is stored in memory along with representations of the typographies and meanings of the sentences. Recognition of these sentences was said to occur by virtue of the fact that the encoded operations were reactivated, memory in such instances including familiarity with both typography and meaning. Kolers underscored the fact that typographic material was recognized after an extended period and took this as evidence that such information is stored in long-term memory. He also presented evidence that the effects of the practice on the speed of reading transformed type are attributable more to the surface characteristics of the text than to their meanings (Kolers 1975a). He concluded from these overall findings that the critical components of memory, by means of which written material is stored and retrieved, are the encoded analyses of graphic patterns rather than the end results of those encodings—the messages contained in the material.

In the study of particular relevance here, Kolers (1975b) compared poor and normal readers on pattern analysis of written sentences employing the transformed text paradigm. Subjects were matched for age (10 to 14 years), grade, school, and sex. They were also administered the WISC vocabulary subtest, and reading ability was measured by the Wide Range Achievement Test (Jastak, Bijou, and Jastak 1965). The poor readers were approximately at the 10th percentile on this test; most of the normal readers were between the 82nd and 91st percentiles.

The most salient finding was that normal readers manifested greater facility in analyzing the typography of the sentences than the poor readers. This was demonstrated on a variety of measures. First, the normal readers remembered proportionally more sentences than the poor readers by virtue of the differences in graphic features characteristic of those sentences. Second, in normal readers recognition was better for sentences initially read in transformed typography than for those in normal typography. This effect was not as pronounced in poor readers, suggesting that their processing of the visual material was not as elaborate as that of the normals. Finally, though the poor readers took substantially longer than the normal readers to read both normal and transformed sentences, the difference in time taken to read these two types of sentences was less for poor readers than for normal readers. In other words, a transformed sentence created less additional handicap for an already handicapped reader than it did for a skilled reader.

Two other findings that emerged from the study are of interest. First, there were no significant differences between the two groups in sentences recognized strictly on the basis of their semantic content. Second, the poor readers made many more errors in reading both normally oriented and transformed text, and an analysis of the types of word substitutions made in reading the material aloud revealed no qualitative differences in grammatical adequacy. In the latter instance, the groups were compared as to the proportion of their substitutions that were paradigmatic (words in the same form class), which Kolers suggests is a measure of grammatical competence.[7] His interpretation of these findings is that poor and normal readers do not differ with respect to language ability.

Kolers concludes that poor and normal readers differ in their ability to analyze and remember graphic patterns, but he rejects the notion that such deficiency implies a basic deficit in visual perception:

The difficulty seems to be associated with the cognitive pattern analyzing operations that first acquire the words from the page, and, perhaps, as Critchley (1964) suggested, in aligning them with their linguistic interpretations; that is, in correlating the graphemic (pictorial) component with the semantic (linguistic) component. In this respect at least, one aspect of reading disability may have a perceptual basis, but it is at a more cognitive level of performance than is usually measured by tests of visual function. It is the level concerned with analyzing or interpreting the graphemes as linguistic marks, but not the level of dealing with words as language or with marks as visual objects. This vague middle ground requires better specification. (1975b, 290)

Kolers' explanations of the findings are to some extent concordant with my own interpretation of the results. I would agree that the poor reader's difficulties in analyzing transformed typography are associated with a breakdown in higher-level cognitive processes rather than in perceptual or first-level processes. I can also agree that such dysfunction may in turn be associated with disorder in aligning or integrating the visual and verbal constitutents of words and sentences. However, unlike Kolers, I suggest that the problems encountered by poor readers in analyzing orthographic structure, either normal or transformed typography, are secondary to the more basic problem of associating visual and verbal symbols. In other words, because the dyslexic's facility in coding is deficient, he does not process the broad variety of linguistic cues necessary for efficient processing of the visual material. He will therefore fail to receive the type of feedback from his efforts at decoding that facilitates more elaborate analysis and thus self-correction. In fact, it seems a reasonable inference that the poor readers' performance in analyzing the transformed text in Kolers' study was partly attributable to the fact that they had less (and more stereotyped) information than the normal readers to assist them in mediating to the more familiar configurations. I would guess that such information normally includes the meaning as well as the

structural relations characteristic of the words and sentences encountered. Efficiency in processing orthographic material implies
a high degree of economy in visual analysis in that the reader is
sensitive to higher-order invariance that facilitates "selective filtering" (Gibson 1971) as well as efficiency in recognition and
discrimination. Such relations may include information about
graphic *(b* versus *d)*, orthographic *(qu)* and graphophonemic
(heat versus *beat)* redundancies as well as the semantic and syntactic rules characteristic of a natural language. The ability to employ this kind of information at an automatic level (LaBerge and
Samuels 1974; Doehring 1976) allows for minimal processing of
the graphic features of letters and words as well as maximum
predictability (Goodman 1969). It is this type of efficiency in
word recognition that no doubt distinguished the normal and
disabled reader in Kolers' study. The inference here is that a poor
reader's knowledge of such redundancies is not as great as that of
a normal reader, with the result that he has a limited repertoire
of cues for visual analysis. The reasons that poor readers have
such knowledge gaps are unclear at the present time, but I think
it would be an error to regard such difficulties as reflective of
visual perceptual deficit in the strict sense.

All these speculations notwithstanding, a simpler explanation
for the poor readers' difficulty with transformed text is their
more basic inadequacy in reading normally oriented text. The
poor readers took significantly longer and made many more
errors than the normal readers in reading both the properly
oriented and the transformed text, which, according to Kolers,
reinforced his contention that these groups differed in basic
pattern-analyzing ability. This interpretation is, of course,
tenuous, given the likelihood that the poor readers' problems in
decoding were attributable to a more basic inability to remember
the verbal components of the written letters and words. In view
of the decoding problems occasioned by the normally oriented
text, it is not surprising that poor readers had more difficulty
than normal readers in deciphering their transformed counterparts.

One final point can be made with regard to Kolers' study:
The evidence he produces to rule out linguistic problems as a
source of reading disability is weak. Comparability of paradigmatic responding would not, by itself, be sufficient reason to

reject the possibility that various types of language difficulties hamper the reading process. Furthermore, even if the phenomenon of paradigmatic responding were as simple as Kolers seems to believe, he has measured it in an age group where even linguistically less skilled children would have already achieved paradigmatic associative behavior. Empirically, a preponderance of paradigmatic responses has been demonstrated as occurring at about age 7 (Entwisle1966); Kolers' subjects had a median age of 12.3. Thus, it may well be the case that verbal skill was a factor that had some influence in determining the results of Kolers' study. Indeed, on the one direct measure of verbal ability employed in this investigation—that is, the vocabulary subtest of the WISC—poor readers had lower scores than normal readers. Kolers suggested that this difference occurred because of long-standing reading and academic problems rather than to differences in language skills, but it is nevertheless possible that the group differences in vocabulary and other measures employed in this study were partly attributable to differences in verbal ability. The ultimate explanation of Kolers' findings is therefore an open issue, but I rather doubt his suggestion that poor readers were less proficient than normal readers in processing transformed typography because of a basic deficiency in pattern analyzing ability. Several studies to be reviewed subsequently provide support for this contention.

5.3.4 Speed of Perceptual Processing

A number of studies having relevance to an evaluation of perceptual deficit explanations of reading disability have compared poor and normal readers on the rate at which they process visual material. These investigations have typically employed both verbal and nonverbal stimuli and have generally assessed the possibility that poor readers are unable to synthesize and store visual information as rapidly as normals. All of the studies to be reviewed indirectly implicate dysfunction at the first stage of visual processing. However, several of them confound perceptual and higher-order cognitive functions, an error that is characteristic of most studies assessing perceptual deficit explanations of reading disability.

Doehring (1968) has reported an elaborate series of reader group contrasts that assessed speed of perceptual processing in addition to a variety of other functions.

Thirty-nine boys with severe reading problems were compared with two other groups of normal readers containing equal numbers of boys and girls. Each group was administered a very large number (N = 109) of neuropsychological tests. These included measures of intelligence, reading and spelling; visual, auditory, and tactile functions; speech and language; visual-motor skills; and visual perceptual speed. The groups were matched on Performance IQ, all other selection criteria being adequate except for the reading measure (sight words), which was not comprehensive. The tests were generally administered in three sessions over two days.

Poor readers were less proficient than normal readers on sixty-eight of the tests and were superior to the normals on five measures. There were no significant differences between the groups on the remaining thirty-six tests. The results were characterized by a great deal of inconsistency in that poor and normal readers were differentiated on some measures of a given process but were equivalent on others assessing the same process. The tests on which the poor readers were superior included four measures of tactual discrimination and a measure of spatial reasoning and visualization (Wechsler-Bellevue Block Designs). What is interesting is that out of the total number of tests that differentiated the groups, roughly 62 percent (by my calculations) had verbal components; 38 percent were nonverbal in nature. Furthermore, in a stepwise regression analysis four of the measures were found to account for most of the variance: word finding, vocabulary, mirror-image reversals, and speed of visual search for a single form (a Greek letter). And of these the first two accounted for approximately 74 percent of the variance, the last two for only 4 percent and 1 percent respectively.

From these results Doehring concluded that poor readers are deficient in the processing of visual and verbal material and placed particular emphasis upon the possibility of a serial order deficiency in this group. Yet the figures can be taken to mean that measures of visual processing differentiated *minimally* between poor and normal readers whereas verbal measures were the more successful discriminators. In fact, the results could readily be interpreted as an indication that speed of visual processing does *not* contribute significantly to our understanding of the etiology of reading disability. Furthermore, many of the measures categorized under visual perceptual speed were highly verbal in nature, including not only single letters and randomly combined letters but pronounceable nonsense syllables and real words as well. Such tasks are confounded by reading ability and clearly put the poor reader at a disadvantage. They therefore cannot be reasonably referred to as measures of visual perceptual speed.

In my estimation Doehring's findings provide indirect support for the suggestion that poor readers do *not* differ from normals in visual spatial processing. Although it is true that the poor readers did not perform as well as the normals on some tests of form perception and figure ground analysis, their performance was comparable to normals on others. Curiously, Doehring suggests that the failure to find differences between poor and normal readers on "simple measures of visual and auditory discrimination" is consistent with Birch's suggestion that reading disability is caused by inadequate development of "higher levels of visual perception" (Doehring 1968, 64). But many of the more complex "perceptual" tasks were composed of letters and words; the results were therefore confounded by the negative learning that no doubt characterizes poor readers' experience with printed material. Furthermore, any inference that the poor readers in this study were deficient in higher-level visual perception would seem to be obviated by the fact that these groups were equated for nonverbal intelligence (Wechsler-Bellevue Performance Scale). The Block Design subtest, in particular, requires a high degree of visual-spatial ability (with respect to both its analytic and conceptual constituents), and on this subtest the poor readers performed significantly better than the normals. Doehring's interpretation would therefore appear unwarranted.

One bothersome feature of Doehring's investigation is the short period of time allotted for administering such a large battery of tests (two days). It would not be surprising to find, under such circumstances, that some of the variance that accounted for differences observed between poor and normal readers was due to attentional and motivational factors rather than to basic process dysfunction. Thus, interpretation of the results of this investigation is problematic, particularly in view of the small number of subjects.

Speed of processing visual material has been assessed in several other studies comparing poor and normal readers on rapid scanning and recognition of letters and words. In one such study Katz and Wicklund (1971) compared poor and normal readers (fifth-graders) on rapid scanning of a probe word embedded in two- and three-word sentences. All stimuli were presented tachisto-scopically for 5-second exposures. Although response latencies were longer for poor readers, their rate of scanning the stimulus words was comparable to normals as measured by parallel in-creases in reaction times to the larger sentences. Katz and Wick-lund concluded that "good and poor readers do not differ in the ability to scan, transform and match words; the differences be-tween the two types of readers occur somewhere else in the chain: in the orientation to the probe, in response decoding, or in the motor portion of the response" (1971, 140).

In a follow-up study employing second- and sixth-graders Katz and Wicklund (1972) attempted to control for possible word en-coding differences in disabled and normal readers by employing letters rather than words as stimuli and by using a manual rather than a vocal response as the index of recognition. Based on the previous findings it was expected that the two groups would differ in efficiency of response selection. Subjects were required to match target letters to single-letter standards, the targets being varied as to number of letters appearing simultaneously. Stimuli were again presented tachistoscopically; in this instance for three-second exposures.

No group differences on response latencies were found under any of the stimulus conditions. There was some indication that both poor and normal reader groups relied exclusively on visual matching rather than on naming for identification. The authors concluded that poor readers are as effective as normal readers in high-speed visual scanning. They suggested in addition that the groups may have been differentiated in the earlier study because of disparities in their ability to retrieve the names of the words presented.

The results of these two studies are consistent with the sugges-tion that poor readers sustain no deficiencies in visual analysis, particularly when the task minimizes interference from verbal encoding. Unfortunately, the findings are equivocal because the reading measures were weak and the authors did not control for possible differences in intelligence and other relevant variables.

However, the results of a study by Steinheiser and Guthrie (1975) are in accord with the results of the Katz and Wicklund studies, and in this investigation the samples were more carefully selected. Dyslexics were compared with two groups of normal readers: one matched for reading level and another matched for age (mean age = 10.3). All were of average or above average intelligence. The selection measures employed to assess reading ability were adequate.

The reader groups were compared in their ability to match graphically similar words *(heat* and *head)*, phonemically similar words *(beat* and *beet)*, and words that were both graphically and phonemically equivalent *(heat* and *beat)*. Subjects were given brief presentations of stimuli in pairs and asked to indicate whether they were the same or different. The dependent variable was reaction time. Disabled readers did not differ from the normal readers in the grapheme identity condition, but their response latencies were greater than the latencies of the normal reader groups on phonemically similar words. The authors concluded that disabled readers have no difficulty in processing the graphic features of words but appear to be deficient in abstracting the phonologic components of these symbols.

Steinheiser and Guthrie (1974) obtained similar results in additional comparisons of poor and normal readers matched for age and reading levels. On visual search tasks employing prose passages and scrambled word strings, poor readers manifested longer latencies than age-matched normals on scanning for target words, letters, and phonemes. However, in comparisons with younger normals matched for reading levels, poor readers had equivalent latencies for target words, shorter latencies for letters, and significantly longer latencies for phonemes. The authors concluded that poor readers' ability to detect the visual features of letters and words is relatively good; apparently they have difficulty in converting graphic symbols into their sound counterparts.

These data add weight to Katz and Wicklund's findings, although they cannot be generalized to poor readers at younger age levels because Steinheiser and Guthrie did not include such children in their samples.

Additional evidence that deficient readers are slow in processing English words comes from a study by Samuels, Begy, and Chen (1975-1976) comparing poor and normal readers on tachistoscopic recognition of words with which all subjects were familiar, as determined in a preliminary session. The words were presented for variable durations and responses were verbal. The main finding was that poor readers had longer response latencies in word recognition than normal readers. In addition, context words *(black)*, presented for longer durations just prior to the brief presentations of the target words *(cat)*, did not facilitate recognition for poor readers as well as they did for normal readers; and the disabled readers were less able than normals in generating (guessing) target words from partial letter cues *(black c_ _)*. The authors concluded that impaired readers are less efficient than normal readers in making use of the various types of information available for word decoding.

This investigation did not control for possible differences between poor and normal readers in response selection. Yet the authors suggest that the poor readers' difficulty in rapid recognition largely accrued on the input side of the word identification task. However, the possibility that speed of processing in such children is more directly related to deficiencies in encoding or production (word retrieval problems) cannot be discounted (see Denckla and Rudel 1976a, 1976b).

Nevertheless, as alluded to earlier, *perceptual inefficiency* in visual processing seems a more plausible description of the difficulty poor readers have in rapid processing of the visual constituents of words than does perceptual deficiency, the more common description. If, for whatever reason, such children are inclined to employ a limited repertoire of cues for decoding, they will inevitably have difficulty in negotiating the complexities characteristic of an alphabetic symbol system. They may therefore be expected to process such material less rapidly than normals, particularly in high-speed recognition tasks, which tend to disrupt the information one typically relies upon to effect discrimination. This is a predictable outcome given that poor readers do not have the flexibility in word decoding characteristic of normal readers, who have a variety of alternative cues for word recognition—cues that may be of either a visual or a verbal nature as Samuels and his associates demonstrated (Samuels et al. 1975–1976).

This explanation is essentially the one I offered to account for the reader group differences found by Kolers (1975b). It would also account for results obtained in a study by Rayner and Kaiser

(1975), which employed a format similar to the one used by Samuels et al. Briefly, Rayner and Kaiser found differences favoring normal readers both in speed of reading and in recognition of altered (mutilated) target words. The common denominator in these three investigations is the disruption of featural information normally employed for decoding, which for the poor reader may be highly stereotyped and circumscribed, leading to inefficiency in visual processing. Such inefficiency, however, would seem to be secondary to more basic deficiencies at higher levels of cognitive processing.

5.3.5 Perception of Spatial Redundancy

Most perceptual deficit explanations of reading disability have incorporated the idea that dyslexics are primarily deficient in form perception and spatial orientation. A distinctly different type of conceptualization that has emerged is that such children are basically impaired in their ability to perceive spatial redundancy. Specifically, in a recent formulation Mason and her associates hypothesize that poor readers are comparable to normal readers in distinguishing the visual features and general shapes of letters and words but are relatively insensitive to the frequency with which specific letters appear in given spatial locations within words (Mason 1975; Mason and Katz 1976). It is, of course, characteristic of an alphabetic symbol system that no letter of the alphabet occurs in all word positions with equal frequency (Mayzner and Tresselt 1965). Thus spatial redundancy inheres in the internal structure of English words, and Mason's assumption is that the normal reader detects and employs such information more readily than the poor reader.

This conceptualization issues from research conducted by Thompson and Massaro (1973) and Massaro (1973, 1975) and carries with it two basic premises: (1) "that the individual letter is the basic perceptual unit, and (2) that redundancy is operative at the stage of identification of distinctive visual features of individual letters" (Mason 1975, 146). The studies by Thompson and Massaro have yielded evidence that casts doubt on previous findings to the effect that a letter is perceived more accurately when presented within the context of a word (or pronounceable nonword) than when it is presented alone or in a letter string devoid of structure (Reicher 1969; Wheeler 1970; Aderman and Smith 1971). Specifically, Thompson and Massaro found that under conditions of brief stimulus exposure, letters presented individually were perceived as well as, or better than, letters presented within the context of words and nonword strings, when redundancy was controlled. They therefore inferred that the single letter is the smallest unit over which feature extraction occurs. They also suggested that knowledge of what specific letters (and letter features) can validly occur at given spatial locations within words facilitates perceptual "synthesis" of individual letters at the primary recognition stage of word identification (Massaro 1975).

Given these findings, Mason contends that redundant spatial location is directly perceived rather than inferred on the basis of information acquired about intraword relationships. She is here distinguishing between *spatial* redundancy and *sequential* redundancy, the latter having to do with the frequency with which one letter precedes or follows another and, more generally, with the constraints that characterize valid spelling patterns in English orthography. A common view is that such patterns facilitate perception because they consist of units larger than the single letter (Lott and Smith 1970; Smith 1971; Gibson and Levin 1975, chap. 7). More specifically, the view is that knowledge of sequential constraints permits economy of visual processing by allowing the perceiver to attend primarily to discriminating cues—that is, the economy results by virtue of the reader's ability to predict, with a high degree of probability, letters that frequently occur in invariant sequences.

Mason challenges this view. Although she agrees that knowledge of predictable letter sequences constitutes categorical information that under certain circumstances might well facilitate the use of "guessing strategies" in perceptual behavior, she suggests that sequential redundancy is actually a special case of spatial redundancy:

If "b" occurs most frequently in the first position, and "a" occurs most frequently in the second position, there is a high probability of the sequence "ba." The question is whether "b" and "a" are independently processed more rapidly because of their redundant positions in the linear array, or whether the sequence "ba" becomes a single perceptual unit. (Mason and Katz 1976, 339)

Mason believes it is the single letters that are independently processed and perceived directly as units. She also believes that
knowledge of the frequency with which letters occur in given
spatial locations augments featural information so as to facilitate
individual letter identification and thus word perception.

In an initial test of her hypothesis, Mason (1975) conducted a
series of four related experiments comparing good and poor readers
on target search tasks employing letter strings that varied with respect to spatial redundancy. The subjects in each study were sixth-
graders selected primarily on the basis of reading ability. The Wide
Range Achievement Test (Jastak, Bijou, and Jastak 1965) was employed for sample selection in all instances. The median grade
equivalents for poor readers ranged from 3.2 to 6.0, those for good
readers from 7.9 to 13.0. Independent samples were selected for
experiments 1 and 2; a third set of subjects was used for both experiment 3 and experiment 4. There were a total of 20 subjects in
the first experiment and 24 subjects in each of the remaining three.

The first study represented a preliminary test of the hypothesis
and simply compared good and poor readers on the speed with
which they searched for a target letter embedded in word or nonword stimuli. The good readers were observed to be faster than the
poor readers only on the word stimuli. It was inferred from these
findings that good and poor readers do not differ in their ability to
"utilize distinctive feature information" but do differ in their ability
to employ redundant information to effect word identification.[8]

The second experiment also employed a letter search task but
presented subjects with word and nonword letter strings varying
in degree of spatial redundancy. The nonword sets were anagrams
of the word sets (seldom, somled, sdelmd) and were of either high
or low spatial redundancy. The word sets were typically of intermediate spatial redundancy. The results of this study were consistent with the results of the previous one in that good readers
were faster than poor readers in locating target letter stimuli only
when the stimulus sets were spatially redundant.

Experiment 3 employed a paradigm that was basically the same
as that used in experiment 2, but the target letters in the three
types of display were counterbalanced to evaluate serial position
effects: All target letters appeared equally often in each serial
position. In addition, each subject was given approximately 100
practice trials prior to the experiment proper. The intent was to
evaluate the question of whether or not highly practiced subjects

would process letter strings simultaneously or from left to right as had been suggested in previous studies that did not counterbalance for target letter position (James and Smith 1970; Kreuger 1970). Contrary to expectations, good readers were faster than poor readers under all three redundancy conditions, with one exception. When target letters appeared in spatial locations where they do *not* often appear, the typical pattern was again observed— that is, good readers had faster search times than poor readers only when the *nontarget* letters were in spatially redundant positions.

Figure 5.11 shows the reaction times, across serial positions, for good and poor readers, collapsed over the three types of display. The difference in the shapes of the curves is striking. In the curve for the good readers, similarity in speed of identifying initial and final letters and the inflated search times in the middle positions make it apparent that they were *not* engaged in serial left-to-right processing. The curve is in fact suggestive of parallel analysis, with redundancy having its most beneficial effect on the letters in

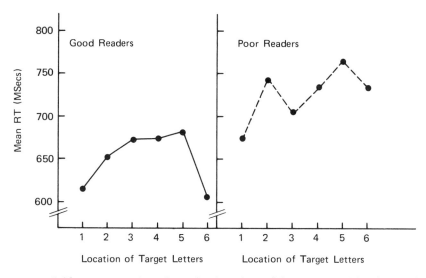

Figure 5.11 Mean reaction times for location of letters embedded in word and nonword stimuli as a function of serial position and reading ability. Each distribution is collapsed over three display types varying in degree of spatial redundancy. All target letters occurred equally often at each serial position. (Reprinted by permission of author and publisher from: Mason, Mildred. Reading ability and letter search time: Effects of orthographic structure defined by single-letter positional frequency. *Journal of Experimental Psychology: General* 104, 2, 146–166. Copyright 1975 by the American Psychological Association.)

the terminal positions. In contrast, the curve for the poor readers shows a (roughly) linear trend suggesting that these subjects *were* inclined toward left-to-right processing. The statistical analyses are consistent with these impressions. Whereas in trend analyses the poor readers manifested (statistically) significant linear effects on the high and intermediate redundancy conditions, the results for good readers yielded only a quadratic effect. These findings suggest that the two groups had decidedly different strategies in processing the letter strings, which would certainly account in part for group differences observed under the high and low redundancy conditions employed in experiments 1 and 2.

Experiment 4 investigated the effects of spatial frequency of the target letters themselves. Two sets of nonword letter strings were employed as stimuli—in one, all letters were located in positions in which they most frequently occur; in the second, letters were located in positions in which they rarely occur. The salient finding in this study is that good readers had faster search times than poor readers only under the high redundancy condition.

Mason (1975) concluded that normal readers are more sensitive to redundancy information and make more effective use of it than poor readers. She suggested that poor readers' difficulties in detecting spatial redundancy are attributable to a more basic disorder in "spatial order perception." Mason acknowledged, however, that these ideas remained to be verified with nonalphabetic material. Consequently, two additional studies were undertaken.

One study attempted to extend the generality of the spatial redundancy hypothesis employing a target search procedure similar to those described. The target items were IBM characters varying in degree and type of redundancy. Two separate contrasts were made, the first with college students and the second with good and poor readers in sixth grade. Reading ability in the sixth-graders was measured by a reading comprehension test, the mean grade equivalents for reader groups being 9.7 and 3.7.

In the initial contrast independent groups of college students (N = 12) were randomly assigned to three test conditions: no redundancy (N), distributional redundancy (D), and spatial redundancy (S). In the D condition twelve IBM characters occurred in stimulus presentations with varying frequency but each character occupied given spatial locations as often as any other character. In the S condition the frequency with which the symbols occurred was equalized but the number of times each appeared in a given spatial location was varied. The N condition equalized both the number of times the twelve symbols were presented and the number of times each appeared in given serial positions. The most important finding was that search times were fastest under the S condition and slowest under the N condition. The D condition was intermediate between the other two, but the difference between the groups exposed to the S and D conditions was not impressive. Serial position effects were significant, the letters in the middle positions occasioning the *fastest* search times under all three conditions. There were significant practice effects from one session to the next.

The study with adults was conducted to establish the fact that redundancy effects could be demonstrated with nonalphabetic stimuli. Having done so, the second contrast, with reader groups, employed only the S and N conditions; poor and normal readers (N = 9 each group) were assigned randomly to one or the other condition. The experimental task was again a letter search; this study was also conducted in two sessions.

Figure 5.12 shows the reader group contrasts under the two conditions, as presented in Mason and Katz (1976, 344). Good and poor readers are comparable under the N condition, but the good readers had more rapid search times under the S condition. This was true in both sessions. Serial position effects were significant for all groups, the fastest search times occurring in the middle portions of the strings. Practice effects were significant, although the influence of serial position was not as dramatic in the second session. The groups were comparable with respect to percentage of error.

Mason and Katz attributed their results to the effects of spatial redundancy rather than to higher-order linguistic variables, since the differences noted under the various conditions were demonstrated using nonalphabetic material. They conjectured that the ability to perceive the spatial location of letters is distinct from the ability to perceive their shapes and that these two functions may be "mediated by different brain regions" (1976, 347). They therefore concluded that the poor readers, though comparable to the good readers in form perception, were less able in perception of spatial redundancy, presumably confirming the suggestion in the previous study (Mason 1975) that poor readers may be suffering from a deficit in spatial order perception.

A final study by Mason and her co-workers more directly

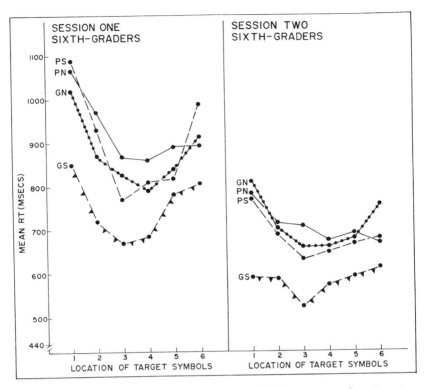

Figure 5.12 Mean reaction times for location of IBM characters, as a function of reading ability, condition of redundancy, serial position, and session. PN = poor readers, no redundancy; PS = poor readers, spatial redundancy; GN = good readers, no redundancy; GS = good readers, spatial redundancy. (Reprinted by permission of author and publisher from: Mason, Mildred, and Katz, Leonard. Visual processing of nonlinguistic strings: Redundancy effects and reading ability. *Journal of Experimental Psychology: General* 105, 4, 338-348. Copyright 1976 by the American Psychological Association.)

evaluated the possibility of a spatial order deficit in poor readers (Mason, Katz, and Wicklund 1975). In one contrast, sixth-grade good and poor readers, again selected on the basis of reading comprehension scores (mean grade equivalent = 9.5 and 3.4 respectively, were tested for immediate recall of consonant letters that were either spatially redundant (phmvld) or randomly arrayed (vmdlhp) and varied in length (four or six letters). The dependent measure in this comparison was memory for the order of letters in a set. Scores for the two groups were not substantially different on the four-item sets, but the poor readers did not perform as well as the good readers on the six-item sets. Both groups performed better when the letters were in spatially redundant arrays.

A second contrast tested an independent sample of sixth-grade good and poor readers (mean grade equivalents = 7.7 and 4.6 respectively) on immediate recall of low redundancy, randomly arrayed consonant letters and digits, each set consisting of eight items. Subjects in this study were asked to remember specific items as well as the order in which these items appeared on a given presentation. The results were at variance with the hypothesis tested. That is, good readers performed significantly better on item as well as order tasks, although the correlation between reading achievement and memory for order was higher than the correlation between reading and item memory (r = .29 versus .08 respectively). The authors concluded that poor readers may sustain a "spatial order perception (or memory) deficit" which impairs the detection and exploitation of positional redundancy as a "source of information for poor readers" (Mason, Katz and Wicklund 1975, 615). **Evaluation of the Spatial Redundancy Theory of Reading Disability** This spatial-order variant of the perceptual deficit explanation of reading disability is not very compelling. Although it is not surprising to find that poor readers are less sensitive than proficient readers to the redundancies inherent in an alphabetic symbol system, I do not believe that such difficulty necessarily implies a basic deficiency in perception. Mason's suggestion that spatial redundancy is directly perceived without recourse to memory seems counterintuitive, and her distinction between spatial and sequential redundancy seems artificial. Although it may be true, as Massaro suggests, that "the utilization of orthographic redundancy can occur during the primary recognition stage of reading" (Massaro 1975, 250), I see no reason why perception of such redundancy is *not* influenced by stored information about the spatial location of individual letters, sequential dependencies, or any other type of invariance (phonologic, semantic, syntactic) characterizing spoken and written language, since it is the availability of such information in long-term memory that determines the way in which the orthography is analyzed. And if it is also true that single letters are the basic perceptual units in reading (Massaro 1973, 1975; Thompson and Massaro 1973),[9] then knowledge of their spatial locations, and of their graphic and linguistic attributes, would seem to be of greater importance in synthesizing letter and word perception than knowledge of contiguously occurring letters. However, the process would still necessitate the retrieval of information about redundant letters from long-term memory, which is to suggest that spatial redundancy is no less a component of memory than sequential redundancy or any other aspect of English orthography.

Assuming then that the detection and utilization of spatial redundancy is as much a memorial as a perceptual process, the question remains, Why are poor readers less attuned to letter positions than normal readers? My explanation of this disparity is the same as that offered earlier to account for reader group differences in spatial orientation and visual analysis of letters and words. To be specific, I suggest that the poor reader demonstrates less facility than the normal reader in acquiring orthographic information because of more basic problems in coding visual material linguistically. As a result of such difficulties, he does not analyze and integrate the internal structure of words as effectively as the normal reader, and therefore does not become as conversant with invariant orthographic relations. This would lead to the prediction that the poor reader's strategies in word analysis would be qualitatively different from those of the normal reader—perhaps more stereotyped, less flexible, and plodding. If so, then one would expect that the poor reader's chances of detecting redundant information on any given sampling of written text would be minimal, certainly compared with those of his more able peers. And because of the different experiences of these two groups in abstracting such invariance, one would expect poor readers to be less favorably disposed to searching for redundancies in a given display, even those embedded in nonalphabetic material.

Interestingly enough, the studies conducted by Mason provide some support for these contentions. In one experiment (Mason

1975, experiment 3) good readers manifested a distinct tendency toward parallel analysis in processing words and letter strings of varying degrees of positional redundancy, whereas poor readers were inclined toward more cumbersome left-to-right processing of the same material (see figure 5.11). Yet in one of the later experiments (Mason and Katz 1976), the shapes of the distributions yielded by nonalphabetic material (IBM characters) were quite different from those yielded by letter and word stimuli, for both good and poor readers. Furthermore, there was a striking similarity in the distributions generated by the nonalphabetic stimuli in the case of both reader groups under redundancy as well as no-redundancy conditions (see figure 5.12). These findings suggest that good and poor readers adopted comparable perceptual strategies when processing nonalphabetic material, differing only in level of performance. However, when processing alphabetic material, the groups were apparently different not only in performance level but also in their perceptual organization of the material.

A reasonable inference from this disparity would be that observed group differences in processing redundant alphabetic material is a consequence of long standing reading problems rather than a primary manifestation of basic perceptual disorder, although the two studies in question provide only indirect support for such a conjecture. It is probable that familiarization with orthographic structure in part accounted for the good readers' tendency to process terminal letters more rapidly than letters in middle serial positions, since they had no doubt learned that letters in initial and final positions provide more information for word identification than those in the middle (see Gibson and Levin 1975, chapter 7). That the poor readers did not adopt these strategies suggests that their experiences with letters and words had yielded qualitatively different kinds of information about word structure—information that obviously made them less efficient in processing spatially redundant letter stimuli. But when the groups were presented with (nonalphabetic) material with which neither had had any prior experience (Mason and Katz 1976), their perceptual attitudes appeared to be quite similar. These results cannot easily be explained in terms of perceptual deficiency in the strict sense, nor in terms of reader group differences in sensitivity to spatial redundancy alone. I am therefore inclined toward the possibility that the qualitative differences observed between good and poor readers in processing redundant letter strings were due largely to experiential factors; I see no reason to infer that poor readers have an underlying deficit in perceiving spatial order.

How then is one to explain reader group differences in level of performance on nonalphabetic material? Aside from the likelihood that the good readers' successful experience in detecting spatial redundancy in English orthography transferred positively to the redundant IBM strings, one cannot discount the possibility that the good and poor readers tested in this study differed in general ability and experience. There is no direct evidence to support this conjecture, the only selection criterion being reading comprehension scores; nevertheless, the fact that the good readers were reading three levels above their grade placement (on the average) suggests that they may have had superior intelligence. Inasmuch as detection of spatial redundancy in the Mason and Katz study could be readily construed as a concept learning task rather than a perceptual task (in the sense in which Mason and Katz used the term), one may justifiably argue that processing was faster for the good readers at least in part because they were conceptually more agile than the poor readers. This suggestion, though admittedly speculative, would seem to be afforded some substance by the dramatic improvement in search times manifested by poor as well as good readers in the second session of the experiment (see figure 5.12). If the poor readers were totally insensitive to spatial redundancy, they should not have shown such improvement. The results, in fact, suggest that considerable learning had taken place from the first to the second session, and it is possible that such learning involved increased awareness of the invariances embedded in the stimuli. Thus, it is likely that factors other than sensitivity to spatial redundancy accounted for the group differences.

Mason's suggestion that poor readers suffer a basic deficit in spatial order perception would seem to receive no support whatsoever from these two studies if my interpretation of the results is correct. Nor does the study by Mason, Katz, and Wicklund (1975), which directly evaluated spatial order memory in poor and normal readers, afford much if any confirmation of the hypothesis inasmuch as group differences were found on measures that assessed memory for item as well as order information. In addition, on at least one of the recall tasks in this study "spatial order perception" was quite possibly confounded with phonetic encoding ability in that spatially redundant items may have been more "pronounceable" than nonredundant items (phmvld versus vmdlhp) even though consonants were used exclusively as stimuli. Thus the authors' interpretation of their findings is in doubt. And, as will be seen in chapter 7, results of research done elsewhere raise further questions about the postulated deficit in spatial order perception.

In view of these arguments I tentatively conclude that the spatial location deficit theory of reading disability, as articulated by Mason, is improbable. The difficulties experienced by poor readers in detecting and utilizing spatial redundancy may be more simply explained as the result of inefficient perceptual strategies occasioned by long-standing reading disorder rather than as a consequence of perceptual deficiency in the strict sense.

5.4 VISUAL MEMORY
Characteristic of virtually all of the perceptual deficit theories is the inference that poor readers sustain significant deficiencies in visual memory. This inference is made either by extension or by definition. In theories that implicate deficiencies at the initial stage of sensory processing (Bender 1956, 1957; Drew 1956; Birch 1962), visual memory is logically included; in theories that emphasize deficiencies in long-term storage the memory deficit is defined as basic (Hinshelwood 1900, 1917; Orton 1925, 1937). However, only Orton is explicit in stating that the orientational and directional problems encountered by dyslexics in word decoding are the result of confusion in retrieving one of two symmetrical (mirror-image) engrams stored in long-term memory. Beyond Orton's conjecture, the theories are not specific about what mechanisms in the memory process might be awry or what stages of memory might be especially problematic in explaining the purported failure of poor readers to store or retrieve visual information.

Given the possibility of visual memory problems, two subtypes of poor readers may be distinguished theoretically. In one group there would be a basic malfunction during initial-stage processing (deficiencies in feature detection, speed of transfer from initial storage, and so on). In the other group there would be dysfunction at the level of short-term memory (problems related to capacity limits or recoding and rehearsal deficits). The studies to be discussed in this section directly assess disorders of the second type. I will attempt to document the contention that dyslexics are *not* characterized by primary deficiency in visual memory and that the results of investigations that have demonstrated differences between poor and normal readers on various memory tasks are confounded by failure to control for more basic deficiencies in other areas.

Recall the unique properties of short-term memory, as illustrated in the processing model in figure 4.1. Short-term memory is believed to be a limited capacity system (four to seven chunks—upper limit for children) of brief duration (up to 30 seconds) requiring active recoding to surmount its upper boundary. The need to do so arises in reading. Because the resting time between saccadic eye movements is no more than 250 msec, one must rapidly encode the information presented in a given fixation before the visual trace is lost. Furthermore, if the number of items presented exceeds the upper limit of one's short-term memory, the information must be recoded in more manageable chunks if it is to be retained for any particular use. And if information must be retained beyond the duration of short-term memory, it must either be deposited in long-term memory or rehearsed and further recoded in a form that will eventually facilitate permanent storage. Although not everyone would agree with this description of the memory process (for example, Craik and Lockhart 1972; Buschke 1975), there is general consensus that there is something akin to a capacity limit on retention over brief periods and that some recoding and organization of stimulus constituents must take place for long-term storage and retrieval.

Reading is an activity that, by definition, requires encoding of alphabetic characters, and poor readers have difficulty in developing this skill. It is therefore not surprising that a number of studies have found differences favoring normal readers in comparing reader groups on short-term memory for verbal material presented visually. Two such studies were discussed in section 5.3.4. (Katz and Wicklund 1971, 1972). In the next section we will review a number of other investigations comparing poor and normal readers on measures of visual memory. The major purpose here will be to contrast the results of investigations that have not controlled for verbal encoding as a possible factor in reading disability with results of several studies conducted in our own

laboratory that have systematically varied experimental conditions so as to separate visual and verbal factors in reader group
contrasts.

Kendall (1948) compared poor and normal readers (ages 6 to
16) on the Graham-Kendall Memory for Designs Test (MFD) and
found no differences between these two groups on measures of
accuracy and orientation. Furthermore, none of the correlations
between reading measures and MFD were significant. However,
since these results were obtained in a normative study, it is likely
that only a small percentage of the readers in the sample were
extremely impaired. Thus the data are inconclusive.

A study by Doehring (1968) comparing dyslexic and normal
readers on a variety of perceptual and cognitive measures has
already been mentioned. Although Doehring's subjects were
differentiated on several tests of visual memory, they were found
to be comparable on other measures of this function. The results
therefore provide no reliable basis for inferring that poor readers,
as a group, are characterized by dysfunction in visual memory.

Lyle and Goyen have conducted a number of studies evaluating
the possibility of visual memory deficits in poor readers, also with
conflicting results. In an initial investigation poor and normal
readers (third-graders) were given brief presentations of letters,
simple lines, and word shapes for immediate, delayed and sequential memory (Lyle and Goyen 1968). Poor readers were found to
be less accurate than normals under all three conditions, but the
groups did *not* differ in number of sequencing and reversal errors.
The authors suggested that reader group disparities may have been
due to differences in speed of coding, although an attempt was
made to minimize verbal mediation by having subjects recite
multiplication tables prior to presentations of test stimuli.

In another study (Lyle 1968) poor readers (age 9 years) were
found to be less able than normals on the Graham-Kendall
Memory for Designs Test. Lyle suggested that the results may have
been due to "minimal cerebral dysfunction" in the poor reader
group. However, the *same* subtests performed as well as normal
readers on all but one of the subtests of the WISC Performance
Scale (Coding) but not as well on the Verbal Scale, these latter
findings being reported in a separate publication (Lyle and Goyen
1969). The authors attributed the results on the WISC to verbal
deficiencies in poor readers. They also pointed out that all of the

subtests that differentiated reader groups require verbalization, except for Coding, which involves association of digits and numerals presented visually. They therefore suggested that verbal processing difficulties may have contributed to the poor readers' performance on this measure, inasmuch as success on this type task may depend heavily upon effective "verbal rehearsal and encoding."

In two later studies these same investigators assessed the effects of incentives on visual recognition and visual learning tasks. In one of these studies (Goyen and Lyle 1971a), normal readers were found to be more accurate than poor readers on immediate memory for wordlike shapes presented briefly (for 10 msec), although differences were found only in 7-year-old subjects and not in 8-year-olds. In a later investigation (Goyen and Lyle 1971b) *no* differences were found between poor and normal readers (ages 6 and 7 years) on visual paired-associates learning involving geometric designs. The authors made note of discrepancies in these two data sets and suggested that the earlier results might have been due either to the use of brief presentations or to the fact that the stimuli were of low discriminability.

In still another study involving 7-year-olds Goyen and Lyle (1973) found that poor readers made more errors than normals in matching geometric forms to standards, stimuli being presented for brief exposures (0.5 sec) under immediate and delayed (2 and 7 sec) recognition conditions. However, the groups were distinguished only when the stimuli were identical, implying a response bias on the part of poor readers rather than trace decay. The magnitude of the differences between the groups was not impressive, undermining the reliability of the findings.

Finally, in their most recent investigation Lyle and Goyen (1975) presented poor and normal readers in first grade (mean age = 6.8 and 6.9 respectively) with rectangular shapes for three exposure durations: (10 msec, 1 sec, and 5 sec). The dependent variable was same/different recognition. The normal readers performed better than the poor readers under the 10-msec and 1-sec conditions but not under the 5-sec condition. The authors conclude that speed of processing rather than short-term memory or form discrimination distinguishes poor readers. They further suggest that reading disability may be related to a perceptual deficit associated with maturational lag.

Their conclusions seem to be unwarranted, for several reasons. First, the use of children in their first year of reading is a highly dubious procedure for identifying severely impaired readers. It is extremely difficult to be certain that children who are functioning below age and grade level at the inception of first grade will maintain that level toward the end of the grade and during their second year; many of the "poor" readers in the sample may have developed normal reading skill later. Furthermore, levels and rates of maturation vary significantly at this age level, so it may be that many of the children in the poor reader group had not yet developed certain of the skills necessary for performance on the tasks employed, particularly the disposition to attend and concentrate. Such deficits would be especially problematic under circumstances that characterize laboratory study. As a matter of fact, the experimental tasks were found to be quite difficult for all the children in the study; when the stimuli were highly similar, none of the subjects in either group performed much better than chance.

A second and closely related reason to distrust Lyle and Goyen's conclusions is that success in reading may have favorably disposed the normal reader toward better performance on the visual recognition task. Learning to read implies the need to develop perceptual and cognitive strategies that tend toward efficiency and economy of visual processing. The successful readers in this study may have begun to acquire such strategies and thereby have had an advantage over the poor readers.

A third factor calling the results into question is the possibility that the disparities between the reader groups were due to differences in encoding or rehearsal abilities rather than to differences in visual processing. Under the brief exposure conditions the poor readers may have been less proficient than the normal readers in *rapidly* coding the stimuli (generating a useful mnemonic) so as to facilitate more efficient detection of distinguishing features among the distracter items. The longer exposure duration, on the other hand, may not have been as taxing in this respect. Thus the authors' interpretation of their findings is open to question. I therefore suggest that this study provides no convincing evidence that poor readers sustain perceptual disorder characterized by a deficiency in rate of visual processing in the literal sense.

The studies by Lyle and Goyen involved relatively careful sampling procedures. Nevertheless, the disparities between poor and normal readers on measures of visual memory are open to question in view of the circumstances under which they were found. Of particular interest are the differences between these groups on tests of visual-spatial processing under conditions that probably involved verbal coding in contrast to those that minimized this influence. In match-to-standard tests involving very brief or limited exposures of visual stimuli, poor and normal readers were often (though not uniformly) differentiated. As thoroughly documented by Calfee (1977) it is under such circumstances that verbal coding is especially useful as an aid to short-term storage. Yet no difference was found between these groups on spatial tasks that did not rely so heavily on speed of processing: WISC Block Design and visual association learning. The Block Design test requires no significant memory factor, and paired-associates learning obviously involves long-term rather than short-term visual memory. Thus one cannot necessarily implicate, on the basis of these results alone, either visual perception or visual memory as major areas of difficulty. In contrast, one may be justified in suggesting that verbal encoding deficiencies may have impaired high-speed storage and retrieval of the visual stimuli in those studies involving very brief exposures, particularly those employing verbal material. Lyle and Goyen's interpretation of at least some of their data (1968, 1969) is consistent with this suggestion.

None of the studies comparing visual memory in poor and normal readers has controlled for possible confounding of results by virtue of deficiencies in verbal encoding. Benton (1962) had earlier mentioned the possibility of "verbal mediation" problems in poor readers and there is enough suggestive evidence in the literature to lead one to give this conjecture serious consideration. Therefore, in pursuing this idea further, members of our laboratory designed a series of studies in which we systematically assessed the influence of verbal mediation upon visual processing. We employed three general strategies.

One approach was to compare dyslexic and normal readers on short-term visual recall of letters and words when instructions were varied to facilitate attendance to either the visual or the verbal features of these stimuli. Consistent with the view that such children do not sustain basic perceptual deficiency, it was expected that poor readers would perform as well as normal readers on visual encoding (copying from visual memory) of the letters and words but not as well as the normals on verbal encoding (naming). This strategy is, of course, consistent with Gibson's (1971) theory of word perception, one component of which is that the featural attributes of words are apprehended sequentially and hierarchically, attendance to one attribute (for instance, graphic features) momentarily precluding attendance to another (phonologic features).

A second approach was to compare disabled and normal readers on short- and long-term memory for letters and words drawn from an unfamiliar orthography. The performance of these two groups was also contrasted with that of children who were familiar with the orthography. The expectation was that poor and normal readers who were unfamiliar with the novel stimulus words would be equivalent on the visual memory tasks but would not perform as well as the children who were acquainted with the alphabet from which the words were constructed and the orthographic and linguistic constituents of the words themselves.

The third approach was to systematically compare reader groups on verbal and nonverbal learning (long-term memory) tasks involving visual constituents. It was anticipated that the performance of poor readers would generally be comparable to that of normal readers on the visual-nonverbal learning tasks but different on the visual-verbal learning tasks.

All three research paradigms were designed to evaluate the contention that the apparent visual processing deficits in poor readers are a secondary manifestation of verbal encoding difficulties in such children and *not* the result of deficiencies in form perception or spatial confusion. Research samples in all instances were selected in accord with the criteria outlined in chapter 2.

In an initial test of this hypothesis (Vellutino, Steger, and Kandel 1972) poor and normal readers between the ages of 9 and 14 (unstratified) were given brief (600-msec) visual presentations of scrambled letters, words of varying length (three, four, and five letters), simple designs, and three-digit numerals and were asked to *copy* them from memory immediately thereafter. They were then presented with the verbal stimuli, again for brief exposures, but this time they were required to *name* each item immediately after presentation. It was found that poor readers performed

considerably better in copying the words than they did in pro-
nouncing and spelling those same stimuli. Their performance was
comparable to the normal readers on the graphic reproduction of
both scrambled letters and words, except for those configurations
that taxed short-term visual memory (the five-letter items). And
there were no differences between reader groups on memory for
simple designs and numerals.

In order to assess Benton's (1962) suggestion that poor readers
at younger age levels may sustain perceptual disorder, a second
study (Vellutino, Smith, Steger, and Kaman 1975) compared the
performance of stratified samples of poor and normal readers, at
age 7 and 11. The major findings of the previous investigation
were replicated. Poor readers generally performed as well as normals in the *copying* of geometric designs and three-, four-, and
five-item scrambled letters, words, and numbers. The only exception was the second-grade poor readers, who began to diverge from
the normals on four- and five-item configurations, quantities
that approximate the capacity limit of visual short-term memory
in young children (Simon 1972). In contrast, the poor readers did
not perform as well as the normals on the pronunciation of word
stimuli or, in the case of second-graders, on naming the letters and
numbers correctly. In neither study were poor readers generally
differentiated from normals in the frequency of orientation,
sequencing, substitution, addition, and omission errors when the
stimuli were graphically reproduced. However, they were inferior
to the normals on these variables when the response was oral.
Representative examples of the type of stimuli employed in both
studies can be seen in figure 5.13.

The decline in both the graphic reproduction and naming of
letters in four- and five-item words observed in second-grade poor
readers (and in some measure in the normal readers) was anticipated on the basis of the results of our initial study. However, we
did not anticipate one finding: poor readers in sixth grade performed as well as normal readers at that grade level (and better
than the second-graders) on both the reproduction and naming
of the letters in *all* stimulus words and all sets of scrambled letters and numerals. It was particularly impressive that the poor
readers often named the letters in a given word in correct sequence,
directly after mispronouncing that same word. These findings
obviously imply intact visual perception and memory in these

REAL WORDS

Three Letter	Four Letter	Five Letter
fly	**loin**	**blunt**
bed	**form**	**drawn**
was	**calm**	**chair**

SCRAMBLED LETTERS

Three Letter	Four Letter	Five Letter
dnv	**jpyc**	**ztbrc**
hbd	**gzfs**	**yfpqg**
mcw	**qvlt**	**qldnr**

NUMBERS

Three Digit	Four Digit	Five Digit
382	**4328**	**96842**
974	**3724**	**31579**
296	**9156**	**86314**

GEOMETRIC DESIGNS

Two Items   Three Items

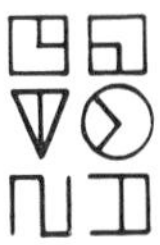

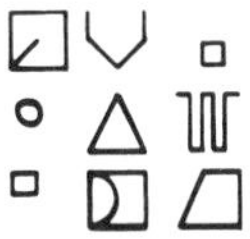

Figure 5.13 Types of verbal and nonverbal stimuli employed in two studies comparing poor and normal readers on visual and verbal encoding. (Vellutino et al. 1972; Vellutino, Smith, and Kaman 1975. Reproduced by permission of the editor of *Child Development*.)

subjects. The results also demonstrate that the sixth grade poor readers were sufficiently well acquainted with the orthographic structures of the words to reproduce their letters accurately in spite of the fact that they could not always pronounce them. Indeed, children in this group, while more proficient than the normal reading second graders on copying and naming the letters in the stimulus words, were no better than the younger normal readers (and sometimes worse) on the pronunciation of those same words. Thus poor readers evidently acquire some knowledge of the visual structure inherent in printed words (albeit less efficiently and less rapidly than normal readers do), even though they experience protracted difficulty in acquiring a stable knowledge of their visual-verbal relationships.

These results clearly indicate that the visual perception of a letter or word does not necessarily parallel its verbal encoding. This was especially evident in the fact that poor readers in both studies generally copied correctly even those words on which they made a large number of apparent spatial and sequential errors in oral reading *(din/bin, cob/cod, sung/snug, lion/loin).* Thus the data support the contention made earlier that the orientation and sequencing errors so often observed in the reading and written language of poor readers may, in fact, be linguistic intrusion errors rather than visual-spatial distortions. In simpler terms, our results indicate that when dyslexics call a *b, d* or *was, saw,* it isn't because they perceive (see) these items differently from the way normal readers do, but because they can't name them correctly. A similar conclusion was reached on the basis of research done elsewhere (Liberman et al. 1971; Shankweiler and Liberman 1972; Allington, Gormley, and Truex 1975).

Inasmuch as our results can be generalized to children at least as young as age 7, the data contradict the hypothesis stated by Benton (1962) and Satz and Sparrow (1970) that poor readers at early age levels—that is, below age 9—suffer from perceptual deficits.

Another point about these two studies that should be emphasized is that the results can readily be interpreted within the context of Gibson's theory of word perception: that the multiple features of printed words are ordered sequentially and hierarchically and that attendance to one set of features momentarily precludes attendance to the others. In our studies the requirement that subjects focus on the visual or the verbal components of the words presented apparently prompted encoding primarily in one or the other medium, as reflected in the differential effects of our procedures. These findings support our thesis that poor readers have selective difficulties in apprehending the *verbal* aspects of written words. Furthermore, the data are in accord with the dual processing theories of a number of other authors (Posner et al. 1972; Crowder 1972; Gazzaniga 1970), who hypothesize that the visual and verbal constitutents of words are stored differentially, letter and word recognition involving the integration and coordination of mechanisms responsible for processing both types of stimuli.

Inasmuch as both of our studies employed letters and words—materials with which poor readers have difficulty—it was felt that the procedures might not permit the strongest test of the hypothesis that such children sustain no deficit in visual perception and visual memory. We therefore designed two other studies comparing poor and normal readers on recall of words of varying length printed in Hebrew, an unfamiliar orthography (see figure 5.9). Since we were also interested in contrasting the effects of visual and verbal encoding, we compared the performance of these subjects with that of normal readers learning Hebrew. These investigations involved children from second through sixth grade (Vellutino et al. 1973; Vellutino, Steger, Kaman, and DeSetto 1975). Word stimuli of various lengths (three, four, and five letters) were presented tachistoscopically, exposure time (in seconds) for each word equaling the number of letters in the word. It was found that poor readers copied the Hebrew words from visual memory as well as the normal readers. However, the performance of both groups was below that of children learning to speak, read, and write Hebrew. The only exception was the three-letter items, on which all groups were equivalent.

A gratuitous result was the observation that the directional (left-to-right) scanning tendencies of poor and normal readers unacquainted with Hebrew were identical, as measured by the frequency of omission errors at the right terminal positions of the Hebrew words. This was in contrast to the right-to-left scanning tendencies of children learning to read and write Hebrew, who were inclined to make their omission errors at the left terminal positions.

Also of interest in these studies was the finding that poor and normal readers did not differ with respect to proportion of orientation, sequencing, omission, and substitution errors, with one exception. On Hebrew letters that were judged (by independent samples) to be disoriented facsimiles of Roman letters (see figure 5.9, item 1B), normal readers were found to make *more* orientation errors than poor readers. This difference was thought to be attributable to proactive interference as a result of the normal readers' more stable experience with Roman letters.

In still another study employing a similar format (Vellutino, Steger, DeSetto, and Phillips 1975), poor and normal readers who were unfamiliar with Hebrew were comparable on the visual recognition of randomly arrayed Hebrew letters, whether presented immediately after initial exposure, twenty-four hours later, or even six months later. In this investigation, as in the others, the non-Hebrew groups did not perform as well as the Hebrew groups. What is remarkable is that the number of children, in each reader group, who recognized several of the Hebrew letters even after six months, is statistically significant (beyond chance) and that the distribution of the recognition scores after this long delay was no different for poor readers than for normal readers.

The results of the studies employing Hebrew letter stimuli provide direct and, we think, convincing evidence that poor readers as a group do not sustain a basic deficiency in either short- or long-term memory for visual forms. Inasmuch as ordering errors were recorded in these studies, it may also be inferred that the groups do not differ with respect to ability to sequence a spatially ordered array when the number of stimuli to be recalled does not unduly tax the limits of short-term memory. In addition, since both of the groups unfamiliar with Hebrew did not recall the stimulus words as well as children learning Hebrew, we may reasonably infer that immediate recall of printed words is to some degree influenced by knowledge of their orthographic and linguistic characteristics.

Of particular interest is the evidence that poor readers are *not* characterized by deficiencies in visual-spatial orientation and directional scanning as suggested by, for example, Orton and Hermann. In fact, the data are in accord with the notion that orientation to visual figures, especially symbolic material, is a stimulus-specific process that varies in accord with learned relations (cf. Ghent and

Bernstein 1961; Gibson et al. 1962; Kolers and Perkins 1969). Thus it seems in error to suggest that the individual is endowed with a homogeneous, inborn capacity that facilitates orientation in the general sense.

That the normal readers in the Hebrew letter studies were inclined to make more orientation errors than poor readers certainly supports this position; so also do our earlier observations that similar appearing words *(was* and *saw)* were encoded differently when subjects were alternately directed to indicate their perception of these words graphically and vocally. Furthermore, these data are entirely consistent with the findings of Liberman and her associates (1971), who suggest that orientational and directional errors are probably attributable to difficulties in verbal encoding rather than to optical reversibility as suggested by Orton.

One other study contrasting reader groups on short-term memory for visual-verbal materials should be mentioned. Liberman and Shankweiler (1978) compared poor and normal readers in second grade on an adaptation of Kimura's (1963) test of memory for recurring figures. Subjects were presented with eight sets of stimulus cards (ten in a set), each set including four recurring stimuli and six nonrecurring stimuli. In presentations of any given set the subject was to indicate which of the stimuli he had seen before. The first set of ten cards constituted the presentation trial; the seven sets that followed were recognition trials. Three different decks of 80 stimuli were prepared (8 sets x 10 cards): nonsense designs, photographed faces, and nonsense syllables. The poor readers were found to be slightly better than the good readers in memory for nonsense designs, and the two groups were comparable in face recognition. However, there was a highly significant difference between poor and normal readers on recognition of recurring nonsense syllables.

Despite identical procedures, neither nonlinguistic visual task differentiated between the good and poor readers, while the language-based visual task did. We would reason that in the nonsense syllable task, though not in the others, the good reader had a clear advantage: he could recode the information phonetically and thus hold it more efficiently in short-term memory. (Liberman and Shankweiler 1978, 21)

Finally, whereas most of the studies already cited directly assessed short-term visual memory in poor and normal readers, only one (Vellutino, Steger, DeSetto, and Phillips 1975) evaluated long-term visual memory in these groups, and no differences were found in this instance. To these findings the results of two other studies can be added. These studies compared poor and normal readers on learning tasks involving visual paired associates, using our third research strategy, namely systematic comparison of dyslexic and normal readers on measures of verbal and nonverbal learning.

In one study (Vellutino, Steger, and Pruzek 1973) it was found that poor readers (grades 4, 5 and 6) did not differ from normals in association learning involving nonverbal stimuli presented in both the visual and auditory modalities; nor were they found to differ on intersensory (visual-auditory) learning tasks, involving nonverbal stimuli. The second study (Vellutino, Harding, Phillips, and Steger 1975) compared poor and normal readers (also in grades 4, 5, and 6) on training and transfer measures employing visual-visual and visual-verbal associates. Although poor readers performed below the level of normal readers on the visual-verbal learning tasks, they were *not* differentiated from normals on visual-visual association learning. On the basis of these two studies, we suggested that reading disability may be due to dysfunction in some aspect of visual-verbal learning and not to either intrasensory or intersensory learning involving nonverbal stimuli. And since comparably selected samples of dyslexic and normal readers were found to differ only on measures involving a verbal component, the disparities observed between the two groups in these studies could not have been due to group differences in general learning ability, attentional or motivational factors, and like variables.

5.5 SUMMARY AND CONCLUSIONS

It is time to synthesize the salient issues regarding visual-perceptual and visual-memory deficit theories of reading disability. Operating within the framework of the memory model in figure 4.1, I will begin by reiterating the point that although the perceptual deficit explanations of reading disability generally implicate dysfunction in the initial (sensory) storage or feature-detection stage of visual processing, only a few have made explicit reference to this stage as the locus of difficulty. In a small number of studies that have attempted to directly assess sensory processing in poor and normal readers the results are conflicting. But none of the studies yielded convincing evidence that poor readers are abnormal in feature detection, trace duration, capacity limits, or any other component of sensory storage. A few better-controlled investigations that also compared poor and normal readers on initial-stage processing yielded no differences between the two groups. Because these studies employed experimental procedures designed to separate the first and second stages of visual memory, they have, in effect, provided a means by which to control for confounding by virtue of possible reader group differences in higher-order cognitive functions. They therefore represent a distinct improvement over most investigations attempting to evaluate the many variants of the perceptual deficit explanation of dyslexia. Indeed it is significant that the results obtained in experiments directly assessing initial-stage processing in poor and normal readers were for the most part negative.

By far the largest collection of studies investigating inferred visual deficits in poor readers have evaluated specific hypotheses through such means as figure-drawing tests, match-to-standard procedures, tests of figure-ground relationships, and measures of high-speed scanning and recognition of both verbal and nonverbal stimuli. The results of these studies are conflicting, and many of the studies are fraught with sampling, methodological, and interpretive problems that leave certain of their findings open to question. Furthermore, none provided adequate controls for confounding that might be associated with the possibility of verbal encoding deficits in poor readers; the failure to provide such controls was particularly problematic in studies comparing poor and normal readers on the high-speed processing of letters and words. A closely related problem in these investigations was the tendency to view inefficient perceptual processing as originating from a basic constitutional defect; yet such difficulty could just as well be construed as a secondary manifestation of the negative learning that is typically associated with long-standing reading disorder. This was particularly true of investigations comparing poor and normal readers on tasks requiring rapid analysis of orthographic structure.

Taken together, the impressions derived from studies attempting both direct and indirect tests of perceptual deficit explanations of reading disability lead to the conclusion that the evidence in support of such explanations is uniformly weak.

The studies contrasting dyslexic and normal readers on short-term visual memory also yielded conflicting results, but the findings of those that systematically compared reader groups on visual (motor) and verbal encoding of written material were much more definitive (Vellutino et al. 1972, 1973; Vellutino, Harding, Phillips, and Steger 1975; Vellutino, Smith, Steger, and Kaman 1975; Vellutino, Steger, Harding, and Phillips 1975). The general picture that emerges from these studies is that poor readers between the ages of 7 and 14 do *not* sustain any deficiency in short- or long-term visual memory and, by extension, have no visual perceptual deficits of the types variously proposed in the literature. In contrast, there was a great deal of evidence indicating that poor readers do have difficulty in processing verbal material. Reader groups consistently differed on learning tasks involving a verbal component but were found to be no different on (visual) nonverbal learning measures or on short term memory tasks that minimized verbal mediation. A striking illustration of this disparity is our finding that poor readers could graphically reproduce letters and words much better than they could name or pronounce them.

It might also be pointed out that perceptual deficit theories of reading disability in which deficient storage of memory engrams or templates is a basic factor (Morgan 1896; Hinshelwood 1900, 1917; Orton 1925, 1937) are at variance with current theorizing in the area of information processing. Briefly, there is considerable evidence in the general literature (Neisser 1967) as well as in the literature concerned specifically with the reading process (Gibson et al. 1962; Pick 1965; Gibson 1971; Smith 1971; Gibson and Levin 1975) that visual as well as other types of information are stored in the form of features rather than as templates or images. Features are the multiform properties of a given stimulus, specific categories of features constituting bundles of information of a specific description. Words contain a variety of types of featural information relating to their graphic, orthographic, phonologic, semantic, and syntactic constituents (Gibson and Levin 1975). Templates, on the other hand, are prototypes representing the broad configurational properties of a given stimulus. Visual templates, for example, represent the shapes or outlines of (visual) figures. Template storage is believed to be uneconomical and probably not the preferred method of storing information. It does not, for example, facilitate reconstruction of categorical information (for example, information about upper- and lower-case letters) as readily as featural storage, which is in greater accord with the generative powers of the human information processor.

In the present context, a feature theory such as Gibson's is much better able than a template theory such as Orton's to explain the differential success of normal and poor readers in visual and verbal encoding of identical stimuli (Vellutino, Steger, and Kandel 1972; Vellutino, Smith, Steger, and Kaman 1975). Whereas Orton viewed *b/d* or *was/saw* errors as the failure to retrieve the template that matched the distal stimulus, our interpretation, which accords with feature theory, is that the perceiver simply could not retrieve the phonologic counterparts of the visual features of the (accurately perceived) stimuli.

The finding that poor and normal readers did not differ on number of items retained when the normal readers had no advantage by virtue of previous learning (as with Hebrew letters) is a strong indication that the two groups do not differ with respect to the capacity limits characteristic of short-term memory. With English words, on the other hand, differences between the groups *were* evident, again suggesting the possibility that poor readers have verbal encoding problems.

There is considerable support for the possibility that poor readers have difficulty in translating visual information into a verbal code, but the studies discussed provide no direct evidence as to the nature of such difficulty. Implied here are basic deficiencies in either storage or retrieval of information from long-term memory, which of course would have secondary effects upon encoding in short-term memory. I am of the opinion that such deficiencies are of a linguistic nature, but there are other possibilities. In chapter 6 we will review the evidence for the intersensory deficit theory of dyslexia as initially postulated by Birch (1962).

Finally, our laboratory undertook to evaluate the perceptual deficit explanations of reading disability in a series of investigations that, by most standards, were carefully designed and controlled. Sample selection was meticulous; salient findings in a given study were replicated in other studies employing essentially identical experimental and sampling procedures; and specific hypotheses were tested by a variety of methodological approaches with independent samples.

We therefore believe that our findings are reliable and can be generalized to the dyslexic, as defined earlier. Indeed our findings pose serious problems for the multitude of perceptual deficit theories of dyslexia that pervade the literature.

Chapter Six

INTERSENSORY
                           INTEGRATION

6.1 EARLY INVESTIGATIONS

The second most popular explanation of dyslexia is the intersensory deficit theory, which associates reading disorder with
difficulties in integrating information from the sensory systems.
This hypothesis was initially proposed by Birch (1962) and later
given support by a large number of studies. Birch's study of
disabled readers was an extension of earlier work with normal children in which he provided some evidence to indicate that the
ability to integrate information from the different sense modalities
increases with chronological age (Birch and Lefford 1963). He
placed such changes within the context of his belief that the sensory modalities undergo significant alteration with respect to
superordinate status, suggesting that proprioceptive (internal)
systems eventually become subordinated to the teleoreceptor (external) systems. Thus Birch accorded sensory dominance a cardinal
role in the ability to establish relationships among the different
senses. These aspects of Birch's theory are open to question
(Milner and Bryant 1970; Friedes 1974), yet there is evidence
that children take some time to grasp the *concept* of intersensory
equivalence and to establish specific liaisons between given modalities (Gibson 1969; Farnham-Diggory 1972; Goodnow 1971a,
1971b). In relation to reading, Birch's theory had considerable
appeal and his seminal studies precipitated a number of investigations providing evidence either for or against his initial findings.

The first study testing the intersensory deficit theory of dyslexia was conducted by Birch and Belmont (1964). The subjects
were 150 poor readers and 50 normal readers comparable in age
(9 and 10 years), sex, and socioeconomic status. Poor readers were

somewhat below the normal readers in IQ, although all were in the normal range. Subjects were required to match auditory patterns (tapped out by an experimenter) with visual-spatial dot patterns presented in multiple-choice arrays (see figure 6.1). The normal readers made significantly fewer matching errors than the poor readers. Since the groups did not differ on the digit span subtest of the WISC, it was concluded that the findings may have been due to reader group disparities in the ability to integrate intersensory information.

In a later study Birch and Belmont (1965) administered the same task to children from kindergarten through sixth grade (N = 220), along with measures of reading achievement and intelligence. It was found that performance in auditory-visual integration (AVI) improved rapidly in the earliest school years but reached an asymptote by fifth grade. Reading achievement

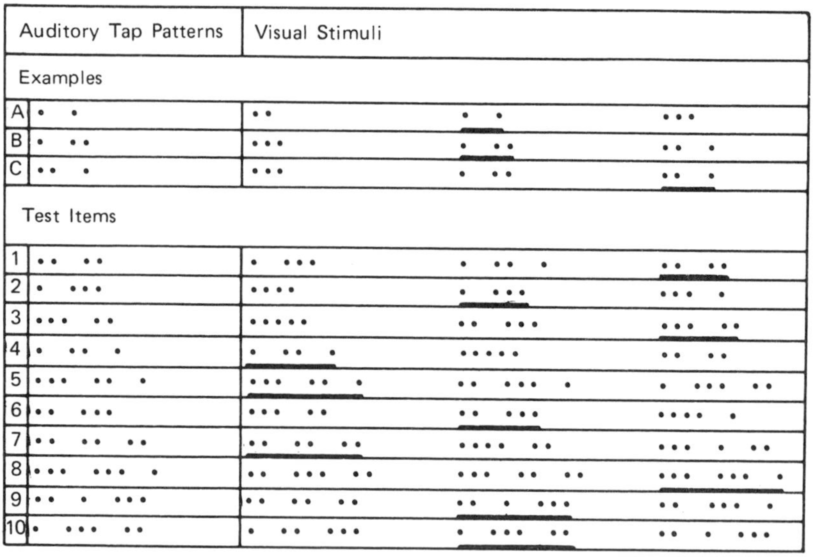

Figure 6.1 Auditory and visual equivalents employed by Birch and Belmont. The experimenter tapped out the pattern on the left and subjects were asked to select its visual counterpart (underlined) on the right; large and small spaces represent approximate time intervals of 1 sec and 0.5 sec respectively. (Reprinted with permission of author and publisher from: Birch, H. G., and Belmont, L. Auditory-visual integration in normal and retarded readers. *American Journal of Orthopsychiatry*, 1965, 34, 852–861.)

correlated with AVI only in first- and second-graders; correlations between IQ and reading increased with age. Correlations between AVI and IQ were substantial in all grades but kindergarten. Birch and Belmont concluded that AVI may be particularly important in acquiring initial skill in reading but that intellectual factors may be more influential later.

Whereas Birch and Belmont's AVI task had involved presentation of auditory stimuli prior to visual matching, Beery (1967) presented visual stimuli first, followed by auditory matching. Subjects were also presented with a lengthened version of the Birch AVI task. Carefully selected samples of poor and normal readers (ages 8 to 13 years; N = 15 each group) were differentiated on all tasks, the normals being the better performers in all instances. (Problems associated with tasks of the type employed in these three studies will be examined later.)

Muehl and Kremenak (1966) employed a similar format, but included intramodal matching (A-A, V-V) as well as two versions of intermodal matching (A-V, V-A). Subjects were 119 first-graders tested at the beginning of the school year. These measures were correlated with end-of-year reading achievement scores, and significant relationships were found between reading and both A-V (r = .52) and V-A (r = .39) matching. In contrast, intramodality measures were not correlated with reading achievement. Intelligence was controlled for, thereby reinforcing the results of Birch's original developmental studies assessing the relation between AVI and reading ability.

One major difficulty with this study is that Muehl and Kremenak did not compare severely impaired readers with normals. The subjects came essentially from a normal population and the results may therefore have limited application to the understanding of the etiology of dyslexia. Perhaps more basic is their failure to control for the possibility that all children tested did indeed grasp the concept of intermodal equivalence. Goodnow (1971a) found that kindergartners had not yet established correspondence rules for judging spatial and temporal stimuli as equivalent, and that first- and second-graders had begun to comprehend these relationships but employed distinctly different strategies in apprehending them. Therefore, it is conceivable that the variability found in reading achievement in the Muehl and Kremenak study was partly attributable to individual differences in conceptual development.

In spite of the positive findings in all these studies, criticisms of Birch's initial investigations were legion. Sterritt and Rudnick (1966) initiated the attack by pointing out that Birch's auditory presentations were not entirely of an auditory nature in that subjects watched the experimenter tap out rhythmic patterns. However, Birch's results were replicated when auditory patterns were presented by a tape recorder; the subjects in this study were fourth-graders. Third-graders were employed in a subsequent study (Rudnick, Sterritt, and Flax 1967), and in this case Birch's AVI test did *not* correlate with reading achievement when the effects of mental age were partialed out. In contrast, a measure of temporal-spatial matching presented visually *was* found to be correlated with reading achievement and so was the modified AVI task presenting auditory stimuli by means of a tape recorder. The subjects in these studies came from essentially normal populations; therefore the data permit no conclusions with respect to AVI in disabled readers.

Another criticism of Birch's investigations was that he did not control adequately for the possibility of *intra*sensory deficits in his subjects, even though reader groups were not found to differ on the WISC memory-for-digits subtest. When Zigmond (1966) employed carefully selected samples of normal and disabled readers, she found that the disabled readers were inferior to the normals on nine measures of *intra*sensory (auditory) functioning, which included both verbal and nonverbal tasks. Not surprisingly, normal readers performed better on six out of seven *inter*sensory tasks too. Thus it was concluded that group differences in intermodal functioning may have been due to differences in intramodal abilities. Bryant (1968, 1974) makes a similar point in two later reviews.

Blank and her associates also provide evidence that the disparities found between poor and normal readers on intersensory matching may have been due to disparities in intramodal abilities—specifically in verbal ability. In two separate experiments they found that poor readers' difficulties in intersensory matching and temporal ordering tasks were due to their limited ability to employ a verbal coding system in the serial organization of stimuli presented to them (Blank and Bridger 1966; Blank, Weider, and Bridger 1968). In contrast, normal readers were apparently more effective in utilizing verbal mnemonics to aid recall. Inasmuch as these results were found with poor readers in both first and fourth grades, Blank concluded that verbal concept deficiencies are present at the onset of reading disability and are a more likely source of the disorder than is dysfunction in cross-modal transfer.

A response to these criticisms appeared in a later study by Kahn and Birch (1968). The interrelations among AVI, IQ, and reading measures were studied in 350 elementary school age boys from grades 2 through 6. Reading achievement measures and AVI were found to correlate moderately in all grades when IQ was uncontrolled, but the correlation for second graders was negligible when IQ was held constant.[1] In order to assess the possible effects of intramodal disorder upon intersensory functioning, children receiving the ten lowest and the ten highest scores on the AVI test were compared on measures of auditory and visual discrimination, auditory memory, and a measure of verbal mediation strategies. No group differences were found on these tasks. Kahn and Birch therefore concluded that the intersensory deficit explanation of reading disability remained intact.

A major weakness of this study is that it was conducted on an essentially normal population and the results could not be generalized to comparisons of dyslexic and normal readers. The same criticism applies to the Birch and Belmont (1965) study. Furthermore, in measuring the effects of verbal mediation on AVI matching, the investigators simply asked subjects what strategies they employed but did not actually record each subject's verbalizations of temporal patterns, as did Blank and her associates (1966, 1968). Thus Kahn and Birch's conclusions that verbal mediation was *not* a factor contributing to reader group differences in AVI is unwarranted.

6.2 STUDIES OF BISENSORY MEMORY

Several investigations of intersensory processing have employed various short-term memory tasks. In an initial study, Senf (1969) compared poor and normal readers between the ages of 8 and 15 on an audiovisual analogue of Broadbent's (1958) dichotic listening technique. In three separate experiments involving free and directed recall, subjects were administered three sets of audiovisual (A-V) stimuli (numbers, common objects, and so on). Items from each set consisted of simultaneous presentations of two different stimuli, one presented visually and the other presented auditorily. Under free-recall conditions subjects were simply told to remember test stimuli regardless of order or mode of presentation. Under directed-recall conditions subjects were asked to recall stimuli in order, either in A-V pairs or by modality. Stimuli were presented at two interpair intervals (0.5 and 2 seconds).

Under the free-recall conditions most subjects were inclined toward modality rather than pair-order responses. However, poor readers were generally characterized by more modality responses than pair-order (A-V) responses, whereas the reverse was true of normal readers. There were no differences in error scores under these conditions. In directed-recall the youngest poor readers (age 9) made more errors within given modalities than did their normal peers but did not differ from the normals in A-V recall. In contrast, all other poor readers did differ from normals in recall of A-V items but were comparable with normals in modality recall. The poor readers' error scores were largely order errors since they were not significantly different from the normal readers on gross memory under any of the conditions. It is particularly interesting that the poor readers appeared to show a distinct preference for recall of stimuli presented auditorily over stimuli presented visually, and their performance was characterized by more errors on the visual stimuli. The pattern of obtained group differences was generally maintained under the two interpair intervals.

Essentially the same results were found in a second study (Senf and Feshback 1970). In this investigation the performance of (comparably selected) poor and normal readers from middle social strata were contrasted with a group of socioeconomically disadvantaged children with reading problems. The disadvantaged youngsters were found to be closer to normals in their performance patterns than to poor readers, but they, like the poor readers, showed a preference for auditorily presented material.

Senf and Feshback suggested that their findings provide some support for the possibility that poor readers cannot effectively organize bisensory stimuli and drew a parallel between their findings and those of studies assessing Birch's intersensory deficit theory of dyslexia (Birch and Belmont 1964; Beery 1967). They also suggested that poor readers, unlike normals, may store information in "two separate memory storage systems" as a result of the failure to translate visual stimuli into auditory representations. Since the pattern of group differences was the same for the two interpair intervals, it was later concluded that memory rather than attention factors could best account for the results (Senf and Freundl 1971).

In a later study the possibility that the modality differences observed in the previous studies may have been due to masking effects (visual stimuli masked by subsequent auditory stimuli) was assessed by staggering serial-order presentations of visual and auditory stimuli (Senf and Freundl 1971). The modality differences obtained with younger children in the previous studies were replicated, thus eliminating sensory masking as an influential variable in accounting for the disparities between the two groups. The study also replicated the earlier findings that poor and normal readers at the youngest age level manifested less difference in A-V pair-order recall than in modality recall. However, contrary to earlier findings (Senf 1969) normal readers performed better than poor readers on measures evaluating gross memory as well as ordered recall. These results call into question Senf's earlier suggestion that poor readers may sustain specific deficiencies in serial-order memory.

It might be asked why reader group differences were found for the younger children in within-modality presentations but not in pair-order (A-V) presentations, whereas for older subjects the reverse pattern was observed. Perhaps the results are due to an interaction between two factors: (1) younger children do not perform as effectively as older children in short-term memory tasks (Hagen et al. 1975) and (2) pair-order recall is more difficult than modality recall even for adults. Thus neither the poor nor the normal readers at the younger age levels could effectively organize the pair-order stimuli and reader group differences emerged only on the within-modality presentations. Older poor readers may have had less difficulty than their younger counterparts in encoding the specific stimuli employed in these studies and were therefore better able to recall items presented within modalities; pair-order recall, being decidedly more complicated, may require more elaborate recoding and rehearsal devices, which older poor readers may not have had at their disposal. This would account for the unique age differences observed in reader group contrasts. Senf and Freundl suggested that the results could be explained either by the salience of the auditory stimuli (as a distracter affecting the groups differently) or by possible deficiencies on the part of poor readers in rapid encoding of visual material. They also considered the possibility of organizational deficits in this group that might impair the proper categorizing of modality-specific stimuli.

These results would seem to weaken the sensory integration deficit theory of reading disability. The similarity of results under modality and pair-order conditions found in all three studies is particularly indicting. The observation that poor and normal readers more often differed in errors on the visual than on the auditory stimuli, under both interpair and modality conditions is also damaging to the theory. What emerges is support of the suggestion (Senf and Freundl 1971) that encoding or organizational problems rather than deficiencies in cross-modal transfer may have accounted for reader group differences in recall. Difficulty in rapidly recoding visual stimuli would certainly impede ability to rehearse this material as well as ability to impose structure for appropriate recall. Such difficulty would readily account for order errors, in that the need to serialize information undoubtedly strains short-term memory more than gross recall. The individual who experienced coding problems in the tasks employed may well have focused upon the auditory modality for preferential recall because it did not involve recoding from one sensory system to another. On the other hand, such a strategy could not have significantly reduced the incidence of either gross or order recall errors when auditory stimuli were to be remembered subsequent to visual stimuli, as was true of the directed-recall conditions. Consequently, an intersensory deficit explanation of reader group differences does not handle these findings as adequately as an encoding deficit hypothesis does.

Parenthetically, it should be noted that the results of the studies by Senf and his co-workers must be accepted with caution because of the failure to employ stringent criteria for sample selection. Therefore, interpretations made on the basis of these findings are necessarily tentative.

The results of several other investigations further undermine the intersensory deficit theory. Vande Voort and Senf (1973) compared more carefully selected samples of poor and normal readers (N = 16, each group; mean age = 9 years) on matching tasks of four types: (1) visual-spatial/visual-spatial, (2) visual-temporal/

visual-temporal, (3) auditory-temporal/auditory-temporal, and (4) auditory-temporal/visual-spatial. Two of the intramodal tasks (1 and 3) discriminated the groups, but the intermodal task (4) did not. The authors suggest that either perceptual or memory factors could have accounted for group differences. Perceptual factors were thought to be a possibility because of a moderately high correlation between Bender Test scores and the V-S/V-S tasks. On the other hand, both the Bender and V-S/V-S tasks correlated significantly with the WISC Full Scale IQ. Yet the Bender did *not* correlate significantly with reading quotients whereas the V-S/V-S task did. Thus V-S/V-S appeared to be related to reading, but the reason for this relation is unclear.

In a separate study Vande Voort, Senf, and Benton (1972) obtained essentially the same results, employing similar experimental and sampling procedures. Poor readers did not perform as well as normal readers on either auditory-auditory or auditory-visual matching tasks. Contrary to the results of the earlier study, the groups did not differ appreciably on visual-visual matching. This investigation evaluated the possible influence of short-term memory in that it employed two age levels and two time delays for matching target stimuli with standards. The authors speculated that a short-term memory deficiency should yield significant time delay x reader group as well as age x time delay x reader group interactions. But since neither interaction was significant, no memory factor seemed implicated. However, there was also no main effect for interstimulus interval, suggesting that the time delays were not sufficiently disparate to assess memory factors.

One additional control for memory was provided in this study through the administration of a separate matching task presenting the auditory stimuli while the visual pattern was in full view. Poor and normal readers were differentiated under these circumstances as well. Consequently the authors suggested that the differences between the two groups were probably not due to memory factors and may have been the result of attentional or stimulus encoding problems possibly associated with "central perceptual deficits" in other areas ("temporal order perception," for instance).

However, the data provided no insight as to what perceptual or encoding deficits might exist in poor readers. Furthermore, to distinguish between stimulus encoding and memory under the conditions in question seems artificial. An auditory temporal pattern must be synthesized or encoded into an integrated unit before it can be matched with a visual pattern; if for any reason a subject has difficulty with such encoding, short-term memory problems can be inferred. The demands on memory would seem even greater if a subject was distracted by the presence of the visual stimulus; in this instance he would have less time to encode the auditory pattern. Therefore, an inference of stimulus encoding deficiencies in poor readers would, by extension, imply memory difficulties in this group under the matching conditions described by Vande Voort, Senf, and Benton (1972).

A later study by Cummings and Faw (1976) provides additional support for the possibility that short-term memory problems characterize poor readers in tasks requiring equivalence judgments. Poor and normal readers, matched for age (10 years), sex, and intelligence were required to make same/different judgments of abstract visual stimuli under three delay conditions and three different stimulus conditions. Subjects were asked to match standard and comparison stimuli consisting of rows of six objects that were (1) identical in form and location, (2) different in location, or (3) different in form. The standard and comparison stimuli were shown simultaneously or with a delay of 1 or 6 seconds between offset of the standard and onset of matching. The standard stimulus was always displayed for 6 seconds, comparison stimuli being presented until the subject made a judgment.

The poor readers performed as well as the normal readers on judgments involving identical stimuli under all three experimental conditions; they were less proficient than the normal readers on judgments of stimuli that were not identical, although group differences were noted only in the two delay conditions.

Cummings and Faw inferred that poor readers are deficient in short-term memory and suggested that the successful performance of these subjects on judgments of *same* may have been due to a response bias. The results would also seem to suggest that poor readers had no difficulty in scanning a visual array for similarities and differences when no demands were made on memory functions. The disparities between reader groups under the delay conditions could have been due to differences in encoding and rehearsal factors, but the possibility of response bias makes this interpretation somewhat tenuous.

The suggestion by Cummings and Faw that poor readers may have been characterized by a bias toward *same* judgments raises some questions as to the validity of the results from the large number of studies employing same/different matching tasks as the dependent variable. It is quite possible that differences between poor and normal readers on such tasks were in many instances attributable to response bias. Indeed it has been found in psychophysical research (Parducci 1965) that responses on tasks that require categorical and dichotomous judgments (good/bad, same/different, and so on) are subject to bias by virtue of the fact that individuals tend to employ both categories with equal frequency. Such bias appears to be a problem in the Cummings and Faw study and could have been operative in many of the other studies employing similar procedures. In view of the fact that those investigations have typically given no indication of whether or not opportunities for response in alternative categories had been balanced, their results can be justifiably questioned.

Another study providing evidence for both intra- and intersensory deficits in poor readers was conducted by Bryden (1972). The subjects (N = 107) were equated for age (9 years), sex, and IQ. Nine matching tasks included various combinations of visual-sequential, auditory-sequential and visual-spatial patterns. Poor readers were found to be less able than normals on all nine tasks. Bryden suggests that the poor readers' deficiencies are not specific to auditory-visual integration or to perception of rhythm but quite possibly to difficulty in verbal coding.

A similar investigation was conducted more recently by Jones (1974). Spatial-temporal matching tasks were employed both within and between the auditory and visual modalities (A-A., V-A, V-A, A-V). Poor and normal readers, matched for age, sex, and IQ (N = 6 each group), were found to differ only on measures of A-A and A-V matching. A second experiment employed the same subjects and the same V-V and A-A tasks, but in this instance various time delays intervened between presentation of the standard and matching stimuli (0, 1, and 10 seconds). The longer delays included either an interpolated task or a rest period. Reader groups did not differ on the V-V tasks but were significantly different on A-A presentations under all delay conditions. The differences were interpreted as possibly due to an inability in poor

readers to code highly abstract auditory sequences. Jones suggested further that group disparities may have been due to memory rather than perceptual factors. These results reinforce Bryden's findings, and the two authors came to similar conclusions.
However, considering the small number of subjects in Jones's
study the reliability of the data is open to question.

A slightly different approach to assessing the intersensory deficit
theory of dyslexia is taken in a study by Shipley and Jones (1969),
who contrasted the performance of poor and normal readers (N =
20 each group) carefully matched for age (11 years), grade (fifth),
and intelligence (mean IQ = 103.8). All subjects were presented
geometric designs and high confusability scrambled letters (such as
p, b, q) for delayed (10 seconds) recognition following 5-second
exposures of each of the stimuli. An auditory distracter (noise)
was presented under three different conditions: (1) during exposure, (2) during the delay period, or (3) during the recognition
test; there was also a control condition with no distracter. Poor
readers did not perform as well as normals under any of the
experimental conditions.

Using many of the same subjects Shipley and Jones attempted
to reinforce their findings by recording evoked brain potentials
(EEG patterns) during single and simultaneous presentations of
light flashes and tones. They predicted that in poor readers the
simultaneous presentations of these stimuli would result in EEG
patterns of reduced amplitudes compared with unimodal presentations. By extension, normal readers were expected to manifest an increase in amplitude in bimodal over unimodal stimulation.
The authors presented data showing that poor readers (only ten
of whom showed any degree of reliability in EEG patterns) manifested either an equal or a reduced amplitude of response under
the bimodal condition. Curiously, no data for normal readers
were presented.

Shipley and Jones concluded from these two sets of findings
that dyslexia is attributable to defects in intersensory integration,
a conclusion that is totally unwarranted. Since the poor readers
performed more poorly than the normals on the visual recognition
tasks under all conditions, it cannot be inferred that the results
were due to dysfunction in intersensory integration. Furthermore,
the results for the geometric designs and scrambled letters were
not separated in the analyses, making it difficult to be certain

that there were not differential effects attributable to the different stimuli. For example, the disabled readers may have performed poorly in remembering confusable letters but had less difficulty in the recognition or recall of geometric designs, as demonstrated in other studies (Vellutino, Smith, Steger, and Kaman 1975). Furthermore, the results could be attributed to reader group differences in stimulus encoding, which would be particularly problematic in delays as long as 10 seconds.

The fact that the authors presented no data for normal readers on EEG patterns invalidates their interpretation of the results derived from poor readers. Moreover, they give no rationale for the expected differences between dyslexic and normal readers on evoked potentials, saying only that an enhanced amplitude in the case of bimodal stimulus presentations was "sometimes observed" with normal readers. This study contributes little to our understanding of dyslexia.

6.3 SPEED OF MODALITY SHIFTING

The studies examined so far have relied heavily upon matching and short-term memory tasks. Other investigators have explored the cross-modal deficit hypothesis by measuring the speed with which subjects can shift attention from one modality to the next.

Raab, Deutsch, and Friedman (1960) presented poor and normal readers (fourth- and fifth-graders) with two auditory stimuli and one visual stimulus: a high tone, a low tone, and a red light. Subjects were asked to keep a telegraph key depressed until a stimulus was presented, upon which they were to quickly release the key. No significant differences were found between reader groups when presentations involved two auditory stimuli (high to low tones), but the normal readers had faster reaction times when presentations involved the visual stimulus and one of the auditory stimuli. The results were thought to be consistent with an intersensory deficit explanation of reading disability.

However, this conclusion would seem to be invalidated by the fact that poor and normal readers differed with respect to both socioeconomic status and intelligence. The failure to equate reader groups on socioeconomic status may risk confounding experimental results by introducing experiential differences that may favor one group over the other in performance situations such as those employed in this study, that is in any situation

that requires task orientation or adaptation to unusual circumstances. As for intelligence, although there was no significant
difference between the disabled and normal readers on mean
IQ scores, the ranges for the two groups were strikingly different: for the normal readers it was from 96 to 148; for the
disabled readers it was from 80 to 110. Thus one can draw no
inferences about group differences in intersensory integration
from these results.

A similar study was conducted later by Katz and Deutsch
(1963), whose subjects were disadvantaged children in first, third,
and fifth grades. Poor readers were again found to have longer
latencies than normal readers for intermodal shifting. These
findings are also questionable because of the use of children from
low socioeconomic populations. However, a more basic problem
with both this study and the earlier one is the rationale prompting
the investigations. It is difficult to understand the logic behind the
use of intermodal shifting as a measure of intersensory integration.
If anything, these tasks would seem to be measuring such diverse
variables as perceptual or response set, ability to attend and concentrate, and general experience. The results of the perceptual
shifting studies tell us very little about intersensory integration,
and the distinctions made between poor and normal readers in
these studies can probably be explained on other grounds.

Some recent work by Blank and her associates provide support
for the latter contention. In two separate investigations they
found that poor and normal readers in third grade differed not
only on *inter*modal shifting but on *intra*modal shifting as well
(Blank, Higgins, and Bridger 1971; Blank, Berenzweig, and Bridger
1975). In both instances poor readers took longer to respond to
stimulus presentations than normal readers. Of particular interest
is the finding in both studies that poor readers' latency scores
were much greater than the normals when the stimuli were relatively complex (colored cartoons versus a single flash of light).
The authors conclude that reader group differences could not be
attributed to deficient intersensory integration and suggest instead
that poor readers might have particular difficulty in processing
complex, meaningful information.

The suggestion is interesting, especially in view of the findings
of other investigators—Goetzinger et al. (1960), Lovell et al.
(1964), and Elkind et al. (1965)—that poor readers did not per-

form as well as normals in picking out given figures from complex backgrounds. The interpretation offered in section 5.3.3. could apply here as well: it was conjectured that the poor reader may be somewhat less efficient than the normal reader in searching a complex visual array because he has had less experience in detecting discriminative relations that will facilitate economy and organization in perceptual processing. The failure to acquire *general orienting attitudes* such as the inclination to search for distinguishing features and invariant relations was cited as an illustrative example (Gibson 1969). Two even more basic sources of inefficiency are sheer disposition to engage a stimulus and flexibility in shifting one's perceptual set. Such attitudes are not unique to reading, but they may not develop in some children partly because of difficulties in learning to read. The inference is that success in reading fosters to some extent the development of the perceptual strategies in question.

Yet it may also be true that lack of appropriate (environmental) experience will impede the development of the orienting attitudes necessary for efficient visual perception of both printed words and nonlinguistic material. This seems a more plausible interpretation of the results of the studies by Blank and her co-workers as well as those of the other investigations employing the perceptual shift paradigm (Raab, Deutsch, and Friedman 1960; Katz and Deutsch 1963), considering their use of economically disadvantaged children as subjects. Thus the findings permit no conclusions regarding intermodal integration in disabled readers as they have been defined here.

6.4 INTERSENSORY AND INTRASENSORY LEARNING
The studies evaluating cross-modal transfer that have so far been examined have all employed tasks requiring processing at the level of short-term memory. Consequently, it is extremely difficult to be certain that reader group differences were not due to verbal encoding deficiencies or that at least some of the disparities on cross-modal transfer tasks were not due to attentional problems.

My associates and I therefore reasoned (Vellutino, Steger, and Pruzek, 1973) that a nonverbal *learning* task entailing the establishment of visual and auditory (V-A) equivalences might circumvent possible confounding due to verbal encoding and attentional problems; a learning task would minimize constraints imposed by short-term memory and would provide subjects with more than one exposure to V-A equivalents. In order to minimize effects of previous learning, novel designs, simple in form, were paired with simple vocalic responses that were devoid of phonetic or linguistic structure (a high or low hum, a cough, a whistle). As a control measure, paired associates were designed for visual-visual (V-V) and auditory-auditory (A-A) presentations. The stimuli for the V-V condition were simple designs, different from the ones employed in V-A learning. The stimuli for the A-A condition consisted of simple environmental sounds (presented by means of a tape recorder) paired with simple vocalic responses. Subjects (N = 30 each group) were poor and normal readers between the ages of 9 and 12 years and were carefully selected on the basis of all of the operational criteria outlined earlier.

We found no differences between poor and normal readers on either the intra- or inter-modality tasks. There was adequate variability on all three measures, so the results could not have been due to the difficulty of the tasks.

Because previous research findings suggested that reader group differences may be unique to situations involving verbal learning, the study was replicated (Vellutino, Steger, Harding, and Phillips 1975) with independent samples (ages 9 to 12 years) selected by identical selection procedures. The (nonverbal) V-A task was again utilized, but in lieu of the intramodal tasks, we substituted a visual-verbal (Vis-Verb) learning measure designed to simulate the process of sight word learning in reading. It consisted of two subtests administered in invariant sequence. The first was designed to approximate object naming (which takes place prior to reading) and paired cartoons and drawings with nonsense syllables: WIB, PEX, MOG, YAG (see figure 8.1.). The second subtest, administered directly after the first, was more akin to sight word learning and paired the nonsense syllables presented on the first task with (novel) letterlike script. Two groups of poor and normal readers in grades 4 through 6 (N = 30 each group) were randomly assigned to either the V-A or Vis-Verb condition.

The previous finding of *no* differences between poor and normal readers in (nonverbal) visual-auditory learning was replicated. For the Vis-Verb task, in contrast, there were significant differences in favor of the normal readers on both the picture-syllable and letter-syllable subtests. These results, along with the results of the earlier study, are contrary to the view that poor readers sustain basic deficiency in cross-modal transfer. They suggest instead that the learning problems experienced by these individuals may be especially evident in the acquisition of relationships that have verbal constituents.

Of particular interest in the second study is the observation that in learning to associate the novel visual stimuli with the nonsense syllables, poor readers substituted actual words for these syllables more often than the normals did. In contrast, the normal readers' response errors were more often unique combinations of the phonemes in particular nonsense syllables (the normal readers might have said /pog/ and /mex/ for *mog* and *pex,* respectively, whereas the poor readers might have said /fog/ and /peck/. These data indicate that poor readers may have inadequate ability to analyze and partition the phonetic elements of the words they hear, as some investigators have suggested (Shankweiler and Liberman 1972; Liberman et al. 1974).

A study by Rudel, Denckla, and Spalten (1976) also compared poor and normal readers on paired associate learning within and between modalities. These investigators had the two groups of 9-year-olds (N = 20 each group) associate Morse code patterns with their letter names, both types of stimuli being presented auditorily. Subjects were also asked to learn the names of Braille letters presented visually as well as tactually. Thus the within-modality condition involved auditory associates and the between-modality conditions involved visual-verbal and tactual-verbal associates. The performance of poor readers was below that of normals under all three conditions. The authors concluded that the results for the poor readers were not attributable to deficits either within or between modalities but rather to the overt or covert verbal requirements of the tasks, particularly name retrieval.

Such an interpretation is, of course, consonant with my own views on the basic difficulties experienced by poor readers in processing intersensory information. Unfortunately, the results of this study are tenuous because of sampling difficulties. Although the groups were equivalent with respect to age and sex, there was no uniformity in the selection measures. The poor readers all attended a special school for dyslexics and the normal readers were said to be reading at grade level or better, but no achievement criteria were presented. The range of IQ scores for poor readers is very wide (WISC, Verbal IQ = 74-110; Performance IQ = 71-136); for normal readers, scores are entirely missing. And there was no information about the socioeconomic and emotional status of the subjects. Thus one cannot be certain that group differences were not due to generalized learning difficulties, or other extraneous factors.

A final study assessing (nonverbal) intersensory integration in normal and poor readers was undertaken in our laboratory (Steger, Vellutino, and Meshoulam 1972). This study evaluates Birch's (1962) suggestion that intersensory deficits would be evident in learning involving not only the modalities that are most directly involved in reading but other sensory systems as well. In order to test this hypothesis, we compared dyslexic and normal readers on tactile-tactile and visual-tactile learning tasks and found no differences between the groups on either comparison. These findings, coupled with the results of the other studies employing learning rather than perceptual or short-term memory tasks, greatly undermine the intersensory deficit explanation of reading disability as defined by Birch and subsequent investigators.

6.5 INTERHEMISPHERIC TRANSFER
We will examine one final explanation of dyslexia under the general rubric of intersensory deficiency. According to this hypothesis intermodal disorder may result from dysfunction in the transmission of information between the two hemispheres of the brain. To be more specific, the implication is that there is particular difficulty in the transfer of information between the left hemisphere, which presumably supports verbal-linguistic functioning, and the right hemisphere, which is believed to be responsible for visual-spatial and other nonverbal functions. This idea emerges largely as an extrapolation from the split-brain studies of Sperry and his associates (Sperry 1964; Gazzaniga, Bogen, and Sperry 1965; Gazzaniga 1970) and the clinical findings of Geschwind and his co-workers in studies of neuropathological disorders in adults (Geschwind 1962, 1968; Geschwind and Fusillo 1966). Both groups of researchers found evidence that lesions at the level of the mid-brain resulted in specific reading difficulties. These difficulties were thought to be a consequence of faulty transmission of visual information across the corpus callosum to the left

(or language) hemisphere. Of particular interest here are the observations of Sperry's group that when split-brain patients were presented with letter and word stimuli exclusively to the right hemisphere, they could not identify them verbally; yet they had no difficulty in copying them. The same stimuli could readily be identified verbally if they were presented exclusively to the left hemisphere (where language functions are concentrated). Similarly, Geschwind and Fusillo found that patients who had suffered damage to the splenium of the corpus callosum could reproduce letters and words graphically but could not readily name them.

These findings are analogous to data obtained in some of the studies conducted in our own laboratory (Vellutino, Steger, and Kandel, 1972; Vellutino, Smith, Steger, and Kaman, 1975). In our investigations the performance of poor readers was better on visual reproduction of letter and word stimuli than on verbal identification of the same stimuli. Although the work of Sperry's and of Geschwind's groups differs from our own with respect to procedures, purposes, and rationale, their results, along with the results of research by Milner (1971), Crowder (1972), and Posner, Lewis, and Conrad (1972), are consistent with the thesis that the visual and linguistic components of printed words are stored differentially, in the right and left hemispheres respectively. If so, then it is conceivable that many of the difficulties encountered by dyslexics in learning to read are in some measure attributable to dysfunction in interhemispheric coordination, perhaps as a result of some developmental anomaly affecting normal transmission. The logical extension of this hypothesis is that *intra*-modality functioning in poor readers would be essentially normal in activities that do not require intercoordination of information stored in the two hemispheres.

In order to evaluate this hypothesis we presented novel symbols (Chinese ideographs) paired with common English words *(house, mother)* to carefully selected samples of poor and normal readers in grades 2 and 6 (Vellutino, Bentley, and Phillips 1978). Stimuli were presented randomly to the right visual field (left hemisphere) or the left visual field (right hemisphere) or, as a control measure, to a central fixation point. In line with an inferred transmission disorder, it was predicted that poor readers would have more difficulty than normals in visual-verbal learning supported unilaterally by the right hemisphere. It was expected further that the groups would not be differentiated in presentations to the left hemisphere and central fixation point. The results did *not* support the hypothesis. Poor readers at both grade levels were less able than normals in all visual field presentations. These differences were not thought to be due to general learning problems in our sample of poor readers, because in previous studies comparably selected samples had differed from normals only on learning tasks involving a *verbal* component (Vellutino, Steger, and Pruzek 1973; Steger et al. 1972; Vellutino, Harding, Phillips, and Steger 1975; Vellutino, Steger, Harding, and Phillips 1975). Instead, we suggested that the disparities observed between the reader groups on the experimental tasks may have been due to verbal-linguistic deficiencies in poor readers. This interpretation was thought to be plausible in that the stimuli to be recalled were presented auditorily and were therefore processed by the left hemisphere. However, since this study is (to my knowledge) the first of its kind employing a population of disabled readers as presently defined, I would prefer to adopt a conservative view and say only that the transmission deficit explanation of reading disability merits further research. Indeed, one other study addressed the possibility of transmission deficiency as a cause of reading disability and obtained positive, though equivocal, results. Yeni-Komshian, Isenberg, and Goldberg (1975) found that poor readers made significantly more identification errors than normal readers in left versus right visual field presentations of numerals and numbers spelled out in words. Yet on dichotic listening tasks the two groups manifested no differences in lateral preference, as reflected in parallel tendencies to recall digits presented to the right ear (left hemisphere) more accurately than digits presented to the left ear (right hemisphere). From this, the authors inferred that poor readers may not be lateralized any less than normal readers (contrary to Orton's theory) and conjectured that reading disability may be due either to a right hemisphere deficiency or to dysfunction in interhemispheric transmission. These findings must be considered tentative, however, since the samples were selected on the basis of weak criteria of reading disability. Furthermore, normal readers performed significantly better than poor readers on *all* tasks. Thus the visual field differences between the groups could be due to sampling error. Nevertheless, the data are suggestive and the study is worth repeating with more stringent sampling criteria.

6.6 SUMMARY AND CONCLUSIONS

Having reviewed most of the important studies of the past ten to fifteen years, I can say with some degree of assurance that there is no conclusive evidence to support the intersensory deficit explanation of reading disability. The theory can be questioned on both empirical and theoretical grounds, and in neither context does it fare very well.

Almost all of the studies bearing on the model of information processing illustrated in figure 4.1 employed tasks that rely heavily upon attention and memory, and in very few cases were attempts made to control for these factors. This was particularly true of studies using ordered recall, a process that especially taxes short-term memory. Consequently, it is difficult to be certain that reader group differences are not attributable to disparities in perceptual set or response bias, encoding difficulties, rehearsal strategies, or any or all variables that may have influenced a subject's ability to retain information long enough to transfer it to permanent memory. It might also be pointed out that a sizable number of studies employed match-to-sample procedures to evaluate cross-modal transfer, often requiring that subjects remember the standard while surveying a large number of alternatives for the correct response. Such procedures may tax memory even when the standard is in full view; it is certain that they are more problematic when matching stimuli must be memorized. Thus it seems highly probable that most if not all of the studies employing match-to-sample techniques were confounded by memorial or attentional factors.

Another problem characteristic of many of the investigations discussed is the failure to control for intramodal differences in poor and normal readers. Bryant makes a convincing case that the results of most of the early studies dealing with cross-modal transfer (Birch's, in particular) are invalidated because of this deficiency in research design. The findings of investigations that did control for intramodal differences in reader groups tend to support Bryant's contention.

Bryant (1974) raises two additional questions that are worth mentioning here. First, he points out that an adequate demonstration that poor readers have difficulty in making judgments of sensory equivalence would necessitate an experimental design involving contrasts of poor and normal readers on three kinds of information: (1) visual and spatial patterns, (2) visual and temporal sequences, and (3) auditory and temporal sequences. These patterns could then be employed in every possible combination involving both intramodal and intermodal judgments. Recall that Bryden (1972) conducted just this type of study and found differences between poor and normal readers in judging sensory equivalence in the case of all of the patterns presented. These findings, of course, further undermine the notion that poor readers may be deficient in cross-modal transfer. They suggest instead that poor readers may be less proficient than normal readers in coding information for temporary storage in short-term memory, a possibility Bryden himself mentions.

The second point made by Bryant is that the results of all of the studies comparing poor and normal readers' judgments of cross-modal equivalence may be irrelevant to an understanding of reading, inasmuch as learning to read does not require that the individual perceive what Bryant calls natural or universal sensory equivalence (1974, 210). It does, however, necessitate the learning of quite arbitrary cross-modal associations, which according to Bryant may constitute a qualitatively different process from judging sensory equivalence in the strict sense. This seems to be a valid distinction, which would of course obviate most of the research conducted in this area.

Inadequate sampling procedures further equivocate the results of many of the studies reviewed. This applies to several investigations providing evidence against the intersensory deficit explanation of reading disability as well as those supporting the hypothesis. It does not seem unreasonable to propose, in this connection, that the results of several of our own studies provide the most definitive evidence against deficiencies in cross-modal transfer as a basic cause of reading disability (Steger et al. 1972; Vellutino et al. 1973; Vellutino, Harding, Phillips, and Steger 1975; Vellutino, Steger, Harding, and Phillips 1975). Our investigations were designed especially to control for (short-term) memory and attention factors, as well as for possible deficiencies in intramodal functioning. In keeping with the point made by Bryant, they also entailed the pairing of arbitrary (cross-modal) associates and therefore constituted a more direct test of the type of intersensory integration that may be involved in learning to read than studies contrasting reader groups on judgments involving natural sensory equivalents. In addition, our sample selection in all instances was in close accord with the operational criteria outlined earlier. The consistent finding in all of these studies was the observation of no differences between poor and normal readers on nonverbal intersensory learning tasks. In contrast, the groups were differentiated on cross-modal tasks that included verbal components. These data indicate that reading disability may be related either to verbal skill deficiencies or to dysfunction specifically associated with the coordination of visual and verbal information, but probably not to cross-modal transfer as defined initially by Birch (1962).

Aside from its failure to derive unequivocal support from the studies conducted to date, Birch's intersensory deficit explanation of dyslexia can be questioned on the basis of its theoretical foundations. Birch assumed that increased liaison among the various sense modalities is age related and occurs conjointly with hierarchical ordering of the sensory systems. Therefore, given sense modalities were thought to have a superordinate role in establishing cross-modal equivalence, not unlike a tutorial or monitoring function whereby one system "teaches" another. However, as pointed out by Friedes (1974) in an extensive review of the literature dealing with cross-modal transfer, there is no convincing support for Birch's theory of sensory dominance. Friedes suggests instead that given modalities are inherently equipped and thus have greater utility than others for processing certain types of information. He further suggests that intersensory integration, during the course of development, probably involves learning to translate information received by one modality into a form appropriate for the modality most adept at processing the information. Friedes reviewed a number of studies that document his position; the research done by Pick is especially worthy of mention. Pick has conducted a series of studies investigating the interaction of sense modalities in effecting perceptual judgments. Adopting a position similar to that of Friedes, Pick (1970) contends that intersensory integration is a unique function of the particular modalities interacting in the development of any perceptual-motor skill. For example, he presents evidence that perception of auditory location is more accurate when monitored by visual information, and he suggests, in explanation of this phenomenon, that all decisions as to location in space entail visual encoding, regardless of sensory pick-up, since the visual system seems best able to facilitate such decisions. Pick reports a series of studies wherein subjects were presented discrepant sensory information and then asked to make perceptual judgments based on the interaction of the two modalities. The major objective of these studies was to investigate the degree to which one type of (sensory) information would supersede another in biasing these judgments. For example, it was found that when someone views his own finger through a wedge prism (in which case the position of the finger is optically distorted), vision biases proprioception in that the subject "locates" his finger closer to the source of the optical position than to the true position. The important observation in the present context is that no sensory system was found to dominate given judgments at any age level. The domination of one system over the other was always determined by the nature of the task, in interaction with the particular modalities involved. Furthermore, it was not possible to predict the interaction of two modalities knowing how each interacted with a third. Such findings would appear to raise serious questions about whether sensory dominance plays any role in the development of intersensory integration as suggested by Birch (Birch and Lefford 1963).

In contrast to Birch's views, Pick suggests that "complex integrated activities" (to which he applies the term *systems*) are determined by general rules and principles that may transcend relations between specific sensory modalities. For example, detecting the invariant relationships existing in temporal patterns presented in more than one modality would seem to be a higher-level function that has little to do with the modalities themselves. Pick's formulations are in close accord with the position taken by Gibson (1969), who suggests that apparent intermodal effects may in fact be determined by amodal information of a higher order and invariant nature. Such information is not believed to be modality-specific and is said to have reference to properties and relations that are not unique to any sensory system. Gibson points out, for example, that the specific properties of the color blue cannot be represented by other than the visual modality, but the property of jerkiness can be readily represented in one modality or another. Gibson deemphasizes the unique qualities of given modalities in intersensory functioning and questions separatist theories, such as Birch's, which suggest that the sense modalities are originally insular and become integrated during the course of development. She also questions the mediating or dominant roles that such theories ascribe to particular modalities in fostering intersensory integration and cognitive development generally.[2]

Finally, Connolly and Jones (1970; Jones and Connolly 1970) adopting a rather pragmatic view, hypothesize that intersensory integration relates to the requirements of the task, but like Pick and Friedes they stress the differential utility of specific modalities for processing given types of information. And, in two very informative publications Goodnow (1971a, 1971b) emphasizes both the conceptual and the experiential aspects of cross-modal transfer, clearly rejecting the idea of hierarchical arrangements among modalities. She provides some useful suggestions to help account for the variability in results characteristic of the cross-modal transfer studies, memory factors and differential sampling of stimulus properties being the two variables earmarked as having the most influence.

It would seem that the intersensory deficit theory of reading disability as originally articulated by Birch (1962) is seriously questioned, if not contraindicated by the weight of both empirical and theoretical evidence. Although differences between poor and normal readers on a variety of cross-modal transfer tasks seem well established, the reasons for those differences are not clear. A number of other possible explanations have been advanced, but the two most often cited as alternatives are dysfunction in serial order recall and deficiencies in verbal processing. In chapter 7 we will review the evidence for the theory that poor readers are characterized by basic deficits in the ordering of serial information.

The possibility that dysfunction in serializing information may be a basic cause of reading disability has long had a great deal of appeal among diagnosticians working with children who have difficulty learning to read and spell. Clinicians and educators commonly suggest that deficiencies in visual or auditory sequencing are characteristic of such children. Their suggestions are generally based on anecdotal and clinical evidence, and typically refer to youngsters who manifest apparent difficulties in serial order recall of information encountered in the natural setting. Indicators of serialization disorder given particular accord by members of this group include phoneme reversals in articulate speech (saying /ephelant/ for *elephant*), sequence errors in oral and written spelling, difficulty on a variety of activities encountered in school learning such as reciting the alphabet or ordering the days of the week and months of the year, and difficulty on more formal measures of sequencing ability, which often involve memory for words, sentences, digits, objects, and designs presented auditorily or visually. Such observations have led to pointed hypotheses that dyslexia is caused by neurological dysfunction resulting in modality-specific sequencing disability unique to either the auditory or visual systems (Johnson and Myklebust 1967; Kirk and McCarthy, 1968; Kolers 1970; Bannatyne 1971; Kirk and Kirk 1971).

Notwithstanding the suggestive evidence provided by informal observation and clinical assessment, serial deficit explanations of reading disability have not, by and large, been formalized and evaluated in the laboratory. Indeed clearly articulated and substantive theories citing serializing deficiencies as underlying causes of reading disorder are not in abundance, and the number of studies dealing specifically with the problem is meager. Clinical accounts are uniformly descriptive, providing little specification as to the relation between inferred deficiencies in serial processing and difficulties in learning to read. And whereas several authors have found significant disparities between poor and normal readers on a variety of serial order tasks only one—Bakker (1972)—has, to my knowledge, advanced a theory of dyslexia that specifically earmarks a sequencing deficit in poor readers as the basic cause of the disorder: specifically, dysfunction in "temporal order perception." Before examining the evidence for serial ordering difficulties in poor readers, it might be useful to review Bakker's theory.

Bakker (1972) accords entity status to temporal order perception and suggests that the ability to perceive and thereby explicate a sequence of events is centrally derived. The latter suggestion was based in part upon the work of Hirsh (1959) and Hirsh and Sherrick (1961), who demonstrated that adult subjects required an interstimulus interval of about 20 milliseconds to detect a succession of two tones. Since the interval did not vary across a variety of stimuli, they concluded that the effect was due to central processing mechanisms. Hirsh (1966) later suggested that speech perception is, in part, determined by the listener's ability to distinguish the order in which phonemes within words are perceived (as in *tacks* versus *task*) and that some individuals may have difficulty in making such distinctions because of dysfunction in the speed of processing acoustic stimuli.

Coupling these observations with the work of Efron (1963) and Milner (1962, 1967), who provided evidence for hemispheric specialization in temporal sequencing, Bakker concluded that temporal order perception takes place in the left hemisphere for verbal stimuli and in the right hemisphere for nonverbal stimuli. By extension, he suggested that the ultimate cause of reading disability is dysfunction in the left or language hemisphere, resulting in deficiency in temporal order perception of verbal stimuli, the implication being that a defect analogous to that proposed by Hirsh may be present in disabled readers. However, Bakker was careful to distinguish this anomaly from language disorder and verbal labeling problems: "Reading-disturbed children do not seem to present any verbal labeling problems nor any temporal ordering problems as such but difficulties which occur 'when verbal items are presented in a time scheme'" (1972, 96). "In other words, the interaction between time and verbal code is disturbed and not so much the main factors" (1972, 67).

In support of his theory Bakker cited the results of several cross-modal transfer studies (Birch and Belmont 1964, 1965; Blank et al. 1966, 1968; Senf 1969) and two of his own earlier investigations (Bakker 1967; Groenedaal and Bakker 1971). The cross-modal transfer studies have typically found differences between poor and normal readers on temporal ordering in both the auditory and visual modalities. Yet the degree to which these differences may be due to malfunction in temporal order perception or to some other factors is open to question.

Interestingly enough, Bakker's early formulations were in concert with Blank's suggestion that temporal order deficits in poor readers are associated with verbal mediation problems (Blank et al. 1966, 1968). In an initial exploration of these relations Bakker (1967) had found that poor readers made more errors than normals on the sequencing of meaningful figures and letters, whereas, in contrast, the groups did not differ in ordering nonverbal stimuli that had no standard or uniform meaning. He had concluded from these results that the disparities were due to reader group differences in verbal mediation ability. A similar conclusion was reached by Groenendaal and Bakker (1971). Since this study and Bakker's Monograph (1972) on temporal order perception were published in close succession, it is curious that the author modified his earlier suggestion that verbal mediation deficits are associated with reading disability. We will look briefly at the studies conducted by Bakker, as reported in the monograph, since their results were offered as primary support for the theory that dyslexia results from a dysfunction in the perception of temporal order.

The first of these investigations provided some evidence for age differences in sequential ordering. A randomly selected population (N = 412) of primary grade children (mean age = 6.3), approximately half boys and half girls, were given serial presentations of pictures of common objects and asked to recall the order in which they were presented. The number of items in a given series varied and there were two different types of presentations: *visual-visual* (V-V) and *visual-auditory* (V-A). Under the V-V condition subjects named the pictures aloud, again in order. Stimulus durations and interstimulus intervals were constant at about 2 seconds each.

Although the V-V condition produced significant differences in performance at two age levels (6.0 and 6.5), the magnitudes of the differences were not striking; there were no other main effects nor any significant interactions. The V-A task, on the other hand, produced more definitive divergence between these age groups and yielded significant sex disparities in favor of the girls. The study was replicated annually over a two-year period with similar results, except that there was no age x sex interaction. Reading scores at the later ages were correlated with scores on both temporal ordering tasks at age six and on the first and second replications. Intelligence scores were also related to these variables. The temporal measures in combination were found to account for 16 to 18 percent of the variance in reading scores; IQ alone accounted for approximately the same percentage. But IQ was also related to the temporal variables, and after IQ was controlled, only 4 percent (approximately) of the variance in reading ability was determined by the temporal order measures. In spite of the low relations between these variables, Bakker concluded that temporal ordering ability at the preschool level is significantly related to reading achievement.

A second study reported in the Bakker (1972) monograph compared normal boys and girls (N = 100) with disabled readers, both groups being of at least average intelligence. The normals varied in age from 7 to 11 years, the disabled readers from 9 to 13 years. All subjects were given serial presentations of 48 sets of letters, three in a set; 16 sets were presented visually, 16 *auditorily*, and 16 *tactually*. The subjects' task was to indicate order of presentation for two of the three letters in a set. The sets were composed of varying combinations of the letters C, D, G, K, V, X, and Z.

In general, the older subjects performed better than the younger ones. Among the 7- and 8-year-olds, girls performed better than boys, but this was not true at later ages. The poor readers did not perform as well as the normals on any of the serial order tasks; neither did they improve their performance as much with age as did the normals. However, reading ability was not consistently correlated with temporal order recall under all modality conditions:

For the normal readers these two variables were related in auditory and tactual presentations but not under the visual conditions; for the poor readers they were related only in auditory presentations. Because of a significant relation between IQ scores and the sequencing tasks, 14 boys from each reader group, matched for IQ, were compared for temporal order recall. The two groups were still found to differ.

Interestingly enough no relations were found between temporal ordering and reading measures in any of the girls' groups. Bakker interpreted this finding as evidence for a "critical" period for such a relation. That is, since girls presumably mature more rapidly than boys in language and other skills related to reading, he reasoned that they might be expected to manifest "temporal order-reading relationships" sooner than boys.

The results obtained in this study are quite variable and therefore constitute only weak evidence for dysfunction in serial recall as a cause of reading disability. Furthermore, the interpretation of the reader group difference is debatable in that temporal order recall may have been influenced to some extent by letter naming difficulties, a possibility in deficient readers even at upper age levels: Recall that Denckla and Rudel (1976a, 1976b) found that poor readers had longer reaction times than normal readers in rapid automatic naming of letters, words, common objects, and other items they could correctly label under normal circumstances. If the poor readers in Bakker's 1972 study were characterized by similar difficulty, apparent order errors might be more accurately attributed to short-term memory problems associated with inefficient encoding.

I will have more to say about the validity of Bakker's theory of dyslexia after reviewing a number of other studies relating serial recall to reading ability.

We have already examined several investigations comparing poor and normal readers on a variety of tests of cross-modal transfer. Many of those studies included experimental measures of serial order, and the majority of them found differences between poor and normal readers on those measures, although interpretations of the results varied. A similar picture emerges in studies specifically designed to assess sequencing ability.

Zurif and Carson (1970) compared carefully selected samples of dyslexic and normal readers (fourth-graders) on a variety of temporal order tasks, including rhythmic patterns presented both visually and auditorily, auditory-visual integration, and dichotic listening for digits (see Kimura 1963). The poor readers made more errors than the normals on all these measures. Reading achievement correlated significantly with all tests of temporal order recall as well as with the dichotic listening tasks; what is more, these measures were significantly related to one another. The authors interpreted the findings as possible evidence that dyslexia is related to "general language disturbances." As an alternative possibility, they suggested that "subtle deficits in temporal processing do not sufficiently alter speech for the change to be noticeable, but adversely affect the process of learning to read by preventing the critical formation of spelling to sound correspondences" (Zurif and Carson 1970, 359). They concluded that it is quite likely that "developmental dyslexia" is associated with difficulty in apprehending temporal order but probably not with cross-modal transfer as might be suggested by the reader group differences found in processing auditory-visual sequences.

The results of the study by Bryden (1972), mentioned earlier, reinforce these findings. Recall that in Bryden's study, poor and normal readers were administered all possible combinations of visual, auditory, and spatial patterns. The performance of poor readers was below that of normals on all of the variables assessed. Moderately high correlations were found between reading ability and the matching tasks *only* in the poor readers, not in the normals, and there was considerable overlap in the reader groups on the experimental tasks. Bryden concluded that the most extremely impaired readers in the sample may have been qualitatively different from the others in that group and may have been supporting general language deficits, which contibuted to reader group differences in pattern matching.

Senf and Freundl (1972) also compared normal and disabled readers on auditory and visual sequential memory. Commenting on the widespread use of the WISC Digit Span subtest in studies comparing reader groups on serial order recall, they underscored the limited usefulness of the test, as constituted, because of the restricted ranges of the scores it typically yields. In order to circumvent this difficulty they designed a modified version of the Digit Span Test with additional items. Presentations were counterbalanced for modality, and subjects were asked

to recall the digits in correct order immediately after each presentation.

The preformance of poor readers was below that of normals on
gross (item) memory, but the groups were not distinguished on
memory for the sequences in which the items occurred. Increasing
trial length more adversely affected the poor readers than the normals. Order errors were more numerous in both groups than gross
errors and were inflated with increases in length of items on given
trials. Visual presentations produced more errors than auditory
presentations, these effects being constant across reader groups.

Senf and Freundl provided no firm explanation of their results
except to point out that the difficulties in serial order recall
characterizing poor readers in this study were evident in both the
visual and auditory modalities. They also noted that the reader
groups manifested rather large differences in gross memory but
not in ordered recall, contrary to findings in earlier studies by Senf
and his associates (section 6.2). This inconsistency suggested that
deficient serial processing was *not* the poor reader's typical performance pattern; instead, poor readers may have been subject to
occasional lapses of attention during which they made a large
number of errors, at other times performing as well as normals.
From these findings they inferred that a central processing deficiency may account for reader group differences rather than
dysfunction in sensory reception or stimulus encoding. Attentional disorder in poor readers was singled out as a possible explanation of observed reader group differences.

Senf and Freundl make the interesting suggestion that gross and
ordered recall, though operationally distinguishable, "may not
reflect different processes" (1972, 512) and may draw upon the
same limited capacity system (see Crossman 1960). They indicate
further that the inconsistent findings that characterized their
comparisons of poor and normal readers on gross and ordered
recall (Senf 1969; Senf and Freundl 1971) may reflect different
response styles of the subjects in given samples rather than differences in sequential ordering ability. The implication is that
temporal order recall is not supported by a unique and different
memory system or capacity but rather by a process characterized
by organizational and rehearsal strategies which differ from those
characteristic of gross memory. This is an important distinction
and will be discussed in greater detail.

A more recent study finding serial order deficits in poor readers was reported by Corkin (1974). Poor and normal readers at three age levels (6-7, 8-9, 10-11) were differentiated on tests of spatial ordering (tapping blocks) under conditions of delayed (6 seconds) recall. The groups were also found to differ on auditory sequencing of digits. Performance on these measures increased with age for both poor and normal readers. Corkin concluded that the results were not attributable to attentional deficits since the groups did not differ when presented with the spatial tasks under immediate recall conditions: "Reading disorders in children may in part grow out of a more general deficit in serial organization that cuts across sensory modalities and stimulus materials" (1974, 353). Mnemonic rather than ordering factors were also considered as possible causes of reader group differences.

Aside from the fact that Corkin's interpretations can be questioned on theoretical grounds, her results are tenuous owing to the fact that reading ability was assessed by teacher judgments rather than by reading achievement measures. Also problematic was the use of a test of intelligence that in part involved reading. Not surprisingly, the poor readers did not perform as well as the normals on this measure. Thus although reader group differences could have been due to intellectual factors, this possibility could not be determined. An additional weakness of the study was the very small number of subjects in each cell (N = 8).

An investigation by Kastner and Rickards (1974) was specifically concerned with the use of verbal mediation in the serial order recall of poor and normal readers. Twelve third-graders were in each reader group. Reading achievement was measured by a group test of silent reading ability. Children scoring at or below the 25th percentile were designated as poor readers, those scoring at or above the 75th percentile were designated as normal readers. Intelligence was determined by the collective judgments of teachers and other school personnel.

The experimental task was taken from the mediational studies designed by Flavell, Beach, and Chinsky (1966). Subjects were presented with small wooden blocks on which were printed either familiar or novel stimuli. The subject's task was to indicate, after a delay of 15 seconds, the precise order in which the examiner had touched each stimulus. Directly following administration of all test stimuli, subjects were asked a number of questions pertaining to their rehearsal and encoding strategies. The final task required that subjects name each of the novel stimulus blocks; naming latency was recorded.

In accord with expectations, normal readers made fewer errors than poor readers in serial recall involving the novel stimuli, but these groups were not found to be different in recall involving the familiar stimuli. None of the poor readers reported any inclination to employ a verbal rehearsal strategy, whereas eight of the twelve normal readers did report the use of such strategies. It is especially interesting, in this connection, that poor readers had slower reaction times in naming the novel stimuli than did the normal readers. Kastner and Rickards concluded that poor readers are less apt to employ verbal encoding strategies for mediated recall than are normal readers, particularly with novel or more abstract stimuli. They also suggested, in line with Blank et al. (1966, 1968), that poor readers may be "deficient in aspects of symbolic representation, specifically in employing verbal codes" (1974, 111).

Because of the authors' failure to control for intelligence, the findings are equivocal. The reading measure employed was also questionable. In addition, inquiring as to a subject's encoding strategies is a rather weak approach for evaluation of trends of this sort. However, the reader group differences in naming the novel stimuli are consistent with the possibility of verbal encoding deficiencies in poor readers and are in accord with work done elsewhere. Nevertheless, because of methodological weaknesses Kastner and Rickards's conclusions must be accepted with reservation.

A study by Davis and Bray (1975) compared poor and normal readers on memory for item and order information employing a modification of the bisensory recall task used earlier by Senf. Davis and Bray suggested that the differences found between reader groups on order versus item errors in the Senf studies may have been confounded by the failure to control for possible interference from multiple recall attempts, considering that *all* items were tested on these trials. The inference is that poor readers may have had more difficulty than normal readers in serial ordering because of output interference rather than from the organization of order information per se. Senf's results were also thought to be contaminated by his measure of order error (order errors as a percentage of total number of errors), given that the total error score included errors of omission and intrusion.

In an attempt to control for output interference, Davis and Bray employed simultaneous presentations of auditory and visual stimuli, as did Senf. Children in each of the groups (N = 24 each group) were presented with a recall probe directly after every trial, and each child was required to report only two of the six digits on that trial. Subjects were asked to recall the auditory-visual stimuli in pairs as well as in isolation (within a modality), and both item and order errors were recorded. Poor readers made more errors than normals on both item and order measures, and both groups made more errors on pair-order recall than on modality recall. Since there were no significant reader group by condition interactions on either item or order measures, the authors concluded that poor readers may not have more difficulty than normals in the organization of serial information but may be generally more deficient in processing information at the level of short-term memory.

These data are, of course, contrary to the suggestion that poor readers are characterized by a specific deficiency in serial ordering. However, the authors employed no uniform criterion of intelligence and used a very liberal criterion for selecting poor readers (below the 45th percentile on a measure of silent reading). Furthermore, there was a relatively large age range among the subjects (7.0 to 10.5 years), the sample was not stratified, and the number of subjects at each age level is not indicated. Therefore the results are tenuous and may not be applicable to the population of poor readers as defined in the present context.

Virtually all of the studies so far reviewed found some differences between poor and normal readers in serial order recall. An investigation by Weiner, Barnsley, and Rabinovitch (1970) found none, however. These investigators presented poor and normal readers with nonverbal measures of visual, auditory, and tactual sequencing, requiring subjects to match the order of items in given standards from memory. The same stimuli were also matched simultaneously. There were no differences between poor and normal readers on any of the measures administered.

The authors interpreted their findings cautiously, indicating that the duration of their presentations (6.75 seconds) may not have been brief enough to differentiate the groups. Perhaps a more plausible explanation of the failure to find group differences is that the poor readers in this study may have been intellectually more capable than the normal readers. Although the group mean IQ scores were not significantly different, the ranges for the two groups differed widely (poor readers IQ = 94 - 126; normal readers IQ = 90 - 108). It is therefore conceivable that the ability of some of the brighter poor readers carried undue weight on the tasks employed.

Finally, certain of our own findings militate against both visual sequential and generalized sequencing deficit explanations of reading disability (Vellutino et al. 1972, 1973; Vellutino, Steger, Kaman, and DeSetto 1975; Vellutino, Smith, Steger, and Kaman 1975). In comparisons of poor and normal readers on immediate visual recall of both familiar and novel visual stimuli (English words, Hebrew words, Roman letters, numbers, and geometric designs) we found no significant differences between these groups on the graphic reproduction of any stimuli, except when the number of items in a given stimulus began to tax the upper limits of visual short-term memory (five-letter words). Since credit was given only if items were reproduced in correct order, we may reasonably suggest that the poor readers in these studies were not characterized either by serial processing deficits of a general nature or by dysfunction in the sequencing of a visual-spatial layout. Instead, the results afford indirect evidence for the possibility that difficulties in both order and item memory would occur when material that taxes capacity limits is not coded and chinked into more economical units for storage in short-term memory. Such a possibility has of course been a confounding variable in many of the studies reviewed here and appears to have been operative in a number of investigations contrasting poor and normal readers on measures involving serial order recall.

7.1 SUMMARY AND CONCLUSIONS

The studies examined in this chapter, along with many reviewed in connection with the intersensory deficit theory of reading disability, are uniform in the finding that poor readers differ from normal readers in serial order recall of various types of sensory stimuli, regardless of the modality in which stimuli are presented. The difference is particularly salient when the amount of information to be recalled taxes short-term memory (Senf 1969; Senf and Freundl 1971, 1972).

The interpretation most often offered in explanation of these findings is debatable, however. There is reason to question the suggestion of Bakker (1972) and others (Doehring 1968; Zurif and Carson 1970; Bannatyne 1971; Corkin 1974) that poor readers sustain either a specific deficiency in temporal order processing or a generalized deficiency in sequencing ability. The assumption implicit in all these suggestions is that the (respective) structures and functions involved in serial order recall and in item recall constitute separate entities in the central nervous system—which seems to be an implausible conceptualization of memory, given what is now known about human information processing. .

Some investigators not only disagree with the view that order and item recall reflect different neurologic entities, but also reject the notion that the two types of processes are operationally distinguishable. Conrad (1964, 1965), perhaps the strongest advocate of this position, contends that order errors are in fact item intrusion errors that are determined by the particular content of the items themselves. More specifically, he suggests that items presented in sequence are stored in the same order in which they were perceived (not necessarily the order of presentation) and would be recalled in that order if they were still available in short-term memory. The failure to recall items in correct sequence is attributed to a decay process characterized specifically by the loss of information about particular features or properties of the items. This generates the prediction that transposition or order errors would be more likely with items that have similar properties than with items that are dissimilar. And Conrad has indeed found that (visually presented) letters that sound alike occasion more transposition errors (CB for BC) than letters with no sound similarities, from which he concludes that serial order and item recall are interdependent rather than independent functions. The ultimate demonstration of the validity of a theory of memory such as Conrad's would, of course, obviate theories of reading disability that distinguish between gross and serial recall. But Conrad's formulations have not been universally accepted either.

Other theorists have suggested that the items of a given array and the order in which they occur might be coded differently. For example Brown (1958) and Crossman (1960) are in general agreement that item and order information are separable components of the same limited-capacity system, and that the recall of either from short-term memory necessitates a trade-off whereby one component is retrieved at the expense of the other. Similarly, Estes (1972) hypothesizes that a representation incorporating both content and sequence is stored at the time of input but that the two types of information are processed differently in short-term memory. In direct contrast to Conrad's position, Estes "assumes that the loss of order information is primary and the loss of item information is derivative" (1972, 180).[1]

Empirical support for the possibility that item and order information are separable emanates from the work of Healy and her associates (Bjork and Healy 1974; Healy 1974, 1975a, 1975b, 1977). Briefly, in these studies recall of the sequences in which items (letters and digits) occurred yielded bow-shaped serial-position curves when the items presented were held constant; in contrast, recall of specific items yielded functions that were flatter and more linear when the sequences in which the items occurred were held constant. Moreover, the likelihood that two items would be transposed (interchanged sequentially) was dependent not only upon the degree to which they were similar but also upon the distance between them. This finding is not entirely consistent with Conrad's suggestion that transposition errors are intrusions from items with similar properties. Healy therefore concluded that theories such as Estes's, which distinguish between item and order information, are better able to explain her findings than theories such as Conrad's, which do not make this distinction.

Although the issue of how item and order information are processed in memory remains unsettled, there is no compelling reason to believe that these two types of representation are supported by distinct neurological systems. It seems more likely that a variety of cognitive functions may be employed in storing and retrieving representations of both content and sequence and that particular functions may be involved in processing information of both types. Of special interest with regard to this contention are Healy's observations that the coding devices employed to recall the order in which specific items occurred depended largely upon the nature of the material to be serialized (1974, 1975a, 1977). She also found support for the possibility that alternate or multiple codes may be applied to such tasks when the need arises: whereas phonemic coding was generally employed in temporal order recall tasks, temporal-spatial pattern codes (patterns contained in the material) were employed in spatial order recall as well as in situations where phonemic coding was disrupted; and in the recall of more complex material both phonemic and pattern codes were frequently employed (1977). these findings are significant in that they emphasize the multiform processing involved in memory for various types of serial information as well as the flexibility of the human information processor in storing and retrieving such information.

Of more general significance in relation to the study of dyslexia, are two implications of Healy's observations: (1) there are apparently no invariant means by which we process serial information of a given type and (2) we do not appear to be equipped with a general ability or capacity for ordering such information. Even though there may be habitual or constrained methods of learning specific sequential relationships (melodic sequences depend upon the auditory modality), the individual has considerable latitude in the devices he employs to encode and organize material for both gross and ordered recall. It would therefore seem to be an oversimplification to suggest, explicitly or implicitly, that distinct neurological systems are responsible for processing information of each type. This conclusion carries with it the assumption that difficulty in remembering one type of information implies difficulty in remembering the other. By extension, theories of reading disability that identify select deficiencies in serial processing (but with gross memory intact) as the major problem area in poor readers are questionable. It is important to emphasize, in this connection, that in almost all of the studies reviewed in this chapter[2] disabled readers were inferior to normal readers on both serial order and gross recall. And in all but one of the studies evaluating reader group differences in serial processing (Davis and Bray 1975), item and order information were confounded. (Indeed an adequate test of the notion that poor readers are deficient only in processing order information would entail a paradigm similar to the one employed by Healy wherein sequential memory was tested holding the items presented constant, and vice versa.) It is therefore likely that children with reading disability have difficulty in memory for given items as well as the order in which they occur.

The specific suggestion made by Bakker (1972) that dyslexics are characterized by deficiencies in temporal order perception can also be questioned on other grounds. In support of this theory, Bakker cited work done by Hirsh (1959) and his co-workers (Hirsh and Sherrick 1961), who had shown that perception of temporal order was not possible at durations shorter than 15 to 20 milliseconds. Since these effects did not vary with the nature of the stimuli, it was inferred that the ability to perceive temporal order is centrally derived. Integrating Hirsh's findings with the results of several studies demonstrating differences between poor and normal readers on serial order recall measures, Bakker formulated a theory of reading disability based on the assumption that poor and normal readers differ on general threshold for perception of temporal order. Yet the evidence that Bakker presented in support of his theory (other than Hirsh's results) is derived from studies that did *not* directly contrast poor and normal readers on temporal order perception, and none employed the type of methodology used by Hirsh (1959), Hirsh and Sherrick (1961), and others (Broadbent and Ladefoged 1959; Fay 1966; Warren 1974) to assess the perception of sequence at varying interstimulus intervals. In fact, all of the studies reported by Bakker, as well as all others reviewed in this chapter, have typically evaluated temporal order recall employing stimulus exposures (and interstimulus intervals) of duration longer than those employed in the studies by Hirsh (1958) and others (Hirsh and Sherrick 1961; Broadbent and Ladefoged 1959; Fay 1966; Warren 1974). Therefore, it seems reasonable to infer that investigations employing the longer durations compared temporal order recall in poor and normal readers at the level of short-term memory, and not at the perceptual level.[3] The likelihood is therefore great that reader group disparities on the serial recall tasks used in the Bakker studies and those reported herein were due to memory and encoding differences rather than to differences in temporal order perception.

An even more basic objection to Bakker's theory is that it appears to rest upon the assumption (following Hirsh) that the elements of an acoustic signal are processed discretely. There is, however, convincing evidence from research conducted by Liberman and his co-workers (1967) that speech perception does not occur as a result of analysis of individual phonemes and that such units may be perceived quite differently in different contexts. Furthermore, these authors have shown that there is no isomorphic relation between the phonologic components of the message perceived and particular segments of the acoustic stream; it appears instead that the speech signal is a complex code that is partly determined by the interrelations among particular phonetic elements that are contiguous. In addition, Liberman et al. provide considerable support for the view that perception of many of the sounds we hear (stop consonants, for instance) is categorical rather than continuous, an indication that speech perception is significantly influenced by higher-order structural principles that themselves are partly determined by variations in the linguistic environment. These findings raise serious questions about (if they do not obviate) conceptualizations such as Hirsh's (1959, 1966), which assume that the perception of speech depends upon the ability to determine the order in which discrete elements of the acoustic signal occur. Thus, by extension, they undermine the theory of reading disability articulated by Bakker, which apparently adopts the same assumption.

More recent evidence against the concept of a general threshold for perception of temporal order, as suggested by Hirsh, is provided by Warren and his associates, who have reported that it was not possible to perceive order within recycled sequences of three or four unrelated items (hiss, tone, buzz), even when each successive item lasted as long as 200 milliseconds (Warren 1968; Warren, Obusek, Farmer, and Warren 1969). These findings suggest that the perception of temporal order at short durations (perhaps in general) is directly related to a perceiver's ability to detect a larger pattern from which sequential information can be derived. A subsequent study by Warren (1974) verified this hypothesis and provided evidence that subjects can be trained to detect order in items presented for a few milliseconds duration, once the overall patterns created by such groupings are detected.

Warren (1974) suggested, in addition, that recall of serialized items of longer duration (250 msec and above) involves the assignment of verbal labels to successive items (as in counting). With extended sequences, organization, encoding, and rehearsal factors are cardinal determinants of serial order recall. It should be emphasized that this process takes place at the level of short-term memory and not at the level of immediate perception. These findings reinforce the remarks concerning the unnecessary distinction made by Bakker (1972) and others between neurological structures responsible for serial order and those responsible for gross recall, further weakening theories implicating deficits in serial processing.

Finally, each of the serial deficit explanations of reading disability discussed, as well as those that have appeared in the clinical literature (Johnson and Myklebust 1967; Bannatyne 1971; Kirk and McCarthy 1968; Kirk and Kirk 1971) can be criticized for failure to specify more clearly the relationships that presumably exist between hypothesized deficiencies in serial processing and deficiencies in reading and related skills. Such detail would seem to be critical, given that the expected correlates and extensions of an ordering deficit may vary, depending upon the way in which that deficit is conceptualized.

Hypotheses such as Bakker's, which suggest that the poor reader cannot perceive distinctions between phonemic sequences, generate predictions about reading behaviors that are different from predictions generated by hypotheses implicating dysfunction in either modality-specific ordering mechanisms (Johnson and Myklebust 1967; Kolers 1970) or nonspecific ordering mechanisms that transcend the sensory systems (Corkin 1974). A response of /taks/ to the printed word *task* tells us little of the derivation of the error, but a perceptual deficit explanation of this and like inaccuracies (saying /deks/ for *desk*) implies a close parallel between confusion in listening and confusion in word decoding, particularly for grapheme sequences that map invariantly onto given phoneme sequences, as in these examples.

On the other hand, a theory that ascribes sequencing deficiencies to dysfunction in the visual system might predict that /taks/ in response to *task,* would occur more often than /kats/ because the latter sequence would probably be more firmly associated with the printed word *cat,* which is distinguished graphically from the other two words. And in contradistinction to each of the other two possibilities, a theory that nonspecific ordering mechanisms are the source of sequencing difficulties leads to the expectation that /task/, /taks/, /akts/, /skat/, /kats/, and other possible combinations of these particular phonemes would be equiprobable responses. Differential predictions such as these have not been observed in accounts addressing the correlates in question, loose references to brain–behavior relations being the more commong characterization of these correlates.

However, even if they were characterized by greater specification of the type indicated, it is doubtful that the serial deficit
hypotheses that have appeared in the literature will ever be validated.

I have already critiqued Bakker's (1972) suggestion that reading
disability is caused by dysfunction in temporal order perception.
My skepticism is increased by the absence of any evidence whatsoever that poor readers actually experience difficulty in perceiving order in linguistic stimuli or that such difficulty—if it in
fact exists—has its parallel in any unique and discernible response
pattern in word decoding. Contrary to what Bakker's theory might
lead one to expect, there is reason to believe that errors in reading
are not isomorphic with errors in listening. Shankweiler and Liberman (1972) have reported results indicating that perception of
speech by reading and perception of speech by ear pose different
problems, and that response patterns observed under one of these
conditions could not readily forecast response patterns that may
be observed under the other. These results would seem to further
undermine the serial deficit theories in contention here.

That poor readers may be characterized by generalized deficiencies in serial processing (Corkin 1974) can be questioned on intuitive grounds. Such a theory inescapably rests on the assumption
that the nervous system is equipped with a serial processor that
records the order in which items are apprehended by given sensory
systems, an assumption that at once oversimplifies a very complex
and little understood aspect of memory and insulates itself from
disproof. The theory does not therefore facilitate specification
of the relation between serial processing and reading ability, nor
does it move us toward an ultimate understanding of the nature of
reading disability.

Whereas the notion of a generalized sequencing deficit is apparently an oversimplification, just the reverse is true of the
notion that deficiencies in serial order recall may be unique to
given modalities. This notion, if taken to its extreme, allows for
the possibility that each sensory system is equipped with specific
mechanisms for processing order and item information. Such
theorizing stretches parsimony beyond reasonable limits, especially when viewed in the light of the ongoing controversy
about the distinction between gross and serial memory. In this

connection, recall that certain of the studies carried out in our own laboratory found no differences between poor and normal readers on measures of immediate visual recall involving serial processing except when upper limits on short-term memory were exceeded. Such evidence undermines both visual and general sequential deficit theories of reading disability.

Perhaps the most basic point to consider in assessing the ultimate validity of sequential deficit explanations of dyslexia is the relative importance of serial processing to word decoding. Although this issue has not been explicitly discussed by authors who promote the various conceptualizations of serial processing deficits discussed, an assumption implicit in each is that the identification and pronunciation of a printed word entails serial (left-to-right) processing of its individual letters. Yet it is not at all clear that word decoding inevitably or optimally takes place in this manner. In fact the degree to which word recognition can be explained by a serial process model is currently a hotly debated issue in the study of normal reading ability (cf. Hochberg 1970; Brewer 1972; Gough 1972), the relevant alternatives being whether a word is recognized through the prior identification of its component letters (Estes 1974; LaBerge and Samuels 1974; McClelland 1976) or through simultaneous processing of its graphic features (Johnson 1975; LaBerge 1976). Space does not permit a detailed account of the points that have been made on either side of this issue nor of the evidence relating to each alternative. Suffice it to say that sequential processing of individual letters and letter sounds may or may not be the necessary means by which words are identified. Obviously the validation of any serial deficit explanation of dyslexia depends, in no small measure, upon the answer to this question. An answer in the affirmative would lend credence to such explanations. An answer in the negative would, of course, reduce their explanatory power.[4] In either event, theories of reading disability that implicate dysfunction in serial order recall as a basic etiological factor rest upon a tenuous foundation and may ultimately be proved incorrect.

Obviously, there is need for greater specification of the nature of the basic process disorders causing the inferred difficulties in serialization and thus in reading. With the exception of Bakker's work, our review of the literature has yielded no serious attempts to add substance to sequential deficit explanations of reading disability, either in definitive conceptualizations of hypothesized deficiencies or in extensive documentation of the validity of specific hypotheses. Indeed most of the hypotheses offered were post hoc interpretations based on isolated findings that, typically, were not replicated. Thus the serial deficit explanations available in the literature cannot be taken seriously at present. The question is an open one, however. Continued research in the area is certainly indicated.

Nevertheless, because of the theoretical and empirical contraindications, I tend to doubt the logic behind the suggestion that reading disability may be caused by a specific disorder in serialization ability—that is, that gross and sequential memory are supported by different neurological structures in different subsystems, poor readers being deficient only in mechanisms responsible for processing sequence. The more appealing view is that item and order information, though perhaps qualitatively different psychologically, are not supported by separable neurological structures.[5] Learning in both instances may require the coordinated involvement of different cognitive processes (multiple codes) as well as similar and dissimilar coding strategies, depending upon the type and complexity of material to be processed (Healy 1977). Implied in this point of view is the possibility that poor readers are impaired in one or more of the psychological systems that may be involved in processing both item and order information. The disparities observed between poor and normal readers on various measures of serial order recall may be attributable to group differences in verbal encoding ability. Such differences could, in turn, be linked to specific impairments in linguistic functioning that may be characteristic of disabled readers. This possibility, in its various aspects, will be the focus of chapter 8.

Chapter Eight   VERBAL PROCESSING

In the discussion thus far, it has repeatedly been suggested that the differences found between dyslexic and normal readers on a great variety of basic process measures are directly or indirectly attributable to disparities in verbal processing ability. This inference was made in my interpretations of results from studies of perceptual functioning, memory, and learning, both within and across various sense modalities. In addition, I have alluded to common underlying deficiencies that apparently handicap poor readers on such diverse tasks as letter and word naming, matching invariant patterns in sequences of lights and tones, and perceiving a variety of figures in correct orientation. The implication in all these instances is that poor readers have deficiencies in both short- and long-term memory, characterized by a paucity or inaccessibility of various types of verbal information—information that would otherwise aid performance on multidimensional tasks by virtue of its coding function.

To be more specific, a child who has difficulty (1) in accessing and relating the semantic or meaning components of physical stimuli (objects, events, and symbols) to their sound counterparts, (2) in explicating the phonetic structure of speech, (3) in developing a functional command of the diverse syntactic usages required for the recognition and production of both spoken and printed words will have difficulty in integrating these complex components of language and will therefore lack skill in their application. Conversely, a rich fund of linguistic information provides a broad variety of implicit mnemonics as well as a variety of contexts that will allow one to readily symbolize or code stimulus input for efficient processing. Those who lack such devices will be especially encumbered when presented with short-term memory tasks requiring rapid coding of information for effective rehearsal and retrieval. For example, a child who synthesizes a temporal pattern through the use of a readily available verbal mnemonic has a distinct advantage over the child who does not have such assistance when processing information in a limited-capacity system. Analogously, the poor reader who mislabels confusable words such as *was* and *saw* or *loin* and *lion* may be inclined to make these errors because he has not coded the critical sound differences characterizing the letter sequences in those words and is thereby forced to recall their names exclusively as whole entities. If for any reason this same child lacks information about the meanings of these words or has not employed them in a variety of grammatical contexts, he will obviously have fewer associations to aid in their discrimination and ultimate recall. The different components of language are thus accorded a significant role in processing stimuli of all types, particularly those of a symbolic and categorical nature.

Given the possibility that difficulties in learning to read do come about because of deficiencies in verbal learning, there remains the problem of determining the nature of such deficiencies and their relationship to the reading process. Existing evidence (Calfee, Chapman, and Venezky 1972; Shankweiler and Liberman 1972) suggest that the major difficulty encountered by poor readers is their limited ability to decode individual words and word parts. Although some authors do not agree with this analysis of the problem (for example Goodman 1969; Smith 1971), there can be little quarrel with the fact that the most severely impaired readers are deficient with respect to both word identification and reading comprehension skills. Such children are of primary interest here.

Assuming that word decoding is the locus of the dyslexic's basic difficulty in learning to read, it becomes necessary to dissect the complex processes involved in acquiring this skill in order to ascertain the factors that may impede such acquisition. Several problem areas present themselves, each relating to a somewhat different aspect of word identification.

One possibility is that dyslexics have basic difficulty in establishing visual-verbal associations. Such difficulty is conceived as unique to verbal learning, and different from the learning of intersensory relationships of a nonverbal nature or association learning in general. In previous chapters reference has been made to research evidence consistent with this contention; that evidence will be discussed in greater detail in the present context.

Another possibility is that dyslexics are dysfunctional in processing one or another of the three components of language: semantics, syntax, and phonology. We will examine each of these components separately. Not only are they semiautonomous systems that may contribute differentially to reading impairment, but the studies evaluating verbal processing have focused on individual components. However, the three are so intrinsically related that they can be conceptualized in isolation from one another only arbitrarily. The reader will see considerable overlap in the discussions of reader group contrasts in these areas.

Finally, several studies have provided retrospective or post hoc evidence for verbal skills deficiencies in poor readers, and a few other studies have yielded correlational evidence in support of the verbal processing hypothesis. I will begin by making brief reference to these investigations.

Research on verbal deficit explanations of reading disability is of an embryonic nature and the evidence does not converge upon a well-defined and comprehensive theory. Although studies in this area are rapidly proliferating, the results to date should be considered preliminary. Ascribing cause-effect relations to given findings is therefore to be avoided, particularly in the case of those that have not been replicated.

8.1 RETROSPECTIVE AND POST HOC STUDIES

According to Benton (1975) the idea that dyslexia may be related to language disorder dates back to McCready (1910) and Bronner (1917), both of whom made note of the frequency with which children who experienced reading difficulties had a history of delayed language. Not until much later, however, was this idea given serious consideration. Rabinovitch (1959, 1968) seems to have been one of the first of the latter-day advocates to draw a parallel between specific language and reading disabilities. He suggested that dyslexics are characterized by subtle language defects that can be observed not only in poor reading ability but in expressive disorders, word-finding difficulties, deficient concept formation, and dysfunction in symbolic learning generally. Rabinovitch's observations were based largely on clinical study of dyslexics, but empirical support for his suggestion emerged subsequently.

Initial support for a possible relationship between reading and language problems was of an indirect nature. To illustrate, Ingram and Reid (1956) found that about half the children diagnosed as dyslexic in a clinical sample of youngsters referred for emotional problems had a history of deviant speech and language development. A similar proportion was reported in a later investigation specifically concerned with children with reading disability (Ingram, Mason, and Blackburn 1970).

In another retrospective study, Lyle (1970) compiled case history data on carefully defined samples of poor and normal readers (N = 54 each group) who were contrasted on a number of developmental variables, including early speech and language difficulties. This survey successfully discriminated children with severe reading disorder from those with normal reading ability. In addition, a history of language disorder was correlated with measures of reversal tendencies in reading, written expression, and memory for designs, as well as with several other tests of verbal ability. Lyle inferred from these results that poor readers may be characterized by a "generalized lag in verbal learning."

These studies suffer from the problems characterizing all retrospective and post hoc analyses. That is, historical accounts are often unreliable and not infrequently tainted by contemporary impressions. Furthermore, descriptions such as "early language difficulties" or "delayed speech" are rather broad and therefore provide little specificity as to the type of verbal deficiencies that may have been characteristic of the children studied. Such information would seem to be relevant to an understanding of the learning problems ultimately encountered by these children. Therefore the results of these investigations provide only suggestive evidence that poor readers sustain linguistic deficiencies that may contribute to their problems in learning to read.

8.2 CORRELATIONAL STUDIES

The possibility that reading disability is correlated with verbal skills deficiencies is consistent with the results of a study by Owen and her associates (1971). These investigators interviewed family members and acquaintances of children sustaining a variety of learning disorders and found that such youngsters were viewed as having less adequate verbal abilities than their siblings and peers. Verbal skills deficiencies were most often observed among children with a history of organic or physical abnormality and those with a low Verbal-high Performance IQ pattern and relatively low IQs (90-99). Children with high IQs (117-154) or emotional problems were not viewed as being verbally deficient.

In one of the earliest studies of its kind, Monroe (1932) compared a sizable number of poor and normal readers (N = 416) on a large battery of tests that included measures of visual, auditory, linguistic, motor, and conceptual functions. The sample was unstratified and encompassed very wide age ranges (6 to 17 years) and intelligence scores (IQs from 55 to 155). Socioeconomic status was quite variable and a significant number of the children had reading difficulties due to extrinsic factors such as sensory acuity problems and emotional disorder. Thus results cannot readily be generalized to the child with specific reading disability.

Nevertheless, the relationships between reading difficulties and developmental language disorders are of interest. Briefly, Monroe (1932) found that for a significant proportion of children in the sample, reading problems appeared to be associated with various types of language disabiltiy. These included auditory discrimination problems, speech difficulties, and verbal deficits characterized, typically, by a limited vocabulary, grammar and syntax problems, poor organizational skills, and deficiencies in general comprehension.

Additional evidence that poor readers have limited verbal abilities is provided by the results of low Verbal-high Performance IQs in poor readers, knowledge of words and verbal concept formation being particularly deficient in the children studied (Belmont and Birch 1966; Warrington 1967; Lyle and Goyen 1969; Huelsman 1970; Owen et al. 1971). Lyle and Goyen suggested that this pattern may *not* be due to the cumulative deficiencies resulting from reading and related learning difficulties, because the discrepancy between these two indices in a sample of poor readers they evaluated did not increase with age. Reinforcing this inference is the observation that poor readers manifesting the low Verbal-high Performance IQ pattern in a sizable number of studies conducted in our own laboratory (1972 to 1975) were consistently differentiated from normal readers on verbal tasks but not on nonverbal tasks.

Several studies have provided support for the possibility that reading disability in school-age children can be predicted by verbal deficits discovered at the preschool level. De Hirsch, Jansky, and Langford (1966) found a significant correlation between language disorder in kindergarten children and reading difficulties in those same children tested in second grade. Jansky and de Hirsch (1972) also tested kindergartners and found significant relations between verbal skills deficiencies manifested at the time of testing and measures of reading achievement obtained in grade 2. The results of both studies are weakened, however, by their sampling procedures as well as by the fact that the reader groups compared were differentiated on a very large number of other predictive measures. The latter finding would lead one to question the assumption that children in these investigations were characterized by specific rather than general learning disabilities, although it is reasonable to surmise that language deficits contributed to such difficulties.

In a longitudinal study by Sampson (1962) fifty children were studied from age 18 months to 8 years. Although a variety of tests of cognitive ability were correlated with reading achievement at age 8, the finding of greatest interest here is the very substantial correlations between the reading measures and measures of speech and language. Predictive correlations (2 to 8 years) ranged from .58 to .69; concurrent indices ranged from .58 to .70. In contrast, correlations between the reading tests and a nonverbal test of intelligence were no higher than .45. This investigation is unique in the length of time the same children were studied. Nevertheless, the findings must be considered tentative because the population evaluated was not well defined.

In summary, retrospective and correlational studies provide indirect and moderately suggestive evidence that poor readers are characterized by verbal skills deficiencies that may be significantly correlated with difficulties in acquiring skill in reading. A number of investigations implicate delayed language development as a possible factor; others provide evidence of a positive relationship between reading ability and tests of verbal functioning such as vocabulary and verbal concept formation. Still other studies yield moderately high correlations between measures of preschool language functioning and reading achievement in the elementary grades. Thus the findings, though tentative, are consistent with a verbal deficit explanation of reading disability.

8.3 ASSOCIATION LEARNING

In earlier sections of this text (5.4, 6.4) we examined several studies comparing disabled and normal readers on learning tasks involving the association and integration of stimuli picked up by various sense modalities. These investigations provide both direct and indirect evidence that children with specific reading disability have no *general* learning deficits. The evidence suggests further that such children can be expected to manifest difficulty in establishing visual-verbal relationships like those required in learning to read. Thus a number of investigations reviewed found no differences between poor and normal readers in paired associates learning involving various inter- and intra-sensory tasks of a nonverbal nature (Goyen and Lyle 1971b; Steger, Vellutino, and Meshoulam 1972; Vellutino, Steger and Pruzek, 1973; Vellutino, Steger, Harding, and Phillips 1975; Vellutino, Harding, Phillips, and Steger 1975). In contrast, studies comparing these groups on various types of verbal learning tasks consistently found differences between them favoring the normal readers (Vellutino, Steger, Harding, and Phillips 1975; Vellutino, Harding, Phillips, and Steger 1975; Rudel, Denckla, and Spalten 1976; Vellutino, Bentley, and Phillips 1978). The investigations conducted in our own laboratory are of particular interest in this connection in that they systematically varied verbal and nonverbal association learning, employing various types of stimuli in contrasts of comparably (and carefully) selected samples of poor and normal readers between second and sixth grade. They also varied stimulus presentations so as to compare these groups on both within- and between-modality learning. Their results (collectively) represent a substantial body of evidence in support of the contention that poor readers have particular difficulty in any learning that involves a verbal component. The general approach employed in two of these studies is especially representative of our research strategy; it may therefore be useful to briefly review their procedures and findings in relation to the present topic.

In both investigations our primary intent was to simulate, in certain respects, the type of visual-verbal learning that may be in-

volved in initial word identification (so-called sight word learning).
In one study poor and normal readers (grades 4, 5, and 6) were
randomly assigned to either a visual-auditory, nonverbal learning
condition or to a visual-verbal learning condition employing two
subtests presented in invariant sequence (Vellutino, Steger,
Harding, and Phillips (1975). The first subtest required the association of nonsense syllables and novel cartoons (see figure
8.1); the second involved the association of those same syllables
with novel script. As predicted, the nonverbal learning condition
did not differentiate the groups, replicating previous findings
(Vellutino, Steger, and Pruzek 1973). However, the poor readers
did not perform as well as the normal readers on either the
picture-naming or the script-naming task, suggesting that they may
be inclined to have difficulty on measures of verbal learning or,
more specifically, on visual-verbal learning.

A gratuitous finding in this study is of particular interest because it was suggestive of one possible problem that these children may encounter in such learning. Specifically, the naming
errors made by the disabled readers in learning to associate the
visual stimuli with nonsense syllables were characterized by more
actual word substitutions (for example, *fog* for *mog*) than were
the naming errors of the normal readers. The normal readers, in
fact, made more errors that were novel combinations of the
individual phonemes making up the stimulus words (*mag* and *yog*

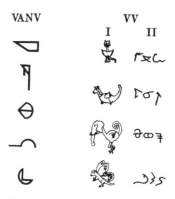

Figure 8.1 Visual stimuli employed in contrasts of poor and normal readers
on visual-auditory nonverbal (VANV) and visual-verbal (VV) paired-associates
learning. (From Vellutino, Steger, Harding and Phillips 1975. Reproduced
by permission of the editor of *Neuropsychologia* and Pergamon Press.)

for *mog* and *yag)* (see table 8.1). This finding suggests that the normal readers were more inclined than the poor readers to code the nonsense syllables phonetically, this suggestion being consistent with the view held by several authors (Liberman and Shankweiler 1978; Perfetti and Lesgold 1978) that poor readers may have difficulty in the phonetic coding of both visual and aural linguistic information. The results are inconclusive on this point, but they do support the more general contention that poor readers perform differentially on measures of verbal and nonverbal learning.[1]

The latter suggestion is reinforced by the results of a second study that evaluated the possibility that poor readers were generally deficient in abstracting invariance in patterned stimuli (Vellutino, Harding, Phillips, and Steger 1975). We were specifically concerned with whether these individuals would have pervasive difficulty in analyzing such information or would manifest a low level of performance only in instances when the stimuli involved a verbal component. Earlier research (Blank et al. 1966, 1968; Kastner and Rickards 1974) had suggested that poor readers may be deficient in verbal classification ability, thereby raising some question as to the generality of such deficiency. It seemed unlikely that a population initially defined as having normal intelligence would be generally impaired in conceptual functioning, but we thought it entirely possible that this group might be selectively deficient in categorical learning that involved abstracting and generalizing verbal relationships. Thus we hypothesized that poor readers would perform less proficiently than normals in apprehending invariant relationships of a verbal nature but would not differ from the normals in apprehending invariant relationships of a nonverbal nature.

We employed a transfer of learning paradigm to test this hypothesis, our intent being to approximate the type of generalization learning involved in acquiring skill in reading (learn *cat, rat, can;* decode spontaneously the word *ran*). A carefully selected sample of poor and normal readers (grades 4 to 6) was administered visual-visual training and transfer tasks, and an independent sample (comparably selected) was presented with visual-verbal training and transfer tasks. The stimuli were novel; those employed under acquisition conditions contained invariant patterns that were retained on the transfer conditions (see figures 8.2 and

Table 8.1
Error patterns of poor and normal readers on visual-verbal paired-associates learning.

	Poor		Normal	
	VVI	VVII	VVI	VVII
A. Types of errors				
Incorrect stimulus pairings	14%	19%	17%	37%
	(3.43)[a]	(3.87)	(2.33)	(3.73)
Syllable substitutions	48%	52%	42%	36%
	(11.13)	(10.53)	(6.00)	(3.70)
No response	38%	29%	41%	27%
	(8.73)	(5.90)	(5.83)	(2.83)
	100%	100%	100%	100%
B. Types of syllable substitutions				
Syllable substitutions that were other nonsense words (phonemic)	54%	57%	71%	74%
Syllable substitutions that were "real words" (semantic)	46%	43%	29%	26%
	100%	100%	100%	100%
C. "Near miss" substitutions				
Syllable substitutions with only one phoneme in error	55%	57%	63%	64%
Syllable substitutions with one phoneme in error that were also "real" word (semantic) substitutions	51%	63%	49%	38%

[a] Figures in parentheses are raw score means.

Source: Vellutino, Steger, Harding, and Phillips 1975, p. 79. (Reproduced with permission of the editor of *Neuropsychologia*.)

8.3). The stimuli were also relatively complex and, in the case of visual learning, provided ample opportunity for subjects to make the types of orientation and sequencing errors that Orton and Hermann believed were reflective of spatial confusion in poor readers.

The children with reading difficulties performed as well as the normal readers on the visual-visual training and transfer tasks but not as well on visual-verbal training and transfer, even after controlling for group differences in intelligence. We concluded that poor readers can successfully process the categorical relationships contained in patterned stimuli when such information is of a nonverbal nature but can be expected to have difficulty in processing patterned information of a verbal nature.

Finally, additional support for a possible relation between verbal learning problems and reading disability is provided by a large number of studies investigating the possibility that dyslexic and normal readers are generally impaired in paired-associates learning. In most of those studies, which have appeared in the literature (Zigmond 1966; Brewer 1967; Gascon and Goodglass

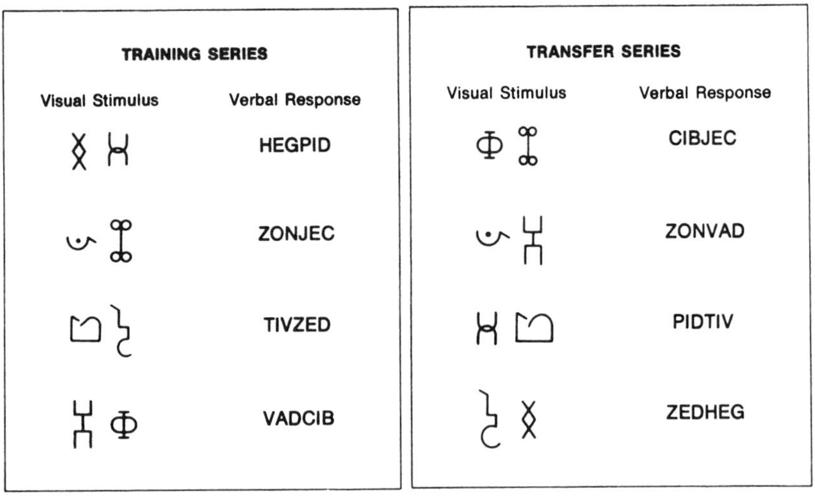

Figure 8.2 Visual and verbal stimuli employed in the training and transfer series used by Vellutino, Harding, Phillips, and Steger (1975). Stimuli in the transfer series constitute different combinations of the stimuli presented in the training series. (Reproduced by permission of the editor of *The Journal of Genetic Psychology*.)

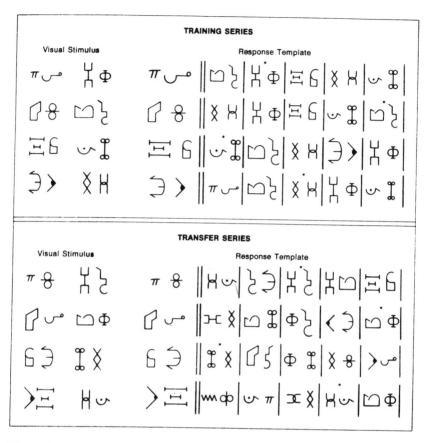

Figure 8.3 Visual stimuli and response templates in the training and transfer series used by Vellutino, Harding, Phillips, and Steger (1975). Stimuli in the transfer series constitute different combinations of the stimuli presented in the training series. (Reproduced by permission of the editor of *The Journal of Genetic Psychology*.)

1970), poor and normal readers were more often differentiated on associative tasks involving verbal components than on tasks involving non-verbal components.

To summarize, there is now a substantial body of evidence that supports the contention that poor readers are less able than normal readers in acquiring visual-verbal relationships, a basic skill prerequisite to learning to read. In contrast, these groups have consistently been found to be comparable on nonverbal learning tasks involving associations both within and between sensory modalities. The studies reviewed included children between second and sixth grades, and most samples were carefully selected in accord with the criteria of (specific) reading disability outlined in chapter 2. Thus the data constitute strong support for the suggestion that reading disability is associated with deficiencies in verbal learning.

The findings are inconclusive as to the nature of such deficits, however. I have suggested that the poor reader's difficulties in establishing visual-verbal associations is a manifestation of his efforts in verbal learning rather than in visual or intersensory (nonverbal) learning and that such dysfunction could be due either to specific difficulty in integrating visual and verbal information or, more generally, to deficiencies in one or more aspects of linguistic functioning. But the only study available that directly evaluated one plausible version of the former hypothesis—that is, dysfunction in interhemispheric transfer—yielded negative results. Yet, assuming for the moment that children with specific reading disability sustain a basic constitutional deficiency, it is entirely possible that problems in integrating visual and verbal information is an *intra*hemispheric anomaly that occurs in spite of normal functioning in callosal transmission, visual processing, and language. This of course is an empirical question that can be answered only with additional research. On the other hand, the possibility remains that poor readers sustain subtle language defects that hamper visual-verbal integration. Evaluation of this possibility will be addressed in the sections that follow.

8.4 SEMANTIC PROCESSING
Successful word identification depends upon, among other things, a child's ability to extract meaning from the words he reads or

attempts to decode. This is true of single-word identification as well as identification of words in running text. In either case the reader's ability to relate a word to a familiar meaning or context will make that word more memorable. On the other hand, ignorance about a word's meaning or incomplete information about the many contexts in which that word may appear will reduce the probability that it will be integrated into an associative network that would readily facilitate recall. Face-valid evidence for the latter issues from the common observation that children with conceptual problems and very limited language ability do not achieve a high level of reading proficiency. The role of meaning in accounting for the word identification problems of specifically disabled readers is not so apparent. Thus a question of no small significance—one that is appropriately addressed here—is whether or not specifically disabled readers have basic dificiencies in processing the meaning of words.

Several authors (Goodman 1969; Kolers 1970; Smith 1971, 1973) are of the opinion that deficient reading ability is the end result of the child's inability to readily derive meaning from written text. Reasons for making this claim have not been detailed to any great extent, except for the suggestion that poor readers are by and large characterized by a disinclination to read for meaning because of the emphasis that many instructional programs place upon single-word decoding. Yet no definitive research supports this notion, at least, none on the population of interest here. Furthermore, to attribute to inadequate instruction alone the severe reading problems experienced by otherwise capable children would seem to oversimplify the problem. Most youngsters in a literate society learn to read regardless of the type of instruction to which they are exposed, and this appears to be true over a broad range of conceptual levels.

Nevertheless, severely impaired readers do have some degree of difficulty in abstracting meaning from printed words, such difficulty being especially apparent in the comprehension of running text. Reading comprehension problems would seem to be a predictable outcome of more basic deficiencies in word decoding, but it is entirely possible that decoding problems themselves are due, in part, to imperfect or inefficient processing of the meanings of individual words. This is essentially the position taken by those who suggest that poor readers are overly attentive to the structural components of written words rather than to their meanings Goodman 1969; Kolers 1970; Smith 1971, 1973). Members of this group argue further that access to the semantic counterparts of orthographic features of printed words is direct and that phonetic-articulatory mediation as a vehicle to word identification and pronunciation is both unnecessary and unnatural.

These arguments again oversimplify the process of learning to read, and they cannot account for the common observation that word decoding ability in many poor readers is defective even when the ability to apprehend meaning is essentially intact. In fact, the evidence from research evaluating semantic processing in poor and normal readers indicates that poor readers do not sustain a basic deficiency in extracting meaning either from individual words or from running text, but are not always as efficient as normal readers in these activities because of significant problems in phonetic encoding or word retrieval.

8.4.1 Semantic Processing and Verbal Encoding: Research Evidence
The results of a recent investigation by Waller (1976) are consistent with the view that poor readers are able to synthesize and abstract the general meanings contained in sentences they read, provided they are able to decode the words in those sentences. The subjects in this investigation were fifth-graders, carefully matched for age, sex, IQ, and other relevant variables. Although reader groups were separated on the basis of reading comprehension rather than oral reading measures (a weakness commented on earlier), the criteria for inclusion in the study were stringent.

The experimental task assessed memory for connected text; subjects were initially required to read simple active declarative sentences and later indicate familiarity with those sentences on a second reading. A semantic integration paradigm (Paris and Carter 1973) was employed to assess the degree to which children were inclined to encode the *meaning* or the *structural* characteristics of the material they read. After reading each sentence on the acquisition trial, each child was given a number of recognition sentences that were (1) identical to some initially read *(true premise);* (2) altered in content, resulting in a change in meaning *(false premise);* (3) altered in content but maintaining meaning *(true inference);* or (4) altered in both content and meaning *(false inference).* Several sentences altered in number and tense markers were also included.

The subject's task was to read each test sentence and indicate whether or not he recognized it as having been read earlier. The sentences were all simple in content and readily deciphered by subjects in both groups, as indicated by the fact that there were no significant differences between them in number of oral reading errors.

Poor readers made no more recognition errors than the normal readers on true premise, false premise, and false inference sentences. In contrast they did make more recognition errors on true inference sentences and sentences characterized by changes in number and tense. Waller inferred from these results that reading disabled children do not sustain general deficiencies in memory. Since they made more errors on the true inference sentences, it appeared that the poor readers in the study must have been encoding meaning as well as the normal readers. However, they did not retain exact verbal strings and important syntactic details (tense markers and indications of plurality) as well as the normals did. The explanation of these differences was that deficient readers may be less inclined than normal readers to employ a verbal code in storing information from material read, relying more heavily upon a visual code for storage. A corollary inference was that details such as tense markers are not as well retained in a visual code as in an auditory code.

The results of a study by Golinkoff and Rosinski (1976) are essentially in accord with Waller's findings. Their primary purpose was to compare skilled and less-skilled readers on semantic processing and decoding of individual words. However, because the subjects were selected on the basis of a reading comprehension test and were only moderately impaired in reading, the findings may not be readily generalized to children with severe reading disability. No other description of the sample was provided, another weakness of the study. Nevertheless the results are suggestive.

The subjects in this investigation were third- and fifth-graders (N = 24 each group). Poor readers were approximately a year to a year and a half below grade level; normal readers were one to two years above grade level. The experimental task compared the groups on measures of single-word decoding and semantic interference. The decoding measure consisted of twenty common first-grade level nouns (animals and objects) and twenty pronounceable nonsense trigrams with low association values. The semantic interference test required that subjects label pictures on which words (or trigrams) were superimposed, some containing words that matched the pictures, others containing words that did not match the pictures. Vocalization latency was the dependent measure in all instances. The specific intent of this study was to evaluate the possibility that poor readers are as sensitive as normal readers to the meanings of printed words though less effective than the normals in word decoding. An affirmative answer to these questions was linked to the prediction that the groups would *not* differ in the time taken to name the pictures containing semantically interfering words but would differ on the word decoding measures. The prediction was confirmed. The authors concluded from these results that poor readers process the semantic information contained in individual words as well as normal readers.

That children with reading problems may not process semantic information with the same degree of speed and efficiency as children who read normally is demonstrated in an impressive series of studies by Perfetti and his associates. Their basic assumption is that the major impediment encountered by poor readers in both reading and listening comprehension is a limited ability to code information phonetically. Put another way, the poor reader is said to have difficulty in "naming a word stimulus and in retrieving semantic information in response to a name" (Perfetti and Lesgold 1978, 177). A consequent problem is limited proficiency in retaining linguistic information in short-term memory—for example, verbatim word strings, specific words or word parts, specific concepts and the like. Poor readers would therefore be expected to have less time and find it more cumbersome to synthesize the interrelated meanings embedded in connected text and would have particular difficulty in abstracting information under time pressures. Put more succinctly, "the poor reader is slower at getting to the point in the comprehension process beyond which exact wording is not needed, but he is also poorer at retaining exact wording" (p. 178).

The subjects employed in all of the investigations by Perfetti and his associates were selected on the basis of reading comprehension rather than oral reading measures and do not necessarily include the most severely impaired readers. The groups contrasted were typically equated on measures of intelligence and only children with normal intellectual ability were studied. In addition, subjects were by and large selected from urban schools. No other descriptions of the samples were provided. Therefore the children studied may not be representative of the severely impaired reader, as described here. Nevertheless, the consistency of the findings in relation to the central hypothesis is compelling. Moreover, the results reported in these investigations (as well as the interpretations of these results) are generally in accord with our own observations, and the children included in our samples *were* severely impaired in reading. Perfetti's findings are also consistent with work done elsewhere. Because of the number of studies to be discussed, the constitution of each sample will not be described in detail.

In the first experiment in this series, Perfetti and Goldman (1976) tested the hypothesis that poor readers sustain no basic deficit in memory for nonverbal stimuli but are characterized by specific deficiency in verbal encoding, which results in short-term memory problems. Such difficulty was thought to be the cause of significant language comprehension problems in poor readers, as might be reflected in "memory for spoken discourse and . . . in the use of linguistic constituents as units of analysis in short term memory" (p. 34). This hypothesis was tested in two separate experiments. Subjects were third and fifth graders characterized as skilled and unskilled readers ($N = 12$ each group). The skilled readers scored a stanine 6 or above; the less-skilled readers were below the 4th stanine. Children in each reader group were matched for intelligence.

The first experiment was designed to assess short-term memory capacity, using a procedure that did not place heavy demands upon verbal encoding ability. The method employed was a probe-digit task devised by Waugh and Norman (1965). Subjects were presented with several lists of thirteen digits, each of which included a probe digit appearing once at changing locations *within* the list and once at the *termination* of the list. The subject's task upon hearing the final probe digit was to recall the digit that had occurred directly after the probe on its first occurrence (in that list). No significant differences were found between poor and normal readers at either grade level on this task, confirming the authors' prediction that the two groups would not differ with respect to auditory short-term memory capacity per se.

The second study employed a probe discourse task analogous to the probe-digit task. It was suggested that listening comprehension requires that one keep track of incoming propositions or concepts in order to integrate them into meaningful configurations (sentences, for instance). Stated differently, individual words and their meanings must be maintained in short-term memory until they can be assimilated into higher-order units of meaning. It was therefore hypothesized that the poor readers would not perform as well as the normal readers on memory for specific words that directly followed a probe word presented in connected text. The hypothesis was confirmed in that the normal readers were better in verbatim recall than the poor readers. It is particularly interesting that recall for both poor and normal readers was better within than across sentence boundaries (Jarvella 1971)[2] suggesting that the two groups employed the structural characteristics of sentences in much the same way. Perfetti and Goldman concluded therefrom that reading and language comprehension difficulties are directly related; they stressed the importance of "effective, automated linguistic codes" as determinants of success in each of these skills.

Results consistent with these findings were obtained by Perfetti, Bell, and Goldman (reported in Perfetti and Lesgold 1978). In this study, oral and silent reading of connected text were the dependent variables rather than discourse listening. Subjects were third- and fourth-grade skilled and less-skilled readers. A memory probe paradigm was again employed to evaluate clause boundary effects in the two groups. In accord with expectations, recall for both reader groups was better within than across (clause) boundaries. However, the less-skilled readers generally did not remember as many target words as the skilled readers. This finding was thought to be consistent with possible deficits in coding and speed of processing in the former group rather than with semantic deficiencies in the strict sense.

The results of several other studies from Perfetti's laboratory comparing reader groups on measures of discourse comprehension are also relevant here. The focus of these investigations was the question of whether or not these two groups would differ in higher-order semantic organization of written text. To illustrate, Berger (1975) found that children with limited reading ability recalled less information about specific content and answered correctly fewer literal questions about the text than did children with normal reading ability. However, the groups did not differ with respect to their recall of propositional content. This finding suggested that skilled and less-skilled readers are comparable with respect to their ability to organize meaningful material globally.

That skilled readers are not necessarily more sensitive to semantic information than less-skilled readers is demonstrated in two other studies reported by Perfetti (Perfetti and Lesgold 1978).[3] In one of these investigations it was found that *thematic* and *context scrambled* material did not differentially affect these two groups (fourth-graders); the skilled readers recalled passages from the text better than the less-skilled readers under both conditions. Similar results were found on a measure of recall for related and unrelated sentences. Of particular interest was the finding that the magnitude of the differences between the reader groups was constant across successive thirds of the passages. Increased divergence toward the end of passages would be predicted if skilled readers were better than less-skilled readers at assimilating previously encoded material into a meaningful context, but such divergence was not observed. In fact the disparities between the groups on each of these measures are more reasonably interpreted as the result of short-term memory factors than of organization of thematic material in long-term memory.

The second study also evaluated the possibility that poor readers are more sensitive to thematic material than normal readers and again made use of previously encoded concepts as a contrast variable. Subjects (fifth-graders) were asked to read sentence pairs differing in the presentation of either given or new information in the second sentence of each pair. The dependent measure was time taken to read sentences that differed with respect to this given/new dichotomy. There was no reader-group by sentence-type interaction, both groups manifesting slower reading times for sentences containing new information. The results were viewed as providing additional evidence that poor and normal readers do not differ in their sensitivity to discourse features. Similar findings were obtained by Straub (1976) with adults and 10-year-old children differentiated on measures of reading ability.

All these studies provide considerable support for the suggestion that poor readers do not process connected text as efficiently as normal readers. There is no reason to believe that these groups differ with respect to their ability to extract semantic information from either written or spoken discourse in the global sense. Rather, the evidence suggests that poor readers are less proficient than normal readers in rapidly coding incoming information for prospective assimilation to existing meanings encoded in either short- or long-term storage. The inference is that comprehension suffers because new material is not effectively coded in working memory, thereby reducing the chances that it will connect with contextual material in permanent memory. Semantic access is therefore slower and more cumbersome and the text may not be fully comprehended.

Additional support for this contention is derived from several investigations comparing skilled and unskilled readers on single-word processing. These more directly assessed the possibility that poor readers are impaired in verbal coding. Since speed rather than accuracy of performance was of special concern, latency scores were typically employed as dependent measures.

Perfetti, Hogaboam, and Bell (reported in Perfetti and Lesgold 1978) raised the question of whether semantic access is an automatic consequence of phonological decoding. An affirmative answer would have obvious implication for poor readers, given the possibility that they sustain deficiencies in phonetic coding. In order to evaluate this possibility, skilled and less-skilled readers (8 and 10 years) were orally presented with single words and were asked to indicate for each word, whether it matched a printed word or a picture stimulus. In a related task the same subjects were presented with a category name (such as *animals*) and asked whether the printed word or picture coincided with that name. The (average) time taken to match spoken and printed words provided a base level for phonological decoding; latencies for matching pictures and spoken words provided a base level for semantic decoding. Response times for matching the categories provided a measure of the speed with which higher-order semantic information is accessed.

There were no statistically significant differences between skilled and less-skilled readers on either picture or word matching when categories were not involved. However, there were substantial differences between these groups on category matching, suggesting that the less-skilled readers were slower in processing verbal concepts than the skilled readers. The authors inferred from these results that semantic integration is partly dependent upon the speed with which a category name is retrieved. The inference, stated more explicitly, is that the name of a category may permit access to semantic information subsumed under that category, whereas difficulty in retrieving the category name may result in labored processing of the meanings associated with that name. The question of whether or not semantic decoding is an automatic consequence of phonological decoding is, by virtue of these findings, answered in the negative, since the less-skilled readers were comparable to the skilled readers in processing lower-order semantic information but were not as efficient as the skilled readers in processing verbal categories.

A final group of studies conducted by Perfetti and his co-workers employed vocalization latencies in comparisons of poor and normal readers on speed of naming a variety of word and nonword stimuli. The primary intent was to demonstrate that a major source of individual differences in reading skill is the rapid decoding of words and subword units.

In the first investigation in this set Perfetti and Hogaboam (1975) tested third- and fifth-grade skilled and unskilled readers of normal intelligence. Subjects came from a working-class neighborhood and there were slight differences between the groups in intelligence. Sex ratios were equivalent.

Each child was presented with high- and low-frequency words, as well as pseudowords and words that varied as to the child's ability to define them (each child could define some but not all of the words). Stimuli were presented randomly by means of a slide projector and response latencies were recorded. Skilled comprehenders manifested faster reaction times than did the less-skilled comprehenders. However, there was less difference between the groups on the high-frequency words than on the low-frequency and pseudowords. The authors suggested that the differences between reader groups were attributable to word decoding ability. They further suggested that speed of decoding is a major factor contributing to reader group differences in reading comprehension, the assumption being that rapid decoding is a basic prerequisite for effective development of comprehension skill.

A similar investigation was conducted by Perfetti, Finger, and Hogaboam (1977) employing third-graders (N = 16 each group).

Of particular interest in this study was vocabulary set size, or, more specifically, the extent to which skilled and less-skilled readers employ knowledge of vocabulary constraints to increase speed and efficiency of decoding. Also of interest were reader group contrasts on speed of naming alphabetic and nonalphabetic material. Skilled readers were expected to manifest shorter latencies than the less-skilled readers in naming alphabetic stimuli, but no differences between the groups were expected in the case of nonalphabetic material. These expectations were in line with a storage rather than retrieval deficit explanation of processing difficulties in poor readers.

In four separate experiments subjects were presented with colors, digits, pictures, and words (respectively) and response latencies were recorded. Digits, pictures, and words varied in number of syllables; digits, colors, and words varied in set size— that is, in the number of possible items in a stimulus set. The twelve months in the year provided an example of the fixed or definite set sizes used; names of animals exemplify the indefinite sets employed in the study. Number of syllables was expected to influence reaction times, consistent with the view that decoding speed varies with size of subword units. The rationale for varying set size was to evaluate the effects of contextual constraints on word identification.

In accord with expectations, skilled and less-skilled readers differed only on the word stimuli. Since no differences were observed in speed of naming colors, digits, and pictures, the authors ruled out response selection (retrieval) or response programming (speech-motor articulation) as significant determinants of reader group differences in vocalization latency. However, in the case of the word stimuli, skilled readers manifested shorter latencies than less-skilled readers and were not as affected as the latter group by the number of syllables in a word or the number of items in a stimulus category. Of additional interest is the fact that the groups were more divergent when syllabic structure of the word stimuli was varied than when semantic set size was varied. The authors suggested, in explanation of this disparity, that the "less skilled reader's ability to use semantic redundancy is rather good" whereas his ability to process phonetically complex material is weak.

Additional support for the view that the poor reader's major difficulty is in word decoding rather than apprehension of semantic content is derived from still another study conducted by Perfetti and his associates (Perfetti et al. 1977). Briefly, they found that vocalization latencies for both skilled and less-skilled readers were shorter within story contexts (heard or read) than in the absence of story contexts and, further, that the reduction of such latencies was greater for the less-skilled when contextual information was provided. It was also found that less-skilled readers could predict target words (which word comes next) as well as skilled readers, the correlations between vocalization latencies and target predictability being approximately -.60 for subjects in both groups. These data suggest that both less-skilled and skilled readers were able to employ context to facilitate the identification of single words and that the two groups used such context to comparable degrees.

The studies by Perfetti and his associates provide substantial support for the contention that inefficiency in semantic processing is a function of more basic deficiencies in verbal encoding. The most general conclusion to be drawn from these investigations is that the locus of difficulty in apprehending meanings is in the phonetic coding of linguistic units no smaller than the word or syllable. This difficulty presumably leads to consequent problems in using the semantic information that may be coded in those units, especially under time constraints. However, the evidence suggests that semantic processing difficulties are of a secondary nature and that poor readers are able to employ contextual information to access global meanings but falter when asked for specific bits of semantic information or verbatim recall of specific words or word strings, each of these items requiring efficient processing in short-term memory.

A finding of particular interest here is that poor readers were *not* characterized by difficulty in name retrieval or response selection (Perfetti et al. 1977). This finding is at variance with the results of other studies demonstrating rapid naming difficulties in poor readers when stimuli consisted of nonalphabetic as well as alphabetic material.

8.4.2 Rapid Naming Studies
Several studies have evaluated the correlates of reading disability within an aphasiological context, their design apparently having been influenced by findings issuing from neuropathological studies

of adult brain-damaged patients (Geschwind 1962; Hecaen 1962; Oldfield 1966; Denckla and Bowen 1973). Among studies adopting this approach, those by Denckla and Rudel (1976a, 1976b) are especially important. These authors conducted a series of exploratory investigations in which dyslexic and normal readers were compared on rapid automatic naming tasks and found to differ on both error and latency measures. Two representative studies will be reviewed.

In one investigation three groups of subjects were compared: a dyslexic group, a group of adequate readers with learning problems in other areas, and a group of normal controls (Denckla and Rudel 1976a). The subjects' ages ranged from 8 to 11 years. The two learning disabled groups (N = 10 each) were matched for age, sex, intelligence, socioeconomic status (middle class), and other extrinsic variables. The dyslexic group was relatively free from any signs of neurological disorder, whereas the other learning disabled group was generally characterized by neurological soft signs. An oral reading test was employed to assess reading achievement. Reading quotients were computed for the two experimental groups based on the ratio of the mean reading age to mental age. Reading quotients for the nondyslexic group ranged from 90 to 110; those for the dyslexic group ranged from 60 to 79. Grade equivalents ranged from 2.8 to 6.5 for the nondyslexics and from "nonreader" to 3.0 for the dyslexics. Thus the poor readers in the dyslexic sample were by and large severely impaired. No standardized measures were available for the normal control group (a weakness of the study), which also consisted of children from middle-class backgrounds.

The stimuli employed in this study were a series of black-on-white drawings of objects (Oldfield and Wingfield 1965) whose names were said to occur within a broad range on the Thorndike-Lorge (1944) frequency count. Subjects were asked only to name the items as rapidly as possible, and response latencies were recorded. Dyslexics made more naming errors than the other two groups, but the difference was greatest with low-frequency words. Perhaps as significant were the types of errors made by the three groups. The proportions of errors for the normal control group were evenly distributed among three categories: circumlocutions, wrong names, and not known. Dyslexics made the largest proportion of their errors in the circumlocution category (41 percent) and approximately equivalent percentages in the other two. In contrast the other learning disabled group made 61 percent of their errors in the wrong-name category and about equal proportions in the other categories. Both the dyslexic and the non-dyslexic learning disabled groups had longer response latencies to the stimulus pictures than the normal controls had.

Denckla and Rudel (1976a) concluded from these results that dyslexic children are "subtly dysphasic." They also suggested that "minimal brain dysfunction" is not always accompanied by dysphasia, in view of the fact that the performance of the neurologically impaired children on the naming tasks was within normal limits. The authors acknowledged that the absence of neurological signs among the dyslexic children rendered it impossible to draw conclusions as to the neuroanatomical basis of the naming difficulty observed, but they speculated that the disorder may reflect left-hemisphere dysfunction.

A second study by Denckla and Rudel (1976b) also compared dyslexic and nondyslexic low achievers with normal controls. Subjects were divided into four subgroups according to age (7 to 12 years). All were selected on the basis of reading and intellectual criteria and came from middle-class backgrounds. They were, in addition, examined for neurological status. Reading ability was operationally defined as the discrepancy between reading age and mental age and a child had to show a discrepancy of two or more years to be included in the study. Thus, the subjects in the sample appeared to be severely impaired in reading. Selection criteria in general seemed adequate.

The subjects in this study as in the one already discussed were administered rapid automatic naming tasks. Stimuli included colors, high-frequency lower-case letters, numerals, and common objects. The dependent measures were error scores and total time taken to complete each stimulus set. Although the groups did not differ in number of errors, they did differ in speed of responding. The dyslexics generally took longer to respond than either of the two other groups assessed; the nondyslexic low achievers were slower than the normal controls. Object naming took more time than any of the other tasks, and color naming was slower than numeral and letter naming. Age differences were also found among all groups, older children generally taking less time to respond than younger children. The results were not thought to be due to generalized slowness in the poor readers, since they were found to be significantly better than the normals on the WISC Performance Scale, all of the measures on that test being timed.

Denckla and Rudel considered the possibility that dyslexia is caused by some anomaly in visual-verbal association which may result in deficient verbal retrieval. Poor speech encoding, visual processing delays, and attentional problems were thought to be possible explanations of the findings.

Several other studies comparing poor and normal readers on rapid naming tasks have yielded results consistent with those obtained by Denckla and Rudel. For example, Spring (1976) tested the hypothesis that memory span impairment is attributable to slow "speech-motor encoding." Subjects (N = 14 each group) were two (nonstratified) groups of boys from 6 to 12 years of age. Criterion measures for selecting poor readers seemed adequate, but intelligence in the normal readers was not measured.

Adopting a two-storage memory model proposed by Atkinson and Shiffrin (1968), Spring hypothesized that items presented for short-term storage are implicitly encoded in a speech-motor response and briefly stored in short-term memory. If the item is rehearsed, it may be transferred into long-term storage and subsequently recalled. If there is limited or no time for rehearsal, the item will be displaced by subsequent input. In accord with this model, unusually slow speech-motor encoding should limit the time available for rehearsal, thereby reducing the number of items transferred to long-term memory and limiting recall to the most recently presented items. Spring therefore predicted that dyslexics would take more time than normal readers to complete rapid naming tasks and would perform below the level of the normals on memory for digits. He also predicted that memory for digits would not account for more of the variance in reading ability than speed of speech-motor encoding.

In order to evaluate these predictions, subjects were given rapid naming tasks employing digits, colors, and pictures of common objects. There were no significant differences between the groups on naming errors, but dyslexics did differ significantly from normals on speed of naming. Specifically, the mean number of responses per second was greater for dyslexics than for normal readers on all naming tasks. The dyslexics were also less accurate than the normals on memory for digits.

However, contrary to initial prediction, the digit-span measure accounted for a small but significant proportion of the variance in reading achievement—variance not determined by speed of encoding. Speed of encoding accounted for a proportion approximately equal to the amount determined by digit span, and both together accounted for more of the variance than either separately. Spring concluded from these results that impaired memory span in dyslexics may be partly, but not wholly, due to speech-motor encoding problems. Thus in this investigation there was evidence that poor readers may experience difficulty in name retrieval (response selection) or in speech-motor articulation (response programming), contrary to the findings of Perfetti, Bell, Hogaboam, and Goldman (1977).

In a second study (Spring and Capps 1974), employing identical sampling procedures and comparable reader groups (7 to 14 years, N = 24 each group), poor readers were observed to make use of rehearsal strategies less often than normal readers on a probe recall task involving memory for visually presented digits. The poor readers also manifested longer reaction times than the normal readers on rapid naming of both verbal and nonverbal stimuli. Interestingly enough, speed of naming was significantly correlated with both rehearsal tendencies and recall of digits. The authors inferred from these results that dyslexics may be characterized by deficiencies in both short- and long-term memory because of limitations in the amount of time available for rehearsal, owing to slowness in "speed of motor encoding."

Unfortunately, failure to assess the intelligence of normal readers equivocates the results of both of Spring's studies, as does the failure to employ uniform measures of reading achievement. The theory advanced in explanation of dyslexia is certainly of interest and the model employed to evaluate this theory seems useful, but the sampling problems permit no generalization to children with specific reading disability.

Additional support for reader group differences on rapid naming tasks can be found in Eakin and Douglas (1971) and in Denckla (1972). These findings coupled with the results of the studies just discussed provide highly suggestive evidence that poor readers sustain basic deficiencies in labeling and naming. Whether the major difficulty is due to malfunction in the storage or in the retrieval of lexical information is not apparent from the data, although such difficulties are not mutually exclusive. It will be recalled that Perfetti et al. (1977) ruled out retrieval or motor programming difficulties as the source of reader group differences in rapid naming since the skilled and less-skilled readers in their studies did not differ on speed of naming colors, pictures, and digits. Yet dyslexic and normal readers did differ on such materials in the studies by Denckla and Rudel (1976a and 1976b), Spring (1976), and Spring and Capps (1974). Two possible explanations of these disparities can be offered. One is that these investigations employed subjects who were qualitatively different with respect to type and degree of processing difficulty. For example, Perfetti's subjects may have been similar to the type of poor reader described by Liberman and Shankweiler (1978)—that is, one who is relatively insensitive to the phonetic structure of printed and spoken words (see section 8.6.2). According to these authors such individuals can be expected to have particular difficulty in coding alphabetic material because of their inefficiency in detecting the grapheme-phoneme invariants embedded in printed words. As a result, they may not readily apprehend such relationships in variable contexts and their efforts at word decoding may be characterized by a limited degree of economy. This explanation would account for the large differences found between the skilled and less-skilled readers in speed of vocalizing multisyllabic words.

In contrast, many of the subjects evaluated in the other rapid naming studies discussed may have had more basic problems in word retrieval, which itself could result in significant encoding problems inasmuch as the rapid coding of incoming material must surely depend in part upon the ability to retrieve information from long-term storage. In other words, subjects in these studies may have had difficulty in both the storage (encoding) and retrieval functions and, in that sense, may have been more severely impaired in verbal processing. The fact that these subjects were apparently more deficient in reading (generally two or more years below level on oral reading tests) than the subjects typically employed in the studies by Perfetti and his co-workers would certainly be consistent with this interpretation. Reinforcing this possibility is the finding in the Spring studies that poor readers were impaired in short-term memory for digits as well as in speed of object naming, which is in accord with many of the studies discussed in previous chapters, which reported reader group differences in short-term auditory memory for nonverbal as well as verbal material. Yet these results contrast with those of Perfetti and Goldman (1976), who found no differences between their skilled and less-skilled readers on memory for digits. Thus, sampling differences may well account for the discrepancies.

The second and perhaps more parsimonious explanation of the disparate results obtained in the rapid naming studies is that the stimuli employed in Perfetti's investigations were more restricted and may have been highly practiced. The other studies, in contrast, employed a larger number and a broader variety of stimulus materials and may have taxed the information processing skills of their subjects more than those Perfetti used. Of course, this interpretation and the first alternative are not mutually exclusive; only additional research can provide a definitive answer to the questions raised.

A final series of studies that seem relevant in this context was reported by Supramaniam and Audley (1976). These authors evaluated the alternative possibilities that disabled readers sustain deficiencies in either visual or verbal processing employing the well-known matching paradigm used by Posner and his associates (Posner et al. 1969). In one condition carefully selected samples of good and poor readers (ages 7 and 8) were given brief presentations of upper- and lower-case letter pairs and pairs of line drawings (animals) and asked to judge whether they were the same or different. Stimuli were prepared so that pairs were physically identical, nominally identical, or different. Both error scores and latencies were obtained. No differences between the groups were observed in making physical (visual) matches, but poor readers made more errors and took longer in making nominal matches.

A second experiment presented comparably selected groups with upper- and lower-case letters, pairs of line drawings in two different orientations, and rebus pairs—that is, a letter and a picture sharing the same name (b and bee). In one condition subjects judged whether stimulus pairs had the same name; in another condition they were asked whether the pairs rhymed. The results for pictures and letters were replicated in that the good readers maintained the advantage in matching name codes. However, greater differences in latencies were found on the rebus material, the differences between the groups being particularly large under the rhyming condition.

These results not only provide additional support for a verbal rather than a visual deficit explanation of reading disability but reinforce the suggestion that poor readers may be characterized by specific difficulty in encoding or retrieving name codes.

8.4.3 Semantic Processing and Knowledge of Words

Finally, there is another sense in which the relationship between semantic processing ability and reading achievement can be made explicit. It seems intuitively sound to infer that an individual with a reasonable knowledge of word meanings or vocabulary has acquired one of the important skills necessary for learning to read. The child with a well-developed vocabulary of the kind he will encounter in school has in effect acquired many of the responses he is expected to code in learning to read and write and, by virtue of such knowledge, has a distinct advantage over the child whose vocabulary is different or whose knowledge of words is inadequate in some way. Given the research reviewed in this section, one can speculate that a good fund of word meanings, although a necessary condition for learning to read fluently, may not be a sufficient condition, because a child who does possess an adequate knowledge of words may nevertheless be hampered by subtle impediments of the types described. Yet I suspect that such knowledge favorably disposes the individual to acquiring reading skills inasmuch as it provides him with a rich network of contextual information that would no doubt enhance both word identification and comprehension.

Considering these points, it is surprising that very little attempt has been made to systematically study the relationship between reading ability and vocabulary in severely disabled readers, particularly in the early stages of acquisition when these relations can be more pointedly evaluated—that is, without incurring the risk of confounding by virtue of the growth in verbal ability that is partly atrributable to knowledge acquired as a consequence of the ability to read. There are, however, a few studies that are suggestive.

Reference was made earlier to the large number of studies (including many of our own) that found that poor readers as young as 7 years of age consistently performed below the level of normal readers on the Verbal scale of the WISC, measures of vocabulary and verbal concept ability being particularly divergent in these groups. In addition, the studies by de Hirsch, Jansky, and Langford (1966) and Jansky and de Hirsch (1972) both found that a number of verbal measures (including vocabulary) administered to kindergartners showed significant positive correlations with second-grade reading achievement. Ravenette (1968) also found substantial correlations between measures of vocabulary and measures of reading, writing, listening, and speaking, as did Monroe (1932), Raulin (1962), Fry (1967), and Schulte (1967). The last two studies are presented in a summary paper by Fry, Johnson, and Muchl (1970) (see section 8.5.3).

Significant relationships between vocabulary and reading ability have been noted in adult college students too. For example, Cromer (1970) observed that individuals with a poor vocabulary who were also poor in reading comprehension did not profit from deliberate efforts to organize text to improve their understanding. In contrast, poor comprehenders matched for vocabulary with good comprehenders on knowledge of words did improve their understanding as a result of organizational aids. Evidently a deficient vocabulary significantly influences one's ability to synthesize information for effective understanding and recall. This is no doubt true of all aspects of linguistic functioning, including, of course, the acquisition of skill in reading. It might also be true that there is an intrinsic relationship between the types of deficits outlined in the studies examined in this section—specifically in word encoding and retrieval—and deficiencies in vocabulary, although such a relationship is not immediately apparent. Additional research investigating correlations that may exist between reading disability and knowledge of words would therefore seem to be an important undertaking.

8.4.4 Summary

In summary, the foregoing results provide considerable support for the view that poor readers do not sustain a primary deficiency in semantic processing when such deficiency is defined as basic malfunction in abstracting the common meanings of individual words, in ability to organize thematic material globally, in sensitivity to meaning-bearing units in phrases and sentences, or in general language comprehension. On the other hand, there is reason to believe that access to specific word meanings or meanings coded contextually is not always efficient in such children, owing to more subtle malfunction in word encoding or retrieval, which in turn results in inefficient processing in short-term memory. Because of these constraints, the semantic information embedded in any given text may not be effectively educed, but such difficulties would seem to be of a secondary nature, at least in the populations of poor readers that have been discussed.

It is of particular interest that inefficiency in apprehending meaning was observed in the processing of spoken as well as written language, implying that the difficulties observed in decoding written text are primarily linguistic in nature. This conclusion is contrary to the alternative theories of reading disorder discussed in earlier chapters. I acknowledge that the strongest body of evidence supporting this conclusion—the studies of Perfetti and his associates—has been obtained with children who by and large appear to be only moderately impaired in reading. Nevertheless, the results of these studies, particularly those data issuing from reader group contrasts in rapid naming, are consistent with work done elsewhere, and the evidence suggests that poor readers of the types studied sustain significant difficulty in the naming function. Thus, assuming that Perfetti's analysis of the role of word naming in semantic access is correct—and it seems plausible—I see no reason why the problems of more severely impaired readers in verbal memory and comprehension would not be comparable. Indeed they should be more pronounced. It would therefore seem that the results discussed have wide generality; certainly they are consistent with the findings supporting a verbal deficit explanation of reading disability discussed in sections 8.1 through 8.3. Research yet to be discussed will reinforce this position.

8.5 SYNTACTIC FACTORS

8.5.1 Syntactic Competence and Reading Disability: Rationale
The ability to comprehend language in the general sense is, of course, an important prerequisite to learning to read. There is no question that children with pronounced language impairments are severely handicapped in their attempts to learn. Such children may be reasonably described as markedly deficient with respect to syntactic competence, when the latter is defined as the ability to employ information about grammatical relationships to effect

understanding of spoken and written language. However, children with specific reading disorder do not, by definition, sustain such global impairments in language. In view of this fact it would be reasonable to question the suggestion that the obstacles these children encounter in learning to read are in any way attributable to syntactic deficiencies.

Yet there is reason to believe that at least some poor readers do not have a fine-grained knowledge of grammatical relationships, even prior to instruction in reading, and it is conceivable that such difficulty could impede progress in all aspects of skill acquisition—word identification as well as comprehension. Children have much to learn in developing linguistic competence, but sensitivity to the rule-bound and recursive qualities of language—that is, to its syntax—is of primary importance to success in this venture. Language is also creative and relative, as well as highly abstract, and it is precisely because of these characteristics that the developing child is constantly confronted with linguistic information of which he has only a partial understanding. The problem of language acquisition is further compounded in that learning to employ the rules of syntax effectively means learning the exceptions to the rules and when and how they are applicable. In his efforts to approximate mature comprehension and use of language, the developing child must frequently alter his conceptualization of linguistic structures and usages to accommodate new information that is incongruent with his previous understanding. In addition, he must learn that particular meanings can be expressed with different words and that different meanings can be expressed with many of the same words in different contexts. Such learning implies a growing awareness of refined distinctions among lexical entries, as when the child learns that content words are frequently categorical and that functors, such as *and, but, because, although, when, how, why,* are highly abstract invariants that carry specific meanings in a variety of contexts. It should be apparent that the acquisition of the complex rule system that facilitates the learning of these complicated relationships—that is, the acquisition of syntax—represents a major developmental achievement. Such complexity holds the potential for imperfect learning, particularly in the case of the more subtle and abstract components of language, and some children experience difficulty in achieving mastery in comprehending and using these constructions. It is just these children who might be expected to have difficulty in one or more aspects of reading.

These remarks should not be taken to mean, necessarily, that deficiencies in a child's knowledge of syntax would occur apart from deficiencies in other linguistic functions; nor do I necessarily believe that syntactic deficiency is of basic constitutional origin. Although these are distinct (and not mutually exclusive) possibilities, they represent hypotheses that are yet to be tested. Consideration of a possible relation between subtle syntactic deficits and reading disability does not depend upon an immediate answer to these questions. In fact an imperfect command of standard English syntax could in some children be associated with limited or inadequate exposure to the language in the preschool years rather than to syntactic problems of organic origin. Such difficulties could also be the result of reading disorder stemming from dysfunction in other areas, which, of course, could lead to restricted opportunities for language enrichment that would be occasioned by the ability to read. In either event, the difficulties in reading that might be associated with deficient syntax would nonetheless obtain; but, as should be apparent, the coexistence of these two problems in children who are normal in other respects would be of special interest. Thus, the primary intent in this section is to present documentation that specific reading disability and deficiencies in syntactic functioning may co-occur in some children and that they may be intrinsically related. However, because research investigating the relation in question is so meager, the discussion will be largely descriptive and will entail no necessary commitment to causal connections in given instances, except perhaps to underscore possible correlates suggested by the data.

8.5.2 Individual Differences in Syntactic Development: Two Illustrative Studies

A number of studies have demonstrated that syntactic development is gradual during early and middle childhood and continues through adolescence (Strickland 1962; Loban 1963; Menyuk 1963, 1964; Hunt 1964, 1965; O'Donnell, Griffin, and Norris 1967; C. Chomsky 1969, 1972). Whether or not such development proceeds in definitive stages is unclear at the present time, but researchers have typically observed large individual differences in the ages at which certain syntactic patterns appear in given children, chronological age being an imperfect predicter of such events. This is an important finding, with implications not only for our understanding of language but for our understanding of related skills such as reading.

In order to provide a context within which to view possible relations that may exist between syntactic functioning and reading disability, we will briefly review two investigations of language development in school-age children which peripherally address the possible connection between reading and language ability. These studies were chosen not only because they provide useful information about normal growth in language and its relation to reading but because their findings led to subsequent studies specifically comparing poor and normal readers on various measures of syntactic ability.

Loban (1963)[4] conducted a longitudinal study that annually evaluated the specific language and cognitive abilities of school-age children (N = 338) from kindergarten through twelfth grade. The sample was stratified to include children from low, middle, and upper socioeconomic groups, and an attempt was made to effect representative sampling and proportional allocation of subjects to given strata according to sex, race, and intellectual ability. Three different samples were defined; one was selected randomly, the other two were classified as high and low language-ability groups on the basis of vocabulary scores.

The intent of the study was to evaluate developmental changes in language and related skills; data were specifically collected in the following areas: (1) vocabulary, (2) use of oral and written language, (3) proficiency in reading and listening, (4) teacher's judgment of skill with language, and (5) background information on health and home environment. The results reported in Loban (1963) were for annual assessments of children from kindergarten through sixth grade. On each occasion the children were interviewed and thereafter asked to respond to six pictures, their responses being tape-recorded and later transcribed for analysis. The children's utterances were initially segmented on the basis of changes in intonation, stress, inflection, and pause, such segments being termed *phonologic units.* These were further subdivided on the basis of semantic-syntactic content—each segment being called a *communication unit,* which is essentially a grammatically independent clause with all of its modifiers. A third unit examined was the child's false starts and hesitations, termed *mazes.*

Two types of analyses were performed. The first level of analysis was structural: Loban ascertained the frequency and variety of use of nine types of complete sentences as well as incidence of partial sentences; the nine patterns were found to be comprehensive in that they accounted for all variations of complete sentences manifested in the samples derived from each subject. In the second level of analysis Loban examined the sentence constituents themselves (types of clauses, types of subjects, objects, complements, types of prediction, and so forth) for their use by children at different ages. The childrens' utterances were also analyzed in terms of their function and style, and transformational analyses (N. Chomsky 1957) were made of the language samples taken from two subjects. Vocabulary was measured by a 100-item word list adopted from Watts (1948). Reading achievement in second and third grade was evaluated by a reading index based on cumulative records; (reading) achievement for children in grades 4 through 6 was assessed employing the Stanford Achievement Test.

The most salient findings from this study are as follows. First, there was a steady increase in verbal fluency each successive year as measured by the total number of words, total number of communication units, and average number of words in communication units. Increases were more pronounced in the high language-ability group, which was consistently superior on these measures, than in the low language-ability group. There was also a steady increase in vocabulary, increments being again greater in the high-ability group than in the low-ability group.

The second major finding was that both linguistic ability groups manifested a decline in the incidence of mazes, or false starts, the high group declining more than the low group over the years. Third, although there were no differences between the groups in use of the nine types of sentence structures, their use of constituents within these structures differed. That is, the low-ability groups employed more incomplete sentence patterns and manifested less sophisticated syntax than the high-ability group, as reflected in the tendency of the latter subjects toward more frequent employment of such items as linking verbs, adverbial clauses, noun clauses, infinitives, verbal phrases, and subordinate clauses. The subjects who were found to be most proficient in language also made much greater use of conditional and suppositional expressions such as *I think* or *I'm not sure,* to communicate tentativeness. They were, in addition, characterized by a more coherent speaking style, as manifested by more subordinations, greater use of subordinating connectives, greater syntactic flexibility and control, and use of language that was generally more substantive and more sophisticated.

A fourth finding of importance was wide variability with respect to the time at which various syntactic patterns emerged in given children, specific constructions being observed across a wide age range. At the same time a greater number and variety of such patterns were observed in the high-ability group than in the low-ability group.

Of particular note, in the present context, is the finding that the children who were less proficient linguistically were much less adequate in reading than those who were highly proficient in language. This was true in the case of children in both the lower and upper grades. In addition, the randomly selected subjects, whose linguistic proficiency was generally intermediate between the high and low language-ability groups, did not read as well as the high-ability group but better than the low-ability group. It is also of interest that the various linguistic measures (oral language, listening, reading, and writing) were highly intercorrelated.

The transformational analyses of the language productions of the two children selected for study discriminated successfully between them. However, since these data come from only two subjects, they must be considered token. Analyses were based on N. Chomsky's (1957) initial formulation of his theory of syntax.

The results of Loban's study, although primarily descriptive and atheoretical, make it clear that syntactic development is not complete when the child begins to learn to read, and continues for some time after. It is also apparent that there are wide individual differences in linguistic sophistication among children in the early and middle childhood years; such differences are manifested not so much in the broad structural patterns characteristic of sentences as in the flexibility with which sentence constituents are employed. In latter day (and more fashionable) parlance, this finding may be a sign that the linguistically sophisticated child may have a better sense of "deep structure" as well as of the relationships between deep structure and transformational rules. This, in effect, enables him to express the same meanings with a greater variety of syntactic usages, as well as to express more subtleties of meaning. Such competence would also enable him to comprehend a broader range of meanings presented in both spoken and written language, which has obvious implications for developing skill in reading. Thus it is not surprising that subjects with more sophisticated language ability were more accomplished in reading than those who were linguistically less competent, and the data provide evidence that syntactic ability and reading skill are intrinsically related. This finding is of special interest in that Loban's (1963) study, so far as I know, is the only one to date that has extensively analyzed linguistic behavior in the same children over an eleven-year period. As noted in his report, linguistic deficiencies were evident in poor readers prior to their initial encounter with reading.

However, the results of Loban's study can be generalized to children with specific reading disability only with some degree of caution, inasmuch as both linguistic competence and reading ability were found to be related to intelligence and socioeconomic level and the author provided no comparative figures for these variables in his high and low language-ability groups. Yet the results are suggestive and entirely consistent with the findings of studies yet to be reported, that contrasted linguistic skills in poor and normal readers who *were* comparable in intelligence and socioeconomic levels (Fry, Johnson, and Muehl 1970; Wiig, Semel, and Crouse 1973; Vogel 1974).

Additional support for the notion that syntactic development extends well into adolescence is provided by two separate studies conducted by C. Chomsky (1969, 1972). In both investigations preschool and elementary-school children were evaluated to determine their understanding of specific aspects of English syntax. We shall focus on the more recent of the two investigations (C. Chomsky 1972), since it specifically concerns the relationship between reading and language.

Thirty-six children from kindergarten through fourth grade were evaluated, each child being selected from a middle socioeconomic school. Subjects were tested for knowledge of nine complex syntactic structures that were judged to be candidates for late acquisition. The common feature among the structures chosen was that they violate widely established patterns in English, thereby prompting generalization error in children who have not yet become conversant with the subtle differences in typical and atypical constructions. An example will better illustrate the point. Consider (from C. Chomsky 1969) the two sentences:

(a) John promised Mary to shovel the driveway.
(b) John told Mary to shovel the driveway.

In (a) it is John who is expected to do the shoveling, but in (b) it is Mary who is expected to do it. C. Chomsky (1969) found this distinction to be difficult for children between the ages of 5 and 8 (roughly speaking), who often interpreted both sentences as meaning that Mary does the shoveling. This is presumably because virtually all verbs that could replace *told* in sentence (b) carry this meaning. Such verbs appear to conform to what has been called the minimum distance principle (MDP) (Rosenbaum 1967), according to which the implicit subject (noun) of the infinitive complement clause is judged to be the noun phrase in closest proximity to that clause. Thus in sentence (b) *Mary* is the implicit subject of the infinitive clause.

The verb *promise* appears to be an exception to the MPD, as can be verified by again examining sentence (a). C. Chomsky suggested that young children have not yet acquired the complex syntactic rules involved in making the distinction in question and will take some time to do so. She further suggested that the acquisition of these rules proceeds in stages approximately as follows. In stage I the tendency is to apply the MDP to sentences containing verbs like *promise,* which do not conform to the typical pattern. In stage II they make errors on those that do conform to the MDP as well as on those that do not. In stage III they begin to avoid the tendency to apply the MDP to verbs like *promise,* but only intermittently. And in stage IV they finally establish the rules necessary to discriminate between typical and atypical structures. C. Chomsky's (1969) initial study provided some support for this progression in children between 5 and 10 years of age.

The intent of the investigation of interest here (C. Chomsky 1972) was to provide further documentation of the stage concept as applied to the acquisition of syntax in children between the ages of 6 and 10. An additional purpose was to examine the relationship of language to intelligence and socioeconomic status was also of interest.

Of the nine syntactic constructions evaluated, three were selected on the basis of previous research (*promise* and *ask*: C. Chomsky 1969; *easy to see*: Cromer 1970) and the rest were selected on the basis of their apparent complexity and plausibility for use with children. Comprehension of these structures was assessed by means of individual interviews. After it was determined that the children knew the meanings of the words presented, each child was required to answer questions or perform actions (with dolls for instance) designed to reveal differential understanding of target and contrast sentences, both of which had identical surface characteristics. Specifically, comprehension of sentences involving *easy to see* were compared with those involving *eager to see; promise* and *ask* sentences were compared with those involving *told;* and sentences substituting *and* for *although* were compared.

Five of the nine constructions appeared to be acquired in an invariant sequence as follows: *easy to see, promise, ask, and, although.* This was viewed as evidence that acquisition of syntactic construction takes place in stages.[5] Since the structures themselves are rather dissimilar in terms of meaning and form class, the results were thought to have considerable generality.

The tendency toward wide variability in acquisition of specific syntactic structures was noted in this study as in the one by Loban. Specifically, children from 5 to 9 years were observed to be at stages I and II, and children from ages 7 to 9 were at stage V. These findings provide additional evidence that chronological age is an imperfect predictor of language acquisition.

However, of particular interest for our purposes, is the observed relationship between measures of the children's experiences in reading and the acquisition of the five syntactic patterns. The reading measures consisted of a standardized inventory assessing literacy experience as well as parent and child interviews, each designed to determine a given child's acquaintance (through either listening or reading) with a variety of reading materials. These measures were then correlated with knowledge of one or more of the five syntactic patterns. The significant finding here is that those who had the most extensive exposure to literary materials proved to be the same children who acquired most or all of the syntactic patterns evaluated. An especially interesting finding is that the preschoolers in high linguistic stages were read to by more people and listened to more stories per week than children at lower linguistic stages.

Because intelligence, age, and socioeconomic level were also found to be related to linguistic performance, comparisons on the literacy measures were made in the case of three children, matched for age, IQ, and socioeconomic status, who were in different linguistic stages. The relationships observed in the first analysis were generally maintained, in that higher stage development was associated with greater exposure to reading material. However, conclusions drawn from the second analysis can only be suggestive, because of the small number of subjects involved in each contrast.

The results of these two studies provide limited support for the contention that reading and language proficiency are highly correlated. They suggest, in addition, that comprehension of the more complex syntactic patterns may be problematic for given children. That such difficulties could conceivably be correlated with reading disorder is suggested in a number of investigations that have specifically evaluated syntactic competence in children with differing abilities in reading. Two studies directly extend from the investigations just discussed.

8.5.3 Studies Evaluating Syntactic Competence in Poor and Normal Readers

The first of these studies was the substance of two doctoral dissertations completed at the University of Iowa (Fry 1967; Schulte 1967) and summarized in a subsequent paper by Fry, Johnson, and Muehl (1970). This investigation compared linguistic functioning in carefully selected samples of poor and normal readers in second grade, employing procedures for procuring and analyzing language samples similar to those Loban had used. The subjects in the study consisted of 36 poor readers and 21 normal readers, whose ages ranged between 7 and 8 years chronologically. The groups were comparable with respect to age, sex, intelligence, and socioeconomic status, and all those sustaining deficiencies in sensory, physical, or emotional problems were excluded from the research sample. Reading achievement measures included tests of word knowledge, word recognition, and comprehension. Thus selection criteria in this study were reasonably adequate.

The basic comparison between poor and normal readers was on an oral language sample derived in response to twenty picture stimuli. Subjects were asked to tell a story about each picture and each response was recorded and transcribed. Fifty responses from each subject were selected for analysis, each a gramatically independent clause. Two general approaches to linguistic analysis were employed. The first was more traditional (descriptive), consisting of a record of such measures as proportion of total words, total different words, type-token ratios (different words to total number of words), types and frequencies of different syntactic patterns, and the like. More detailed analyses were made of the syntactic structures of each independent clause (termed *communication units*), employing methods used by Strickland (1962), Loban (1963, as described above), and Kean (1965). The responses were analyzed as to types and frequencies of syntactic usages, which included constituents of dependent and independent clauses.

The second method of analysis was based upon N. Chomsky's 1965 grammatical model and was essentially a comparison of the two reader groups on the type and number of transformational rules employed to arrive at a given phrase or sentence. Statistical tests included contrasts of group mean differences as well as correlations of various measures with reading scores.

The descriptive analysis yielded 14 variables that distinguished the poor and normal readers, 8 favoring the normal readers and 6 favoring the poor readers. However, the specific differences on these variables were complementary and can be synthesized in the form of certain general performance patterns separating the groups. First, the normal readers were characterized by larger speaking vocabularies and greater fluency than the poor readers. These differences were indexed by a higher stimulus-to-output (in words) ratio, more frequent use of word categories, greater number of different words, better organization of ideas, and greater elaboration generally.

A second major finding from the descriptive analysis was that the sentences produced by the two reader groups were often structurally different from one another. For example, the normal readers tended to use modification in the predicate position more often than poor readers, who used more modification in the subject positions. These tendencies appeared to be linked to a more general pattern of group differences with respect to type of subordination manifested in their protocols. To illustrate, the normal readers were more inclined than the poor readers to use phrases as indirect objects, direct objects, or predicate nominatives; the poor readers used more phrases related only to the subject, especially nominal compounds (*This monkey and that monkey and the other monkey are talking.*)

The normal readers' productions were also characterized by greater flexibility and more complexity in syntactic usage than those of the poor readers, as manifested in a high general incidence of movables (parts of sentence with no fixed position) and greater use of clauses as direct objects, indirect objects, and subject-verb complements (words or phrases which elaborate the meanings of subjects or complete the sense of verbs). Normal readers also employed subject-verb-object constructions (that is, complete sentences) more often than poor readers. These findings are, of course, analogous to the results obtained by Loban in contrasts of high and low language-ability groups.

The structural disparities observed in the language of poor and normal readers could well have been related to a third difference found between the two groups: a difference in the content of the sentences they produced. Specifically, the poor readers tended to employ sentences of the "existence" type more often than normal readers, being generally more inclined to simply describe obvious characteristics of a given stimulus without elaboration rather than to create and detail a story in response to that stimulus. This tendency would, in part, account for a higher incidence, for poor readers than for normal readers, of linking verbs followed by subjects (*there's the stool*), expressions of place (*there's the stool over there*), phrases related only to the subject (*three baby chicks are eating some food*), and clauses related only to the subject (*three baby chicks who are eating some food*). Since the reader groups were equated for intelligence, the lack of substance in sentences produced would appear to be related to linguistic rather than conceptual deficiencies.

Finally, discriminant function analyses indicated that the variables that best predicted reading scores (in combination) were number of different words used, frequency of use of clauses in a predicate position, and movables expressing cause or condition, the normal readers employing the latter construction less often than the poor readers (although normal readers generally used more moveables, as noted above).

The transformational analysis was also successful in separating the reader groups. (It should be noted that the subjects were not identified as to reader group membership until the analysis had been completed.) The quantifications in this analysis consisted of such items as the total number of transformational rules (T-rules) needed to account for the communication units produced, the total number of T-rules used, the total number of different T-rules used, and the total number of T-rules used excluding those that generated existence type sentences. Reporting only the salient results derived from these contrasts, it was found that poor readers used more contractions, violated subject-verb agreement in number more often, used more nominal compounds, and used more existence sentences than did normal readers. Excluding existence sentences, normal readers generally employed a greater number of transformations than did the poor readers. They also employed more transformations per communication unit. Discriminant function analyses performed on the transformation data indicated that the frequency of subject-verb number *dis*agreement predicted reading achievement better than any other variable or combination of variables ($r = .41$).

The results from the transformational analysis are generally in accord with the results derived from the descriptive analysis, in that both were characterized by less sophisticated and more descriptive linguistic constructions on the part of poor readers rather than grammatically elaborated language. Interestingly enough, the higher incidence of subject-verb disagreement in this group suggests the possibility of poorly developed morphological usage in children with reading problems, a linguistic deficiency that has been shown in other studies to be significant in differentiating poor and normal readers (Brittain 1970; Wiig, Semel, and Crouse 1973; Vogel 1974).

These findings are consistent with the results of the studies by Loban (1963) and C. Chomsky (1972). All three investigations provide support for the notion that there are significant individual differences in linguistic competence among children with differing abilities in reading. The combined results can also be taken as evidence for the hypothesis that reading disability and syntactic inadequacy may be correlated. The conclusions drawn by Fry, Johnson, and Muehl (1970) were that language deficits such as those observed in their study could impair both word recognition and comprehension by limiting the number and variety of "verbal labels and mediators" available for acquiring the coded relations involved in learning to read; they cited the results of Blank and her associates (1966, 1968) as being consistent with their own. Pointing out that their findings do not resolve the question of cause-effect relationships, they nevertheless conjectured that language disorder may be a causal factor in cases of reading disability. I might add that the finding of pronounced linguistic deficits in children at the beginning stages of reading speaks for the possibility that specific language disability is causally related to reading disorder and not just the result of cumulative deficiencies associated with long-standing reading problems.

Consistent with the foregoing are the results of a recent investigation conducted by Goldman (1976). The design and procedures employed in this study directly extended from the studies by C. Chomsky (1969, 1972). Goldman's primary intent was to contrast listening and reading comprehension for sentences that either follow or do not follow the minimum distance principle (MDP), as a function of skill in reading. An additional purpose was to examine the reliability of Chomsky's stage theory of syntactic development.

The subjects in this investigation were third, fourth, and fifth graders (N = 96), selected on the basis of a test of reading comprehension. Intelligence tests were administered to each subject, but no other selection criteria were employed and no further description of subject characteristics was provided. The entire sample was divided into thirds, comprising high, middle, and low reading-ability groups. The high and low groups differed with respect to age and intelligence, but this circumstance was not thought to be critical because IQ was not found to be highly correlated with the language measures.

Two separate experiments were conducted. In experiment 1, comprehension of the *promise* and *tell* constructions employed by C. Chomsky were the dependent measures, and the procedures she used in her studies were adopted, except that all subjects were presented with sentences containing these constructions under both listening and reading conditions. The most significant finding in this experiment is that the low-ability readers did not perform as well on the *promise* construction as the middle- and high-ability groups, under either listening or reading comprehension conditions. In contrast, the groups did not differ appreciably on the reading comprehension of *tell* sentences (the more common structure) and the differences on the *tell* sentences were minimal under the listening condition. Furthermore, although there was a low (but significant) correlation between intelligence and *promise* sentences, the correlation between reading skill and the *promise* constructions was considerably higher, under both experimental conditions. This pattern was maintained when *tell* sentences and the stage variable were the dependent measures. There was no substantial relationship between age and the other variables assessed in this study. Experiment 1 provided some verification for Chomsky's stage theory, but only for the listening condition.

Because there was some question of confounding by virtue of the use of lists containing both *promise* and *tell* constructions, a second experiment compared blocked presentations of these variables with mixed lists. Half the subjects in the sample responded differently on the blocked and mixed lists, suggesting the need for some degree of caution in interpreting results from the two types of presentations. However, the reader group differences were maintained in this second contrast, underscoring the reliability of initial results.

Goldman's findings are certainly of interest in the present context, and they complement the findings of Chomsky's 1972 study, which correlated syntactic functioning and reading with a somewhat different focus. Aside from the reservations already expressed in reviewing the other studies, conclusions drawn from Goldman's results must be tempered by the fact that the magnitude of group differences in reading ability is not apparent in this study, because silent reading tests were employed for sample selection rather than oral reading tests. Furthermore, the high-skill and low-skill groups differed in both age and intelligence and these variables may have influenced the results to some extent. Nevertheless, the data are suggestive and certainly accord with the results of the other three studies reviewed. In fact the combined results of the four studies discussed thus far could be taken as strong support for the hypothesized relationship between reading ability and syntactic development.

8.5.4 Inflectional Morphology and Reading Ability

Consistent with the possibility that some poor readers may be basically impaired in acquiring certain of the more subtle aspects of English grammar are the results of three studies evaluating the relation between reading achievement and knowledge of English morphology. One branch of morphology (inflectional morphology) is concerned with the system of bound morphemes (inflections) that indicate case, number, gender, person, tense, aspect, and so on. Inflectional morphemes are suffixes such as tense markers, plural markers, and possession markers. Occurrence of these bound morphemes is governed by syntactic rules, and the precise form an inflection takes is determined by morphophonological rules. Developmental studies (Berko 1958; see also Palermo and Molfese 1972) have shown that the child's ability to employ grammatical inflections is yet another illustration that language is very definitely a complex categorical skill that takes some time to develop, and age-appropriate use of inflections apparently reflects the fact that a child has begun to internalize the more abstract and fine-grained system of rules necessary for understanding and producing grammatically sophisticated language. Correct use of inflections requires the coordination of large amounts of semantic, syntactic, and phonologic information and thus requires an intimate acquaintance with the comprehension and production rules characteristic of those linguistic subsystems. It is therefore significant that some investigations have found evidence for an intrinsic relationship between reading ability and facility in using morphology.

Brittain (1970) presented first- and second-graders with a modified version of Berko's (1958) test of morphological usage. Subjects were from suburban communities and came predominately from middle-class families. There were an unequal number of boys and girls in the sample (29 boys and 27 girls, first grade; 17 boys and 35 girls, second grade); the median ages for first- and second-graders were 7.1 and 8.0 respectively; all subjects were of average or above average intelligence. Because this was a correlational study, there was no specific grouping on the basis of reading ability.

The salient findings that emerged from this investigation are as follows. Although neither grade level nor sex differences clearly separated the groups, there was definitive support for the prediction that morphological development proceeds from the simple to the complex and is elaborated with experience. Of more importance, in the present context, are the correlations between the language measure and composite reading scores, which included tests of word recognition, word analysis, and comprehension. Briefly, significant positive correlations were found between both these measures in separate analyses for boys and girls, as well as for the groups combined. The correlations in first grade ranged from .39 to .46; in second grade they were considerably higher, .71 to .74. Furthermore, the correlations between reading and inflectional performance were generally higher than the correlations between reading and intelligence, and were maintained even after controlling for intelligence. Brittain concluded from these findings that the children who have not mastered the morphophonological rules of their language may be characterized by a "genuine linguistic retardation which would be expected to hamper their progress in the reading aspect of the language arts" (1970, 47).

Brittain's findings are reinforced by the results of a study conducted by Wiig, Semel, and Crouse (1973). The subjects in this investigation were groups of poor and normal readers who were 9 years of age, as well as 4-year-olds who were considered either "high" risk or "low" risk children. The poor readers were comparable to the normal readers on intelligence and other relevant selection criteria. Reading achievement was assessed on the basis of a composite reading measure and a test of spelling ability. The sampling procedures for these groups thus appeared to be adequate. The 4-year-old children were classified as high-risk and low-risk on the basis of case history data indicating the presence or absence of neurological signs. (The selection criterion for the 4-year-olds was obviously weak, considering the fact that the validity of case history data cannot be assured.)

As in Brittain's study, the experimental test of morphology designed by Berko (1958) was the task on which the groups were compared. Briefly, the poor readers gave fewer correct responses on this test than did the controls. Furthermore, there was virtually no parallel between the two groups with respect to differential facility with particular morphological usages. In fact, the individual patterns of difficulty in the poor reader group were idiosyncratic and unpredictable, whereas in the normal reader group they could generally be predicted. Also evident in the nor-

mal readers was the tendency to transfer phonological conditioning rules across morphological categories, a sign that the
normal readers' knowledge of grammatical inflections was more
stable than that of the poor readers.

Turning to the 4-year-olds, the high-risk children were observed
to have less acquaintance with morphology than the low-risk
children. This finding suggested a possible relationship between
early language deficiencies and later predicted learning disability.
An interesting bit of evidence to further support this possibility
is the finding that possessives, adjectival inflections, and the
third-person singular of verbs occasioned the greatest difference
between the 9-year-old poor and normal readers, and the same was
true in comparisons of high- and low-risk 4-year-olds, suggesting
a continuum of deficits across the two age levels. No interpretation of this finding was offered. The authors concluded that verbal
skills are significantly impaired in disabled readers and recom-
mended remediation to correct such deficiencies no later than
kindergarten or first grade.

Finally, Vogel (1974) compared normal and dyslexic children
on a large battery of tests measuring a variety of syntactic abilities.
Some of these measures were standardized; others were designed
by the experimenter. The subjects in this study were second-
graders and appear to have been carefully selected on the basis of
all relevant exclusionary criteria. Reading achievement criteria
were also adequate, although final sample selection was based on
a reading comprehension test.

The assessment battery consisted of nine measures of oral
syntax, which included tests of abiltiy to detect intonational
variations, recognition of grammaticality, comprehension of
syntax, knowledge of morphology (real words and nonsense
words), linguistic closure (sentence completion employing correct
grammar), and sentence repetition.

The dyslexics were inferior to the normal readers on seven out
of the nine measures employed in the study, including the test
of morphology. Vogel concluded that syntactic deficiencies and
reading disability are intrinsically related. However, she underscored the experimental nature of many of the tests administered
and cautioned that her findings should be considered tentative
rather than definitive. Nevertheless, Vogel's results on the various
measures she employed are consistent with the results of the

other studies discussed and may therefore be reliable. In all three studies testing the use of inflectional morphology, poor readers were found to be less proficient than normal readers. And it should be pointed out that the study reported by Fry, Johnson, and Muehl (1970) also yielded a higher incidence of subject-verb disagreement among poor readers than among normal readers.

8.5.5 Syntactic Competence, Word Decoding, and Comprehension

Thus far, we have reviewed a number of investigations which have directly compared poor and normal readers on various aspects of syntactic functioning. These studies evaluated both the perceptive and productive components of language and poor readers were found to be less proficient than normal readers on the variables assessed, suggesting that at least some of these children may sustain basic inadequacies in syntactic development. This seems a distinct possibility inasmuch as several of the investigations reviewed included subjects specifically chosen on the basis of reading ability, who were carefully selected in accord with the exclusionary criteria discussed earlier (Fry, Johnson, and Muehl 1970; Wiig, Semel, and Crouse 1973; Vogel 1974). Furthermore, all but one of the studies discussed (Goldman 1976) evaluated children who were in the early stages of reading acquisition (second grade and below), which suggests that the linguistic deficits observed in these children were not the result of protracted reading disorder. Thus the results can be reasonably viewed as suggestive, if not conclusive evidence in support of the hypothesis in question.

It is instructive to supplement these observations with relevant findings from studies specifically contrasting poor and normal readers on their ability to employ syntax to decode written language. These investigations provide no direct evidence to support the contention that poor readers may be characterized by deficiencies in syntactic competence, and subjects were not generally selected in accord with the operational criteria outlined earlier. However, they do add substance to the argument that knowledge of linguistic structure influences all aspects of reading.

A series of experiments was undertaken by Cromer, Wiener, and their associates to evaluate the hypothesis that poor readers are characterized by a general propensity toward inefficient use of language in both reading comprehension and word identification. Such difficulties were said to be manifested in anomalous tendencies toward the use of idiosyncratic cues for word decoding, inadequate use of contextual information, word-by-word reading, and lack of economy in processing. Three studies were conducted with children. In one of their initial investigations, Cromer and Wiener (1966) predicted that poor readers would make more syntactic errors and produce more uncommon responses than would good readers in reading connected text orally. This hypothesis was tested with fifth-graders (N = 48) selected on the basis of reading comprehension and intelligence measures (mean grade equivalent = 3.8 poor readers, 5.7 good readers; IQ range 94–121). Basic contrasts were made employing the Cloze techinque used by Taylor (1953). The Cloze procedure essentially evaluates comprehension of syntax, and requires that the subject fill in words randomly deleted from sentences. Children in both groups were also administered a word association test.

The poor readers scored lower than the good readers on the sentence deletion task, from which it was inferred that they were not as atuned to the syntactic information contained in the text as their normal reading peers. The poor readers also gave more uncommon responses than the good readers on both the Cloze task and the word association test. The authors concluded from these findings that "cue elaboration is somehow deviant" in poor readers, and "does not match most printed material" (Cromer and Wiener 1966, 9).[6]

A second study (Oaken, Wiener, and Cromer 1971) evaluated the relationship between reading comprehension and word identification. Good and poor readers were asked to read two separate selections, one of which contained words they had learned to identify beforehand. It was predicted that the ability to identify the words in a given passage would not appreciably affect comprehension of that passage in the poor reader group, owing to inferred difficulties in processing syntactic information. As a contrast variable, normal readers were presented with degraded as well as intact material, and it was expected that their comprehension *would* suffer when the material was degraded. Listening comprehension was also assessed in this study, the two reader groups being presented with both intact and degraded text. Degrading of written text consisted of presenting subjects with transcripts of *poor* readers' reading of four passages aloud including pauses, false

starts, errors, mispronunciations, omissions, and other imperfec-
tions. Degrading of auditory material employed essentially the
same procedure. Intact auditory material consisted of good
readers' renderings of specific passages.

Subjects were fifth-graders (N = 96) chosen on the basis of
silent reading measures and group-administered intelligence tests.
Individuals in each group were matched for sex, age, intelligence,
and school program. The mean grade equivalent for good readers
was 6.1, that for poor readers was 3.2. Thus sample selection was
generally adequate, except for the use of silent reading tests.

It was found that learning to identify the words beforehand did
not substantially improve reading comprehension in poor readers,
verifying the authors' contention that word identification is a
necessary but not a sufficient condition for effective reading
comprehension. Not surprisingly, the good readers performed
better than the poor readers under all conditions except the
optimal auditory condition. The authors suggested that the poor
readers' difficulties in reading comprehension may have been due
to the way in which they approached the organization of the
material rather than to a basic defect in linguistic processing,
particularly since the groups did not differ in auditory comprehension. However, the design of the study did not provide any
means by which this distinction would be made.

Both of these studies provide evidence suggesting that poor
readers have difficulties in reading comprehension because of inefficiency in using syntactic information. The relationship between these variables is of course face valid and the problems that
one might encounter in comprehending connected text because of
deficiencies in syntax are readily apparent. What may not be so
apparent is the relationship between syntactic information and
single-word decoding. The common stereotypes are that word
identification directly involves the association between either a
word's graphic and semantic features or its graphic and phonologic features. Yet all words also carry syntactic information that
may facilitate their identification, both when they appear within
the context of sentences and when they are presented in isolation. For example, the child who has made the subtle distinctions
in use and meaning among function words such as *and, but,
although,* and *because* need not rely exclusively upon accurate
association of the graphic and phonologic constituents of these

words for their identification, but the child who has not firmly made these distinctions will be likely to encounter difficulty in identifying these words, particularly since many of them do not lend themselves to the application of grapheme-phoneme correspondence rules as an alternative approach to decoding.

Wiener and Cromer (1967) have discussed alternative means by which syntactic information may facilitate single-word identification in running text. Briefly, they suggest that knowledge of linguistic structure may limit response possibilities in four ways: (1) by constraining alternative responses to words in given form classes, (2) by constraining the contexts in which a given word can be embedded, (3) by reducing the amount of information that must be processed in parsing lexical alternatives, and (4) by providing immediate feedback when the response word is not consonant with the grammatical and semantic constituents of the message.

The most obvious way in which syntactic information can aid in identifying individual words presented out of narrative context is to have previously associated those words with their use in sentences. Thus knowing that *was* is a verb as well as an abstract representation of a past event may serve as a mnemonic to help distinguish it from *Sam* if the latter is known to be a proper noun.

A second possibility is suggested in a theory of lexical memory articulated by Miller (1969). Briefly, Miller hypothesizes that the lexicon may be organized not only on the basis of semantic feature information but also on the basis of information about the grammatical relationships into which given words may enter. To be more specific, the spoken and written representations of the concept "cat," refer to the substantive features that place it in a particular class (living, animate, nonhuman, feline) as well as to the grammatical properties that depict those features in sentential form: "a cat *is* an animal" (inclusion relationships), "a cat *has* whiskers" (part-whole relationships), "a cat *purrs* (functional relationships). Miller suggests that such information is coded with a given word along with information about its essential qualities and that both determine the categorical and hierarchical structure of words in an associative network. Thus, the lexical response that occurs in the presence of a given stimulus (say, on a word association or word identification task) is determined as much by the word's syntactic features as by its semantic characteristics, and response production is not unlike filling in a part that is missing from a sentence.

If this formulation is correct, it would seem that the child who has not firmly associated various syntactic constructions with the types of meanings that are permissible within the context of those constructions may have difficulty in employing grammatical relationships as a heuristic for efficient word decoding. The results of the third investigation in the series by the Cromer and Wiener group is of interest in this context (Steiner, Wiener, and Cromer 1971). Whereas the study by Oaken, Wiener, and Cromer evaluated the effect of word identification on reading comprehension, this investigation assessed the effect of comprehension training on word identification. On the strength of the belief that poor readers may simply organize contextual information less efficiently than normal readers, it was expected that helping them structure discourse material beforehand might improve their identification of individual words in a passage. Good readers, however, were not expected to profit as much from such structure, since it was assumed that they already utilize context cues to good advantage.

The subjects were fifth-graders (N = 24 each group) selected by means of the same matching procedures used in the investigation just described (mean grade equivalents = 3.2 poor readers, 6.0 good readers). Each subject read aloud four different passages under four experimental conditions: stories presented either one word at a time or in paragraphs, with or without comprehension training. Comprehension training consisted of presenting each subject with an aural summary of a specific passage before having him read it.

Aside from the observation that the good readers made fewer errors in word identification than the poor readers under all stimulus conditions, the most significant finding of this study is that the prior organization of contextual information did not significantly reduce word identification errors in poor readers, either under the word or paragraph reading conditions. This reinforced the authors' contention that poor readers tend to treat words as unrelated items and are not inclined to utilize syntactic information and other contextual cues to organize word strings into larger units. A particularly interesting finding was that presenting a synopsis of a selection beforehand actually occasioned normal readers a higher proportion of word identification errors than they made in reading a selection to which they had no prior exposure. Evidently, the advanced organization of the material prompted a more economical approach to reading comprehension whereby these subjects processed less visual information, to the apparent detriment of single-word identification. The authors ascribed no cause-effect relationships to the results except to suggest that reading difficulties in the poor readers "encompass the entire range of language signaling devices and not just problems of identifying individual lexical items" (Steiner, Wiener, and Cromer 1971, 510).

The results of the studies on comprehension and word identification support the contention that poor readers experience significant difficulties in employing syntactic information to extract the message from printed text. The data provide no clues to aid in determining basic causality, but they do add to the growing body of evidence that suggests that effective use of one's linguistic abilities is of the utmost importance in acquiring skill in all aspects of reading. Furthermore, the results are consonant with the possibility that poor readers sustain a variety of syntactic difficulties that impede their progress, either as a result of the failure to develop effective use of (syntactic) information they potentially have at their disposal or because of some basic defect that hinders development in this aspect of language. Additional research is needed to distinguish between these possibilities, although it should be apparent that they are not mutually exclusive.

There are still other research findings to support the notion that reading problems may accrue, in part, because of deficient use of syntax. Briefly, Guthrie (1973) evaluated the use of context in groups of poor and normal readers (age 10) and a younger group of normal readers (age 7). Subjects were presented with a modified Cloze procedure which required that they select one of three lexical alternatives for sentence completion. For example:

$$\text{Both} \left\{ \begin{array}{l} \text{horses} \\ \text{flowers} \\ \text{talk} \end{array} \right\} \text{lifted their ears.}$$

Four types of words were employed as alternatives: nouns, verbs, modifiers, and functors. All sentences appeared within the context of larger passages selected from basal texts. The poor readers performed below the level of both normal reader groups in choosing the lexical alternatives that made sentences grammatically correct. Poor readers had difficulty on this task even when they could identify all the words in a given sentence. Guthrie suggested that some poor readers may sustain a "primary comprehension disability" whereas others may be basically deficient in word decoding.

Weinstein and Rabinovitch (1971) found that children who sustained mild reading impairment did not recall syntactically coherent nonsense sentences any better than syntactically incoherent sentences. Good readers, on the other hand, recalled nonsense sentences that approximated English syntax better than those that had no syntactic structure. These findings emphasize the importance of learning to employ syntax to good advantage in processing verbal material. They also suggest that even children who are less severely impaired in reading may have some degree of difficulty in employing syntactic information effectively.

The results of two studies employing somewhat unusual procedures also support the possibility that poor readers are not optimally atuned to syntactic structure. Denner (1970) employed a technique used by Farnham-Diggory (1967). Poor and normal readers learned to associate pictographic material with several words that could be used in sentences. After learning these associations, subjects were asked to combine the items in each pictographic representation syntactically and to respond, through action, to a directive communicated by the pictographs. Denner found that poor readers did not perform as well as normal readers on this task and were more inclined than the normals to respond to each word as an individual stimulus.

The second of these studies was conducted by Clay and Imlach (1971). They observed that poor readers made little use of the suprasegmental features of juncture, pitch, and stress in the oral reading of given passages, though normal readers did employ this information in reading the same passages. It was suggested, in explanation of these findings, that the poor readers in the sample were not disposed toward processing linguistic cues in sentential and intersentential units.

The hypothesized relation between various aspects of syntax and reading ability is further strengthened by the results of studies demonstrating that both meaning and syntax are important determinants of the way in which normal children process words in print. This is evident in consistent observations that the reading errors made by such children are not at all random and are quite frequently determined by the syntactic and semantic characteristics of the words and sentences they read (Goodman 1969; Clay 1968; Biemiller 1970; Weber 1970).

Finally, it should be noted that the observation of reader group disparities in the use of linguistic context for word identification and sentence comprehension reported in the studies discussed in section 8.5.5 (and also reported by Samuels et al., 1975–1976, section 5.3.4) is contrary to results obtained by Perfetti et al. (1977, section 8.4.1), who found that poor readers employed contextual information as effectively as normals in word decoding. The reasons for the discrepancy in these findings are not clear, but it may well be attributable to sampling differences (Perfetti studied moderately impaired readers), and to some extent to methodological differences. It remains for further research to clarify the disparate results obtained in these studies.

8.5.6 Summary

In this section I have attempted to lend credibility to the notion that reading disorder in some children may be significantly correlated with basic deficiencies in knowledge of syntax. I have made the assumption that a limited acquaintance with grammatical relationships, specific syntactic structures and usages, and the rules by which words are meaningfully employed in sentences can have a deleterious effect not only upon the understanding and production of spoken and written sentences but upon the storage and retrieval of individual lexical entries, whether embedded within sentences or presented separately. This assumption is based primarily upon another assumption: that a word's memorability is determined in part by the connecting links that are established between its multiple features and the contexts in which it may be found. Thus, access to that word's location in the lexicon and, thereby, the ultimate identification of the word should be dependent upon the accurate encoding of its syntactic as well as its semantic, phonologic, graphic and orthographic features. If the child has significant difficulty in acquiring information about the syntactic characteristics of specific words or about syntactic environments in which they may be found, he could conceivably have difficulty in organizing their multiple features into an associative network that would stabilize identification, primarily because of the negative learning that is an inevitable consequence of such information gaps.

These formulations are admittedly speculative and somewhat intuitive; very few studies have addressed the relations in question, with the population of interest here. Supporting evidence is largely correlational in nature, issuing both from investigations that have compared disabled and normal readers on various measures of linguistic functioning and from those that have contrasted these groups on their use of syntax in reading comprehension, word identification, and memory for sentences. In all these instances poor readers were less proficient than normals. But the strongest support for the hypothesized relation between reading disability and deficiencies in syntax is provided by studies of children who have had limited experience in reading (ages 7 and below). In these investigations disabled and normal readers are consistently differentiated on various measures of linguistic functioning, including knowledge of words, knowledge of specific syntactic constructions, ability to use words categorically, ability to organize words into meaningful expressions, facility with grammatical inflections, and linguistic sophistication in general. (Sampling procedures in these studies were adequate for defining the child with specific reading disorder.)

The results of studies of children with more experience in reading (fourth- and fifth-graders) provide only tentative support for the possibility that syntactic deficiencies may occasion reading problems, since causal relationships are more difficult to define in the case of those with long-standing reading disorder. Moreover, sampling procedures in some of those studies were inadequate. Nevertheless, their findings emphasize the possible ways in which syntactic competence may influence different aspects of reading; they therefore strengthen the central component of my position. Combining the data from these studies with those from the studies of younger children provides what can be viewed as ample justification for pursuing the problem further.

Finally, the observation in several of the investigations reviewed, that poor readers were less proficient than normal readers in their use of grammatical inflections is especially interesting. The etiology of such difficulty is not apparent and it is conceivable that limited knowledge of morphology is simply a reflection of more general deficiencies in acquiring transformational rules. On the other hand, it is possible that this problem issues from a specific deficiency in coding information phonetically, which of course underscores the position, taken by a number of researchers, that reading problems in some children may be associated with phonologic deficits.

8.6 PHONOLOGIC FACTORS

The possibility that reading disability is associated with malfunction in processing the phonologic components of printed words has been a popular notion among investigators concerned with the origins of reading problems in young children and has also had a great deal of currency among practitioners. As any teacher of beginning readers will verify, many children experience considerable difficulty in learning to relate varying combinations of printed letters to their sound counterparts, some even laboring with the conceptual aspects of this skill.

The traditional explanation for such disorder is that at least some poor readers sustain basic deficiencies in the discrimination of speech sounds, which affects their ability to employ an analytic approach to word identification. Wepman (1960, 1961) has been the chief proponent of this point of view and his work has had widespread acceptance among educators and clinicians.

A significantly different formulation proposed by several other investigators is that poor readers have difficulty in mapping alphabetical symbols to sound because of the failure to code linguistic information phonetically (Downing 1973; Elkonin 1973; Shankweiler and Liberman 1976; Rozin and Gleitman 1977; Gleitman and Rozin 1977; Liberman and Shankweiler 1978). The more general problem underscored by this group in explanation of reading disability is the poor reader's limited awareness of the phonetic structure of spoken words.

8.6.1 Auditory Discrimination

The most popular explanation of reading disability implicating phonologic processing deficits is Wepman's (1960, 1961) discrimination theory. This author suggested that a sizable number of beginning readers might be significantly impaired in their efforts at learning to read because of deficient auditory discrimination of speech sounds, presumably as a result of a developmental lag selectively affecting speech perception. Wepman apparently conceptualized auditory discrimination as a perceptual skill partly dependent upon, but not guaranteed by, auditory acuity. Children were said to be typically characterized by gradual development in auditory discrimination until approximately 8 years of age; but (according to the theory) some children may fall significantly behind their peers in the maturation of this skill, thereby creating a disposition toward difficulty in learning to read, especially when they have been exposed to instructional approaches leaning heavily upon phonics.

In an initial test of his theory Wepman (1960) employed a measure consisting of 40 pairs of words, of which 10 pairs were identical and 30 pairs differed in a single phoneme *(pin/pen)*. The child's task was to judge whether the words in each pair were the same or different. In studying randomly selected groups of children in first and second grade, Wepman found that many of those youngsters who were deficient on this test were also low achievers in reading. From these results he inferred that a significant number of children in the early grades may have auditory discrimination problems that interfere with learning to read. He therefore suggested that beginning readers be screened for the possibility of discrimination difficulties using a measure such as the one he had used (Wepman 1958). He reaffirmed this position in a subsequent paper (Wepman 1961).

In spite of its popularity among practitioners, there has been no convincing evidence to substantiate the validity of Wepman's theory. Two studies that appeared after the initial presentation of the theory (Deutsch 1964; Katz and Deutsch 1967) claimed support for auditory discrimination as an individual difference variable that might significantly affect academic learning, but the results of these studies are questionable because they were derived primarily from disadvantaged populations.

More indicting is a study by Dykstra (1966). Dykstra examined investigations evaluating the realtionship between reading ability and auditory discrimination and found that the range of correlations between these two variables was rather large but most were of low magnitude. Because of the ambiguity in the literature, he undertook a large-scale study with stratified samples of first-graders (N = 632). Seven measures of auditory discrimination were employed as predictor variables, along with a group-administered intelligence test. Two indicators of reading achievement (word recognition and comprehension) were the criterion measures. The predictive battery was administered at the beginning of first grade and criterion testing was conducted at the close of the school year. The salient finding in this study was that correlations between reading achievement and auditory discrimination were uniformly low, few reaching .40. Furthermore, there were very low correlations among the various measures of auditory discrimination, suggesting that the concept does not generate clear-cut assessment procedures. The test of intelligence predicted reading achievement better than all the tests of discrimination combined. Dykstra concluded that auditory discrimination may not be a significant factor in learning to read and suggested that assessment and remediation of this function may not be worthwhile.

However, there are even more compelling reasons to doubt the validity of Wepman's theory, the most basic being the possibility that poor readers, as a group, do not sustain specific deficiencies in auditory discrimination—barring any real problems in auditory acuity. Shankweiler and Liberman (1972) have shown, for example, that poor readers who made many errors in reading minimally contrasted words *(pin/pen)*, vocalized these same words with little difficulty when they were presented orally. Similarly, Blank (1968) found that poor readers in first grade did not perform as well as good readers when asked to make same/different judgments on oral presentations of similar sounding words *(pin/pen)* (Wepman 1958), but performed as well as the good readers when they were asked to *vocalize* word pairs rather than indicate only whether they were the same or different.

These studies suggest that measures (such as Wepman's test) that require relative judgments of same and different may yield spurious impressions of auditory discrimination ability in young children. Additional support for this possibility comes from a study by Kamil and Rudegair (1972), who presented kindergartners and first graders with repeated contrasts on pairs of nonsense syllables *(bob/dod)* over multiple testing sessions and found significant improvement in auditory discrimination scores. This was also the case when the items from the Wepman test were presented repeatedly (over several successive days). Kamil and Rudegair therefore suggested that initial error rates on tests of auditory discrimination such as Wepman's may be unreliable indicators of (auditory) discrimination ability when employed with very young children.

In view of all these results, it may be reasonable to ask what factors account for the poor performance frequently found among poor readers on tests of auditory discrimination requiring dichotomous judgments of equivalence. Blank (1968) suggests that such tests are far more complex than they seem and necessitate the development of such cognitive skills as the "ability to overcome impulsivity (Kagan 1965), the ability to mediate a response through conceptualization (Blank and Bridger 1964, 1966) and the ability to see a word as separate from its context (Goody and Watts 1963)."

It would be hazardous to apply these remarks to more stringently defined populations of poor readers. Yet the points made are of interest because they succinctly summarize the conceptual and methodological problems associated with tests (such as the Wepman) that require complex judgments from young children. I agree with Blank's analysis, especially since my associates and I have encountered similar problems in employing such measures in our own study of phonologic deficiencies in children. Furthermore, the cognitive skills Blank underscores in interpreting her data are quite similar to the "general orienting attitudes" cited earlier in explanation of poor readers' failure to perform adequately on complex visual tasks such as the Gottschaldt embedded figures test (Gottschaldt 1926).[7]

The results of the studies discussed thus far are contrary to the suggestion that deficiencies in auditory discrimination, as conceptualized by Wepman and others, are a significant cause of reading disability. Nevertheless, it may yet be true that poor readers have less ability than normal readers to explicate phonemic differences in similar sounding words that they implicitly discriminate. Stated differently, it is possible that poor readers are as sensitive as normal readers to the names of words as wholes but are less aware than normal readers of the component sounds that make up those names, in which instance it may be that they perceive words as syllabic or articulatory units but have little or no awareness of their phonetic structure. Yet detection of phonemic differences in minimal contrast words such as *pin* and *pen* requires just this kind of sensitivity. Thus, by extension, segmentation of words into their constituent phonemes may be an important prerequisite to the acquisition of grapheme-phoneme correspondence, a skill that a number of workers in the field consider to be basic to word identification.

8.6.2 Phonetic Coding and Phonemic Segmentation

Several investigators have suggested that some children with reading problems may be deficient in the degree to which they are aware of the linguistic structure of speech (Liberman 1971; Mattingly 1972; Savin 1972; Downing 1973; Elkonin 1973; Gleitman and Rozin 1977; Rozin and Gleitman 1977; Liberman and Shankweiler 1978). Members of this group generally view reading as a second-order language-based skill and consider the ability to decode printed symbols to be largely dependent upon the learner's success in establishing phonetic or sound representations of those symbols. Indeed, Mattingly (1972) considers reading "parasitical" on spoken language. He postulates that the acquisition of skill in reading requires that the internal structure of one's own language be made explicit and has coined the term *linguistic awareness* to refer to the individual's conscious knowledge of the types and levels of linguistic processes characterizing spoken utterances. A similar suggestion has been made by Liberman and Shankweiler (1978) and by Rozin and Gleitman (1977).

Liberman and Shankweiler and their associates have provided the most definitive evidence for this point of view. The basic assumption they make is that reading and writing require an explicit knowledge of the phonetic structure of both the spoken and the printed word, without which children can be expected to have difficulty in mapping alphabetic symbols to sound. Specifically, a child must discern that a word can be segmented into constituent phonemes and that graphic symbols represent phonemes rather than syllables or some other unit of speech. Such knowledge is sharply distinguished from the ability to discriminate similar sounding pairs of words, which is the more conventional description of phonologic deficiencies in poor readers. Thus some children may be able to discriminate between spoken words such as *pin* and *pen* but remain unaware of the fact that each contains three separate units. Conversely, those who can segment words into phonemes are believed to have an *implicit* awareness of the phonetic contrasts necessary for word decoding. The theory therefore suggests that the child's analysis of the internal structure of words must be fine-grained and his knowledge of speech sounds made *explicit* if he is to develop facility in relating varying combinations of written letters to their sound counterparts. Liberman and Shankweiler (1978) point out, however, that such awareness is a rather formidable accomplishment for young children, since phonemes are not acoustically represented in discrete units but are assimilated into the structure of the syllable (Liberman et al. 1967). A simple trigram such as *cat* represents three phonetic segments but only one acoustic segment. This makes it exceedingly difficult for the child to "encounter" and explicate the phonemic components of the words he hears, particularly since in varying contexts attendance to given sounds is selective and economical. Furthermore, the beginning reader must not only learn how to analyze words in order to detect their separate sound components, he must eventually develop skill in synthesizing those components into articulatory units that render the word pronounceable—that is, into units at the level of the syllable, which some consider to be the basic unit of articulation (Liberman et al. 1967).

A second assumption made by this group, one even more germane to the understanding of how children acquire skill in reading, is that speech is a natural and most efficient vehicle for learning to read. It is hypothesized that graphic symbols are typically recoded into a phonetic representation at some level of processing and that the basic task of the beginning reader is to establish a link between these symbols and their spoken counterparts. The poor reader is viewed as one who is not naturally disposed toward recoding visual information auditorily, as well as one who has not been sensitized to the phonetic structure of speech.

In an initial test of this hypothesis, Shankweiler and Liberman (1972) found that poor readers made more errors in *reading* given words than they did in repeating the same words read to them and that the types of errors made in the two instances differed. In reading, most of the errors were in the medial and final positions and more often on vowels than on consonants; in oral repetition, errors were evenly distributed across positions and fewer errors occurred on vowels than on consonants. It was also found that when asked to read nonsense syllables, poor readers substituted actual words for them more often than normal readers did. Shankweiler and Liberman suggest, on the basis of these findings, that auditory discrimination of spoken words is quite different from the phonemic segmentation required for decoding written language and that poor readers may not have developed a conscious awareness of this distinction. As a result, such children are inclined to treat all words as unit syllables, which becomes problematic, considering the orthographic and phonetic complexities involved in mapping alphabetic symbols to sound. I might point out here that the poor readers' tendency to substitute actual words for nonsense syllables in this study is similar to the response pattern observed in a comparison of poor and normal readers on paired-associate learning involving nonsense syllables (Vellutino, Harding, Phillips, and Steger 1975). Both findings provide indirect support for the phonemic segmentation hypothesis.

In further studies, Liberman and her associates offer more direct support for the theory. To illustrate, Liberman et al. (1974) evaluated children in nursery school, kindergarten, and first grade and found that the ability to analyze spoken words phonemically develops gradually. Specifically, these youngsters were better able to count the syllables in polysyllabic words than to count the phonemes in monosyllabic words. In addition, of the first graders assessed, those who had the greatest amount of difficulty in phonemic segmentation proved to be deficient in reading; those who had no difficulty in phonemic segmentation were the best readers.

In following up on these same children one year later, it was discovered that half of those in the lowest third of the class in reading achievement had failed the phonemic segmentation task the previous year, but among children in the top third of the class in reading ability none had failed in phonemic segmentation (Liberman et al. 1977). The generality of these findings are extended by studies recently completed by Helfgott (1976), Zifcak (1976), and Treiman (1976), who assessed widely varying school populations, employing diverse procedures, each finding substantial correlations between phonemic segmentation ability and early reading achievement.

A series of experiments was conducted later by Liberman and her associates in order to evaluate the hypothesis that poor and normal readers differ in the degree to which they employ phonetic coding in short-term memory. Reference was made earlier to a study by Liberman and Shankweiler (1978, section 5.4) which found evidence of phonetic recoding problems in poor readers: the poor and normal readers differed in their recognition of printed nonsense syllables presented repeatedly, but recognition in these groups was equivalent in the case of repeated presentations of pictorial material. It was concluded that the groups differed in their ability to code the nonsense words phonetically rather than in visual recognition per se.

Another evaluation of this hypothesis employed a procedure similar to the one devised by Conrad (1964, 1965), comparing poor and normal readers on recall of phonetically confusable (rhyming) and nonconfusable (nonrhyming) letters (Liberman et al. 1977). The expectation was that the rhyming letters would occasion more recall errors than the nonrhyming letters in those who employ an auditory code in short-term memory.

Subjects were three groups of second-graders separated on the basis of the word recognition subtest of the Wide Range Achievement Test (Jastak, Bijou, and Jastak 1965). One group consisted of children reading two years above grade placement (superior readers, N = 17), another consisted of marginally impaired readers (N = 16), and the third of poor readers (N = 13). The latter two groups included children averaging one-half to a full year of reading retardation and were "roughly" equated with superior readers in mean age and IQ (no measure reported).

Subjects were given tachistoscopic presentations of strings of five upper-case letters in simultaneous exposures of three seconds duration each. Half of the sets were composed of rhyming consonants (drawn from the letter set B, C, D, G, P, T, V, Z) and half of nonrhyming consonants (drawn from the set H, K, L, Q, R, S, W, Y). There were two experimental conditions: immediate and delayed recall, the delay extending for 15 seconds; there was no intervening task, giving subjects ample opportunity for rehearsal (many subjects were observed mouthing the syllables silently). Responses were scored for both item intrusions and serial order.

Subjects in all groups made more errors on the rhyming letters than they did on the nonrhyming letters, the level of performance in the marginal and poor reader groups being roughly equivalent under the two experimental conditions. However, the magnitude of the difference between performance on rhyming and non-rhyming letters was greater in the superior readers than it was in either of the other two groups, indicating that the rhyming letters were more confusing for the superior readers than for the low achievers. Furthermore, the superior readers were only slightly better than the marginal and poor readers on the rhyming letters, but much better than these subjects on the letters that did not rhyme. In addition the differences in performance between the rhyming and nonrhyming letters was greater under the delayed recall condition than under the immediate recall condition for all subjects, but the disparity was more pronounced for normal readers. A similar pattern was observed in analyses of serial position errors.

Liberman and her co-workers interpreted these results as providing evidence for their suggestion that normal readers are more inclined than poor readers to code visual material auditorily (Liberman et al. 1977). They suggested further that the results could not be due to general memory or serial order deficits in poor readers because there was much less difference between the groups on memory for confusable items. They were careful to point out that poor readers must, to some extent, employ a phonetic code in processing visual materials because they (as well as the superior readers) erred more on the rhyming letters. It was therefore inferred that poor readers must have a weak or defective representation of the phonetic code.

In order to extend the generality of these findings to coding in the auditory modality, a second study was designed employing the same subjects (Shankweiler and Liberman 1978). In this investigation the same materials were presented by a tape recorder. In addition, a visual analogue of the auditory condition was employed using visual serial presentations. Results were much the same. That is, phonetically similar materials had a more adverse effect upon recall in the superior reader than in the poor reader. The authors inferred that coding difficulties in poor readers are not limited to the processing of visually presented information.

Because the results obtained in these studies could have been due to reader group differences in rehearsal strategies, another study was designed to evaluate the effects of phonetic similarity upon verbal memory, eliminating rehearsal as an influential variable (Mark et al. 1977). The subjects were second-grade good and poor readers (N = 15 good readers and 14 poor readers) carefully selected on the basis on individually administered tests of reading (comprehension and word recognition) and intelligence (Wechsler 1974). A false recognition paradigm was employed as the experimental task and degree of phonetic similarity (rhyming and nonrhyming words) was the independent variable. Two lists were prepared, an acquisition list containing words that were similar and dissimilar in sound, and a recognition list containing all of the words on the acquisition list plus an equal number of words not included on that list. Half of the words on the recognition list rhymed with half of the words on the acquisition list. An attempt was made to construct the lists so that visual similarity among the stimulus words was minimal. The experimental task was straightforward. After a subject read aloud each word on the acquisition list, he was presented with the recognition list (to read aloud) and simply asked to indicate whether or not each word was one that had been on the first list presented. All words that could not be decoded by the poor readers were dropped from the analysis.

The results were consonant with earlier observations. Briefly, good readers manifested a greater tendency than poor readers to report that words on the recognition list rhyming with words on the acquisition list had been read earlier. This was true in the case of both false positives and false negatives. Liberman et al. reaffirmed their earlier contention that poor readers differ in their ability to code information phonetically.

The foregoing results constitute strongly suggestive evidence that at least some poor readers may sustain significant difficulties in employing a phonetic code for effective processing in short-term memory. These experiments are especially impressive in that related processes (phonemic segmentation and phonetic coding) were evaluated employing a variety of methodologies and the different strategies consistently yielded reliable data. Furthermore, sample selection in most respects was quite adequate. Thus the results are not to be dismissed and the theory is worth considering.

Findings consistent with the phonetic coding theory are reported by Farnham-Diggory and Gregg (1975), although their investigation did not specifically evaluate this theory. Inasmuch as the subjects employed in reader group contrasts (fifth-graders, N = 12 each group) were from low socioeconomic urban areas and selection criteria were weak (performance on 24 sight words), the results cannot be generalized to children with specific reading disability. Nevertheless, the data are of interest because of the authors' attempt to design experimental tasks that specifically assessed particular skills necessary for efficient word decoding, and their description of the process provides a useful account of how a phonetic code might be employed in identifying printed words.[8]

To illustrate, according to a model they present, in decoding a single word the child (1) initially attends to the first visual segment of a word (spelling cluster), (2) retrieves an auditory associate from long-term memory, (3) places that associate in short-term storage while attending to the next segment of the word, and (4) proceeds sequentially in this fashion until he reaches the end of the word, at which time the "auditory particles" he has retrieved from long-term memory are integrated. The word is then pronounced, employing appropriate adjustments in articulation and stress. Such processing was said to rely heavily upon chunking operations in which redundant letter combinations are perceived and matched with their auditory counterparts. Also thought to be important was short-term memory for both visual and auditory materials, particularly as it is subject, during reading, to the possible effects of interference from material previously encountered. Finally, it was suggested that efficient reading is also dependent upon *memory scanning*, whereby the individual tracks information he has already apprehended for its edifying and organizational utility as well as for efficient integration with incoming material. Such scanning is presumably necessary for word identification as well as sentence comprehension (Sternberg 1969; Chase and Calfee 1969).

Farnham-Diggory and Gregg employed three separate tests of the capacities they identified. First, in order to assess the possibility that poor readers are not as sensitive as normals to letter combinations (chunks or spelling clusters), subjects were presented with the letters B, K, M, and S and told to construct letter patterns of their own invention. After a series of patterns had been constructed, subjects were asked to describe their rules for assembling given patterns and were credited for the number of different letter combinations they assembled.

Second, memory span was evaluated by presenting subjects with several trials of visual and auditory recall for various letter series composed of random arrangements of B, K, M, and S. The trials were counterbalanced for order of visual and auditory presentations. This procedure allowed a comparative assessment of build-up of and release from proactive inhibition in both reader groups, as a function of the shift in modality. The memory span task encompassed ten trials. Error scores and reaction times were recorded.

Third, on the memory scanning task subjects were again presented with random series of the same letters, but this time were asked to answer one of four questions: (1) What letters came first? (2) What letters came last? (3) What letter came before ——? (4) How many ——s were there? Ten instances of each question were prepared and balanced across trials. Error scores and reaction times were recorded on this measure as in the case of memory span.

Poor readers generally did not perform as well as normals on the pattern construction tasks. The major finding of interest was that short-term memory function (memory span) manifested a sharper decline across trials in poor readers than it did in normal readers. The poor readers also showed less release from proactive inhibition than the normal readers on modality shift trials. Both groups had somewhat lower means (across trials) under the visual than under the auditory presentation conditions. It is of particular interest here that the rate and magnitude of decline for poor readers under the visual condition was significantly greater than under the auditory condition, but the differences in performance levels in these two situations were not as great in the normal readers. It is conceivable that the normal readers were more inclined than the poor readers to code the stimulus letters auditorily in the case of both the visual and auditory presentations, which would account for the minimal differences found in the performance of the normal readers under these two conditions. Poor readers on the other hand may have employed a visual code to store the visually presented letters. The visual system, according to some authors (Conrad 1964, 1965; Baddely 1966), is not as well suited to short-term storage as the auditory system. If the auditory system is better suited to short-term storage than the visual system and if poor readers in this study did not employ an auditory code to store the visual stimuli presented, then the cumulative deficiencies that accrued among poor readers under the visual conditions might be explained.

The distribution of errors made by poor readers on the memory scanning task was comparable to that for normal readers, and there were no significant differences between the groups on this variable. However, there were apparent differences between them on speed of processing the letters. Although both poor and normal readers took longer with questions about letter sets presented auditorily than with questions about letter sets presented visually, this difference was greater in poor readers. As the trials proceeded, the poor readers took increasingly longer to respond under the auditory condition. Yet, though the poor readers were somewhat slower than the normal readers to respond to auditorily presented letter stimuli, they were somewhat faster than the normals in responding to visually presented material. This finding seems consistent with the suggestion that poor readers may have been more inclined than normal readers to employ a visual code for recall.

It is important, in this connection that the largest proportion of the variance on the reading task (errors in word recognition) was determined by auditory span and auditory scanning. The authors concluded from these and the other results that the reading process relies heavily upon adequate functioning in auditory short-term memory and auditory scanning ability. These capacities were said to be particularly important in the service of (a) "place-keeping functions, (b) eye-guiding functions, and (c) chunking functions, relieving the load on STM [short-term-memory] through language mechanisms of redundancy, familiarity, and sequential probabilities" (Farnham-Diggory and Gregg 1975, 296).

Even though these results cannot readily be generalized to children with specific reading disability, they are consistent with the general view that various components of reading are greatly dependent upon adequate ability to process verbal material, especially at the level of short-term memory. Thus extrapolating from Farnham-Diggory and Gregg's model, one can predict that the effects of verbal skills deficiencies would be especially pronounced at the beginning stages of reading, when the child's decoding skills are not well developed and efficiency in visual processing is at its nadir. During this period reciprocity between information stored in short- and long-term memory is not very fluid, often taxing the limits of short-term memory owing to the low level of automatic responding in word decoding (LaBerge and

Samuels 1974; Doehring 1976). Farnham-Diggory and Gregg make particular note of the differential involvement of specific memory skills at different stages of reading development and underscore the utility of current models of reading—for example, that of LaBerge and Samuels (1974)—which stress the need of automaticity in letter and word processing as a requisite for overcoming natural limits in short-term memory; that is, the ability to process given word features at an automatic level allows one to focus upon other word features in need of more detailed analysis. Their remarks are certainly relevant to our problem; the study would be well worth replicating with more stringently defined samples of disabled readers.

8.6.3 Summary

In summary, the results of recent studies comparing phonologic processing in poor and normal readers suggest that the conventional explanation of such deficiencies, citing auditory discrimination problems as the basic disorder, may be untenable. An alternative possibility is that some poor readers are relatively insensitive to the phonetic structure of both spoken and printed language and may therefore be expected to have difficulty in acquiring representations that depend directly upon such sensitivity—in mapping alphabetic symbols to speech, for instance. Such difficulty would also provide a plausible explanation of at least some of the problems encountered by poor readers in short-term memory tasks, particularly those of a verbal nature. Indeed, these findings add weight to the contention of Perfetti and his associates that unskilled readers are inclined to be inefficient in processing semantic information because of phonetic encoding difficulties. Confirmation of these findings in further research could also prove to be heuristic for understanding many of the types of errors made by poor readers in both reading and written expression. In the latter connection, findings made by members of my own laboratory are pertinent (Vellutino, Steger, and Kandel 1972; Vellutino et al. 1973; Vellutino, Steger, Kaman, and DeSetto 1975; Vellutino, Smith, Steger, and Kaman 1975) along with results in an earlier study by Liberman and her associates, (1971) both of which suggested that the orientation and sequencing errors commonly attributed to poor readers *(b/d, was/saw)* may actually be linguistic rather than perceptual distortions, the latter being the more common explanation of such malfunction.

It is also conceivable that the inflectional errors made more often by poor readers than normal readers are partly attributable to phonetic coding problems in poor readers (Brittain 1970; Fry, Johnson, and Muehl 1970; Wiig, Semel, and Crouse 1973; Vogel 1974). In any event, the results available are suggestive and continued research in this area is indicated. An important caveat is in order, however: phonetic coding and phonemic segmentation problems may characterize only some poor readers, whereas others may be troubled by difficulties in semantic or syntactic processing. It should be apparent that these problems are not mutually exclusive.

8.7 SUMMARY AND CONCLUSIONS

When a child is presented with a single printed word to identify—for example, *plus*—and responds with a semantically related word—*add, subtract, minus,* or *divide* (a type of response that is not uncommon)[9] —it is likely that his errors are caused by intrinsic or experiential deficits that deprive him of a sufficient variety and number of phonetic cues for correct identification. It is also possible that he has not firmly associated the word's syntactic characteristics with its graphic and orthographic features, information that could conceivably be put to good advantage to assist in response selection. On the other hand, it is clear that the child has recognized the stimulus as a familiar visual configuration and has sufficient awareness of its meaning to generate responses in the same taxonomic class.

However, if the child's response to the word *plus* had been *plum*, the derivation of the error would be more difficult to discern. The child may have employed only graphophonemic cues to decode the stimulus (albeit imperfectly), but it could also be true that he relied in part (or exclusively) upon meaning as a vehicle for word retrieval. In the latter case it might be suggested that *plum* was a familiar lexical entry whereas *plus* was either nonexistent in that child's lexicon or not sufficiently elaborated, semantically and syntactically, to have been a readily available alternative.

In any event, it seems apparent that response errors of the types outlined are complexly determined and could occur under one of three circumstances: (1) when the child lacks information about one or more of the features of both stimulus and response words, (2) when he does not have ready access to such information, or (3) when he has both information gaps and lexical access problems. It is likely that the third circumstance represents the situation in the case of the child who has had reading problems of any duration: it must certainly be true that inadequate knowledge of featural information would result in lexical access problems (because of the paucity of verbal mediators), whereas dysfunction in lexical access would result in information gaps because of the negative learning that would inevitably accrue as a result of retrieval problems.

Implied in these remarks is a conceptualization that depicts word identification as an interactive process whereby the various features of given lexical entries become interrelated over time and eventually come to serve both a *cuing* and a *monitoring* function. In the first instance (cuing) specific word features may act as proper stimuli for either mediating or terminal responses; in the second instance (monitoring) they provide contextual information that increases the accuracy and efficiency of response selection, by virtue of confirmatory or negative feedback. Confusing *plus* with *plum* or *was* with *saw* will in some contexts create semantic incongruity, which for normal readers typically leads to the learning of discriminating cues that eventually eliminate their tendency to confuse such pairs: knowledge of the final consonant sounds in the first two words and of the initial consonant sounds in the second pair, for example. The failure to acquire such information or difficulty in retrieving it rapidly and efficiently will increase the probability of generalization error, particularly in the case of words that have many overlapping visual features.

Wickens (1970) has provided a useful paradigm that may help to elucidate these distinctions. He points out that words are encoded on several dimensions, connotative as well as denotative, as a result of experience with and knowledge about their referents. He assumes that the more psychologically similar these dimensions or classes, the more they will interfere with one another in short- and long-term memory. Gibson (1971) has articulated a similar conceptualization of featural encoding, but she also stresses the fact that attending to one set of word features momentarily precludes attending to another. It follows then that letters *(b/d)* or words *(was/saw, plus/add, plus/plum, dog/cat)* that can be readily placed in a variety of classes have the potential for considerable confusion, unless the reader has sufficient distinguishing cues available to help him mediate to the correct response. Furthermore, the reader's accuracy is determined by his ability to both acquire and interrelate characteristics of a given type, which of course implies a fluid exchange of information between long- and short-term storage and flexibiltiy in shifting focus from one word to another.

In line with these conjectures, successful recall of the name of a printed word can be characterized as the end result of an elaborate series of cross-referencing maneuvers whereby information from the featural categories encoded in that word is retrieved in successive operations, each being determined by (1) the circumstance under which the word is presented, (2) the knowledge one has already acquired about specific word features, and (3) the feedback received from a particular operation performed. Again using *plus* as an example, if the orthographic information contained in a specific (word) stimulus is initially associated with its semantic content and the response is a substitution in the same taxonomic class *(add, subtract, minus, divide)*, it may be assumed that this error is partly due to the failure to employ information from other featural categories to aid in discriminating among alternatives from that class. A correct response, in this instance, may be facilitated if the orthographic and semantic features of the stimulus word are cross-referenced with its phonologic and syntactic features as well as with the orthographic, phonologic, and syntactic features of the other words in the class.

If the stimulus word is presented individually, the most efficient means for preventing or correcting a semantic generalization error would be to draw upon knowledge that may have been acquired about the sounds associated with the letters or combinations of letters in that word. For example, knowledge of the *pl* cluster in the word *plus* would effectively eliminate such taxonomic alternatives as *add, subtract, divide,* and *minus.* But if either *s* or *u* were the only letter-sound associates available in that word, the potential for confusion exists in that certain of the category words contain one or both of these sounds. Syntactic information might then be solicited, as when the child spontaneously calls up the word *sign* as yet another association to the stimulus word, which in turn prompts recall of words that are grammatically paired with the new associate *(plus sign, minus sign, addition sign, subtraction sign)*. This type of processing could conceivably lead to the determination that only two words in this group have an *s* sound in the final position *(plus* and *minus)*, and that information could subsequently facilitate the awareness that only one of these words begins with the letter *m*, a (letter) sound with which the child may be familiar. This, of course, would terminate the discrimination and could also become the occasion for learning the *pl* blend. It should be apparent that such an instance the child is able to utilize implicit knowledge of the functional differences among the words in the arithmetic class in question *(plus sign* versus *add sign)*; it appears, further, that he has some awareness that the printed word *plus* is associated with one of a small group of lexical entries in the same grammatical class.

If, on the other hand, the stimulus word is encountered within the context of a sentence, the (semantic) response error would be initially detected as a result of feedback from the semantic-syntactic environment in which it occurred, and it would be quite likely that this feedback would precipitate cross-referencing of the semantic and syntactic features of related lexical entries. In the case of the word *plus,* such processing would be limited to words used as nouns, verbs, or adjectives, each having reference to arithmetic operations. The semantic and syntactic features of the stimulus may thereafter be cross-referenced with its graphic and phonologic features to effect a correct response.

The illustrations just given should underscore the fact that the child is required to deal with multiple classes of lexical information (Wickens 1970; Gibson 1971) stored in both long- and short-term memory, and must search featural categories effectively if he is to decipher a single word or word part, let alone a communication embedded in a phrase or sentence. Indeed, there must be a fluid interchange of information stored in the two systems in order for the reader to process the manifold constituents of a printed symbol and interpret them meaningfully. Farnham-Diggory and Gregg (1975) provide a useful example of such processing. They suggest that decoding a given word *(par ti cu lar)* might require analysis in chunks or particles, a strategy that may be commonly employed by beginning and intermediate readers. In this instance, attention would be alternately focused upon given word features while those already apprehended are stored in short-term memory for later integration with information in long-term store. Thus, the reader may attend sequentially to specific visual constituents of the word, holding each in short-term store while searching long-term memory for phonemic associates of each constituent. The process is even more complicated in that the sound particles retrieved from long-term memory must also be held in temporary storage while visual analysis proceeds. The reader is dealing, in such instances, primarily with the visual and phonologic information contained in the word, but the decoding process could also be characterized by reference to the word's semantic and syntactic associates to varying or lesser degree. If this same word were read within the context of a phrase or sentence, semantic and syntactic information might provide initial access to the word, with phonologic information employed to complete the identification process and confirm the accuracy of the response.

In any event, the example should serve to emphasize the importance of reciprocity among the memorial systems in word decoding, especially as it may influence the child's ability to rapidly shift his attention from one word feature to the next in searching for specific bits of information that might facilitate a critical discrimination.

It should be apparent from the above that the identification of words in print is a complex process that depends upon the amount and type of featural information already acquired, as well as on the accessibility of given word features that may be potentially available as discriminating cues. This, of course, carries with it the assumption that a richly elaborated network of lexical features would provide the best chance for rapid and efficient word encoding and retrieval; a limited knowledge of featural attributes would render these processes slow and cumbersome.

The child who eventually becomes a fluent reader may be described as one who implicitly and explicitly engages in effective cross-referencing of graphic, orthographic, and linguistic information both because he has little difficulty in acquiring such information and because he is disposed toward using it elaboratively. Indeed expanding one's knowledge of word features would seem to promote the active and deliberate use of cross-referencing strategies, whereas the successful use of such strategies typically and frequently occasions new learning. In time, the process no doubt becomes well integrated and economical, characterized by the use of precisely the type and amount of information necessary to effect identification (LaBerge and Samuels 1974).

The poor reader, on the other hand, is characterized by limited cross-referencing of word features, both because he lacks the (featural) information necessary for engaging effectively in this activity and because he has developed neither the explicit nor the implicit inclination to do so. It is my contention that such difficulties are the result of basic deficits in one or more aspects of linguistic functioning, and/or specific impairment in visual-verbal integration. The research reviewed in this chapter provides both direct and indirect evidence to support this contention, as manifested in significant disparities between poor and normal readers on various measures of verbal processing. The findings encompass dysfunction in short- and long-term memory for both meaningful and nonmeaningful verbal material, deficiencies in verbal classification, visual-verbal association learning, and difficulties in rapid naming of both concrete and symbolic stimuli.

Specific language deficits are manifested in unique patterns of expression characterized by immature sentence structure, frequent use of literal rather than categorical descriptions, deficient verbal organization, limited knowledge of words, inadequate knowledge of morphological usage, and lack of verbal fluency. Suggested difficulties in phonologic processes include dysfunction in phonemic segmentation as well as limited sensitivity to the phonetic structure of language and its relation to the printed word.

There is also retrospective and post hoc support for early language impairment in poor readers, and a few studies provided at least suggestive evidence that verbal deficits detected at the preschool level can be predictive of later difficulties in reading and related school subjects.

Inferred disorders include deficiencies in semantic access, word retrieval, speech-motor encoding, language comprehension, and phonetic representation. A theme commonly encountered in these studies is that poor readers may be characterized by malfunction in verbal coding, which results in processing difficulties at the level of short-term memory. Such difficulties could, of course, contribute to reading problems because of the critical role of short-term memory in facilitating the integration of new information with information that already exists in long-term storage. Some investigations provided evidence that observed differences between poor and normal readers on various memory tasks are secondary to verbal coding deficits and *not* due to generalized memory problems or (general) limitations in processing patterned stimuli. The inference is that poor readers are not equipped with automatized and overlearned verbal devices that are readily available when it becomes necessary to synthesize information for economical storage and rehearsal. A corollary implication is that the verbal information needed for effective short-term processing is either limited in amount or frequently inaccessible.

The research findings, in sum, provide strongly suggestive evidence that reading disability is caused by basic inadequacies in one or more aspects of linguistic functioning. Such inadequacies would undoubtedly have an adverse effect on the cross-referencing process, leading in turn to dysfunction in word identification, which I view as the most critical problem in severely impaired readers. The evidence available does not permit definitive conclusions as to the primary etiology of the linguistic deficits encountered in poor readers, but the fact that they have been observed in very young children at the beginning stages of reading or prior to any exposure to the reading process suggests that they are *not* necessarily the result of long-standing reading difficulties. They are also presumed to be of a subtle rather than a global nature, being manifested in such characteristics as a limited vocabulary, less elaborated knowledge of the contextual meanings of words, imperfect knowledge of syntax, limited awareness of the phonologic attributes of spoken and printed words, and limited sensitivity to the nature and structure of the language generally. Such skills I consider to be of primary importance for developing fluency in reading. Indeed, it is entirely possible that, barring those whose reading problems are the result of extrinsic variables outlined in chapter 2 or of specific dysfunction in visual-verbal association, virtually all poor readers may be characterized by significant deficits in verbal ability.

The role of attention in learning to read has been referred to only in passing, and primarily in relation to its importance in initial storage of information to be processed. Attention factors are critical in acquiring skill in reading, a fact that may not be fully appreciated until one considers the multifaceted nature of word perception (Gibson 1971). The concern here is not with attention defined simply, as exemplified in descriptions that make reference to fixation upon specific spatial locales, eye movements, and like variables. Such activities certainly identify a basic component of attention, and apprehension of stimuli to be interpreted necessarily depends upon efficient direction of the sensory apparatus. In the present context attention must be conceptualized as a more complex phenomenon; it may be more usefully defined as the effective distribution of one's cognitive capacities and energies in the interest of efficient and economical analysis of specific types of information to be apprehended. The implication is that attention is a selective process characterized by the neglect or filtering out (Broadbent 1958) of information irrelevant to discrimination.

Gibson (1969, 1971) has long emphasized the selective nature of attention in her study of perceptual learning and most pointedly in relation to reading. She believes that the information contained in printed words is processed sequentially and hierarchically, so that attendance to one set of features precludes attendance to another. In reading, focal attention is directed toward the letter, word, or sentence constituents that afford the best chance of decoding the communication. Thus, effective reading at all stages of development involves the flexible shifting of focus not only from one word (or word part) to the next but also from one word feature to another, as in the cross-referencing operations described in chapter 8.

LaBerge and Samuels (1974) have designed a model of letter and word perception that stresses the importance of focal attention in acquiring relations that are not firmly established or, to use their term, *automatized*. Like Gibson, LaBerge and Samuels suggest that focal attention can activate only one constituent code (visual, phonologic, semantic, syntactic) at a time, the attended code or feature being said to contain information that is not strongly associated with information stored in long-term memory. Thus (focal) attention is judged to be particularly important in new learning, where the acquisition of critical and stabilizing relationships often entails the discrimination of stimuli with common or overlapping features. Interestingly enough, this model includes a mechanism for peripheral attention to automatized relationships contained in a given array, thereby implying that a significant degree of parallel processing takes place simultaneously with the serial processing of focal stimuli. Such a component is not included in Gibson's theory of word perception, but both theories heavily emphasize the role of selective attention.

These remarks may be given additional substance by reference once again to the memory model in figure 4.1. As the pairs of bidirectional arrows indicate, processing at all stages of memory depends upon attentional processes, the relationships between attention and each of the stages being reciprocal. Thus, focal attention to given word features is the initial determinant of what is permanently stored, while information in long-term storage largely influences attendance to featural information of one type or another. And, as suggested by some authors (Craik and Lockhart 1972; Buschke 1975), intelligible perception of some stimuli may require various types and levels of processing before contact with information in long-term memory can be made. It therefore becomes appropriate to inquire whether or not there is any evidence that attentional deficits may hamper poor readers in acquiring the types and amounts of information that they need in order to learn to read.

9.1 PRIMARY ATTENTION FACTORS

Two possible types of attentional problems might be considered. The first type is what will be called a *primary* attention deficit.

This type of disorder could conceivably characterize a significant proportion of children with reading and other achievement difficulties and may be the result of either basic neurological deficiencies affecting the arousal system (Malmo 1959) or personality factors, both of which may disrupt a child's ability to sustain attention or attend selectively and efficiently.

9.1.1 Neurological Factors

Attention problems resulting from neurological deficiencies are illustrated in a study by Dykman et al. (1970). These investigators found that children with learning disabilities (most of whom had reading difficulties) made many more errors and took longer to learn a simple conditioned response than normal controls. There were also differences between the disabled learners and normal controls in time taken to respond to stimuli presented. Some, designated as hyperactive, were inclined to respond impulsively and manifested shorter response latencies than the normals; others, said to be hypoactive, took longer to respond. Thus both groups of learning disabled children were characterized by attentional problems, though the nature of the difficulty was qualitatively different in each case.

Interestingly enough, these authors suggested that one deficiency that may exist in such children is the failure to develop inner speech and, thereby, adequate verbal mediating skills, following the theorizing of Vygotsky (1962) and Luria (1961). The inference is that language serves, among other things, a directive or monitoring function that significantly influences an individual's behavior pattern in most situations and quite possibly in the somewhat artificial circumstances characterizing the experimental conditions in the study by Dykman and his associates (1970).

The possibility that many children with learning disabilities have short attention spans associated with neurological disorder has been a commonly accepted view among many workers in the field (Strauss and Lehtinen 1947; Bender 1956, 1957, 1975; Johnson and Myklebust 1967) and may be an apt description of some children who sustain reading difficulties. Every effort should be made to exclude such children from initial studies of specific reading disability, because they can be expected to have *general* learning probelms and their inclusion in such investigations may constitute a confounding variable. On the other hand, the deleterious effect of an attention deficit upon reading ability should be considered in developing remedial programs for poor readers.

9.1.2 Personality Factors

Personality factors may also be a source of difficulty in effecting optimal attention to relationships that must be acquired if one is to become a fluent reader. Reference has already been made to the cumulative deficits that inevitably accrue in the case of severe emotional disorder, or even in children with subtle adjustment problems (2.1.4); in particular, the difficulties associated with measuring the effects of the latter have been emphasized.

A similar problem inheres in the suggestion made by a number of authors that reading difficulties may be associated with individual variations in "cognitive style," variations that can either facilitate or impede efficiency in perception and learning. Kagan (1965) provided some evidence that elementary-school children with reading problems were inclined to be more impulsive than successful readers, who were described as reflective in visual matching tasks. Several other investigators (Stuart 1967; Wineman 1971) correlated reading achievement measures with performance on embedded figures tests (Witkin et al. 1962) and concluded that poor readers are more "field dependent" than normal readers, in this instance relating personality differences to efficiency of perceptual processing. I have already commented on alternative explanations of contrasts between poor and normal readers on embedded figures tests and need not dwell on the problem. Furthermore, in none of these studies were samples selected in accord with the operational criteria employed in identifying children who may qualify as specifically disabled in reading. It might be added that studies of cognitive style are fraught with interpretive and methodological problems, the concept itself being vague and not easily defined, either theoretically or operationally (Dubois and Cohen 1970; Kogan 1971, 1973). In the present context, cognitive style would seem to have little utility as an interpretive hypothesis in that there is no apparent reason to believe that individual differences on this dimension would affect reading, selectively.

Nevertheless, it is reasonable to suggest that reading achievement problems in some children may be due to ineffectual approaches to the task, which may themselves be due to more subtle adjustment problems. In any event, such difficulties stand as possible confounding variables that are difficult to avoid in the study of specific reading disability.

9.2 SECONDARY ATTENTION FACTORS

The second type of attention problem will be called *secondary* attention deficit and is defined by the type of inefficiency in focal attention that inevitably accrues when the information network necessary for optimal efficiency in perception is not developing adequately. For example, the young child who sees the word *loin* and says /lion/ has attended to letter and configurational information but not to the directional or phonologic cues he must ultimately employ to respond correctly. It was proposed earlier that many of the findings in the visual scanning and speed of (perceptual) processing studies could be explained in terms of such lapses. The general point to be made here is that, in reading, focal attention becomes increasingly more efficient with increased amounts of relevant information to apply to the decoding process. The poor reader, lacking such information, is bound to be woefully inefficient in deploying his attention; thus he fails to make critical discriminations.

A useful illustration of a secondary attention deficiency is provided in a recent study by Willows (1974), who compared carefully matched samples of good and poor readers on their ability to read continuous text selectively. The subjects were sixth-graders (N = 104) with at least average intelligence. Children from each group were randomly assigned to a selective reading or control condition and asked to read one of two different types of passages, after which they were asked a number of questions to evaluate comprehension. In the selective reading condition subjects were presented with double-spaced passages typed in black ink with words in red ink typed between the lines. In the control condition, the same passages were presented but without the words in red. Subjects in the selective reading condition were told to ignore the red words between the lines and each was informed beforehand that he would be checked for comprehension. Dependent variables were oral reading errors, intrustion errors, non-intrusion errors, reading time, and time to read and answer questions.

The most significant finding was that poor readers in the selective reading condition did not perform as well as poor readers in the control condition on any of the measures evaluated. They also performed below the level of normal readers on all but one of the variables (intrusion errors, in the selective reading condition). Furthermore, the differences between the reader groups was of greater magnitude under the selective reading condition than under the control condition. These findings indicate that poor readers have significantly greater difficulty than normal readers in attending selectively to the material they read. Willows suggested that such children may be much too inclined to focus upon the visual components of words rather than to attend selectively to the material in accord with the meanings embedded in the text. That normal readers are generally more disposed than poor readers to selective attendance to printed words is provided additional support by the interesting finding that normal readers made *more* intrusion errors on the selective reading passages than did poor readers, indicating that the normal readers sampled the text to validate linguistic expectancies rather than reading it word by word as the poor readers did.

The results of this study are consistent with the notion that children with reading problems sustain secondary attention deficits. However, I consider such deficits to be the result of factors that contribute to reading disability rather than the cause of this disorder.

Kinsbourne (1970) contends that poor readers' difficulties with the proper orientation of symmetrical letters is more accurately classified as an attentional than as a perceptual problem. He points out that orientation is lowest on the hierarchy of discriminating cues and that ultimate stabilization of positional constancy depends upon the acquisition of information that consistently directs the child's attention to positional differences in printed letters (such as *b* and *d*) that are identical save for orientation. If the poor reader does experience difficulty in the verbal coding of letters and words, he might be expected to have difficulty in stabilizing positional constancy because of the inability to employ verbal mediating devices that would alert him to the phonemic differences in written characters.

What are being called secondary attentional problems occur because of information gaps that perpetuate inefficiency in perceptual processing—inefficiency that will attenuate only with accumulation of the information necessary for making critical discriminations economically (information about orthographic redundancies, grapheme-phoneme invariants, word meanings, and so on). The difficulties created by secondary attention deficits are not less problematic than those that may be caused by primary attention deficits, and both types may contribute to reading disorder in a given child.

It cannot be denied that attentional deficiencies may well result in learning problems regardless of the basic causes of such deficiencies. And they stand as prospective confounding variables that could invalidate the results of even the most meticulous research. Furthermore, there are no obvious measures to help assess attentional problems in poor readers. This lack is disconcerting, considering that some degree of difficulty in attention can almost always be inferred in most low achievers. Thus, it seems that the researcher's only means of controlling for inadequate attention in subjects in a given sample is replication and cross-validation of results with independent samples, varying contrasts within a sound theoretical context. Unfortunately, very few studies currently available have adopted this strategy and even their findings could be equivocated by lurking attentional problems in subjects included in their samples.

Part Three **GENERAL SUMMARY
AND CONCLUSIONS**

Chapter Ten

TOWARD A VERBAL PROCESSING THEORY OF DYSLEXIA

10.1 DEFINITION OF A RESEARCH POPULATION

We have examined a large number of studies evaluating the major conceptualizations of the etiology of specific reading disability—or dyslexia, as it is called. It is now time to attempt a synthesis and integration of the questions raised throughout this text.

This review was initiated with a discussion of the problems associated with defining a research population. It was pointed out that while *dyslexia* is a generic term that signifies no specific or clear-cut causal factors, it is commonly used in reference to severe reading disorder in children who are apparently normal in other respects. Theoretically, specific reading disability is attributable to developmental problems of basic constitutional (neurological) origin; but because there are no definitive criteria by which its identifying characteristics can be unequivocally specified, the origin, and indeed the very existence, of such disorder remains to be verified in laboratory study.

Accordingly emphasis has been placed on the need to circumscribe research samples so as to distinguish between children whose reading problems result from impairment in abilities that are uniquely related as components of the reading process (visual and verbal functions, for example) and children who are poor readers because of impediments that are not unique to reading. Therefore, it was suggested that the study of dyslexia is best undertaken in severely impaired readers who have at least average or above average intelligence, who sustain no sensory acuity problems, gross brain damage, or pronounced emotional or social disorders, and whose learning difficulties are not due to inadequate instruction or socioeconomic disadvantage. This strategy constitutes definition by exclusion and is inherently weak in that it provides little positive information for clearly defining specific reading disability. However, given our lack of understanding of the nature of this problem, it would appear that the investigator has little choice but to employ the method of exclusion in identifying a research population in order to maximize the probability of studying the variables of primary interest.

A number of difficulties associated with operational definition of exclusionary criteria were pointed out. Measures for directly assessing many of these criteria are not readily available. For example, there are currently no empirically validated instruments that can be usefully employed to quantify such important factors as degree of emotional adjustment, adequacy of instruction, or opportunity for learning. Among indirect methods for operationalizing these variables, particular note was made of the importance of conducting replication studies with comparably selected subjects as alternative means of controlling for sampling error. Another possible way to effect such control is to use a variety of experimental paradigms in independent tests of the same hypotheses.

With respect to reading behaviors, it seems likely that the probability of studying the intrinsically impaired reader would be greatest in (otherwise normal) children who encounter extreme difficulty in identifying single words and consequently have difficulty with all other aspects of reading. Because the most severely impaired children in this group are typically observed to be markedly deficient not only in the decoding of whole words but also in the analysis of their component sounds, it is suggested that the term *dyslexia* should be reserved for children with severe and pervasive difficulties in all aspects of word decoding, contrary to the practice of those who apply the term to children who appear to be deficient only in whole word learning or only in word analysis (Johnson and Myklebust 1967; Boder 1970, 1971; Ingram, Mason, and Blackburn 1970; Mattis, French, and Rapin 1975). It is therefore essential that the study of the disorder entail sampling procedures that measure skill in both oral reading and word analysis. It also seems important to employ achievement standards that are stringent enough to insure selection of the most seriously deficient readers, since the learning problems of children who sustain only mild or moderate impairments in reading appear to be more often due to extrinsic than to intrinsic factors.

The necessity of considering the unique properties of a particular metric was discussed in connection with measures of reading achievement, and the problems associated with those metrics most commonly employed (grade equivalents and percentile ranks) were highlighted. It was concluded that the use of one or another procedure for sample selection is not nearly as critical as (1) the reliability of findings obtained with a given achievement index and (2) the interpretations ascribed to those findings within the constraints imposed by the particular characteristics of a specific metric.

Two additional issues can be addressed in relation to the sampling and definitional problems associated with the study of dyslexia.

First, it should be apparent from the review of the literature that investigations evaluating the same or similar hypotheses typically yielded differential results when comparable sampling procedures were not used in selecting poor and normal reader groups. This pattern was particularly evident in the multitude of investigations contrasting these groups on tests of visual-motor functioning. Studies that employed stringent sampling criteria (those that excluded clinic cases as well as emotionally disturbed and disadvantaged children) found no differences between disabled and normal readers in visual-motor skills, whereas those using more liberal selection procedures did find such differences. This disparity is instructive in that it underscores a weakness characteristic of these and many other studies reviewed: the assignment of causal relationships to results where relations may be only correlational. To be more specific, the visual-motor difficulties sometimes observed in poor readers, typically measured by figure-drawing tests, have been traditionally interpreted as a sign of neurological immaturity characterized by deficient integration of the visual and motor systems. This notion has had great currency over the years, especially with those who believe that veridical perception presupposes such integration. Yet, as we have seen, there is reason to doubt that there is any intrinsic relationship between visual-motor dysfunction and reading disability. Indeed as suggested by Symmes and Rapoport (1972), some children manifest both types of disorder, but that does not necessarily imply a causal connection between the two.

These remarks should not be taken to mean that all of the conflicting results observed in the literature are attributable to sampling differences. That would be an oversimplification, particularly since many investigations that did yield disparate findings employed comparable selection procedures. It is nevertheless true that the majority of studies reviewed did *not* employ stringent sampling criteria and interpretations of their results are therefore open to question. This is an important fact to underscore inasmuch as a number of these studies have been widely referenced in support of particular theories of reading disability, studies investigating perceptual and perceptual-motor correlates of the disorder being most often cited (Goins 1958; Silver and Hagin 1960; de Hirsch, Jansky, and Langford 1966; Jansky and de Hirsch 1972). Appeal to such studies as the justification for articulating or subscribing to a given etiological theory is ill-founded.

A second issue associated with the definitional problems is the question of whether or not reading difficulties in otherwise normal children may be rationally attributed to developmental disorders of basic constitutional (neurologic) origin. The answer to this question must necessarily be guarded, given the indirect means by which support for specific reading disability as a concept has been documented. Indeed, after reviewing a large number of studies investigating the neurological correlates of developmental dyslexia, Benton (1975) concludes that there is no convincing evidence to support the notion that the disorder is associated with disturbed neurology. Nevertheless, it is quite possible that reading disability in some children is caused by organic disturbance of some degree and kind. Consistent with this possibility is the general observation that poor and normal readers have repeatedly been found to differ on tests of basic processing employed in studies that have attempted to control for confounding due to extrinsic factors. Also suggestive are the results of studies finding both quantitative and qualitative differences between specifically disabled readers and impaired learners from different populations. Reference was made earlier to Senf and Feshbach's (1970) observation that on bisensory memory tasks poor readers who were socioeconomically disadvantaged functioned more like normal readers than like specifically disabled readers selected on the basis of exclusionary criteria. Similarly, on rapid-naming tasks, Denckla and Rudel (1976a) found quantitative and qualitative differences between dyslexics and children who sustained learning problems in areas other than reading. Interestingly enough, performance patterns in nondyslexic underachievers were similar to those observed in children who achieved normally in all areas. The nondyslexic problem learners were also characterized by neurological soft signs, but this was not generally true of children from the other two groups.

A particularly impressive indication that reading disorder in some children may be associated with basic developmental difficulties is the finding by members of our laboratory that severely impaired readers at both younger and older age levels (7 through 14 years) were reliably observed to be deficient in some basic process areas but not in others. Poor readers consistently performed below the level of normal readers on tasks that relied heavily upon verbal encoding, but were comparable to the normal readers on tasks that were not greatly influenced by verbal ability. These disparities were observed in separate studies employing independent samples, different experimental paradigms, and a variety of verbal and nonverbal stimuli. Given the selective nature of the reader group differences noted in these investigations and the consistency with which such differences were found, it may be reasonably conjectured that the poor readers were impaired by neurological dysfunction affecting some aspect of verbal processing.

On the other hand, it is entirely possible that the specific performance patterns observed in the studies in question were attributable to group differences in previous experience. To illustrate the contrast, in one study (Vellutino, Steger, Harding, and Phillips 1975) normal readers performed better than poor readers in learning to associate nonsense trigrams with both cartoon figures and letterlike (novel) script. It was also found that the poor readers' errors were characterized by more semantic substitutions (*fog* for *mog*) than those of the normal readers, whose errors were more often phonemic substitutes. Such inaccuracies could have occurred because of some type of organic disorder affecting the encoding or retrieval processes, but they may be more simply explained as the poor readers' lack of experience in attuning themselves to the phonetic properties of the stimulus words, in which case neurological dysfunction need not be inferred. This illustration may, in fact, reflect a more general problem: the inability of poor readers to develop effective strategies for processing and synthesizing information in short-term memory. Liberman and Shankweiler's (1978) suggestion that such children do not code information phonetically may exemplify this problem. Similarly, several investigators have found that deficient readers are less effective than normal readers in using verbal rehearsal strategies to aid recall on short-term memory tasks (Blank and Bridger 1966; Blank, Weider, and Bridger 1968; Kastner and Rickards 1974; Torgesen and Goldman 1977). Again, though such difficulties may be related to more basic neurologic deficits affecting verbal encoding ability, they may as readily be attributed to the poor readers' failure to acquire an implicit disposition to employ efficient coding and organizational devices when the task demands it. In neither of these cases are the possibilities mutually exclusive. But they are not easily differentiated.

We are therefore left with relatively crude operational criteria for circumscribing a research population—criteria that do not unequivocally separate those children whose reading difficulties are largely attributable to subtle experiential deficits (that is, in spite of adequate instruction and exposure) from those who may be impaired because of neurological dysfunction. It is therefore essential that the researcher exercise caution in ascribing given findings to either organic disorder or inadequate experience, while at the same time endeavoring to develop the means for distinguishing between these two sources of difficulty. In any event, the question remains open and will probably not be answered in the immediate future.

Researchers and practitioners would do well to consider Applebee's (1971) suggestion that terms such as *dyslexia* and *specific reading disability* have utility only in reference to "reading retardation which we have not been able to explain" (Applebee 1971, 94), which obviously underscores the relative and tentative nature of these terms as well as our lack of understanding of the disorders to which they apply. Until there are more definitive criteria to aid in distinguishing between constitutional and experiential origins of reading difficulty in young children, investigators must be content with analyses of the problem at the level of overt behavior. They would do well to limit their generalizations accordingly.

10.2 ALTERNATIVE THEORIES

10.2.1 Visual versus Verbal Deficiency

Discussions of the various explanations of the etiology of dyslexia have encompassed both single-factor and multifactor theories, converging upon four areas of difficulty most frequently hypothesized: *visual perception and visual memory, intersensory integration, serial order recall,* and *verbal processing.* We have examined research evaluating each of these alternatives within the framework of a synthesized model of the stages of memory (figure 4.1).

We began with theories that earmark visual perceptual deficiency as the probable cause of reading disorder. Problem areas most often cited in perceptual deficit theories include abnormalities in form perception, spatial orientation, and visual pattern analysis. Studies concerned with inferred deficiencies in these areas have typically employed figure-drawing, visual matching, and figure-ground tests to evaluate given functions, and visual search tasks to compare poor and normal readers on speed and accuracy of processing.

The results of most of these investigations were equivocal, owing to sampling, procedural, and interpretive difficulties. Especially problematic was the failure to control for reader group differences in previous experience or specific abilities such as verbal and motor skills. In addition, many of these studies employed experimental methods that confounded discrimination with short-term memory processes, this error being most often made in those investigations that employed visual matching as the contrast variable. Interpretations of results were particularly ambiguous in studies comparing poor and normal readers on speed of processing printed letters and words, stimuli with which poor readers have a history of difficulty. Perceptual deficiency cannot readily be inferred in such instances, given the likelihood that children who have had chronic difficulty in word decoding will have acquired inefficient strategies of visual organization, which would no doubt hamper them on the types of tasks employed in the studies in question.

Virtually all perceptual deficit explanations of reading disability implicate dysfunction in initial-stage (sensory storage) processing, but only a few investigators have explicitly mentioned and directly assessed this possibility. Adopting conceptualizations and experimental paradigms taken from research conducted in the study of visual information processing, these investigators have typically made reference to the possibility that reading disability may be caused by deficiencies in functional and structural characteristics of the visual system such as feature analysis and synthesis (form perception), capacity limits, and trace duration. Their rationale was straightforward and their methodology was unique. Specifically, poor and normal readers were contrasted on various measures of visual discrimination and visual memory during the first 300 milliseconds following the termination of a given stimulus. Since this duration roughly approximates the amount of time the visual afterimage is available, procedures requiring judgments or discriminations within this limit presumably evaluate reader group differences on direct analysis of the stimulus rather than coding ability.

The few studies comparing disabled and normal readers on initial-stage processing yielded conflicting evidence, but the results of the majority were negative. Furthermore, those investigations that reported positive findings did not adequately control for response bias; those in which the findings were negative were better controlled.

Synthesis of the results of studies that directly or indirectly assessed the perceptual skills of poor and normal readers led to the conclusion that there is no compelling reason to believe that reading difficulties are in fact caused by dysfunction in visual processing. Indeed, the data can readily be taken as an indication that such theories are ill-conceived.

The strongest support for this conclusion was derived from the results of a number of investigations conducted in our own laboratory. Briefly, poor readers between the ages of 7 and 14 were found to be no different from normal readers on measures of short- and long-term visual memory when the effects of verbal mediation were minimized. Especially impressive in these studies is our observation that poor readers were comparable to normal readers in graphically reproducing spatially confusing letters and words *(b/d, was/saw, calm/clam)* from memory after only a brief visual exposure to these stimuli, even though the same subjects misnamed these items when they were asked to read rather than copy them. These findings suggest that poor readers have no basic difficulties in visually discriminating such configurations; they are unable to remember their names.

Another important finding is that poor readers were comparable to normal readers on nonverbal learning tasks that in some instances involved only visual stimuli. Yet they performed consistently below the level of normal readers on learning tasks that contained a verbal component. These data constitute strong support for the contention that reading disability is not caused by any basic deficiency in visual perception or visual memory. They also provide indirect evidence that poor readers may be basically impaired in some aspect of verbal processing.

Aside from the lack of empirical support for perceptual deficit theories of reading disability, there are even more elementary reasons for doubting the validity of such conceptualizations. First, it is well to underscore the nature of the reading process itself and to point out that reading is primarily a linguistic skill, contrary to traditional views that vision is the dominant system in decoding words in print (Young and Lindsay 1971). Indeed, in closely examining the basic functions involved in learning to read it becomes clear that this enterprise taxes the visual and linguistic systems unequally. The reason is not only that the learner is required to process three different types of linguistic information (semantic, syntactic, and phonologic) and only two different types of visual information (graphic and orthographic) but because he has to remember a good deal more about the linguistic attributes of words than about their visual attributes—a contention supported by the fact that in reading, the visual symbols are stationary, which in effect necessitates only discrimination and not reproduction of the graphic counterparts of words. A word's linguistic constituents, in contrast, must be reproduced as well as discriminated. Stated differently, reading essentially requires recognition of or familiarity with the visual components of words in print, but it requires recall or reproduction of their verbal components. Recall involves the recollection of much more detailed information than recognition (Underwood 1972); it would therefore seem that the reading process places greater demands on verbal memory than it does on visual memory.

This argument is afforded additional support by the fact that the orthographic structure of written English actually allows for a good deal of economy of visual processing, given the redundancy characterizing an alphabetic symbol system. Such redundancy is reflected in the iterative use of a limited number of alphabetic characters (26 letters in English) and in the high frequency with which certain combinations of these characters (*qu, ch, tion, and, is, but,* and so on) are encountered. Normal readers soon learn to capitalize upon this quality of English orthography in the interest of limiting the amount of visual information they process to effect discrimination. Indeed Rosinski and Wheeler (1972) have found that children become quite conversant with the orthographic structure of printed English no later than third grade, and it is significant that by this time most have become highly skilled in word decoding.

The dominant role of the linguistic system in learning to read is, perhaps, most pointedly emphasized in the fact that reading, by definition, involves the recoding of one's natural language, and, children learning to read are required to decode to that language. Consequently, their discrimination of graphic symbols is in no way arbitrary and is structured (indeed monitored) by their growing knowledge of visual-verbal relations—that is, the names of printed words and the sounds associated with their component parts—as well as by their more basic knowledge of and facility with language. Thus the child who is not only familiar with the meanings of given words and knows something of their use in sentences but who also knows the sounds associated with individual letters or combinations of letters in those words (like the initial consonant sounds in *was* and *saw*) will have little difficulty discriminating between them. It is assumed that critical visual discriminations are ultimately made by virtue of the fact that attention is implicitly drawn to the distinguishing sound features of particular words, the availability of the information necessary to make those discriminations being a requisite component of this process. If, for any reason, such information is not readily available to the reader, discrimination will be global, as in the case of children who call *was, saw* (and vice versa) on a chance basis.

It should not be concluded that I underestimate either the complexity of English orthography or the amount of discrimination learning that must take place before the child becomes a fluent reader. Nor do I deny the fact that word decoding in poor readers is often characterized by inaccuracy or inefficiency in visual discrimination. However, I reject the notion that such difficulties are attributable to primary (neurologic) dysfunction in visual perception or visual memory. I adopt this position partly in view of the fact that there is no convincing evidence to support a visual deficit explanation of reading disability (and some convincing evidence against it) but more basically because the visual system is not normally required to do a great deal of remembering in reading, unless of course the learner develops no effective means for optimizing the amount of visual information processing necessary for word decoding. I suggest that the latter circumstance obtains in severely impaired readers because of basic difficulties in storing and retrieving the linguistic counterparts of the visual symbols they are required to discriminate. As a result of such difficulties they do not systematically and efficiently dissect the orthography so as to readily acquire the invariant (visual-verbal) relationships that will facilitate economy in visual processing and maximize the probability of accurate discrimination. Thus they often attempt to process either too little or too much (visual) information and, as a result, the discrimination process suffers.[1]

Visual inadequacies of this sort are more accurately classified under *perceptual inefficiency* as a descriptive rubric, rather than under *perceptual deficiency*. Perceptual inefficiency in this instance implies idiosyncratic attention to information that does not optimally facilitate discrimination, such inefficiency resulting from more basic difficulties in verbal learning. It has nothing to do with distortion or disorientation of the visual stimulus as a result of organic disorder.

The second reason for doubting the validity of perceptual deficit explanations of reading disability is based as much on logic as on theoretical and empirical evidence. I am inclined to reject hypotheses that dyslexics are literally subject to types of visual anomalies that have been variously proposed: optical reversibility, spatial disorientation, figure–ground difficulties, and the like. If the visual system were so disordered, the difficulties in question should be pervasive—they should be apparent in all aspects of daily living and not just in symbolic learning. Yet there is no reason to believe that this is the case. Furthermore, the suggestion of some authors (Orton, for example) that visual perceptual difficulties occur only when linguistic symbols are being processed would seem to be an implausible explanation of *b/d* or *was/saw* kinds of confusions, especially since there are more parsimonious explanations of such errors.

I reject in particular the notion that poor readers are spatially disoriented—by far the most popular theory of reading disability— on the grounds that directional set is almost certainly a learned rather than an inborn phenomenon. Directionality is a relative rather than an absolute function; it develops largely in reference to quite arbitrary coordinates. What spatial deficit theorists loosely refer to as the development of the "directional sense" may be better characterized as the acquisition of well-integrated responses to situation-specific stimuli (concrete or symbolic) that typically have functional utility. Such responses are acquired, they are not inherited. Thus it would seem to be in error to suggest that spatial confusion associated with neurological dysfunction is the underlying anomaly common to such diverse behaviors as mirror writing, erratic and regressive scanning in reading, dysfunction in naming the left and right sides of the body, and calling *b*, *d*. Interestingly enough, what *is* common to all of the examples just given is the integration of spatial and verbal coordinates. Consistent with the point of view articulated throughout this text, it is suggested that the difficulties poor readers experience in stabilizing these relationships originate from dysfunction in verbal mediation, quite possibly associated with more basic deficiency in some aspect of verbal processing. A number of studies that have been reviewed afford support for this possibility (sections 5.3.1, 5.4).

Perhaps the most basic reason for questioning perceptual deficit explanations of reading disability is that they appear to rest on a fundamental misunderstanding of the nature of the perceptual process. Implied in most of these theories is the belief that perception is an organismic entity that matures like any other structure or function of the body, as exemplified in motor development and physical growth. These theories also assume that perceptual functioning is characteristic of a particular "stage" in cognitive growth, midway between sensorimotor and conceptual development and, further, that there is strict linear ordering of qualitatively different experiences associated with each stage to form an integrated network of hierarchical relationships.

One argument against this conceptualization is that "perception is not an entity, but an abstract and generic category which has reference to the recognition of a given stimulus as well as the meaning(s) one ascribes to it. Thus, while it can be reasonably viewed as a dynamic, interpretive process which can be significantly altered by previous learning, set, increments of knowledge, or a change in context, perception does not have thing value" (Vellutino et al. 1977, 377).

A closely related argument is that the relation between perceptual and conceptual functioning is, in all likelihood, reciprocal rather than sequential. What we already know significantly affects what and how we perceive, which is to say that the interpretation of a given stimulus always takes place within a context. Contextual information determines not only the meanings we attach to specific objects and events but the extent to which we selectively attend to their constitutent features (what we look at; what we listen to). Conversely, perceptual differentiation—that is, making more fine-grained discriminations—significantly alters our understanding or interpretation of a particular stimulus, which in turn affects the way we perceive it at given points in time. To cite an example employed earlier (section 2.1.1), the child who can identify the printed words *fat* and *her* may be initially inclined to perceive these words as separate units when they are encountered for the first time in the word *father,* but this will probably not be true when the child learns that father is itself a single unit with a pronunciation quite different from that of either of the words learned earlier. However, I do not believe, in this instance, that the child's perceptual boundaries change because of structural and functional alterations in general growth processes (maturation or decentration), as Elkind, Horn, and Schneider (1965), have suggested, but because he has acquired specific mediating relations that selectively attune him to featural information that will facilitate critical distinctions.

To illustrate, I suspect that visual reorganization of the letters in *fat* and *her* ultimately depends upon the learner's ability to phonetically recode these letters as subunits of the new word *father,* inasmuch as this information has functional value for identifying the word and for segmenting its constituent letters into qualitatively different units of perception. When the letters *a, t,* and *h* occur in *father,* they sound quite different from the way they sound when they occur in the environments provided by *fat* and *her.* Reliable coding of these differences significantly influences focal attention to orthographic information in each of the words, which in turn facilitates perception of the new word apart from the familiar words embedded in it. Thus, knowledge of and selective attention to the *th* blend in *father* may be important for initial reorganization of the letters in *fat* and *her,* since unit perception of this cluster effectively dissolves the boundary between their respective letters *t* and *h.* The *th* blend also occurs at the syllabic division of the spoken word *father,* and syllabication is a natural vehicle for partitioning the letters in the old words so as to synthesize perception of the new word. Similarly, the *fa* combination in *father* not only sounds different from the way it sounds in *fat,* it also occurs at the syllabic juncture of *father* and receives the most stress. Thus it too may serve to alter focal attention and perceptual reorganization of the letters in the words learned previously.

The general point being made here is that the visual and linguistic systems interact reciprocally in discriminating and identifying printed words, which of course implies that visual organization of the component letters does not efficiently take place apart from the reader's knowledge of their linguistic associates. Given that the child's task in learning to read is to decode print to his spoken language, it would seem that for the normal reader the linguistic system plays the dominant role in determining word perception. By extension, difficulty in processing linguistic information or in interrelating the visual and verbal constituents of printed words will result in idiosyncratic and inefficient organization of their graphic and orthographic features, as manifested in the types of generalization errors typically made by poor readers.

I therefore suggest that, given adequate visual acuity, and thus adequate form discrimination, perceptual organization of alphabetic characters is largely determined by the child's ability to cross-reference and integrate the visual and linguistic components of words and word parts. Visual perception in this context is best conceived as directly tied to linguistic information, which significantly influences the organization of graphic and orthographic features of the printed words encountered. It should also be viewed as a dynamic process that is constantly undergoing change with the broadening of the child's knowledge of the visual-verbal relations involved in code acquisition. Word perception conceived in this way of course obviates the perceptual deficit explanations of reading disability that have appeared in the literature.

10.2.2 Intersensory versus Visual-Verbal Integration

The possibility that reading difficulties are caused by deficient integration of the sensory systems has been a popular theme in the literature, from the publication of Birch's (1962) seminal paper on the topic up to the present time. Indeed this hypothesis has been widely researched and its popularity is second only to the view that dyslexia is attributable to basic disorder in visual perception. The theory, in brief, is that at least some poor readers may be subject to dysfunction in the ability to integrate information received through various sense modalities. Such difficulty presumably stems from developmental problems of unknown origin and has been thought to be a general deficiency that would be observed in cross-modal learning involving any of the sensory systems, not only those involved in reading.

The initial studies testing this hypotheses were conducted by Birch and his associates. These investigations essentially entailed cross-sectional comparisons of poor and normal readers on match-to-sample tests requiring equivalence judgments, with patterned information presented in the auditory and visual modalities. Observation of reader group differences on such tasks led to a proliferation of studies employing similar procedures, as well as to studies employing various other measures of sensory integration.

We have examined most of the important studies that appeared in the literature during the past ten to fifteen years; critical analyses of the findings led to the conclusion that there is no substantial support for the intersensory deficit theory of reading disability as initially articulated by Birch. Virtually all of the studies offering supportive evidence for the hypothesis were confounded by memory and attention factors, and most failed to control for the possibility of reader group differences in intramodal functioning as well. Inadequate sampling procedures were characteristic of many of the investigations and further equivocated results supporting the theory.

At the same time, studies that did attempt to remedy the control problems discussed did *not* find support for Birch's hypothesis. Particularly indicting are the results of studies issuing from our own laboratory, since they were specifically designed to control for short-term memory and attention factors and also evaluated the possibility of reader group differences in intramodal processing. In all of these investigations, poor readers consistently performed as well as normal readers on paired-associates learning involving material devoid of linguistic structure, presented both within and between various sense modalities. In contrast, poor readers did not perform at the level of the normals on learning tasks involving a verbal component. These findings accord with the results of studies by Blank and others, which found that poor readers' difficulties on measures of both cross-modal transfer and serial processing were due to more basic deficiencies in verbal encoding. In fact, the combined results of these and our own investigations provide highly suggestive evidence that poor readers may be characterized by dysfunction in one or more aspects of verbal processing.

A more basic contraindication to the results of most studies evaluating the cross-modal deficit theory of reading disability is their use of procedures requiring judgments of intersensory equivalence. As pointed out by Bryant (1974, 210) reading involves the association of rather arbitrary symbols with linguistic counterparts, but it does not necessitate the ability to perceive "natural" or "universal" equivalences in objects represented in different modalities. This of course further equivocates the theory in question.

The intersensory deficit explanation was found wanting on theoretical grounds also. For one thing, the theory rests on the assumption that information processing in humans is characterized by hierarchical organization of the sensory systems, sensory integration presumably involving a comparatively active (and dominant) role for the teleoreceptor systems, especially vision. This would seem to be a questionable notion, given research findings indicating that sensory dominance is relative, in all likelihood being determined by the modality best equipped to process information of a given type (Pick 1970; Friedes 1974). It has also been suggested (Gibson 1969; Pick 1970) that the establishment of equivalence among the senses (judging temporal patterns as equivalent in different modalities) depends more upon the coding of invariant relationships *amodally*—that is in some abstract form—than it does upon the unique properties of given senses or the ways in which they may cross-communicate. In other words, judgments of intersensory equivalence may depend primarily upon the ability to store categorical and invariant relationships that transcend specific modalities, the implication being that such information performs a mediational function in the assignment of equivalent meanings to the same concept coded in different sensory systems.

On the other hand, whereas it is true that sensory equivalence implies the ability to abstract essential information represented in given sensory codes, it may also be true that the ability to cross-reference these representations develops somewhat apart from the ability to associate higher-order invariants with particular sensory symbols. For example, the printed word *chair* has an auditory counterpart, and it is possible for both the visual and auditory components of this word to be successfully related to the concept they symbolize without being successfully associated with each other. Yet reading requires that all of these relationships materialize, thus qualifying the suggestion that cross-modal transfer depends only upon the ability to store amodal invariants.

Nevertheless, it would seem from the evidence available that the intersensory deficit theory of dyslexia, as originally proposed by Birch, is seriously questioned, if not obviated, and may ultimately be discarded.

The possibility remains, however, that some disabled readers may be characterized by circumscribed difficulties in *visual-verbal* integration (instead of generalized intersensory dysfunction) in the absence of significant disorder within the visual and linguistic systems. For example, given the likelihood that the hemispheres have differential responsibility for processing the visual and verbal components of printed words, it is conceivable that dyslexia in some children is caused by disruption in the transmission of these two types of information across the hemispheres. Such dysfunction could plausibly account for word identification problems as well as for the naming and labeling difficulties observed in poor readers in controlled laboratory study (Denkla and Rudel 1976a, 1976b). So far as I know, only one investigation has directly assessed the possibility of transmission deficits in a rigorously defined population of dyslexics (Vellutino, Bentley, and Phillips 1978), and the results were negative. Nevertheless, in view of the fact that technology in this area is still crude, I suggest that the hypothesis is still viable and should be further evaluated.

Finally, select disorder in visual-verbal integration could also originate from transmission deficits within rather than across hemispheres. The cross-referencing of visual and linguistic symbols may be problematic because the neural pathways transmitting these two types of information within the hemisphere supporting language are not optimally connected, whereas those transmitting information across the hemispheres function normally. Pursuit of these alternatives obviously implies refined (operational) definition of normalcy in the subsystems involved in reading and in the transmission of information across the hemispheres. Such requirements pose methodological problems of considerable magnitude, but there would appear to be utility in attempting to overcome these problems, since the hypotheses in question have never been extensively evaluated and it may be instructive to do so.

10.2.3 Serial Order Recall versus Verbal Encoding

The third conceptualization of dyslexia addressed was dysfunction in serial order recall. Serial deficit explanations of reading disability have long had a great deal of currency among practitioners, but only in recent years have researchers become interested in the problem. To date, however, neither group has provided a comprehensive theory that clearly specifies the relations that may exist between deficiencies in serial processing and dysfunction in reading. Nor has either group elaborated upon the nature of inferred difficulties in sequential memory which presumably result in reading disorder. Clinical accounts are descriptive rather than substantive and typically make vague reference to brain-behavior relations that do not readily lend themselves to experimental verification. A common theme in such accounts is the assumption of modality-specific serial order deficits manifested in qualitatively different error patterns in reading and related skills. Beyond informal observations of serialization difficulties in school-related activities (reciting the alphabet, reversing numerals, ordering the days of the week) and on standardized tests involving memory for order (digit span, memory for designs), there has been no comprehensive documentation of the existence of differential error patterns in serial processing that are unique to given sensory systems.

Laboratory study of sequential deficit explanations of reading impairment has yielded little more substance than clinical evaluation has. Only Bakker (1972) has attempted to articulate a coherent theory of dyslexia implicating sequential deficiencies as a basic causal factor. This conceptualization suggests that poor readers are deficient in perceiving temporal order in verbal stimuli and assumes a close parallel between the types of serial errors made in listening and those made in reading. This theory also implies (although Bakker never explicitly states it) that the individual phoneme is the unit of speech perception, which would account, presumably, for the inferred similarities between auditory and visual error patterns. These ideas are questionable on theoretical and empirical grounds, in light of research demonstrating that the invididual phoneme is not the unit of speech perception.

The theory is also undermined on the strength of evidence that there may not be a close parallel between the types of sequencing errors made in listening and reading (Shankweiler and Liberman 1972), as well as by the fact that results offered in support of temporal order and other serial deficit hypotheses are generally equivocal, indirect, and meager. Only a few studies could be found that specifically addressed the possibility that poor readers sustain a circumscribed deficiency in serial processing, and only a fraction of these were conducted within a given theoretical framework. Most yielded only post hoc speculations about particular types of disorder, such as temporal order difficulties (Senf 1969; Zurif and Carson 1970) dysfunction in visual sequencing (Senf 1969), and generalized deficit in sequential memory (Corkin 1974).

Nevertheless, in almost all of the studies that did directly evaluate the possibility that dyslexia is associated with deficiencies in serial order recall, poor readers consistently performed *below* the level of normal readers on various measures involving memory for order. Although these results were interpreted by some as support for a serial deficit explanation of reading disability, there are two contraindications to such an interpretation.

First, in practically all of the studies in which gross and order memory were recorded, poor readers performed below the level of the normal readers on memory for given items as well as on memory for the order in which those items were presented. This includes investigations comparing disabled and normal readers on measures of cross-modal transfer as well as investigations more directly concerned with measuring sequencing ability. These findings cast doubt on the assumption that difficulties in remembering sequence constitute a specific disability that may occur even when gross memory is intact. Instead, they suggest that poor readers are deficient in both types of recall.

The second contraindication is that virtually none of the studies evaluating serial order memory in impaired and normal readers attempted to control for the possibility of group differences in verbal encoding. It is therefore difficult to be certain that the disparities observed between poor and normal readers were actually attributable to dysfunction in the (hypothesized) serial processor rather than to the poor readers' inability to employ verbal mnemonics to aid recollection. Several studies found that reading disabled children, who were not as proficient on measures of sequencing ability as their more able peers, were also less proficient in employing verbal rehearsal strategies for coding and storing information for later recall.

Aside from the lack of substantial empirical support for serial deficit explanations, certain other questions can be raised about their validity. As noted earlier, each incorporates the notion that gross and serial memory are supported by neurologically distinct entities. However, this is related to the more basic question of whether item and order information are qualitatively different, which turns out to be a controversial theoretical issue that has not yet been resolved (cf. Conrad 1964, 1965; Healy 1974, 1975a, 1975b, 1977). Furthermore, the validity of a sequential deficit explanation of reading disability rests in part on the implicit assumption that printed words are identified through the serial processing of their individual letters. Yet the role of serial letter processing in word identification is also controversial (cf. Brewer 1972; Gough 1972). It would therefore seem that sequential deficit conceptualizations are on tenuous ground, theoretically as well as empirically. In their present form the hypotheses either oversimplify the problem or violate parsimony, as exemplified, respectively, in accounts that ascribe reading problems to generalized sequencing deficits in poor readers or to modality-specific deficits unique to the visual or auditory systems.

Nevertheless, because the various aspects of reading do, in some measure, necessitate the coding and functional use of order information (as in distinguishing between *was* and *saw* or *loin* and *lion*), a serial-processing deficit explanation of reading disability would appear to have some face validity, and I fully acknowledge the utility of research investigating the derivation of sequencing errors. However, to explain the observed inaccuracies simply as a disorder in sequencing is to be circular and uninformative. What is needed is greater specification of the nature of inferred serialization problems in poor readers and better explication of relationships that may exist between serial processing deficiencies and various aspects of reading. Furthermore, a theory of reading disability implicating basic disorder in sequencing ability will not be a viable explanation of the difficulties poor readers encounter in learning to read and the types of inaccuracies they typically manifest unless it has more explanatory value and is more consistent with the empirical facts than those currently available. There is reason to believe that sequencing errors account for only a small percentage of the errors made by poor readers in their efforts at word decoding (Shankweiler and Liberman 1972); there is even greater reason to doubt the assumption—central to such a theory—that poor readers sustain a specific deficiency in processing order information.

Finally, I tend to doubt the logic behind the basic premise that gross and order memory are supported by neurologically distinct entities; I am more inclined toward the view that item information and order information, though perhaps qualitatively different, as suggested by some authors (Estes 1972; Healy 1974, 1975a, 1975b, 1977), may come by those differences because they are respectively derived from featural and relational (structural) characteristics of the items in a given array (see note 5, chapter 7). It is also likely that these two types of information may be represented in a variety of ways; in some instances they may involve the coordinated use of multiple sensory codes; in others, the use of specific codes that may be particularly effective for processing given types of stimuli. Reading obviously involves the coordinated use of visual and verbal representations. In view of the arguments advanced thus far, I consider it quite likely that dysfunction in storing and retrieving the types of item and serial information that are involved in acquiring this skill is basically attributable to deficiencies in verbal encoding ability.

10.2.4 Verbal Processing

This brings us to the fourth and final explanation of reading disorder: that dyslexics may sustain specific deficits in one or more aspects of verbal processing.

It has been repeatedly suggested throughout this book that poor readers are not as proficient as normal readers in coding information verbally and, further, that this deficiency in verbal coding accounts, to a large extent, for the differences observed between poor and normal readers on a broad variety of basic process measures. The implication is that people rely heavily upon linguistic devices to help store and retrieve various types of information, and that poor readers experience significant difficulty on both short- and long-term memory tasks because they lack facility in employing such devices to aid recall. This is not to imply that language is the only coding mechanism used for processing information; there is considerable evidence to the contrary (Kroll 1975; Healy, 1974, 1975a, 1975b, 1977). I do believe, however, that because of its generative and abstract quality, language is a marvelously convenient and natural vehicle for symbolizing the things to which we are exposed.

Verbal coding mechanisms are particularly useful for processing information in short-term memory, wherein material is often stored temporarily and rehearsed for later integration with incoming stimuli, prior to permanent deposit in long-term memory. Indeed this type of processing is entailed, in some degree, in almost everything we do, including every aspect of reading, from single-word analysis to sentence and paragraph comprehension. It therefore follows that success in acquiring skill in reading is heavily dependent upon the ability to code information verbally— even more, the essence of the process is the coding of language itself. Thus reading requires not only intact language ability, but metalinguistic ability; which is to say that it is of importance to have explicit knowledge about language in addition to the implicit knowledge necessary for functional use of language.

The case can be stated more definitively. It seems quite likely that given normal intelligence, intact visual and auditory acuity, and adequate exposure to and investment in reading as a process, success in learning to read depends, first, upon *linguistic ability in general* and, second, upon the *ability to make one's knowledge of language explicit.* By extension, deficiencies in any aspect of linguistic functioning will presumably result in difficulty in reading.

By general language ability, the first basic prerequisite, I have in mind such capacities as a rich fund of lexical information—that is, a substantial knowledge of words and the ability to use those words in appropriate contexts. A good vocabulary implies facility in associating specific concepts with verbal representations, a basic skill in language acquisition. There is abundant evidence to support a high correlation between vocabulary and reading ability; it may therefore be true that deficient knowledge of words is causally related to reading disability in some children. Here it is important to distinguish between knowledge of the meanings of specific words deliberately taught, in isolation, to the beginning reader and the possession of a rich vocabulary acquired from the ongoing stream of language to which the child is constantly exposed and which provides an elaborate associative network that may facilitate word encoding and retrieval, owing to the ready availability of verbal mediators. The former is static whereas the latter is dynamic and contextual; thus a rich vocabulary would seem to be a prerequisite for success in all aspects of reading, including word decoding.

General language ability also includes the ability to rapidly retrieve words representing given concepts when the necessity arises. I am referring here to the *naming* function which raises the more general question of how we remember the names of things—the question that may, in the most germane sense, constitute the central problem in the study of dyslexia. A growing number of investigations have been concerned with this problem, most finding significant differences between poor and normal readers in rapid naming of objects, printed words, pseudowords, and various other representations. These data suggest that disabled readers may indeed experience significant difficulty in word retrieval, both in speaking and in reading.

General language ability entails the ability to organize verbal concepts categorically, which implies the ability to distinguish and interrelate similar and dissimilar verbal meanings occurring in the form of either individual words or groups of words. The obvious importance of semantic categorizing to the comprehension of spoken and printed words underscores the necessity of determining whether children with reading problems have difficulty in apprehending the meanings of individual words or in apprehending the ideas expressed in words, as in connected text. The evidence available suggests that in both listening and reading comprehension, impaired readers may organize and recall global meanings as well as normal readers, but they have less ability to recall particular items of information or groups of words expressing such information. They are also less proficient in remembering individual words, whether these are presented within the contexts of sentences, in categorical groupings, or in unrelated groups. Such findings seem to imply that poor readers sustain subtle deficiencies in semantic memory, but the nature of such disorder is unclear. There is some suggestion in the literature that deficient memory for particular words and ideas is attributable to phonetic encoding deficiencies, which result in short-term memory problems. However, it may also be the case that some children are subject to basic difficulties in word finding, which would implicate dysfunction in lexical retrieval, perhaps related to qualitative differences in the structure of the lexicon. These disorders are not mutually exclusive, but much more research is needed to distinguish between them. In any event, an elaborate network of verbal concepts, ready access to those concepts, and the ability to interrelate them would seem to be necessary conditions for successful reading.

General language proficiency implies an adequate command of syntax, specifically, adequate comprehension of grammatical relationships, a working knowledge of the interrelationships among parts of sentences, and age-appropriate comprehension of various syntactic constructions and usages.

The semantic and syntactic components of language obviously provide meaningful context that aids the decoding of words embedded within sentences; the implicit feedback provided under these circumstances normally helps to stabilize the learning of those words. What is not so apparent is how knowledge of syntax facilitates the coding and decoding of printed words presented individually. One obvious way is to associate a particular word with its use in a sentence. Such information is probably more implicit than explicit, but it is quite likely that it can be employed as a useful mnemonic when the necessity arises.[2] Another way was proposed by George Miller (1969), who suggests that a lexical entry contains information about the syntactic as well as the semantic relationships into which a word may enter, coded in sentential form: remembering that word is in some respects not unlike completing a sentence. Kintsch (1974) adopts a similar position. If these authors are correct, imperfect understanding of a word's use in sentences and the associated constraints on meaning could conceivably lead to word encoding difficulties or lexical access and retrieval problems.

Support for these conjectures is provided by observations in the literature that poor and normal readers differ in the complexity of the language they use, implying less sophistication on the part of the poor readers in knowledge and use of grammar. Specific reference was made to research indicating that poor readers take longer than normal readers to comprehend the more complex grammatical constructions, particularly those that violate usages typically found in the language. There is also reason to believe that disabled readers are less capable than normal readers in their knowledge and use of both transformational and morphological rules. Children with reading problems have, in addition, been found to differ from normal readers in their use of syntax to aid word decoding. These data are correlational in nature and admittedly scant. However, they are suggestive and are certainly consistent with the notion that difficulties in word identification and other aspects of reading could be associated with deficiencies in syntax, at least in the case of some children.

Finally, general language ability implies proficiency in coding information phonetically and in associating phonetic codes with their stimulus counterparts (Shankweiler and Liberman 1972; Liberman and Shankweiler 1978). Severe cases of receptive language disability seem to be characterized by pronounced limitations in this function, but the child with specific reading disorder is not so impaired, at least not obviously. However, there is empirical support for the possibility that some poor readers sustain a subtle deficiency in phonetic coding, which hampers them on a variety of functions, including reading. This type of disorder is to be distinguished from dysfunction in auditory discrimination, the more traditional explanation of auditory perception problems in poor readers. In fact, the evidence suggests that dyslexics who have intact auditory acuity are able to discriminate words quite well at the level of the syllable, but because of inefficiency in employing phonetic information representationally, such children do not implicitly analyze the internal structure of those same words. This presumably accounts for the difficulties encountered by poor readers in mapping alphabetic symbols to sound.

Phonetic coding problems have also been associated with reader group differences on a variety of short-term memory tasks as well as on memory for words embedded in spoken and printed sentences. The results are therefore suggestive, and dysfunction in phonetic coding may indeed be a plausible explanation of the difficulties some children encounter in learning to read.

The second basic prerequisite for successful reading is the ability to make one's language explicit. The reference here is to what some theorists have alternatively termed *linguistic awareness* (Mattingly 1972) and *metalinguistic awareness* (Gleitman and Rozin 1977; Rozin and Gleitman 1977) to depict the individual's conscious knowledge of and sensitivity to the internal structure of language. As noted by these and other authors (Shankweiler and Liberman 1972; Liberman and Shankweiler 1978), reading places greater demands upon one's linguistic abilities than does oral communication, because it requires that the child assimilate much more detailed structural information about words and sentences than is normally required in spoken discourse; these authors contend that it is the poor reader's insensitivity to the internal structure of spoken and printed words that leads to difficulty in alphabetic mapping and thus in code acquisition. This is a useful description of a general problem that characterizes virtually all poor readers.

Just the reverse appears to be true of children who read normally. The fluent reader is a verbal gymnast, who is able to employ a variety of linguistic devices for word identification and for extracting the messages embedded in the text. Such a child has acquired a richly elaborated network of lexical features to provide alternative vehicles for decoding, and he engages, both implicitly and explicitly, in an active cross-referencing of visual and linguistic information to achieve success in this enterprise. He is able to do so not only because he has little difficulty in acquiring such information but also because he is disposed toward using it elaboratively and flexibly.

The poor reader, on the other hand, lacks such ability, I suggest, because of subtle and specific impairments in one or more aspects of linguistic functioning. Inferred deficiencies discussed in the literature encompass the semantic, syntactic, and phonologic components of reading, but the evidence available does not allow any definitive conclusions as to which of these areas of possible dysfunction is etiologically more significant. Indeed the components of language are so interwoven that their differential effects on the reading process are not readily detected, in either the poor or the normal reader. For example, a youngster who experiences difficulty in naming words as wholes (for instance, *cat, rat*), would have difficulty in detecting graphophonemic and orthographic invariance in those and like words (*fat, hat,* and so on), which would certainly impede acquisition of the rules necessary for effective word analysis and decoding. Conversely, difficulty in word analysis—that is, in relating letter clusters to their sound counterparts—would no doubt hamper whole word naming. In other words, the problems poor readers experience in interrelating the *semantic-syntactic* and *orthographic* components of printed words impair their ability to acquire information that would allow them to effectively interrelate the *phonological* and *orthographic* components, and vice versa. In contrast, proficient readers make effective and economical use of all of their linguistic and cognitive abilities in decoding any bit of printed material, and one cannot easily discern or separate the particular devices they employ in doing so. Thus there is need for greater explication of the relationships between specific linguistic functions and various aspects of the word identification process.

10.3 AREAS FOR FUTURE RESEARCH

Research on verbal processing is still at a seminal stage and much remains to be learned. There are, however, certain logical extensions of findings currently available, and it may be useful to outline those areas of inquiry that merit further consideration.

In the first place, it would seem worthwhile to add more detail about the relationship between knowledge of words and word decoding. It would be of particular interest to ascertain the mediational potential of an enriched lexicon—that is, the degree to which an elaborated network of associated word meanings actually facilitates word identification, by comparison with knowledge of the meanings of given words in the absence of broad contextual knowledge about those words. The question, put more simply, is whether or not a good vocabulary has any direct influence on the decoding process, and if so, what is the nature of this influence. Word enrichment as an aid to word identification seems intuitively sound, but there is virtually no direct evidence to substantiate its utility for this purpose.

Continued study of the degree to which poor readers have difficulty in other aspects of processing semantic information would be useful. For example, although there seems to be no convincing evidence that these children are deficient in apprehending general ideas, there is some suggestion that they are inefficient in doing so; more specifically, it may be that they frequently lose information in short-term memory because of phonetic coding problems. The results supporting this hypothesis were compiled largely by Perfetti and his associates and they are indeed strongly suggestive. Unfortunately, the findings to date are largely indirect. It would be useful to have some outside evidence of whether those who manifest inefficiency in semantic processing are subject to phonetic coding problems as well. Furthermore, Perfetti's subjects were only moderately impaired in reading. Severely disabled readers might well have more pronounced difficulties on the types of tasks employed in his studies than those tested, quite possibly because of more basic problems in language comprehension. Additional research is needed to clarify these issues.

It is also important to pursue further the correlates and extensions of inferred naming difficulties in poor readers. Ideally, additional study of the problem would be undertaken within the context of a comprehensive theory of lexical access and retrieval. Unfortunately, few of the rapid naming studies discussed earlier incorporated such a theory, and we are, by and large, left with descriptive and post hoc explanations of the results. There is consequently an obvious need for a theoretical model that could account for and integrate results from relevant studies conducted to date, as well as generate hypotheses that will lead to a better understanding of the reasons some poor readers have apparent difficulty in name retrieval.[3]

Dysfunction in naming may be subsumed under verbal memory deficits as a more general area of hypothesized difficulty in poor readers, and certain other aspects of this problem area could be usefully explored. One important distinction that has been made in the study of verbal memory is that between *storage* and *retrieval* of verbal information. That this distinction is not a superfluous one is readily demonstrated in the occasional difficulty we all experience in recalling a specific verbal concept or proper name known to be stored in permanent memory. It is not clear from the findings to date whether the poor reader's apparent difficulty in verbal recall is the result of storage or retrieval problems or some admixture of both. Whereas some studies have presented evidence indicating that recall problems in such children may be attributed to encoding or storage deficits, others provided support for the possibility that they are due to retrieval difficulties. More specifically, it has been suggested that poor readers do not code or register the phonologic features of spoken and printed words as well as normal readers and are therefore less effective in employing such information as retrieval cues. On the other hand, it is conceivable that poor readers may be characterized by qualitative differences in the structure and organization of the lexicon and in the ways in which verbal concepts are processed for recovery subsequent to permanent storage. These two disorders are not mutually exclusive; they may also weigh unequally in different children. Thus the distinction merits further exploration.

In summary, there is a pressing need for reader group contrasts on various aspects of semantic memory. It would be useful to replicate those studies that have yielded promising results, employing more stringent sampling criteria than in most conducted to date. I should point out, in this connection, that researchers have been very actively involved in recent years in the study of semantic processing in normal children and adults (Bransford and Franks 1971; Paivio 1971; E. Clark 1973; H. Clark 1973; Jenkins 1974; Hagen, Jongeward, and Kail, 1975; Ghatala and Levin 1976; Pressley 1977; Rumelhart and Ortony 1977). Investigators studying semantic memory in poor readers would do well to draw upon this literature for theoretical foundations and promising research methodologies.

Continued study of the possibility of phonologic deficiencies as a source of reading disorder is certainly indicated. In examining the evidence derived from reader group contrasts on linguistic functioning, it becomes apparent that phonetic coding deficits have been more extensively researched than alternative explana-

tions of verbal processing difficulties in poor readers. Yet interpretations of results in some of these investigations are open to
question. This was true, for example, of the promising studies
conducted by Perfetti and his associates, which offered only indirect evidence for a phonetic coding deficit explanation of
reading group differences in semantic memory. Thus there is need
of further elucidation of such findings.

There is also need for additional exploration of how phonetic
coding difficulties may relate to the more general problem of
linguistic awareness. Do these two descriptors constitute different
rubrics for essentially the same problem, both being caused by
experiential gaps that create a disposition toward inefficient processing? Or are phonetic coding deficits reflective of more basic
developmental problems that would obtain even if a child were
more sensitive to the phonetic structure of the language? One
obvious way to pursue an answer to this question is to attempt
to instill linguistic (phonemic) awareness in children with reading
difficulties, in the interest of determining the extent to which
such training influences the coding function. To my knowledge,
no such study has been conducted, and it would seem useful to
investigate this possibility.

Finally, the relationship between phonologic deficiencies and
various other aspects of verbal memory needs to be explored more
thoroughly. It is possible, for example, that word retrieval and
semantic memory problems are directly related to dysfunction in
phonetic coding and thus to problems in cross-referencing the
phonemic and prosodic features of words and sentences with their
semantic and syntactic counterparts. These possibilities have not
been directly investigated in reader group contrasts, and it seems
important to do so. A good illustration of the type of clarification
needed here is the ambiguity occasioned by the reliable differences
found between disabled and able readers on knowledge of inflectional morphology. It is possible that such difficulty arises because
of phonologic disorder that impedes the acquisition of morpho-
phonemic conditioning rules; but it may also be that the difficulty
reflects a more basic deficiency in syntactic competence. It seems
likely that there is an interaction here; evaluation of this interaction, as it relates to reader group differences in morphology, may
tell us something about the nature of reading disability.

Of the limited number of studies evaluating linguistic functioning in poor and normal readers, few have directly addressed
the possibility that reading disorder may be related to deficiencies
in syntactic competence. No doubt syntax has been overlooked
because the dyslexic typically manifests no disorder in language
comprehension that can be discerned in spoken discourse. Yet
there is reason to believe that some poor readers may sustain more
subtle deficits in grammatical competence that may impede the
development of skill in reading. The evidence is meager, however,
and the hypothesis needs to be explored more thoroughly.

Perhaps the most important area of inquiry here is the relation
between various aspects of syntactic ability and the word identification process. Although there is some reason to believe that
poor readers do not make effective use of contextual information
to aid word decoding, the nature of this difficulty is not apparent.
The evidence available suggests that such disorder is the result of
experiential impediments, but this interpretation may not be
applicable to all poor readers. It may be, for example, that some
children have basic language comprehension problems that affect
their ability to use context to assist in word retrieval. This possibility has not been extensively evaluated, and it would therefore
seem useful to do so.

Given the absence of gross deficiencies in language comprehension in the population of interest here, one may justifiably
inquire what specific aspects of syntactic ability might be problematic. Unfortunately, the literature provides little to assist in
answering this question, although the results of the few studies
available do hint at areas of difficulty that might be further explored. Reference has already been made to research indicating
that poor readers have less facility than normals in using grammatical inflections (Brittain 1970; Wiig, Semel, and Crouse 1973;
Vogel 1974); I speculated that such difficulty could be attributed
either to phonologic or syntactic deficits. Assuming the latter
alternative, it might reasonably be suggested that some dyslexics
have impaired ability to apprehend and make use of the rule-
bound qualities of language, a problem that should be especially
evident in the acquisition of the more abstract and complex syntactic constructions. Thus, in addition to difficulty in the use of
grammatical inflections, it would be anticipated that poor readers

might be slower than normals in acquiring facility with functionally invariant words (such as *and, but, although, when, how, if*), lexically derived words (*speak/speaker, bomb/bombardier:* Chomsky 1970; Kintsch 1972), words that carry syntactic markers depicting identical surface structure but different deep structure complexity (*digging* versus *growling:* Polzella and Rohrman 1970), and any construction that calls for a fine-grained analysis of subtle changes in syntax to represent different meanings and shades of meanings. By extension, difficulty in the comprehension and use of such words might significantly influence the speed and efficiency with which a child learns to identify them. This hypothesis can be tested directly, but to my knowledge no studies have attempted to do so.

These suggestions are consistent with the results of at least three investigations, one that found differences between poor and normal readers in their use of transformational rules (Fry, Johnson, and Muehl 1970) and two that differentiated these groups on their comprehension of complex grammatical constructions (Vogel 1974; Goldman 1976). These findings have not, to date, been replicated, and speculations must remain tenuous without additional research exploring in greater depth the parameters in question.

In addition to more detailed evaluation of specific language comprehension problems in poor readers, there would seem to be some utility in continued study of their expressive language skills. There is at present only one such investigation (Fry, Johnson, and Muehl 1976) in the literature, and it yielded significant differences between impaired and able readers on a variety of measures of syntax. The reliability of these findings should be assessed and similar contrasts should be undertaken with children at different age and grade levels.

This suggestion brings into focus the need for longitudinal as well as cross-sectional study of the linguistic skills of poor as compared with normal readers. There is some reason to believe that deficient readers are characterized by specific language impairments prior to learning to read (see, for example, de Hirsch, Jansky, and Langford 1966; Jansky and de Hirsch 1972). Extensive documentation of this possibility is, without question, necessary to an ultimate understanding of the relation between language and reading ability.

Finally, any serious study of the linguistic correlates of dyslexia must be concerned with the interrelationships among the various components of language, as well as with the effects of deficiencies in one or more of these components upon both linguistic functioning and reading ability. Semantic, syntactic, and phonologic processes as separate areas of inquiry can only arbitrarily be divorced from language as a representational system. Although there is some degree of autonomy among these subsystems, and thus sufficient justification for studying them individually, language as a functional skill depends upon their successful interaction. A deficiency in one linguistic process can be expected to have a deleterious effect upon the others and, by extension, upon given aspects of reading. It may be that the various components of language do not carry equal weight with respect to their influence upon particular aspects of reading, but this is an empirical question for which there are only intuitive answers, given the paucity of research specifically addressing the issue. Furthermore, the investigation of this and the other questions raised is constrained by our limited knowledge of normal language development in school-age children (Loban 1963; Menyuk 1963, 1964; C. Chomsky 1969, 1972). It is therefore imperative that attempts to understand the differential effects of linguistic functions upon the development of skill in reading be broad-based, to include conceptualizations that emerge from the study of normal and abnormal language ability as well as normal and abnormal reading ability. Indeed research in all these areas can only be complementary.

Chapter 9 addressed the problem of attentional deficits as factors that may potentially contribute to reading failure. There is no question that poor attention can lead to difficulties in learning to read, but in studying the etiology of reading disability, a distinction must be made between *primary* attentional problems due to motivational or constitutional (neurological) factors and *secondary* attentional problems resulting from the inability to acquire information that will selectively attune one to relationships that will facilitate critical distinctions (like the initial consonant sounds in *was* and *saw*). A primary attentional deficit may contaminate any given data set and thereby equivocate one's findings; thus every effort should be made by researchers to control for such contamination. A secondary attentional deficit is an inevitable consequence of imperfect learning in any given area, and researchers cannot readily control for such difficulties, the net effect being that their presence often leads to misinterpretation. The astute investigator can nevertheless attempt to understand the origin of secondary attentional problems in order to avoid the tendency to attribute faulty discrimination to an organically derived *deficit* in perception when such difficulties may be more accurately attributed to *inefficiency* in perception resulting from the inability to attend selectively to information that maximizes the probability of accurate discrimination. Although I have no doubt that some of the "perceptual" problems observed in poor readers are caused by primary attentional problems, I suspect that most of them are instances of secondary attentional deficit.

As I approach the end of this long discourse, let me express the hope that it will prove to be an effective spur to needed research in at least some of the areas of inquiry that are important to the understanding of specific reading disability. Before terminating it, however, two final points are pertinent.

10.4 FURTHER COMMENT ON THE QUESTION OF MULTI-FACTOR THEORIES AND THE NEUROLOGICAL BASES OF READING DISABILITY

In the review of the literature, it became evident that multifactor explanations of dyslexia presently enjoy a greater number of advocates than in past years, when unitary deficit theories such as Orton's and Bender's held sway. Multifactor theories typically assume that dyslexia can be caused by dysfunction in one or another of the sensory or motor processes involved in learning to read. Implicit in most of these conceptualizations is the notion that such disorders constitute distinct neuropsychological syndromes characterized by qualitatively different performance patterns in specific aspects of reading and in skills, such as spelling, that are intrinsically related to reading.

Although it may be reasonable to assume that specific types of reading disorder may be linked to different antecedent conditions, given the complexities of this process, it does not seem reasonable to assume that each of these deficiencies is associated with a particular neurological syndrome. Nor is it likely that dysfunction in any one of the sensory or motor systems typically involved in reading (vision, language, speech-motor articulation) necessarily results in reading disability.

Boder's conceptualization of dyslexia provides a useful illustration. She separates dyslexics into subgroups on the basis of two different types of reading and spelling errors, issuing theoretically from neurological dysfunction affecting the visual and auditory systems. Whole-word decoding is believed to take place through the visual modality, whereas the decoding of word parts (phonetic analysis) is said to be supported primarily by the auditory modality. Boder suggests that the "visually impaired" dyslexic (called dyseidetic) is not very good at whole-word learning, is prone to make a large number of "visual discrimination" errors *(was/saw, clam/calm)*, and is unduly inclined to read and spell phonetically, presumably because of inferred difficulties in visual perception and memory. On the other hand, the "auditorily impaired" dyslexic (called dysphonetic) is said to be less analytic and more global in his approach to reading and spelling because of deficiencies in phonetic analysis. A third subgroup described by Boder is believed to be characterized by both visual and auditory deficits and is poor at both whole-word learning and word analysis.

In my estimation, Boder's theory rests on a weak foundation, primarily because the differential error patterns observed in the oral reading and spelling of poor readers can be more simply explained by instructional and experiential deficiencies than by neurological dysfunction. A child may fail to develop skill in whole-word learning or in word analysis either because he has not received a balanced reading program emphasizing the utility of both strategies for decoding (Chall 1967) or because of an implicit tendency to construe the decoding process as either a holistic or an analytic enterprise. In neither instance is it necessary to postulate the existence of neurological disorder as a causal factor. Indeed, Baron (1979) has provided evidence indicating that individual differences in reliance upon phonetic rules for word decoding as opposed to word-specific associations arise largely from differences in approach to instruction.

It may be true that whole-word strategies of identification are qualitatively different from part-whole strategies, in that each draws upon specific relationships established between different word features.[4] Even so, it seems incorrect to equate difficulties in whole-word learning with dysfunction in visual processing, on the one hand, and difficulties in word analysis with dysfunction in auditory processing, on the other. Both are clear-cut examples of visual-verbal learning, neither being more dependent on one modality or the other. Boder's theory is therefore questionable on grounds of parsimony. The same is true of other multifactor theories of dyslexia that incorporate similar conceptualizations of word identification (for example, Myklebust and Johnson 1962).

Further concern over the rationales employed in distinguishing subgroups of poor readers is generated by multifactor theories holding that dysfunction in any one of the sensory and motor systems involved in reading can result in dyslexia. For example, on the basis of a single study, Mattis, French, and Rapin (1975) claimed to have isolated *three* types of dyslexia: one believed to be caused by language deficiencies, which they found to be in highest incidence; a second presumably caused by speech-motor and graphomotor difficulties, observed in a slightly lower proportion of the sample; and a third said to be the result of visual-perceptual and visual-motor difficulties, observed in a very small proportion of this same sample.

Consistent with the view expressed throughout this book, I am not surprised that a sizable proportion of the children sustained language deficiencies, which, I suspect, did indeed contribute to their reading problems. I rather doubt, however, that either speech-motor deficits or so-called visual-perceptual and visual-motor problems were primary causes of the reading difficulties in the other children tested. As for speech-motor deficits, many children with even severe motor deficiencies (many cerebral palsied children) become quite literate, providing that they have had the benefit of adequate instruction. On the other hand, children with significant motor deficiencies are often denied the benefit of adequate instruction in reading because their ability to learn to read is belied by their motor handicaps (Schonell 1956). It is possible that such children were included in the study by Mattis, and his co-workers.[5] I of course question the role of visual processing deficits as a significant cause of reading disability. However, the more general point to be made here is that a given skill does not require the use of our sensory, cognitive, and motor abilities in equal measure, and this constrains the etiological factors that may be logically considered as prospective causes of reading disability. Speech-motor, visual-motor, and visual discrimination problems may be correlates of a severe reading disability and may even constitute secondary factors that compound the problem, but I do not believe they are primary causes of the disorder. I therefore question the validity of the neuropsychological "syndromes" defined by Mattis et al. (1975) and, by extension, conceptualizations that incorporate the notion that dysfunction in any one of the subsystems involved in reading can cause dyslexia.[6]

This point of view should not be taken to mean that I reject the possibility that reading disability may be caused by a variety of basic process disorders, in effect comprising qualitatively different subgroups of disabled readers. This is an empirical question, and it is an open one. Indeed, I have alluded to the possibility that deficiencies in various aspects of linguistic functioning or a specific disorder in visual-verbal association learning could constitute significantly different causes of reading disability, although I expect that specific difficulties may not contribute equally to the disorder.[7] I also recognize that other explanations are viable; for example, the serial order deficit theory of dyslexia, which has not been adequately evaluated. However, it seems reasonable to suggest that hypothesized causes of reading disability must be plausible not only from the standpoint of their theoretical, empirical, and logical validity but also from the standpoint of the essential importance to the reading process of the basic functions they implicate. Vision and speech articulation are typically involved in reading but are not essential to it; linguistic ability and the ability to relate linguistic symbols to coded representations *are* essential to reading. Thus the search for etiological factors must accord with these constraints in order to be a successful enterprise. The multifactor theories currently available do not, by and large, do so.

Given the foregoing considerations, it seems obvious that delineating neurologically distinct syndromes as separate causes of specific reading disability, while a valid enterprise with both theoretical and practical significance, should entail meticulous definition of the behaviors defining these syndromes, particularly as regards their relevance and essential importance for developing skill in reading. It would be wise for investigators to take care to distinguish between primary and secondary causation and to assiduously avoid the unnecessary proliferation of neuropsychological syndromes as explanatory devices. Such proliferation is an inevitable consequence of a tendency to ascribe ultimate (neurological) causes to a reading disability before its more immediate (psychological) correlates have been well defined.

10.5 ON REMEDIATION

Up to this point I have made no direct reference to the practical implications of empirical findings emerging from the study of dyslexia, and have not done so because my primary purpose was to discuss the important theoretical and research issues emanating from such studies. However, I do feel concern over current practice in the field of learning disabilities. Specifically, I have been concerned that those who suggest that reading disability is caused by basic disorder in neuropsychological processes have promoted the widespread use of a variety of "diagnostic" and "treatment" procedures designed to correct hypothesized deficiencies in such processes as a prerequisite to direct instruction in reading (Kephart 1960; Getman 1962; Barsch 1965; Johnson and Myklebust 1967; Bannatyne 1971; Kirk and Kirk 1971; Cruickshank 1972; Frostig and Maslow 1973). On the strength of inferred disorders in visual-motor integration, cross-modal transfer, serial order recall, auditory discrimination, and various other basic functions, practitioners commonly involve impaired learners in training programs designed to correct "deficiencies" in each of these areas and, more basically, to foster neurological "readiness" for learning. Such programs typically include gross and fine motor training, visual and auditory discrimination training, optical exercises, cross-modal integration training, activities designed to improve sequential memory, and a variety of other perceptual-motor activities that, typically, have only a remote relation to reading.

In my estimation, remedial procedures derived from the basic process models of learning disability currently in vogue have little or no utility for correcting reading problems. Indeed much of the research presented in this volume either obviates or casts serious doubt on the validity of such models and, by extension, the training programs that issue from them. Furthermore, a number of studies have directly tested the effectiveness of basic process training upon growth in reading and other academic areas and the results have been uniformly negative (Robinson 1971; Hartman and Hartman 1973; Hammill, Goodman, and Wiederholt 1974).

And although it may be speculated, in line with my own bias, that direct stimulation in various aspects of linguistic functioning may have utility for remediating reading difficulties, the fact remains that my conjectures about relationships that may exist between anomalies in language and reading disability have not yet been extensively documented. We are further constrained in such a venture by the limited progress that has been made in determining the sources of individual differences in verbal ability in the normally developing child, let alone children who, theoretically, support (specific) language impairments that may result in specific reading disability. Without additional study of the effects of linguistic stimulation upon various aspects of reading, I would be hesitant to suggest categorically that general language enrichment or direct training to improve semantic, syntactic, or phonological competence will improve reading ability.

On the other hand, my perspective does have some clear-cut implications for instruction, suggesting a number of general guidelines that seem both intuitively sound and conservative, while at the same time allowing for further exploration of remedial techniques that may eventually prove useful.

First, inasmuch as I have strongly emphasized the poor reader's limitations in cross-referencing the multiple features of words (graphic, orthographic, semantic, syntactic, phonologic), it seems apparent that the practitioner might try to ascertain the degree to which the child lacks information about such features and attempt to correct deficiencies when they are found. This recommendation implies a *direct* approach to assessment and remediation, which means that in both evaluating and correcting a reading disorder, it would be far more profitable to conceptualize the reading process and the learner's competence in units that most closely approximate the skills and subskills we ultimately wish to teach him, rather than to "subdivide these variables into basic sensory and intersensory processes involved in learning that skill, but not unique to it" (Vellutino et al. 1977, 381). In other words, the practitioner should assess the child's deficiencies in the various components of reading (word analysis skills, whole word decoding, comprehension skills, and so on) and attempt to remediate these rather than waste time remediating inferred process disorders such as apparent dysfunction in basic visual and auditory discrimination.

Consistent with the speculation that poor readers may lack information about word features is the possibility that some instructional programs may be inclined to place undue emphasis upon one or another strategy for word identification. This suggests the need for a well-balanced approach to remedial instruction, with equal emphasis upon whole-word and analytic strategies for decoding, in addition to pointed attempts to provide learners with as much information as possible about the meanings of words they encounter in print and use of those words in sentences. Care should be taken to present such words both within the context of sentences to enrich their meanings and in isolation to promote analysis of internal structure. Some time might be well spent in visual discrimination of critical differences in printed letters and words, placing particular emphasis upon developing familiarity with orthographic and graphophonemic invariants. However, such training should not take place out of context, the primary purpose of all these exercises being to provide the child with alternative means for decoding.

Inasmuch as many poor readers may not have made explicit the phonemic structure of spoken and printed words, in the interest of mapping (alphabetic) symbols to sounds, a third remedial strategy would be for the practitioner to spend some time in direct training of phonemic segmentation and awareness. The specific procedures employed in such a training program might roughly correspond to those suggested by Downing (1973) and Elkonin (1973), but the major objective is clear-cut—to assist the child to develop facility in dissecting a word's sound structure so as to foster more meticulous symbol-sound and sound-symbol association. A corollary procedure is to spend some time in direct teaching of these associations, taking care to present letter sounds and their combinations in accord with the way they are perceived in the natural language. This means that letter sounds will be taught within the context of syllables, with the exception of certain vowel sounds (/a/ in *cat*), which can be readily taught in isolation. Such learning will expand the child's repertoire of graphophonemic and other graphophonic invariants, (morphological units), which in turn will increase the probability of generalizing these relationships across variable contexts. The failure to generalize is, of course, one of the poor reader's major stumbling blocks.

General language enrichment could well prove to be a useful adjunct to remedial reading, but it might be most defensibly undertaken on an experimental basis, given the constraints mentioned. Furthermore, such activity should be relevant to the remedial program in order to achieve its most beneficial effect. For example, direct instruction to expand the child's vocabulary might be helpful but would no doubt have greater utility if linked to code acquisition as a related enterprise. In such instances, deliberate attempts might be made to familiarize the child with the phonologic, orthographic, and syntactic characteristics of given vocabulary words, in the interest of establishing firm associations among the multiple features of each word and thus more facile cross-referencing of these features.

A similar example is provided in the presentation of derivative forms, that is, words that have a common semantic and orthographic base (one "lexical spelling"), but which differ with respect to their syntactic and phonologic characteristics: *bomb, bombard, bombardier.* Direct teaching of the different meanings of such words, their uses in sentences, and the differences in their spellings and oral pronunciations would allow the learner to more readily predict given pronunciations in print by virtue of his knowledge of the relations among these words in his natural vocabulary.[8]

A language enrichment program might also include teaching the child something of the functional differences between content words (nouns, verbs, adjectives, and most adverbs) and function words (all the "little words": conjunctives, prepositions, articles, and so on), providing him with activities that would facilitate sensitivity to the idiosyncratic nature of content words and the invariant and abstract qualities of the function words. Such activities might include pointed listening to sentences using specific words of both types, exercises requiring that the child generate sentences or complete incomplete sentence frames using such words appropriately, discussions of the meanings of sentences using specific words as well as the meaning of the words themselves, and lessons that necessitate reading the same words in isolation and in the context of sentences. All of these activities would seem to be helpful in developing the child's linguistic intuitions and enriching the meanings of vocabulary words taught, particularly those (such as the function words) that are more difficult to grasp.

A language enrichment program might also provide the child with ample opportunity to hear and use language, which obviously implies involving him in activities in which he listens to spoken discourse (as in hearing stories told and being read to) and creating circumstances wherein he is encouraged to express himself in words. Other strategies might include direct teaching of lexical interrelationships (synonyms, antonyms, homonyms, and so on), exercises that facilitate elaborated use of new words (use of those words in different contexts), exercises that sensitize the child to the invariances in spoken and written language (invariant meanings using different words and sentences, invariant use of specific syntactic constructions, morphological invariance, orthographic and graphophonemic invariance), and involving the child in any situations that render the structure and unique characteristics of language itself the object of study.

These are just a few of the pedagogical principles that issue from certain of the hypotheses I have entertained as to the origin of reading difficulties. I have stressed the need to interrelate word features, placing particular emphasis upon the cross-referencing of visual and linguistic constituents of printed words. I have also emphasized the importance of explicating both the structural and the functional components of language as well as the necessity of enriching linguistic skills within the context of reading. Obviously I believe that deficiencies in these areas hamper the child's progress in reading. It remains for future research to verify or reject these speculations.

NOTES

NOTE TO CHAPTER 1

1. The term *dyslexia* is arbitrarily employed as a convenience, owing to its widespread use in application to children with severe reading problems. Its employment should not be taken as evidence that the author is committed to any particular description or characterization of such children. The reader should also be alerted that the terms *dyslexia, specific reading disability, reading disability, poor readers* and similar terms are employed interchangeably throughout this text.

NOTE TO CHAPTER 2

1. For purposes of evaluating word analysis skills in poor and normal readers, we have in each of our studies employed a brief test (35 items) of phonetic decoding ability employing nonsense syllables (Bryant 1965). This measure has proved reliable over the years and has consistently yielded means and standard deviations of comparable magnitude for all groups tested. However, the test is still in experimental form and there are currently no published norms. We have therefore employed it for post hoc comparisons of subjects included in research samples rather than as a selection device. This procedure has allowed us to determine that severely impaired readers sampled on the basis of the oral reading test employed in our studies (Gilmore 1968) were extremely deficient in word analysis as well (see table 2.1).

NOTE TO CHAPTER 3

1. Orton believed that his theory had wide applicability in explanation of a variety of other developmental difficulties. For example, he attempted to generalize its essential features to spoken language, suggesting that confused or mixed dominance could account for such disorders as stuttering and speech reversals (saying /ephelant/ instead of /elephant/).

NOTES TO CHAPTER 5

1. Satz's theory can also be criticized on logical grounds. It is difficult to understand why, within the context of a hypothesized lag in general maturation,

a dyslexic who exhibits developmental retardation in somatosensory and perceptual motor functions would not also manifest language and conceptual deficiencies if these processes emerge in tandem, ontogenetically. The theory seems to suggest that dyslexics and normals should *not* be different in these more complex functions upon beginning to learn to read, and, further, that they are not of primary importance to successful achievement at this stage of development. Yet neither assumption appears to be tenable. Language in a normal child is relatively well developed by the time he begins to learn to read and it would therefore be expected that a general maturational delay would have a significant impact on such development. In addition, there is increasingly greater evidence (see sections 8.1 and 8.2) that early language deficiencies are present in many children who later become poor readers, contrary to the position taken by Satz, and that such deficits have a deleterious effect on reading. These facts alone would seem to obviate Satz's theory.

2. To provide a broader context within which to place this argument, the reader is referred to the substantial literature dealing with the developmental lag between perceiving and performing, as it is called (Maccoby and Bee 1965; Bee and Walker 1968; Olson 1970; Arnheim 1972; Golomb 1973).

3. A good example of the type of conceptual knowledge that might facilitate performance on both visual-motor and reading measures is sensitivity to invariance in the orientation or sequencing of identical figures. Individual differences in the implicit knowledge that the word *same* had reference to such invariance was clearly evident in a study of prereading skills in kindergartners and first-graders reported by Calfee (1977). Similar findings emerged in a study by Caldwell and Hall (1969), as will be noted in the discussion of spatial and directional confusion as a hypothesized cause of reading disability (see sections 5.2.2 and 5.3.1 for more detailed discussions of these two studies).

4. The term *transfer skills* applies, in the present context, to an implicit knowledge of basic visual-motor generalizations that eventually serve to facilitate the copying and spontaneous reproduction of graphic material to which the child may be exposed: discrimination and execution of horizontal, perpendicular, and oblique lines, curved- versus straight-line figures, and directional changes, in addition to such general concepts as awareness of positional and sequential invariance, size, spacing, and like heuristics.

5. *Directional sense* might be more accurately viewed as a complex of higher-order cognitive skills than as a perceptual function, since it appears to involve much more than the perception of spatial relations or *spatial awareness* in the sense in which these terms are employed in the literature concerned with reading disability. This suggestion will become intelligible if the reader considers the abilities that must underlie a successful journey to and from an unfamiliar destination with the aid of directions provided by someone familiar with the route. Such a feat must surely depend in part upon an implicit knowledge of such heuristic concepts as relativity and reversibility, in addition to the ability to synthesize and code serial information, which itself depends partly upon the ability to relate spatial and verbal representations.

Automatizing the maneuvers necessary to traverse the route successfully need only imply rote serial learning with appropriate executions made at certain choice points; but the ability to execute these maneuvers in one trial as well as the ability to assist someone else in doing so depends upon the conceptual and memorial skills referred to. When reconsidered in the present light, directional sense would seem to be a nonentity or, at very least, an oversimplified conception of a very complex process.

6. The author is indebted to his daughter, Anne, who at the age of 7 provided him with this insight.

7. Here Kolers has adopted a distinction made by some authors (e.g., Ervin 1961; McNeil 1970) between two types of responses typically solicited in the laboratory by free-association tasks: paradigmatic associations are words in the same form class as the stimulus word (*boy*-girl); syntagmatic associations are words that may be found to be contiguous to the stimulus word in a functionally meaningful phrase (e.g., boy–plays). Because paradigmatic substitutions were found to be more prevalent in older children and syntagmatic substitutions more prevalent in younger children, McNeil suggested that preponderance of the former type may be a sign of growing linguistic competence. However, this may be a vastly oversimplified distinction, as pointed out in a recent review by Nelson (1977).

8. Good and poor readers did not differ in percentage of errors in any of the four contrasts made by Mason (1975). This would appear to support her conclusion that the reader groups in these studies were comparable with respect to form perception.

9. The suggestion that the single letter constitutes the basic unit of perception in word recognition has not received widespread acceptance and represents a controversial issue in reading research (cf. Reicher 1969; Wheeler 1970; Aderman and Smith 1971; Smith 1971; Thompson and Massaro 1973; Massaro 1973, 1975; Gibson and Levin 1975; Healy 1976). However, this issue can be set apart from the issue of spatial redundancy as conceptualized by Mason and applied to poor and normal reader contrasts. My critique of Mason's formulations is not necessarily incompatible with the notion that the single letter is the basic perceptual unit, but at this point I consider the question to be completely open.

NOTES TO CHAPTER 6

1. This finding is somewhat contrary to results obtained by Birch and Belmont (1965), who found that reading achievement and AVI were correlated only up to second grade. However, the correlation found beyond this grade level in the Kahn and Birch study may have been due to the fact that the AVI test employed had a greater ceiling than those used in previous studies, since the number of items was doubled.

2. I might mention, in addition, such mediation theories of intersensory integration as Piaget's (Piaget and Inhelder 1956) and the Soviet psychologists Leontiev (1957) and Zinchenko (1966), all of which stress the dominant role

of the motor systems in perceptual and cognitive development, as well as the position taken by Ettlinger (1967) who has stressed the role of language in mediating cross-modal transfer.

NOTES TO CHAPTER 7

1. Of all of the theorists addressing the distinction between memory for content and sequence, Estes (1972) comes closest to suggesting that the processing of information of each type is supported by separable neurological structures. He has articulated a model for coding temporal events which has as its main feature the establishment of associations between featural characteristics of items in given arrays and superordinate contextual codes—termed *control elements*. Control elements are considered to be abstract constructs representing either some transient element of the stimulus input or more stable structures in long-term memory (the spoken word /cat/ which generates the sequence *c, a, t*). The order of particular items is said to be preserved in short-term memory by means of reverberatory loop mechanisms that reactivate the sequence in which the items occur—that is, by virtue of a cyclic interchange between the control element and the items themselves. In this model item information consists of the particular features of the characters in a string (visual, phonetic, etc.) whereas order information is generated by the reactivation of the sequence by means of the reverberatory mechanisms. Loss of order information from short-term memory is said to occur as a result of disturbances in the timing of recurrent activations of the individual elements in a sequence (for instance, from intervening material). Such disturbances are said to result in interchanges in the order of items, particularly those in close proximity to one another, or those that have similar properties. Disruptions in timing could also result in other types of (item) intrusions or in errors of omission. Loss of item information is therefore viewed as a consequence of basic dysfunction in reverberatory mechanisms that automatically register the order in which given items were presented. It should be clear that such mechanisms could be readily viewed as physiological entities that could be awry in poor readers. However, it might be pointed out that Estes's conceptualization has been articulated within a psychological context, and can be evaluated without reference to specific organic mechanisms. It would therefore seem that reference to Estes's theory in support of organic deficit explanations of serial processing disturbances in poor readers is premature.

2. Senf (1969) found evidence for specific difficulties in poor readers in bisensory memory for serial information, from which he inferred that poor readers may be selectively impaired in recall of serial information. However, in Senf's later studies the results were not replicated, suggesting that initial findings were artifactual.

3. It is in the understanding of such phonomena as the ability to perceive temporal order in a succession of stimuli of brief durations that Crowder's (1972) and Massaro's (1975) respective conceptualizations of precategorical

store and synthesized memory are particularly useful (see discussion of basic process model in chapter 4).

4. Two bits of evidence provide support for the possibility that a serial deficit theory of dyslexia may not have much explanatory value. First, Shankweiler and Liberman (1972) found that sequence errors on word lists containing a high proportion of reversible words (*not*, *pat*, etc.), accounted for only 15 percent of the total number of errors, whereas mispronunciation of consonants and vowels accounted for 75 percent. These data suggest that ordering difficulties may not constitute a basic cause of dysfunctional reading and may in fact be a result of deficits in other areas.

The second bit of evidence is less direct. Briefly, S. J. Samuels and his associates (personal communication) have found that component letter processing is more characteristic of unskilled readers than is simultaneous processing of letter and word features, whereas the reverse is true of skilled readers (see also our discussion of Mason, 1975, section 5.3.5). This finding may be interpreted to mean that serial processing of letters is a naive approach to word decoding that must be significantly modified if progress is to be made in this enterprise. The logical extension of this interpretation is that a strict rendering of the order of the letters in a printed word is not only unnecessary for word recognition but may to some extent impede the process. The implications for a serial deficit theory of reading disability should be obvious.

5. The particular items in a printed letter string may be encoded and retrieved with reference to their membership in given featural classes (graphic and phonologic). However, the encoding and retrieval of the sequential arrangement of those letters is a more complex process which may depend not only upon the featural characteristics of each letter but also upon the particular relations that are established between the letters, especially insofar as their appearance in a given order has functional value. The retrieval of both types of information also depends in part upon capacity limits in short-term memory, the particular coding devices and rehearsal strategies employed, and the degree to which the letter string has higher-order structure. Thus the specific letters, or letter combinations, retrieved in the random string *pntlehae* might be those whose graphic and phonologic features happen to be most salient at the time of presentation. However, the recall of the order of these letters would be determined also by the individual's chunking strategies, or, in other words, the degree to which structure can be imposed on the letters in the string, as well as by primacy and recency phenomena characteristic of short-term memory. The differential reliance upon featural and structural cues on a given recall trial may, in such instances, be partly responsible for the disparities in the shapes of the error curves generated by item and order information observed by Healy (1974, 1975a, 1975b, 1977). On the other hand, these curves should be in closer correspondence in the case of the letter string *elephant*, which contains the same letters arranged in higher-order structures that are inherent in the language and in the orthography rather than imposed by the individual. It should be clear from these illustrations that the recollection of item and order information is dependent not so much

upon qualitative differences in specific neurologic substructures but upon the interaction of a variety of cognitive and stimulus variables that determine the salience of given items as well as groups of items placed in specific relationships.

NOTES TO CHAPTER 8

1. These findings may be interpreted within the context of recent research by Kimura (1973), who, with the use of dichotic listening tasks, demonstrated a left-ear (right-hemisphere) superiority for nonlanguage sounds such as coughing, laughing, and crying, but a right-ear (left-hemisphere) advantage for speech sounds. Coupling these results with our own data and with the results of research done elsewhere (Gazzaniga 1970; Milner 1971; Posner et al. 1972; Crowder 1972), it might be reasonably theorized that poor readers are essentially normal in right-hemisphere processing but deficient either in left hemisphere functioning or in coordinating and interrelating visual and verbal information stored, respectively, in the right and left hemispheres.

2. Jarvella (1971) found that recall for words within sentence and clause boundaries was greater than recall across such boundaries, suggesting that thematic material is more readily organized within semantic-syntactic units.

3. Three experiments employing procedures similar to those already described are discussed in greater detail in Goldman, Hogaboam, Bell, and Perfetti (1977). The results obtained in these studies were essentially the same as those discussed here, thereby reinforcing the authors' position.

4. A comprehensive review of this literature can be found in Palermo and Molfese (1972).

5. It is doubtful that the orderly acquisition of the specific structures evaluated by C. Chomsky (1969, 1972) would classify as a stage phenomenon in the sense discussed by Wohlwill, who distinguishes between *stage* and *sequence* as developmental constructs. See Wohlwill (1973, chapter 9) for a comprehensive treatment of this distinction.

6. As an alternative explanation, one might speculate that idiosyncratic responding in poor readers may have been the result of word finding problems which created difficulty in employing contextual information. If so, then the poor readers might be less idiosyncractic when contextual information is provided, as in the Cloze condition. The figures reported in the Cromer and Weiner (1966) study provide no information as to this possibility, but the hypothesis would seem to be worth testing.

7. Further calling into question inferences of auditory deficiencies based on the Wepman test are the results of Vellutino, DeSetto, and Steger (1972), who suggested that the structure of this test creates the possibility of measurement error due to response bias (Parducci 1965), inasmuch as it does not balance the number of identical and nonidentical items. To explore this possibility two versions of the Wepman test were administered—one standardized and one balanced for same/different items (20/20). Two randomly selected

samples of elementary-school children were given one or the other version of the test, and it was found that the standard Wepman occasioned more "errors" than the balanced version, thereby questioning the validity of the test in its present format.

8. I do not necessarily accept Farnham-Diggory and Gregg's (1975) conceptualization of word decoding, particularly as it might apply to the advanced reader. However, their description of the complexity of component processes involved in reading, in relation to reader group differences on measures designed to evaluate these processes, seems instructive.

9. The child who made this error was a 14-year-old severely impaired reader whose efforts at word decoding were fraught with semantic substitution errors of this type. He also had difficulty with all other aspects of reading and appeared to have a basic problem in name retrieval, both in oral language and reading. Indeed, it was the response patterns observed in this youngster that initially piqued my interest in the possibility that severe reading disability is associated with basic dysfunction in naming and labeling.

NOTES TO CHAPTER 10

1. It seems reasonable to suppose that even the poor reader would, in some measure, draw upon the redundant nature of English orthography as an aid to visual discrimination, although not as efficiently as normal readers. In fact there is at least suggestive evidence (Vellutino, Smith, Steger, and Kaman 1975) that poor readers acquire an implicit knowledge of high-frequency letter clusters long before they have learned their sound counterparts. I suspect, however, that such knowledge is acquired more slowly in poor readers, because it does not have the functional value that it has for normal readers.

2. A striking illustration of this likelihood is provided in the response of a 7-year-old I observed. When asked to identify the single printed word *but*, the child exclaimed, "Now I know that word goes in between other words a lot, and I know what it means, but I can't remember what you call it." The child obviously had a good deal of information about the word, including some knowledge of its syntax, but did not successfully retrieve its phonologic components.

3. Interestingly enough, Forster (1976) has articulated a model of lexical access, certain important dimensions of which are compatible with our own initial speculations as to the nature of the word identification process. Briefly, Forster adopts a search rather than a direct access or associative model of word recognition that likens the process to the workings of a reference library. The "books" in the library are analogous to the entries in the lexicon or "master file"; the catalogues are analogous to one of three major "access files," which contain the words included in the lexicon indexed by their *orthographic, phonologic,* and *semantic-syntactic* features; and the reference numbers are analogous to "pointers" in the access files, which provide information as to where to find specific entries in the lexicon or master file. As in locating a book in the library, a lexical entry can be accessed by reference to

one or another category of featural information stored in the respective access files, that is either through print, sound, or meaning. Entries in each of these files can be found in "bins" containing items of a similar description, listed in accord with their frequency of occurrence. When a word stimulus is presented, initial perceptual operations convert it into a format compatible with the access codes and a bin "number" (salient letter clusters, syllables, meanings) is computed. The appropriate bin is then searched for a stimulus match. When the match is found, a "pointer" indicates its location in the "master file," or lexicon, and the recognition process is complete. Because the lexicon contains all the information available about a word, its featural characteristics can be "cross-referenced" for purposes of discrimination and recall. It should be apparent to the reader that Forster's description of the word recognition process is similar to our own; his model serves as a good example of the type we have in mind.

4. It would seem that a whole-word approach to decoding more directly involves the development of relations among orthographic, semantic, and syntactic word features, whereas phonetic analysis more directly relates the orthographic and phonologic components of printed words. Baron (1979) suggests that these disparities in decoding strategy are manifested in two respective tendencies: to make errors that preserve the meanings of given words (responding /kitty/ for *cat*) or to make errors that adhere to spelling–sound correspondence rules. However, both strategies are imperfect in that each fails to incorporate featural information that maximizes the probability of discrimination and identification. Thus the failure to distinguish between *was* and *saw* represents not so much a visual discrimination error as it does the inability or disinclination to cross-reference the visual, semantic, syntactic and phonologic features of those words.

5. In addition to the logical and theoretical contraindications to this conceptualization (see section 10.4) the results from which it was derived can be questioned on methodological grounds. For one thing, the study included both brain-damaged and "developmental" dyslexics, the largest proportion comprising the brain-damaged subjects (53/82). This fact alone casts doubt on the conclusions drawn, since many of the subjects may have been multiply handicapped rather than specifically disabled in reading. In fact, it is possible that most children in the sample were multiply handicapped in that all were clinic cases referred for learning and behavior disorders.

Another difficulty with this study is that the intellectual criterion used for sample selection may have been too liberal, given that subjects had to have an IQ of only 80 or better. And several of the criterion measures were questionable, particularly the use of figure-drawing tests and the Raven Progressive Matrices (Raven 1962) for the measurement of visual perception. Figure-drawing tests confound motor and discrimination abilities; the Raven test confounds perceptual and conceptual ability.

But perhaps most indicting is the fact that the constitution of subgroups is dubious in that there were few significant differences on critical variables between the small number of "developmental dyslexics" (N = 29) and adequate readers, who, incidentally, were also judged to be "brain-damaged." Interestingly enough, the only differences found between these groups were on measures of naming, sentence repetition, and sound blending, all of which are linguistic functions. On the other hand, there were a larger number of differences between the brain-damaged dyslexics and the (brain-damaged) adequate readers, but these differences presented no consistent pattern. There were also no disparities observed between these groups on the measures of "visual perception." Thus, it appears that the subgroups that Mattis et al. (1975) claimed to have isolated were based upon post hoc and informal analysis of individual profiles, rather than on stable group trends. Considering, in addition, the fact that the developmental dyslexic group (which might be the only specifically disabled subjects in the study) included only twenty-nine subjects, one can reasonably question the reliability and statistical validity of the findings and thereby the investigators' claim that they isolated distinct subgroups of dyslexics, manifesting clearly defined neuropsychological syndromes.

6. A study conducted by Doehring and Hoshko (1977) represents the most recent attempt to provide documentation of the existence of subgroups of dyslexics. Employing a factor analytic technique that clusters children in accord with similarity of individual profiles, these authors claimed to have isolated four types of poor readers, characterized by difficulties in (1) oral reading, (2) auditory-visual letter association, (3) auditory-visual association of words and syllables, and (4) visual matching. However, the results of this study cannot possibly provide support for a multifactor approach to the understanding of dyslexia, because they were derived from various measures of rapid reading skill employing letter and word stimuli. As pointed out by Applebee (1971, 99), it is tautological and thus invalid to employ reading measures to define qualitatively different types of disabled readers. Thus Doehring and Hoshko's (1977) definition of subgroups of dyslexics is highly questionable.

7. At the risk of going beyond available research evidence and basing speculations largely upon clinical observations, I would estimate that the largest proportion of disabled readers are characterized by significant impairment in mapping alphabetic symbols to sound, perhaps because of basic difficulty in phonetic encoding, as suggested by Liberman and Perfetti, among others. Such children do appear to be deficient with respect to phonemic awareness, as manifested in pronounced difficulty in analyzing the internal structure of spoken and printed words. Children with phonetic encoding problems may initially acquire a modest number of words they are able to recognize on sight, but they soon encounter difficulty and may ultimately become severely impaired. This is because of an implicit tendency to rely too much upon word meanings as the vehicle for word decoding and the consequent failure to make effective use of graphophonic redundancies to aid this function and to facilitate economy and efficiency in visual processing. Spoken language in such children is not ostensibly impaired and may even be relatively normal, at least with respect to verbal concept formation and grammatical competence.

Nevertheless, subtle deficiencies in verbal memory would be expected in this group because of phonetic encoding problems.

A smaller proportion of poor readers seems to encounter reading difficulties because of the tendency to be overanalytic in their approach to word decoding. Children in this group are not, by and large, as seriously impaired as those who have more basic coding problems, but without a reorientation of their approach to the decoding process, in time they suffer more severe deficiencies. These youngsters typically do not have an age-and-grade appropriate repertoire of whole words that they can rapidly recognize on sight. General language ability in such children is usually intact.

A very small number of children appear, in my experience, to be hampered by pronounced word retrieval problems. These youngsters are apparently more severely impaired than children in the other groups mentioned and can be observed to have name finding difficulties in spoken as well as written language, along with fluency problems and verbal memory deficits in general. They also appear to have as much difficulty learning the sounds associated with word parts as they do in remembering whole-word labels, since the basic deficiency seems to be in relating the phonologic components of words to objects or representations of any kind. Linguistic functioning in such children is characterized by an aphasoid quality (using this term somewhat loosely) reminiscent of the word finding difficulties characteristic of some adult aphasic patients. Interestingly enough, spoken language in youngsters of this description may, on the surface, appear to be quite normal, because of basic grammatical competence and a reasonably good knowledge of words. It is in the more demanding linguistic functions such as reading and writing that their language difficulties become apparent.

Even smaller proportions of specifically disabled readers would appear to encounter word decoding problems because of a limited knowledge of words or deficiencies in grammatical competence, although the incidence of such difficulties would obviously be inflated in children from language deprived environments. These youngsters, and those with varying admixtures of the other types of defects, may be hampered by specific causes of reading difficulty that are qualitatively different than the problem areas outlined. Additional research is obviously needed to distinguish among these hypothesized categories of reading disability and to more definitively catalog their major characteristics.

Certain of the categorizations described here roughly approximate those suggested by Boder (1970, 1971) and others (Myklebust and Johnson, 1962), for example, children with phonetic coding problems versus those who are inclined to be overanalytic. However, I attribute both disorders to malfunction in verbal processing and do not believe that difficulties in whole-word learning are a manifestation of visual processing disorder. Nor do I believe that either of these problems is necessarily attributable to underlying neurological impairment, although this possibility is not ruled out in some circumstances.

8. Carol Chomsky makes the same point and I acknowledge her influence on my thinking. A quote from her excellent paper on the topic is instructive:

A serious possibility, following from these hypotheses, is that one of the important ways to improve reading might be to enrich the child's vocabulary so as to enable him to construct for himself the underlying representations of sound that correspond so closely to the written form. As far-fetched as this possibility may seem at first, it ought to be given serious consideration in light of the close tie that exists between English phonology and English orthography. The orthography assumes a fairly sophisticated degree of internal organization of the sound system of the language. Extending the child's vocabulary to include Latinate forms and polysyllabic derived forms is one of the best ways to provide him with the means of constructing the phonological system of his language more fully as he matures. He ought to become familiar with word groups such as *industry-industrial, major-majority, history-historical-historian, wide-width, sign-signature,* etc., and have their relationships made explicit to him. In general, connections should be brought out among words that he already knows but may not yet have classified together, and new words should be introduced for the purpose of establishing new connections. His awareness of these relationships and the variant phonetic forms that words assume in different contexts will facilitate and accelerate his internalization of the phonology of his language. (1970, 302)

REFERENCES

Aderman, D., and Smith, E. E. (1971) Expectancy as a determinant of functional units in perceptual recognition. *Cognitive Psychology* 2, 117-129.

Allington, R. L., Gormley, K., and Truex, S. (1976) Poor and normal readers achievement on visual tasks involving high frequency, low discriminability words. *Journal of Learning Disabilities*, 9, 292-296.

Almy, M. C. (1966) *Young children's thinking—Studies of some aspects of Piaget's theory.* New York: Teachers College Press, Columbia University.

Almy, M. C. (1974) Your children's thinking and the teaching of reading. In R. B. Ruddell, E. J. Ahern, E. M. Hartson, and J. Taylor, eds., *Resources in reading—language instruction.* Englewood Cliffs, N.J.: Prentice Hall.

Alwitt, L. F. (1963) Decay of immediate memory for visually presented digits among nonreaders and readers. *Journal of Educational Psychology* 54, 3, 144-148.

Anapolle, L. (1967) Visual training and reading performance. *Journal of Reading* 10, 372-382.

Angoff, W. (1971) Scales, norms, and equivalent scores. In R. L. Thorndike, ed., *Educational measurement*, 2nd ed. Washington, D.C.: American Council on Education.

Applebee, A. N. (1971) Research in reading retardation: Two critical problems. *Journal of Child Psychology and Psychiatry* 12, 2, 91-113.

Arnett, J. L. (1977) Early visual information processing as a function of age and of reading ability. Doctoral dissertation, University of Manitoba.

Arnheim, R. (1972) *Visual thinking.* Berkeley: University of California Press.

Atkinson, R. C., and Shiffrin, R. M. (1968) Human memory: A proposed system and its control processes. In K. W. Spence and J. T. Spence, eds., *The psychology of learning, and motivation, Vol. 11.* New York: Academic Press.

Averback, E., and Coriell, A. S. (1961) Short-term memory in vision. *Bell Systems Technical Journal* 40, 309-328.

Baddeley, A. D. (1966) Short-term memory for word sequences as a function of acoustic, semantic, and formal similarity. *Quarterly Journal of Experimental Psychology* 18, 362–365.

Bakker, D. J. (1967) Temporal order, meaningfulness, and reading ability. *Perceptual and Motor Skills* 24, 1027–1030.

Bakker, D. J. (1970) Temporal order perception and reading retardation. In D. J. Bakker and P. Satz, eds., *Specific reading disability: Advances in theory and method*. Rotterdam: Rotterdam University Press.

Bakker, D. J. (1972) *Temporal order in disturbed reading-developmental and neuropsychological aspects in normal and reading-retarded children*. Rotterdam: Rotterdam University Press.

Bannatyne, A. (1971) *Language, reading and learning disabilities*. Springfield, Ill.: Charles C. Thomas.

Baron. J. (1979) Orthographic and word specific mechanisms in children's reading of words. *Child Development* 50, 60–72.

Barrett, T. C. (1965) The relationship between measures of prereading visual discrimination and first-grade reading achievement: A review of the literature. *Reading Research Quarterly* 1, 51–78.

Barsch, R. H. (1965) *A movigenic curriculum*. Madison: Wisconsin State Department of Instruction, Publication No. 25.

Bee, H. L., and Walker, R. S. (1968) Experimental modification of the lag between perceiving and performing. *Psychonomic Science* 11, 127–128.

Beeley, A. L. (1918) *An experimental study of left-handedness*. Chicago: University of Chicago Press.

Beery, J. (1967) Matching of auditory and visual stimuli by average and retarded readers. *Child Development* 38, 827–833.

Beggs, D. L., and Hieronymus, A. N. (1968) Uniformity of growth in the basic skills throughout the school year and during the summer. *Journal of Educational Measurement* 5, 91–97.

Belmont, L., and Birch, H. G. (1965) Lateral dominance, lateral awareness, and reading disability. *Child Development* 36, 1, 57–71.

Belmont, L., and Birch, H. G. (1966) The intellectual profile of retarded readers. *Perceptual and Motor Skills* 22, 787–816.

Bender, L. A. (1938) *Visual Motor Gestalt Test and its clinical use*, Research Monograph No. 3. New York: American Orthopsychiatric Association.

Bender, L. A. (1956) *Psychopathology of children with organic brain disorders*. Springfield, Ill.: Charles C. Thomas.

Bender, L. A. (1957) Specific reading disability as a maturational lag. *Bulletin of the Orton Society* 7, 9–18.

Bender, L. A. (1975) A fifty-year review of experiences with dyslexia. *Bulletin of the Orton Society* 25, 5–23.

Benton, A. L. (1962) Dyslexia in relation to form perception and directional sense. In J. Money, ed., *Reading disability: Progress and research needs in dyslexia.* Baltimore: Johns Hopkins Press.

Benton, A. L. (1975) Developmental dyslexia: Neurological aspects. In W. J. Friedlander, ed., *Advances in neurology, Vol. 7.* New York: Raven Press.

Benton, A. L., and Kemble, J. D. (1960) Right-left orientation and reading disability. *Psychiatry and Neurology* 139, 49–60.

Bereiter, C., and Engleman, S. (1966) *Teaching disadvantaged children in the preschool.* Englewood Cliffs, N.J.: Prentice-Hall.

Berger, N. S. (1975) An investigation of literal comprehension and organizational processes in good and poor readers. Doctoral dissertation, University of Pittsburgh.

Berko, J. (1958) The child's learning of English morphology. *Word* 14, 150–177.

Biemiller, A. (1970) The development of the use of graphic and contextual information as children learn to read. *Reading Research Quarterly* 6, 75–96.

Binet, A., and Simon, T. (1950) The development of intelligence in children. *L'Annee Psychologique* 11, 163–244.

Birch, H. (1962) Dyslexia and maturation of visual function. In J. Money, ed., *Reading disability: Progress and research needs in dyslexia.* Baltimore: Johns Hopkins Press.

Birch, H., and Belmont, L. (1964) Auditory-visual integration in normal and retarded readers. *American Journal of Orthopsychiatry* 34, 852–861.

Birch, H., and Belmont, L. (1965) Auditory-visual integration, intelligence and reading ability in school children. *Perceptual and Motor Skills* 20, 295–305.

Birch, H., and Gussow, J. D. (1970) *Disadvantaged children—health, nutrition, and school failure.* New York: Grune and Stratton.

Birch, H., and Lefford, A. (1963) Intersensory development in children. *Monographs of the Society for Research in Child Development* 28, 5 (Whole No. 89).

Bjork, E. L., and Healy, A. F. (1974) Short-term order and item retention. *Journal of Verbal Learning and Verbal Behavior* 13, 80–97.

Blank, M. (1968) Cognitive processes in auditory discrimination in normal and retarded readers. *Child Development* 39, 1091–1101.

Blank, M., Berenzweig, S., and Bridger, W. (1975) The effects of stimulus complexity and sensory modality on reaction times in normal and retarded readers. *Child Development* 46, 133–140.

Blank, M., and Bridger, W. H. (1964) Cross-modal transfer in nursery school children. *Journal of Comparative and Physiological Psychology* 58, 277-282.

Blank, M., and Bridger, W. H. (1966) Deficiencies in verbal labeling in retarded readers. *American Journal of Orthopsychiatry* 36, 840-847.

Blank, M., Higgins, T. J., and Bridger, W. H. (1971) Stimulus complexity and intramodal reaction time in retarded readers. *Journal of Educational Psychology* 62, 117-122.

Blank, M., Weider, S., and Bridger, W. (1968) Verbal deficiencies in abstract thinking in early reading retardation. *American Journal of Orthopsychiatry* 38, 823-834.

Bloom, B., Davis, A., and Hess, R. (1965) *Compensatory education for cultural deprivation*. New York: Holt, Rinehart & Winston.

Boder, E. (1970) Developmental dyslexia: A new diagnostic approach based on the identification of three subtypes. *Journal of School Health* 40, 289-290.

Boder, E. (1971) Developmental dyslexia: A diagnostic screening procedure based on three characteristic patterns of reading and spelling. In B. Bateman, ed., *Learning disorders*. Seattle: Special Child Publications.

Bransford, J. D., and Franks, J. J. (1971) The abstraction of linguistic ideas. *Cognitive Psychology* 2, 331-350.

Brewer, W. F. (1967) Paired-associates learning of dyslexic children. Doctoral dissertation, University of Iowa.

Brewer, W. F. (1972) Is reading a letter-by-letter process? In J. F. Kavanagh and I. G. Mattingly, eds., *Language by ear and by eye*. Cambridge, Mass.: The MIT Press.

Briggs, C., and Elkind, D. (1973) Cognitive development in early readers. *Developmental Psychology* 9, 279-280.

Brittain, M. M. (1970) Inflectional performance and early reading achievement. *Reading Research Quarterly* 6, 1, 34-48.

Broadbent, D. E. (1958) *Perception and communication*. New York: Pergamon Press.

Broadbent, D. E., and Ladefoged, P. (1959) Auditory perception of temporal order. *Journal of Acoustical Society of America* 31, 1539.

Brock, F. (1966) Chronicle on orthoptic history covering 25 years of practice. *Optometric Weekly* 10, 17.

Bronner, A. F. (1917) *The psychology of special abilities and disabilities*. Boston: Little, Brown.

Brown, J. (1958) Some tests of the decay theory of immediate memory. *Quarterly Journal of Experimental Psychology* 10, 12-21.

Bryan, T., and Bryan, J. (1975) *Understanding learning disability*. Port Washington: Alfred Publishing Company.

Bryant, N. D. (1965) Characteristics of dyslexia and their remedial implication. *Exceptional Children* 31, 195-199.

Bryant, P. E. (1968) Comments on the design of developmental studies of cross-modal matching and cross-modal transfer. *Cortex* 4, 127-128.

Bryant, P. E. (1974) *Perception and understanding in young children.* New York: Basic Books.

Bryden, M. P. (1972) Auditory-visual and sequential-spatial matching in relation to reading ability. *Child Development* 43, 824-832.

Buschke, H. (1975) Short-term retention, learning, and retrieval from long-term memory. In D. Deutsch and J. Deutsch, eds., *Short-term memory.* New York: Academic Press.

Caldwell, E. C., and Hall, V. C. (1969) The influence of concept training on letter discrimination. *Child Development* 40, 63-71.

Calfee, R. C. (1977) Assessment of independent reading skills: Basic research and practical applications. In A. S. Reber and D. L. Scarborough, eds., *Towards a psychology of reading.* Hillside, N.J.: Erlbaum Associates.

Calfee, R. C., Chapman, R., and Venesky, R. L. (1972) How a child needs to think to learn to read. In L. W. Gregg, ed., *Cognition and learning in memory.* New York: John Wiley and Sons.

Calfee, R. C., Cullenbine, R. S., dePorcel, A., and Royston, A. (1971) Further exploration of tests of basic prereading skills. Paper presented at American Psychological Association Convention, Washington, D.C.

Carter, D. B. (1970) Vision and learning disorders. In Carter, D. B., ed., *Interdisciplinary approaches to learning disorders.* New York: Chilton Book Company.

Cattell, J. McK. (1885) Ueber die Zeit der Erkennung und Benennung von Schriftzeichen Bildern und Farben. *Philosophische Studien* 2, 635-650.

Cattell, J. McK. (1900) Time and space in vision. *Psychological Review* 7, 325-343.

Chall, J. (1967) *Learning to read—The great debate.* New York: McGraw-Hill.

Chase, W. G., and Calfee, R. D. (1969) Modality and similarity effects in short term recognition memory. *Journal of Experimental Psychology* 81, 510-514.

Childs, B., Finucci, J. M., and Preston, M. S. (1978) A medical genetics approach to the study of reading disability. In A. Benton and D. Pearl, eds., *Dyslexia: An appraisal of current knowledge.* New York: Oxford University Press.

Chomsky, C. (1969) *The acquisition of syntax in children from 5 to 10.* Cambridge, Mass.: The MIT Press.

Chomsky, C. (1970) Reading, writing, and phonology. *Harvard Educational Review* 40, 287-309.

Chomsky, C. (1972) Stages in language development and reading exposure. *Harvard Educational Review* 42, 1–33.

Chomsky, N. (1957) *Syntactic structures.* The Hague: Mouton and Company.

Chomsky, N. (1965) *Aspects of the theory of syntax.* Cambridge, Mass.: The MIT Press.

Claiborne, J. H. (1906) Types of congenital amblyopia. *Journal of the American Medical Association* 47, 1813–1816.

Clark, E. V. (1973) What's in a word? On the child's acquisition of semantics in his first language. In T. E. Moore, ed., *Cognitive development and the acquisition of language.* New York: Academic Press.

Clark, H. H. (1973) Space, time, semantics, and the child. In T. E. Moore, ed., *Cognitive development and the acquisition of language.* New York: Academic Press.

Clark, M. M. (1976) *Young fluent readers.* London: Heinemann Educational Books.

Clarke, B. R., and Leslie, P. T. (1971) Visual-motor skills and reading ability of deaf children. *Perceptual and Motor Skills* 33, 263–268.

Clay, M. (1968) A syntactic analysis of reading errors. *Journal of Verbal Learning and Verbal Behavior* 7, 434–438.

Clay, M., and Imlach, R. H. (1971) Juncture, pitch and stress as reading behavior variables. *Journal of Verbal Learning and Verbal Behavior* 10, 133–139.

Coleman, J. S. (1966) *Equality of educational opportunity.* Washington, D.C.: U.S. Department of Health, Education and Welfare.

Conners, C. K. (1970) Cortical visual evoked response in children with learning disorders. *Psychophysiology* 7, 418–428.

Connolly, K., and Jones, B. (1970) A developmental study of afferent-reafferent integration. *British Journal of Psychology* 61, 2, 259–266.

Conrad, R. (1964) Acoustic confusions in immediate memory. *British Journal of Psychology* 55, 75–84.

Conrad, R. (1965) Order error in immediate recall of sequences. *Journal of Verbal Learning and Verbal Behavior* 4, 161–169.

Corkin, S. (1974) Serial-ordering deficits in inferior readers. *Neuropsychologia* 12, 347–354.

Cox, M. B. (1976) The effect of conservation ability on reading competency. *The Reading Teacher* 30, 3, 251–258.

Craik, F., and Lockhart, P. (1972) Levels of processing: A framework for memory research. *Journal of Verbal Learning and Verbal Behavior* 11, 671–684.

Critchley, M. (1964) *Developmental dyslexia.* London: Heinemann.

Critchley, M. (1928) *Mirror-writing.* London: Kegan Paul.

Critchley, M. (1970) *The dyslexic child.* Springfield, Ill.: Charles C. Thomas.

Cromer, W. (1970) The difference model: A new explanation for some reading difficulties. *Journal of Educational Psychology* 61, 6, 471–483.

Cromer, W., and Wiener, M. (1966) Idiosyncratic response patterns among good and poor readers. *Journal of Consulting Psychology* 30, 1, 1–10.

Crossman, E. R. F. W. (1960) Information and serial order in human immediate memory. In C. Cherry, ed., *Information theory: Fourth London symposium.* London: Butterworth.

Crowder, R. G. (1972) Visual and auditory memory. In J. F. Kavanagh and I. G. Mattingly, eds., *Language by ear and by eye.* Cambridge, Mass.: The MIT Press.

Cruickshank, W. M. (1968) The problems of delayed recognition and its correction. In A. H. Keeney and V. T. Keeney, eds., *Dyslexia: Diagnosis and treatment of reading disorders.* St. Louis: C. V. Mosby.

Cruickshank, W. M. (1972) Some issues facing the field of learning disability. *Journal of Learning Disabilities* 5, 380–383.

Cummings, E. M. and Faw, T. T. (1976) Short term memory and equivalence judgments in normal and retarded readers. *Child Development* 47, 286–289.

Curry, L., Ross, R., and Calfee, R. C. (1973) Components of visual matching skills in prereaders. Paper presented to American Psychological Association.

Davidson, H. P. (1935) A study of the confusing letters B, D, P, and Q. *Journal of Genetic Psychology* 47, 458–468.

Davis, S. M., and Bray, N. W. (1975) Bisensory memory in normal and reading disability children. *Bulletin of the Psychonomic Society* 6, 572–574.

Dearborn, W. F. (1931) Ocular and manual dominance in dyslexia. *Psychological Bulletin* 28, 704–715.

de Hirsch, K., Jansky, J., and Langford, W. (1966) *Predicting reading failure.* New York: Harper & Row.

Denckla, M. B. (1972) Color-naming defects in dyslexic boys. *Cortex* 8, 164–176.

Denckla, M. B. (1978) Minimal brain dysfunction. In J. S. Chall and A. F. Mirsky, eds., *Education and the brain.* Chicago: University of Chicago Press.

Denckla, M. B., and Bowen, F. P. (1973) Dyslexia after left occipito-temporal lobectomy: A case report. *Cortex* 9, 321–328.

Denckla, M. B., and Rudel, R. (1976a) Naming of pictured objects by dyslexic and other learning disabled children. *Brain and Language* 3, 1–15.

Denckla, M. B., and Rudel, R. (1976b) Rapid 'automatized' naming (R.A.N.): Dyslexia differentiated from other learning disabilities. *Neuropsychologia* 14, 471–479.

Denner, B. (1970) Representational and syntactic competence of problem readers. *Child Development* 41, 881–887.

Deutsch, C. P. (1964) Auditory discrimination and learning: Social factors. *Merril-Palmer Quarterly* 10, 277-296.

Deutsch, C. P. (1967) Learning in the disadvantaged. In W. Harris, ed., *Analyses of concept learning.* New York: Academic Press.

Deutsch, D., and Deutsch, J., eds (1975) *Short-term memory.* New York: Academic Press.

Deutsch, M. (1963) The disadvantaged child and the learning process. In A. H. Passow, ed., *Education in depressed areas.* New York: Teachers College, Columbia University.

Deutsch, M. (1965) The role of social class in language development and cognition. *American Journal of Orthopsychiatry* 35, 78-88.

Di Lollo, V. (1977) On the spatio-temporal interactions of brief visual displays. In R. H. Day and G. V. Stanley, eds., *Studies in perception.* Perth: University of Western Australia Press.

Dodge, R. (1905) The illusion of clear vision during eye movement. *Psychological Bulletin* 2, 193-199.

Doehring, D. G. (1968) *Patterns of impairment in specific reading disability.* Bloomington: Indiana University Press.

Doehring, D. G. (1976) Acquisition of rapid reading responses. *Monographs of The Society for Research in Child Development* 41, 2, 1-54.

Doehring, D. G., and Hoshko, I. M. (1977) Classification of reading problems by the Q-technique of factor analysis. *Cortex* 13, 281-294.

Downing, J. (1973) *Comparative reading: Cross national studies of behavior and processes in reading and writing.* New York: Macmillan.

Drew, A. L. (1956) A neurological appraisal of familial congenital word-blindness. *Brain* 79, 440-460.

Dubois, T. E., and Cohen, W. (1970) Relationship between measures of psychological differentiation and intellectual ability. *Perceptual and Motor Skills* 31, 411-416.

Dykman, R. A., Walls, R. C., Suzuki, T., Ackerman, P. T., and Peters, J. E. (1970) Children with learning disabilites: Conditioning, differentiation, and the effect of distraction. *American Journal of Orthopsychiatry* 40, 766-782.

Dykstra, R. (1966) Auditory discrimination abilities and beginning reading achievement. *Reading Research Quarterly* 1, 3, 5-34.

Dykstra, R. (1967) The use of reading readiness tests for prediction and diagnosis. In T. C. Barrett, ed., *The evaluation of children's reading achievement.* Newark, Del.: International Reading Association Publications.

Eakin, S., and Douglas, V. I. (1971) "Automatization" and oral reading problems in children. *Journal of Learning Disabilities* 4, 31-38.

Efron, R. (1963) Temporal perception, aphasia, and déjà vu. *Brain* 86, 403-424.

Eisenberg, L. (1966) The epidemiology of reading reatardation and a program for preventive intervention. In J. Money, ed., *The disabled reader.* Baltimore: Johns Hopkins Press.

Elkind, D. (1964) Ambiguous pictures for the study of perceptual development and learning. *Child Development* 35, 1391-1396.

Elkind, D. (1976) Cognitive development and reading. In H. Singer and R. B. Ruddell, eds., *Theoretical models and processes of reading.* Newark, Del.: International Reading Association.

Elkind, D. A., Horn, J., and Schneider, G. (1965) Modified word recognition reading achievement and perceptual de-centration. *Journal of Genetic Psychology* 107, 235-251.

Elkind, D., Koegler, R., and Go, E. (1962) Effects of perceptual training at three age levels. *Science* 137, 755-756.

Elkind, D., Koegler, R., and Go, E. (1964) Studies in perceptual development. II: Part-whole perception. *Child Development* 35, 81-90.

Elkind, D., and Scott, L. (1962) Studies in perceptual development. I: The de-centration of perception. *Child Development* 33, 619-630.

Elkind, D., and Weiss, J. (1967) Studies in perceptual development, III. Perceptual exploration. *Child Development* 38, 553-561.

Elkonin, D. B. (1973) "U.S.S.R." In J. Downing, ed., *Comparitive reading: Cross national studies of behavior and processes in reading and writing.* New York: Macmillan.

Entwisle, D. R. (1966) *The word associations of young children.* Baltimore: Johns Hopkins Press.

Erdmann, B., and Dodge, R. (1898) *Psychologische Untersuchungen über das Lesen.* Halle: M. Neimeyer.

Erikson, C. W., and Collins, J. F. (1968) Sensory traces versus the psychological moment in the temporal organization of form. *Journal of Experimental Psychology* 77, 376-382.

Erlenmeyer. (1879) Die schrift, grundzuge ihrer physiologie und ihrer pathologie, Stuttgart, 1879. In M. Critchley, ed., *Mirror-writing.* London: Kegan Paul, 1928.

Ervin, S. M. (1961) Changes with age in the verbal determinants of word association. *American Journal of Psychology* 74, 361-372.

Estes, W. K. (1972) An associative basis for coding and organization in memory. In A. W. Melton and E. Martin, eds., *Coding processes in human memory.* Washington, D.C.: Wintons.

Estes, W. K. (1975) The locus of inferential and perceptual processes in letter identification. *Journal of Experimental Psychology: General* 104, 2, 122-145.

Ettlinger, G. (1967) Analysis of cross modal effects and their relationship to language. In C. H. Millikan and F. L. Darley, eds., *Brain mechanisms underlying speech and language.* New York: Grune and Stratton.

Eustis, R. S. (1947) Specific reading disability. *New England Journal of Medicine* 237, 243-349.

Farnham-Diggory, S. (1967) Symbol and synthesis in experimental reading. *Child Development* 38, 223-231.

Farnham-Diggory, S. (1972) The development of equivalence system. In S. Farnham-Diggory, ed., *Information processing in children.* New York: Academic Press.

Farnham-Diggory, S., and Gregg, L. W. (1975) Short term memory function in young readers. *Journal of Experimental Child Psychology* 19, 2, 279-298.

Fay, W. H. (1966) *Temporal sequence in the perception of speech.* The Hague: Mouton and Company.

Ferinden, W. E., and Jacobson, S. (1970) Early identification of learning disabilities. *Journal of Learning Disabilities* 3, 589-593.

Fildes, L. G. (1921) A psychological inquiry into the nature of the condition known as congenital word-blindness. *Brain* 44, 286-307.

Fildes, L. G. (1923) Some memory experiments with high-grade defectives. *The British Journal of Psychology* 14, Part 1, 39-56.

Finucci, J. M., Guthrie, J. T., Childs, A. L., Abbey, H., and Childs, B. (1976) The genetics of specific reading disability. *Annals of Human Genetics* 40, 1-23.

Fisher, D. F., and Frankfurter, A. (1977) Normal and disabled readers can locate and identify letters: Where's the perceptual deficit? *Journal of Reading Behavior* 9, 1, 31-43.

Flavell, J., Beach, D., and Chinsky, J. (1966) Spontaneous verbal rehearsal in a memory task as a function of age. *Child Development* 37, 283-299.

Flavell, J., and Wohlwill, J. F. (1969) *Formal and functional aspects of cognitive development.* In D. Elkind and J. M. Flavell, eds., *Studies in cognitive development.* New York: Oxford University Press.

Flax, N. (1970) The contribution of visual problems to learning disability. *Journal of the American Optometric Association* 41, 841-845.

Flom, B. (1963) The optometrist's role in the reading field. In M. Hirsch and R. Wick, eds., *Vision of children.* New York: Chilton Books.

Flom, M. (1970) Statistical considerations. In D. B. Carter, ed., *Interdisciplinary approaches to learning disorders.* New York: Chilton Books.

Forster, K. I. (1976) Accessing the mental lexicon. In R. J. Wales and E. Walker, eds., *New approaches to language mechanisms.* Amsterdam: North-Holland.

Fox, F. J., Orr, R. R., and Rourke, B. P. (1975) Short-comings of the standard optometric visual analysis for the diagnosis of reading problems. *Canadian Journal of Optometry* 37, 57-61.

Friedes, D. (1974) Human information processing and sensory modality: Cross-modal functions, information complexity, memory, and deficit. *Psychological Bulletin* 81, 284-310.

Frith, I. (1972) Components of reading disability. Doctoral dissertation, University of New South Wales.

Frostig, M. (1961) *The Marianne Frostig Development Test of Visual Perception*. Palo Alto: Consulting Psychologists Press.

Frostig, M., and Maslow, P. (1973) *Learning problems in the classroom: Prevention and remediation*. New York: Grune and Stratton.

Fry, M. A. (1967) A transformational analysis of the oral language structure used by two reading groups at the second grade level. Doctoral dissertation, University of Iowa.

Fry, M. A., Johnson, C. S. and Muehl, S. (1970) Oral language production in relation to reading achievement among select second graders. In D. J. Bakker and P. Satz, eds., *Specific reading disability: Advances in theory and method*. Rotterdam: Rotterdam University Press.

Furness, E. L. (1956) Perspectives on reversal tendencies. *Elementary English* 33, 38–41.

Galifret-Granjon, N. (1952) Le Problème de l'organisation spatiale dans les dyslexies d'évolution. In N. Nanent, ed., L'Apprentissage de la lecture et ses troubles. Paris: Presses Universitaires de France.

Gardner, H. (1975) *The shattered mind*. New York: Alfred A. Knopf.

Gascon, G., and Goodglass, H. (1970) Reading retardation and the information content of stimuli in paired associate learning. *Cortex* 6, 417–429.

Gates, A. I. (1922) The psychology of reading and spelling with special reference to disability. *Teachers College Contributions to Education #129*, New York: Teachers College, Columbia University.

Gates, A. I. (1939) An experimental evaluation of reading readiness tests. *Elementary School Journal* 39, 497–508.

Gates, A. I. (1940) A further evaluation of reading readiness tests. *Elementary School Journal* 40, 577–591.

Gates, A. I., Bond, G. L., and Russell, D. H. (1939) *Methods of determining reading readiness*. New York: Bureau of Publications, Teachers College, Columbia University.

Gazzaniga, M. S. (1970) *The bisected brain*. New York: Appleton.

Gazzaniga, M. S., Bogen, J. E., and Sperry, R. W. (1965) Observations on visual perception after disconnection of the cerebral hemisphere of man. *Brain* 88, 221–236.

Gerstmann, J. (1940) Syndrome of finger agnosia, disorientation for right and left, agraphia and acalculia. *Archives of Neurology and Psychiatry* 44, 398–408.

Geschwind, N. (1962) The anatomy of acquired disorders of reading. In J. Money, ed., *Reading disability: Progress and research needs in dyslexia*, Baltimore: Johns Hopkins Press.

Geschwind, N. (1968) Neurological foundations of language. In H. R. Myklebust, ed., *Progress in learning disabilities.* New York: Grune and Stratton.

Geschwind, N., and Fusillo, M. (1966) Color-naming defects in association with alexia. *AMA Archives of Neurology* 15, 137-146.

Gesell, A. (1924) *The mental growth of the preschool child.* New York: Macmillan.

Gesell, A. (1952) *Infant development.* New York: Harper & Row.

Gesell, A., and Amatruda, C. S. (1947) *Developmental diagnosis,* 2nd ed. New York: Hoeber.

Gesell, A., and Thompson, H. (1934) *Infant behavior: Its genesis and growth.* New York: McGraw-Hill.

Getman, G. N. (1962) *How to develop your child's intelligence.* Luverne, Minn.: Announcer Press.

Ghatala, E. S., and Levin, J. R. (1976) Children's recognition memory processes. In J. R. Levin and V. L. Allen, eds., *Cognitive learning in children: Theories and strategies.* New York: Academic Press.

Ghent, L. (1960) Recognition by children of realistic figures presented in various orientations. *Canadian Journal of Psychology* 14, 4, 249-256.

Ghent, L. (1961) Form and its orientation: A child's-eye view. *American Journal of Psychology* 74, 177-190.

Ghent, L., and Bernstein, L. (1961) Influence of the orientation of geometric forms on their recognition by children. *Perceptual and Motor Skills* 12, 95-101.

Gibson, E. J. (1969) *Principles of perceptual learning and development.* New York: Appleton.

Gibson, E. J. (1971) Perceptual learning and the theory of word perception. *Cognitive Psychology* 2, 351-368.

Gibson, E. J., Farber, J., and Shepela, S. (1967) Test of a learning set procedure for the abstraction of spelling patterns. *Project Literacy Reports* No. 8, 21-30.

Gibson, E. J., Gibson, J. J., Pick, A. D., and Osser, H. (1962) A developmental study of the discrimination of letter-like forms. *Journal of Comparative and Psysiological Psychology* 55, 897-906.

Gibson, E. J., and Levin, H. (1975) *The psychology of reading.* Cambridge, Mass.: The MIT Press.

Gibson, E. J., Osser, H., and Pick, A. D. (1963) A study of the development of grapheme-phoneme correspondences. *Journal of Verbal Learning and Verbal Behavior* 2, 142-146.

Gilmore, J. V. (1968) *Gilmore Oral Reading Test.* New York: Harcourt Brace Jovanovich.

Glanzer, M., and Cunitz, A. R. (1966) Two storage mechanisms in free recall. *Journal of Verbal Learning and Verbal Behavior* 5, 351-360.

Gleitman, L. R., and Rozin, P. (1977) The structure and acquisition of reading, 1: Relations between orthographies and the structure of language. In A. S. Reber and D. L. Scarborough, eds., *Toward a psychology of reading. The proceedings of the CUNY conferences.* New York: Wiley.

Goetzinger, C. P., Dirks, D. D., and Baer, C. J. (1960) Auditory discrimination and visual perception in good and poor readers. *Annals of Otolaryngology, Rhinology, and Laryngology* 69, 121-136.

Goins, J. T. (1958) Visual perceptual abilities and early reading progress. *Supplementary Educational Monographs* No. 87, University of Chicago.

Goldman, S. R. (1976) Reading skill and the minimum distance principle: A comparison of listening and reading comprehension. *Journal of Experimental Child Psychology* 22, 123-142.

Goldman, S. R., Hogaboam, T. W., Bell, L. C., and Perfetti, C. A. (1977) Short-term discourse memory during reading and listening. Preprint, University of Pittsburgh.

Golinkoff, R. M., and Rosinski, R. R. (1976) Decoding, semantic processing, and reading comprehension skill. *Child Development* 47, 252-258.

Golomb, C. (1973) Children's representation of the human figure: The effects of models, media, and instruction. *Genetic Psychology Monographs*, 87, 197-251.

Goodenough, F. L. (1954) *Measurement of intelligence by drawings.* Chicago: World Book Company.

Goodman, K. S. (1965) Dialect barriers to reading comprehension. *Elementary English* 42, 853-860.

Goodman, K. S. (1969) Analysis of reading miscues: Applied psycholinguistics. *Reading Research Quarterly* 5, 9-30.

Goodnow, J. J. (1971a) Matching auditory and visual series: Modality problem or translation problem? *Child Development* 42, 1187-1201.

Goodnow, J. J. (1971b) The role of modalities in perceptual and cognitive development. In J. P. Hill, ed., *Minnesota Symposium on Child Psychology, V.* Minneapolis: University of Minnesota Press.

Goody, J., and Watt, I. (1963) The consequence of literacy. *Comparative Studies in Society and History* 5, 3, 304-305.

Gordon, H. (1920) Left-handedness and mirror writing, especially among defective children. *Brain* 43, 313-368.

Gottschaldt, K. (1926) *Über den Einfluss der Ehrfahrung auf die Wahrenhmung von Figuren*, Psychologische Forschung 8, 261, 261-317.

Gottschalk, J., Bryden, M. P., and Rabinovitch, M. S. (1964) Spatial organization of children's responses to a pictorial display. *Child Development* 35, 811-815.

Gough, P. B. (1972) One second of reading. In J. F. Kavanagh and I. G. Mattingly, eds., *Language by ear and by eye.* Cambridge, Mass.: The MIT Press.

Goyen, J. D., and Lyle, J. (1971a) Effect of incentives and age on the visual recognition of retarded readers. *Journal of Experimental Child Psychology* 11, 266–273.

Goyen, J. D., and Lyle, J. (1971b) Effect of incentives upon retarded and normal readers on a visual-associate learning task. *Journal of Experimental Child Psychology* 11, 274–280.

Goyen, J. D., and Lyle, J. (1973) Short-term memory and visual discrimination in retarded readers. *Perceptual and Motor Skills* 36, 403–408.

Gray, W. S. (1917) Studies of elementary school reading through standardized tests. *Supplementary Educational Monographs* No. 1, University of Chicago.

Gray, W. S. (1921) Diagnostic and remedial steps in reading. *Journal of Educational Research* 4, 1–15.

Groenendaal, H. A., and Bakker, D. J. (1971) The part played by mediation processes in the retention of temporal sequences by two reading groups. *Human Development* 14, 62–70.

Gulliksen, H. (1950) *Theory of mental tests.* New York: Wiley.

Gummerman, K., and Gray, C. R. (1972) Age, iconic storage, and visual information processing. *Journal of Experimental Child Psychology* 13, 165–170.

Guthrie, J. T. (1973) Reading comprehension and syntactic responses in good and poor readers. *Journal of Educational Psychology 65,* 3, 294–299.

Haber, R. N. (1969) *Information-processing approaches to visual perception.* New York: Holt, Rinehart & Winston.

Haber, R. N., and Standing, L. G. (1969) Direct measures of short-term visual storage. *Quarterly Journal of Experimental Psychology* 21, 43–54.

Hagen, J. W., Jongeward, R. H., and Kail, R. V. (1975) Cognitive perspectives on the development of memory. In H. W. Reese, ed., *Advances in child development and behavior, Vol. 10.* New York: Academic Press.

Hagin, R. (1954) Reading retardation and the language arts. Doctoral dissertation, New York University. Publication 12216, University Microfilms, Ann Arbor, Mich.

Hallgren, B. (1950) Specific dyslexia: A clinical and genetic study. *Acta Psychiatrica et Neurologia* 65, 1, 287.

Hammill, D., Goodman, L., and Wiederholt, J. L. (1974) Visual-motor processes: Can we train them? *The Reading Teacher* 27, 469.

Harris, A. J. (1957) Lateral dominance, directional confusion and reading disability. *The Journal of Psychology* 44, 283–294.

Harris, A. J., and Sipay, E. R. (1975) *How to increase reading ability.* New York: McKay.

Hartman, N. C., and Hartman, R. K. (1973) Perceptual handicap or reading disability? *The Reading Teacher* 26, 684.

Healy, A. F. (1974) Separating item from order information in short-term memory. *Journal of Verbal Learning and Verbal Behavior* 13, 644–655.

Healy, A. F. (1975a) Coding of temporal-spatial patterns in short-term memory. *Journal of Verbal Learning and Verbal Behavior* 14, 481–495.

Healy, A. F. (1975b) Short-term retention of temporal and spatial order. *Bulletin of the Psychonomic Society* 5, 57–58.

Healy, A. F. (1976) Detection errors on the word *the:* Evidence for reading units larger than letters. *Journal of Experimental Psychology: Human Perception and Performance*, 1976, 2, 235–242.

Healy, A. F. (1977) Pattern coding of spatial order information in short-term memory. *Journal of Verbal Learning and Verbal Behavior* 16, 419–437.

Hebb, D. O. (1949) *The organization of behavior*. New York: Wiley.

Hecaen, H. (1962) Clinical symptomatology in right and left hemispheric lesions. In V. B. Mountcastle, ed., *Interhemispheric relations and cerebral dominance*. Baltimore: Johns Hopkins Press.

Hecaen, H., and de Ajuriaguerra, J. (1964) *Left-handedness, manual superiority and cerebral dominance*. Translated by E. Ponder. New York: Grune and Stratton.

Helfgott, J. (1976) Phonemic segmentation and blending skills of kindergarten children: Implications for beginning reading acquisition. *Contemporary Educational Psychology* 1, 2, 157–169.

Hendrickson, L. N., and Muehl, S. (1962) The effect of attention and motor response pretraining on learning to discriminate B and D in kindergarten children. *Journal of Educational Psychology* 53, 5, 236–241.

Hermann, K. (1959) *Reading disability*. Copenhagen: Munksgaard.

Hermann, K., and Norrie, E. (1958) Is congenital word-blindness a hereditary type of Gerstmann's syndrome? *Psychiatria et Neurologia* 136, 59–73.

Hinshelwood, J. (1900) Congenital word-blindness. *Lancet* 1, 1506–1508.

Hinshelwood, J. (1917) *Congenital word-blindness*. London: H. K. Lewis.

Hirsh, I. J. (1959) Auditory perception of temporal order. *The Journal of the Acoustical Society of America* 31, 759–767.

Hirsh, I. J. (1966) Audition in relation to perception of speech. In E. C. Carterette, ed., *Speech, language and communication*, vol. III, *Brain function*. Berkeley: University of California.

Hirsh, I. J., and Sherrick, C. E. (1961) Perceived order in different sense modalities. *Journal of Experimental Psychology* 64, 1–19.

Hochberg, J. (1970) Components of literacy: Speculations and exploratory research. In H. Levin and J. P. Williams, eds., *Basic studies on reading*. New York: Basic Books.

Hogben, J. H., and Di Lollo, V. (1974) Perceptual integration and perceptual segregation of brief visual stimuli. *Vision Research* 14, 1059-1069.

Hollingshead, A. B., and Redlich, F. (1958) *Social class and mental illness.* New York: Wiley.

Holt, E. B. (1903) Eye movement and central anesthesia. *Psychological Review Monograph Supplements* 4. Vol. 4, January 1903.

Huelsman, C. B., Jr. (1970) The WISC subtest syndrome for disabled readers. *Perceptual and Motor Skills* 30, 535-550.

Huey, E. B. (1908) *The psychology and pedagogy of reading.* Reprint. The MIT Press, Cambridge, Mass., 1968.

Hunt, K. W. (1964) Differences in grammatical structures written at three grade levels, the structures to be analyzed by transformational methods. Report to the U.S. Office of Education, Cooperative Research Project No. 1998, Tallahassee, Florida.

Hunt, K. W. (1965) *Grammatical structures written at three grade levels.* NCTE Research Report No. 3. Champaign, Ill.: National Council of Teachers of English.

Huttenlocher, J. (1967a) Discrimination of figure orientation: Effects of relative position. *Journal of Comparative and Physiological Psychology* 63, 359-361.

Huttenlocher, J. (1967b) Children's ability to order and orient objects. *Child Development* 38, 1169-1176.

Ilg, F. L., and Ames, L. B. (1965) *School readiness: Behavior tests used at the Gesell Institute.* New York: Harper & Row.

Ingram, T. T. S., Mason, A. W., and Blackburn, I. (1970) A retrospective study of 82 children with reading disability. *Developmental Medicine and Child Neurology* 12, 271-281.

Ingram, T. T. S., and Reid, J. F. (1956) Developmental aphasia observed in a department of child psychiatry. *Archives of Disorders of Childhood* 31, 161.

Inhelder, B., and Piaget, J. (1953) *The growth of logical thinking from childhood to adolescence.* New York: Basic Books.

International Reading Association. (1972) Report of Disabled Reader Committee. *The Reading Teacher* 26, 341.

James, C. T., and Smith, D. E. (1970) Sequential dependencies in letter search. *Journal of Experimental Psychology* 85, 56-60.

Jansky, J., and de Hirsch, K. (1972) *Preventing reading failure—Prediction, diagnosis, intervention.* New York: Harper & Row.

Jarvella, R. J. (1971) Syntactic processing of connected speech. *Journal of Verbal Learning and Verbal Behavior* 10, 409-416.

Jastak, J. (1934) Interferences in reading. *Psychological Bulletin* 31, 244-272.

Jastak, J., Bijou, S. W., and Jastak, S. R. (1965) *Wide Range Achievement Test.* Wilmington, Del.: Guidance Associates.

Jeffrey, W. (1958) Variables in early discrimination learning, 1: Motor responses in the training of a left-right discrimination. *Child Development* 29, 269-275.

Jenkins, J. (1974) Remember that old theory of memory? Well, forget it! *American Psychologist* 29, 785-795.

Johnson, D., and Myklebust, H. (1967) *Learning disabilities: Educational principles and practices.* New York: Grune and Stratton.

Johnson, N. F. (1975) On the function of letters in word recognition: Some data and a preliminary model. *Journal of Verbal Learning and Verbal Behavior* 14, 17-29.

Jones, B. (1974) Cross-modal matching by retarded and normal readers. *Bulletin of the Psychonomic Society* 3, 3A, 163-165.

Jones, B., and Connolly, K. (1970) Memory effects in cross-modal matching. *British Journal of Psychology* 61, 267-270.

Kagan, T. (1965) Reflection–impulsivity and reading ability in primary grade children. *Child Development* 36, 609-628.

Kahn, D., and Birch, H. G. (1968) Development of auditory-visual integration and reading achievement. *Perceptual and Motor Skills* 27, 459-468.

Kamil, M. L., and Rudegeair, R. E. (1972) Methodological improvements in the assessment of phonological discrimination in children. *Child Development* 43, 1087-1091.

Kastner, S. B., and Rickards, C. (1974) Mediated memory with novel and familiar stimuli in good and poor readers. *The Journal of Genetic Psychology* 124, 105-113.

Katz, L., and Wicklund, D. (1971) Word scanning rates for good and poor readers. *Journal of Educational Psychology* 62, 138-140.

Katz, L., and Wicklund, D. (1972) Letter scanning rate for good and poor readers in grades two and six. *Journal of Educational Psychology* 63, 363-367.

Katz, P. A., and Deutsch, M. (1963) Relation of auditory-visual shifting to reading achievement. *Perceptual and Motor Skills* 17, 327-332.

Katz, P. A., and Deutsch, M. (1967) The relationship of auditory and visual functioning to reading achievement in disadvantaged children. Paper presented to the Society for Research in Child Development, New York.

Kavanagh, J. F., and Mattingly, I. G. (1972) *Language by ear and by eye.* Cambridge, Mass.: The MIT Press.

Kawi, A. A., and Pasamanick, B. P. (1958) Association of factors of pregnancy with reading disorders in childhood. *Journal of the American Medical Association* 166, 1420-1423.

Kean, J. M. (1965) An exploration of the linguistic structure of second and fifth grade teachers' oral classroom language. Doctoral dissertation, Kent State University.

Kendall, B. S. (1948) A note on the relation of retardation in reading to performance on a memory-for-designs test. *Journal of Educational Psychology* 39, 370-373.

Keogh, B. K. (1965a) Drawing and copying tasks for differential diagnosis of children with atypical development. Paper presented at the Western Psychological Association, Honolulu, Hawaii.

Keogh, B. K. (1965b) The Bender Gestalt as a predictive and diagnostic test of reading performance. *Journal of Consulting Psychology* 29, 83-84.

Keogh, B. K. (1968) The copying ability of young children. *Educational Research* 11, 1, 43-47.

Keogh, B. K. (1970) Early identification of children with potential learning problems. *Journal of Special Education* 4, 3, 307-365.

Keogh, B. K., and Becker, L. D. (1975) The Bender-Gestalt for educational diagnosis. *Academic Therapy* 11, 1, 79-82.

Kephart, N. (1960) *The slow learner in the classroom.* Columbus: Charles E. Merrill.

Kerpelman, L. C., and Pollack, R. H. (1964) Developmental changes in the location of form discrimination cues. *Perceptual and Motor Skills* 19, 375-382.

Kerr, J. (1897) School hygiene in its mental, moral and physical aspects. *Journal of the Royal Statistical Society* 60, 613-680.

Kimura, D. (1963) Speech lateralization in young children as determined by an auditory test. *Journal of Comparative and Physiological Psychology* 56, 899.

Kinsbourne, M. (1970) The analysis of learning deficit with special reference to selective attention. In D. J. Bakker and P. Satz, eds., *Specific reading disability; Advances in theory and method.* Rotterdam: Rotterdam University Press.

Kinsbourne, M., and Warrington, E. K. (1963) The developmental Gerstmann syndrome. *Archives of Neurology* 8, 490-502.

Kintsch, W. (1972) Abstract nouns: Imagery versus lexical complexity. *Journal of Verbal Learning and Verbal Behavior* 11, 59-65.

Kintsch, W. (1974) *The representation of meaning in memory.* New York: Wiley.

Kirk, S. A., and Kirk, W. D. (1971) *Psycholinguistic learning disabilities: Diagnosis and remediation.* Chicago: University of Illinois Press.

Kirk, S. A., and McCarthy, J. J. (1968) *The Illinois Test of Psycholinguistic Abilities.* Urbana: University of Illinois Press.

Kleiman, G. M. (1975) Speech recoding in reading. *Journal of Verbal Learning and Verbal Behavior* 14, 323-339.

Koffka, K. (1935) *Principles of Gestalt psychology.* New York: Harcourt, Brace.

Kofsky, E. (1968) A scalogram study of classificatory development. In I. E. Sigel and F. H. Hooper, eds., *Logical thinking in children.* New York: Holt, Rinehart & Winston.

Kogan, N. (1971) Educational implicatons of cognitive styles. In G. S. Lesser, ed., *Psychology and educational practice.* Glenview, Ill.: Scott, Foresman.

Kogan, N. (1973) Creativity and cognitive style: A life-span perspective. In P. B. Baltes and K. W. Schaie, eds., *Life-span developmental psychology.* New York: Academic Press.

Kohler, W. (1929) *Gestalt psychology.* New York: Liveright.

Kolers, P. A. (1968) The recognition of geometrically transformed text. *Perception and Psychophysics* 3, 57-64.

Kolers, P. A. (1970) Three stages of reading. In H. Levin and J. P. Williams, eds., *Basic studies in reading.* New York: Basic Books.

Kolers, P. A. (1974) Remembering trivia. *Language and Speech* 17, 324-336.

Kolers, P. A. (1975a) Specificity of operations in sentence recognition. *Cognitive Psychology* 7, 289-306.

Kolers, P. A. (1975b) Pattern-analyzing disability in poor readers. *Developmental Psychology* 11, 3, 282-290.

Kolers, P. A. (1976a) Pattern-analyzing memory. *Science* 191, 1280-1281.

Kolers, P. A. (1976b) Reading a year later. *Journal of Experimental Psychology: Human Learning and Memory* 2, 554-565.

Kolers, P. A., and Ostry, D. J. (1974) Time course of loss of information regarding pattern analyzing operations. *Journal of Verbal Learning and Verbal Behavior* 13, 599-612.

Kolers, P. A., and Perkins, D. N. (1969) Orientation of letters and errors in their recognition. *Perception and Psychophysics* 5, 265-269.

Koppitz, E. M. (1964) *The Bender Gestalt Test for Young Children.* New York: Grune and Stratton.

Koppitz, E. M. (1975) Bender gestalt test, visual aural digit span test and reading achievement. *Journal of Learning Disabilities* 8, 3, 154-158.

Koppitz, E. M., Sullivan, J., Blyth, D. D., and Shelton, J. (1959) Prediction of first grade school achievement with the Bender gestalt test and human figure drawings. *Journal of Clinical Psychology* 15, 164-168.

Krise, E. M. (1949) Reversals in reading: A problem in space perception. *Elementary School Journal* 49, 278-284.

Krise, E. M. (1952) An experimental investigation of theories of reversals in reading. *Journal of Educational Psychology* 43, 408-422.

Kroll, N. E. A. (1975) Visual short-term memory. In D. Deutsch and J. A. Deutsch, eds., *Short term memory.* New York: Academic Press.

Krueger, L. E. (1970) Search time in a redundant visual display. *Journal of Experimental Psychology* 83, 391-399.

Kussmaul, A. (1877) Disturbance of speech. In H. vonZiemssen, ed., *Clycopaedia of the practice of medicine*, vol. 14. Translated by J. A. McCreery. New York: William Wood.

LaBerge, D. (1976) Perceptual learning and attention. In W. K. Estes, ed., *Handbook of learning and cognitive processes*, vol. 4. Hillsdale, N.J.: Erlbaum Associates.

LaBerge, D., and Samuels, S. J. (1974) Toward a theory of automatic information processing in reading. *Cognitive Psychology* 6, 293-323.

Labov, W. (1967) Some sources of reading problems for Negro speakers of nonstandard English. In A. Frazier, ed., *New directions in elementary English*. Champaign, Ill.: National Council of Teachers of English.

Lachmann, F. M. (1960) Perceptual-motor development in children retarded in reading ability. *Journal of Consulting Psychology* 24, 427-431.

Lashley, K. S. (1929) *Brain mechanisms and intelligence.* Chicago: University of Chicago Press.

Lashley, K. S. (1938) The mechanism of vision: XV. Preliminary studies of the rat's capacity for detail vision. *Journal of Genetic Psychology* 18, 123-193.

Lawson, L. (1968) Ophthalmological factors in learning disabilities. In H. R. Myklebust, ed., *Progress in learning disabilities*, vol. 1. New York: Grune and Stratton.

Leontiev, A. N. (1957) The nature and formation of human psychic properties. In B. Simon, ed., *Psychology in the Soviet Union.* Stanford: Stanford University Press.

Liberman, A. M., Cooper, F. S., Shankweiler, D., and Studdert-Kennedy, M. (1967) Perception of the speech code. *Psychological Review* 74, 431-461.

Liberman, I. Y. (1971) Basic research in speech and lateralization of language: Some implications for reading disability. *Bulletin of the Orton Society* 21, 71-87.

Liberman, I. Y., and Shankweiler, D. (1978) Speech, the alphabet and teaching to read. In L. Resnick and P. Weaver, eds., *Theory and practice of early reading.* New York: Wiley.

Liberman, I. Y., Shankweiler, D., Fischer, F. W., and Carter, B. (1974) Explicit syllable and phoneme segmentation in the young child. *Journal of Experimental Child Psychology* 18, 201-212.

Liberman, I. Y., Shankweiler, D., Liberman, A. M., Fowler, C., and Fischer, F. W. (1977) Phonetic segmentation and recoding in the beginning reader. In A. S. Reber and D. Scarborough, eds., *Toward a psychology of reading. The proceedings of the CUNY conferences.* Hillsdale, N.J.: Erlbaum Associates.

Liberman, I. Y., Shankweiler, D., Orlando, C., Harris, K. S., and Berti, F. B. (1971) Letter confusion and reversals of sequence in the beginning reader: Implications for Orton's theory of developmental dyslexia. *Cortex* 7, 127-142.

Liss, P. H., and Haith, M. M. (1970) The speed of visual processing in children and adults: Effects of backward and forward masking. *Perception and Psychophysics* 8, 396-398.

Loban, W. (1963) *The language of elementary school children.* NCTE Research Report No. 1. Urbana, Ill.: National Council of Teachers of English.

Lott, D., and Smith, F. (1970) Knowledge of intraword redundancy by beginning readers. *Psychonomic Science* 10, 343-344.

Lovell, K., Gray, E. A., and Oliver, D. E. (1964) A further study of some cognitive and other disabilities in backward readers of average non-verbal reasoning scores. *British Journal of Educational Psychology* 34, 275-279.

Lovell, K., Shapton, D., and Warren, N. S. (1964) A study of some cognitive and other disabilities in backward readers of average intelligence as assessed by non-verbal test. *British Journal of Educational Psychology* 34, 58-64.

Luria, A. R. (1961) *The role of speech in the regulation of normal and abnormal behavior.* Oxford: Pergamon Press.

Lyle, J. G. (1968) Performance of retarded readers on the memory-for-designs tests. *Perceptual and Motor Skills* 26, 851-854.

Lyle, J. G. (1969) Reading retardation and reversal tendency: A factorial study. *Child Development* 40, 832-843.

Lyle, J. G. (1970) Certain antenatal, perinatal, and developmental variables and reading retardation in middle class boys. *Child Development* 41, 481-491.

Lyle, J. G., and Goyen, J. (1968) Visual recognition, developmental lag, and strephosymbolia in reading retardation. *Journal of Abnormal Psychology* 73, 25-29.

Lyle, J. G., and Goyen, J. (1969) Performance of retarded readers on the WISC and educational tests. *Journal of Abnormal Psychology* 74, 105-112.

Lyle, J. G., and Goyen, J. D. (1975) Effect of speed of exposure and difficulty of discrimination on visual recognition of retarded readers. *Journal of Abnormal Psychology* 8, 673-676.

Maccoby, E. E. and Bee, H. (1965) Some speculations concerning the lag between perceiving and performing. *Child Development* 36, 367-378.

MacGinitie, W. H. (1969) Evaluating readiness for learning to read: A critical review and evaluation of research. *Reading Research Quarterly* 4, 396-410.

Malmo, R. B. (1959) Activation: A neuro-psychological dimension. *Psychological Review* 66, 367-386.

Malmquist, E. (1960) *Factors related to reading disabilities in the first grade of the elementary school.* Stockholm: Almqvist and Wiksell.

Mark, L. S., Shankweiler, D., Liberman, I. Y., and Fowler, C. A. (1977) Phonetic recoding and reading difficulty in beginning readers. *Memory and Cognition* 5, 623–629.

Mason, M. (1975) Reading ability and letter search time: Effects of orthographic structures defined by single-letter positional frequency. *Journal of Experimental Psychology: General* 104, 146–166.

Mason, M., and Katz, L. (1976) Visual processing of non-linguistic strings: Redundancy effects and reading ability. *Journal of Experimental Psychology: General* 105, 338–348.

Mason, M., Katz, L., and Wicklund, D. A. (1975) Immediate spatial order memory and item memory in sixth-grade children as a function of reader ability. *Journal of Educational Psychology* 67, 610–616.

Massaro, D. W. (1973) Perception of letters, words, and nonwords. *Journal of Experimental Psychology* 100, 349–353.

Massaro, D. W. (1975) *Understanding language: An information-processing analysis of speech perception, reading, and psycholinguistics.* New York: Academic Press.

Mattingly, I. G. (1972) Reading, the linguistic process, and linguistic awareness. In J. F. Kavanagh and I. G. Mattingly, eds., *Language by ear and by eye.* Cambridge, Mass.: The MIT Press.

Mattis, S., French, J. H., and Rapin, I. (1975) Dyslexia in children and young adults: Three independent neuropsychological syndromes. *Developmental Medicine and Child Neurology* 17, 150–163.

Mayzner, M. S., and Tresselt, M. E. (1965) Tables of single-letter and digram frequency counts for various word-length and letter-position combinations. *Psychonomic Monograph Supplements* 1, 2.

McCarthy, D. (1954) Language development in children. In L. Carmichael, ed., *Manual of child psychology,* 2nd ed. New York: Wiley.

McClearn, G. E. (1977) Comments on Dr. Freya Owen: Dyslexia—Genetic aspects. Paper presented at the National Institute of Mental Health conference, Bethesda, Md.

McClelland, J. L. (1976) Preliminary letter identification in the perception of words and non-words. *Journal of Experimental Psychology: Human Perceptions and Performance* 3, 80–91.

McCready, E. B. (1910) Biological variations in the higher cerebral centers causing retardation. *Archives of Pediatrics* 27, 506–513.

McGrady, H. J. (1968) Language pathology and learning disabilities. In H. R. Myklebust, ed., *Progress in learning disabilities.* New York: Grune and Stratton.

McNeill, D. A. (1970) *The acquisition of language: The study of developmental psycholinguistics.* New York: Harper & Row.

Menyuk, P. (1963) Syntactic structures in the language of children. *Child Development* 34, 407–422.

Menyuk, P. (1964) Syntactic rules used by children from preschool through first grade. *Child Development* 35, 533–546.

Miller, G. A. (1956) The magical number seven, plus or minus two: Some limits on our capacity for processing information. *Psychological Review* 63, 81–97.

Miller, G. A. (1969) The organization of lexical memory: Are word associations sufficient? In G. A. Talland and N. C. Waugh, eds., *The pathology of memory*. New York: Academic Press.

Milner, A. D., and Bryant, P. D. (1970) Cross-modal matching by young children. *Journal of Comparative and Physiological Psychology* 71, 453–458.

Milner, B. (1962) Laterality effects in audition. In V. B. Mountcastle, ed., *Interhemispheric relations and cerebral dominance*. Baltimore: Johns Hopkins Press.

Milner, B. (1967) Brain mechanisms suggested by studies of temporal lobes. In C. H. Millikan and F. L. Darley, eds., *Brain mechanisms underlying speech and language*, New York: Grune and Stratton.

Milner, B. (1971) Interhemispheric differences in the localization of psychological processes in man. *British Medical Bulletin* 27, 272–277.

Money, J. (1966) On learning and not learning to read. In J. Money, ed., *The disabled reader: Education of the dyslexic child*. Baltimore: Johns Hopkins Press.

Monroe, M. (1932) *Children who cannot read*. Chicago: University of Chicago Press.

Morgan, W. P. (1896) A case of congenital word-blindness. *British Medical Journal* 11, 378.

Morrison, F. J., Giordani, B., and Nagy, J. (1977) Reading disability: An information-processing analysis. *Science* 196, 77–79.

Muehl, S., and Kremenak, S. (1966) Ability to match information within and between auditory and visual sense modalities and subsequent reading achievement. *Journal of Educational Psychology* 57, 230–239.

Myklebust, H. R., and Johnson, D. J. (1962) Dyslexia in children. *Exceptional Children* 29, 14–25.

Neisser, A. (1967) *Cognitive psychology*. New York: Appleton.

Nichols, A. S. (1947) *To optometry this 1946 yearbook*. Published by the author.

Nielsen, H. H., and Ringe, K. (1969) Visuo-perceptive and visuo-motor performance of children with reading disabilities. *Scandinavian Journal of Psychology* 10, 225–231.

Nodine, C. F., and Evans, J. D. (1969) Eye movements of prereaders containing letters of high and low confusability. *Perception and Psychophysics* 6, 39–41.

Nodine, C. F., and Lang, N. J. (1971) The development of visual scanning strategies for differentiating words. *Developmental Psychology* 5, 221–232.

Norman, D. A. (1972) The role of memory in the understanding of language. In J. F. Kavanagh and I. G. Mattingly, eds., *Language by ear and by eye.* Cambridge, Mass.: The MIT Press.

Oakan, R., Wiener, M., and Cromer, W. (1971) Identification, organization, and reading comprehension for good and poor readers. *Journal of Educational Psychology* 62, 1, 71–78.

O'Donnell, R. C., Griffin, W. J., and Norris, R. C. (1967) *Syntax of kindergarten and elementary school children: A transformational analysis.* NCTE Research Report No. 8. Champaign, Ill.: National Council of Teachers of English.

Oldfield, R. C. (1966) Things, words and the brain. *Quarterly Journal of Experimental Psychology* 18, 340–353.

Oldfield, R. C., and Wingfield, A. (1965) Response latencies in naming objects. *Quarterly Journal of Experimental Psychology* 17, 273–281.

Olson, D. R. (1970) *Cognitive development: The child's acquisition of diagonality.* New York: Academic Press.

Olson, D. R., and Baker, N. E. (1969) Children's recall of spatial orientation of objects. *The Journal of Genetic Psychology* 114, 273–281.

Olson, W. C. (1949) *Child development.* Boston: Heath.

Orton, S. T. (1925) "Word-blindness" in school children. *Archives of Neurology and Psychiatry* 14, 581–615.

Orton, S. T. (1931) Special disability in spelling. *Bulletin of the Neurological Institute of New York* 1, 2.

Orton, S. T. (1937) *Reading, writing and speech problems in children.* London: Chapman and Hall.

Orton, S. T., and Gillingham, A. (1933) Special disability in writing. *Bulletin of the Neurological Institute of New York* 3, 1–32.

Over, R., and Over, J. (1967) Detection and recognition of mirror-image obliques by young children. *Journal of Comparative and Physiological Psychology* 64, 467–470.

Owen, F. W. (1978) Dyslexia: Genetic aspects. In A. L. Benton and D. Pearl, eds., *Dyxlexia: An appraisal of current knowledge.* New York: Oxford University Press.

Owen, F. W., Adams, P. A., Forrest, T., Stolz, L. M., and Fisher, S. (1971) Learning disorders in children: Sibling studies. *Monographs of the Society for Research in Child Development* 36, No. 4.

Paivio, A. (1971) *Imagery and verbal processes.* New York: Holt, Rinehart & Winston.

Palermo, D. S., and Molfese, D. L. (1972) Language acquisition from age 5 onward. *Psychological Bulletin* 68, 409–428.

Parducci, A. (1965) Category judgment: A range-frequency model. *Psychological Review* 72, 407–418.

Paris, S., and Carter, A. (1973) Semantic and constructive aspects of sentence memory in children. *Developmental Psychology* 9, 109–113.

Pavlov, I. P. (1927) *Conditioned reflexes.* London: Oxford University Press.

Perfetti, C. A., Bell, L. C., Hogaboam, T. W., and Goldman, S. R. (1977) Verbal processing speed and reading skill. Paper presented at the Psychonomics Society, Washington, D.C.

Perfetti, C. A., Finger, E., and Hogaboam, T. W. (1978) Sources of vocalization latency differences between skilled and less-skilled readers. *Journal of Educational Psychology, 70,* 5, 730–739.

Perfetti, C. A., and Goldman, S. R. (1976) Discourse memory and reading comprehension skill. *Journal of Verbal Learning and Verbal Behavior* 14, 33–42.

Perfetti, C. A., and Hogaboam, T. W. (1975) The relationship between single word decoding and reading comprehension skill. *Journal of Educational Psychology* 67, 461–469.

Perfetti, C. A., and Lesgold, A. M. (1978) Discourse comprehension and sources of individual differences. In M. A. Just and P. A. Carpenter, eds., *Cognitive processes in comprehension.* Hillsdale, N.J.: Erlbaum Associates.

Piaget, J. (1961) *Les mécanismes perceptifs: Modèles probabilistes, analyse génétique, relations avec l'intelligence.* Paris: Presses Universitaires de France.

Piaget, J. (1963) *The psychology of intelligence.* New York: Littlefield, Adams.

Piaget, J., and Inhelder, B. (1956) *The child's conception of space.* New York: Humanities Press.

Piaget, J., and Morf, A. (1958) Les isomorphismes partiels entre les structures logiques et les structures perceptives. In J. Piaget, ed., *Études d'Epistémologies génétique.* Paris: Presses Universitaires de France.

Pick, A. D. (1965) Improvement of visual and tactual form discrimination. *Journal of Experimental Psychology* 69, 331–339.

Pick, A. D., and Frankel, G. W. (1974) A developmental study of strategies of visual selectivity. *Child Development* 45, 1162–1165.

Pick, H. L. (1970) Systems of perceptual and perceptual motor development. In J. P. Hill, ed., *Minnesota symposia on child psychology,* Vol. 4. Minneapolis: University of Minnesota Press.

Pinard, A., and Laurendeau, M. (1970) A scale of mental development based on the theory of Piaget: Description of a project. In I. J. Athey and D. O. Rubadeau, eds., *Educational implications of Piaget's theory.* Lexington, Mass.: Ginn.

Pollock, R. H. (1965) Backward figural masking as a function of chronological age and intelligence. *Bulletin of the Psychonomic Society* 3, 2, 65–66.

Pollock, R. H., Ptashne, R. I., and Carter, D. J. (1969) The effects of age and intelligence on the dark interval threshold. *Perception and Psychophysics* 6, 50–52.

Polzella, D. J., and Rohrman, N. L. (1970) Psychological aspects of transitive verbs. *Journal of Verbal Learning and Verbal Behavior* 9, 537–540.

Pope, P., and Snyder, R. T. (1970) Modification of selected Bender designs and interpretation of the first graders' visual-perceptual maturation with implications for Gestalt theory. *Perceptual and Motor Skills* 30, 263–267.

Posner, M. I., Boies, S. J., Eichelman, W. H., and Taylor, R. L. (1969) Retention of visual and name codes of single letters. *Journal of Experimental Psychology Monographs* 79, 1–13.

Posner, M. I., Lewis, J. L., and Conrad, C. (1972) Component processes in reading: A performance analysis. In J. F. Kavanagh and I. G. Mattingly, eds., *Language by ear and by eye.* Cambridge, Mass.: The MIT Press.

Pressley, M. (1977) Imagery and children's learning: Putting the picture in developmental perspective. *Review of Educational Research* 47, 585–622.

Preston, M. S., Guthrie, J. T., and Childs, B. (1974) Visual evoked responses (VERs) in normal and disabled readers. *Psychophysiology* 11, 452–457.

Raab, S., Deutsch, M., and Friedman, A. (1960) Perceptual shifting and set in normal school children of different reading levels. *Perceptual and Motor Skills* 10, 187–192.

Rabinovitch, R. D. (1959) Reading and learning disabilities. In S. Arieti, ed., *American handbook of psychiatry.* New York: Basic Books.

Rabinovitch, R. D. (1968) Reading problems in children: Definitions and classification. In A. Keeney and V. Keeney, eds., *Dyslexia: Diagnosis and treatment of reading disorders.* St. Louis: C. V. Mosby.

Raulin, A. E. (1962) Study of the relationship between silent reading and oral vocabulary of elementary school children. Doctoral dissertation, New York University.

Raven, J. C. (1956) *Standard progressive matrices.* New York: Psychological Corporation.

Raven, J. C. (1962) *The Raven Progressive Matrices.* New York: Psychological Corporation.

Raven, R. J., and Salzer, R. T. (1974) Piaget and reading instruction. In R. B. Ruddell, E. J. Ahern, E. M. Hartson, and J. Taylor, eds., *Resources in reading-language instruction.* Englewood Cliffs, N.J.: Prentice-Hall.

Ravenette, A. T. (1961) Vocabulary level and reading attainment. *British Journal of Educational Psychology* 31, 96.

Rayner, K., and Kaiser, J. S. (1975) Reading mutilated text. *Journal of Educational Psychology* 67, 301–306.

Reicher, G. (1969) Perceptual recognition as a function of meaningfulness of stimulus material. *Journal of Experimental Psychology* 81, 275–280.

Reinhold, M. (1963) The effect of laterality on reading and writing. *Proceedings of the Royal Society of Medicine* (London) 56, 203–206.

Renshaw, S. (1930) The errors of cutaneous localization and the effect of practice on the localizing movement in children and adults. *Journal of Genetic Psychology* 29, 493–496.

Renshaw, S. (1939–1965) *Psychological optics*. Series 1 through 25.

Roach, E., and Kephart, N. (1966) *The Purdue-Perceptual-Motor Survey*. Columbus, Ohio: Charles E. Merrill.

Roberts, K. P. (1976) Piaget's theory of conservation and reading readiness. *The Reading Teacher* 30, 3, 246–250.

Robinson, H. M. (1946) *Why pupils fail in reading*. Chicago: University of Chicago Press.

Robinson, H. M. (1971) Perceptual training: Does it result in reading improvement? Paper presented at the convention of the International Reading Association, Atlantic City, N.J.

Rosen, C. L. (1966) An experimental study of visual perceptual training and reading achievement in first grade. *Perceptual Motor Skills* 22, 979–986.

Rosen, C. L., and Ohnmacht, F. (1968) Perception, readiness, and reading achievement in first grade. In *Perception and Reading*. Proceedings of the 12th Annual Convention of the International Reading Association. Newark, Del.

Rosenbaum, P. S. (1967) The grammar of English predicate complement construction. Cambridge, Mass.: The MIT Press.

Rosinski, R. R., and Wheeler, K. E. (1972) Children's use of orthographic structure in word discrimination. *Psychonomic Science* 26, 97–98.

Rosner, J. (1972) The development and validation of an individualized perceptual skills curriculum. Learning Research and Development Center, University of Pittsburgh.

Rozin, P., and Gleitman, L. R. (1977) The structure and acquisition of reading, 11: The reading process and the acquisition of the alphabetic principle. In A. S. Reber and D. L. Scarborough, eds., *Toward a psychology of reading. The proceedings of the CUNY conferences*. New York: Wiley.

Rudel, R. G., Denckla, M. B., and Spalten, E. (1976) Paired associate learning of Morse code and Braille letter names by dyslexic and normal children. *Cortex* 12, 61–70.

Rudel, R. G., and Teuber, H. L. (1963) Discrimination of direction of line in children. *Journal of Comparative and Physiological Psychology* 56, 892–898.

Rudnick, M., Sterritt, G. M., and Flax, M. (1967) Auditory and visual rhythm perception and reading ability. *Child Development* 38, 581–588.

Rumelhart, D. E., and Ortony, A. (1977) The representation of knowledge in memory. In R. C. Anderson, R. J. Spiro and W. E. Montague, eds., *Schooling and the acquisition of knowledge.* New York: Wiley.

Salapatek, P., and Kessen, W. (1966) Visual scanning of triangles by the human newborn. *Journal of Experimental Child Psychology* 3, 155–167.

Sampson, O. C. (1962) Reading skill at eight years in relation to speech and other factors. *The British Journal of Educational Psychology* 32, 12–17.

Samuels, S. J. (1972) The effect of letter-names knowledge on learning to read. *American Educational Research Journal* 1, 65–74.

Samuels, S. J., Begy, G., and Chen, C. C. (1975–1976) Comparison of word recognition speed and strategies of less skilled and more highly skilled readers. *Reading Research Quarterly* 1, 73–86.

Satz, P., and Friel, J. (1974) Some predictive antecedents of specific reading disability: A preliminary two-year follow-up. *Journal of Learning Disabilities* 7, 437–444.

Satz, P., Friel, J., and Rudegeair, F. (1974a) Differential changes in the acquisition of developmental skills in children who later become dyslexic: A three-year follow-up. In D. Stein, J. Rosen, and N. Butters, eds., *Plasticity and recovery of function in the central nervous system.* New York: Academic Press.

Satz, P., Friel, J., and Rudegeair, F. (1974b) Some predictive antecedents of specific reading disability: A two- three- and four-year follow-up. *The Hyman Blumberg Symposium of Research in Early Childhood Education.* Baltimore: Johns Hopkins Press.

Satz, P., and Sparrow, S. S. (1970) Specific developmental dyslexia: A theoretical formulation. In D. J. Bakker and P. Satz, eds., *Specific reading disability: Advances in theory and method.* Rotterdam: Rotterdam University Press.

Satz, P., Taylor, H. G., Friel, J., and Fletcher, J. M. (1978) Some developmental and predictive precursors of reading disabilities: A six year follow-up. In A. L. Benton and D. Pearl, eds., *Dyslexia: An appraisal of current knowledge.* New York: Oxford University Press, pp. 313–348.

Savin, H. B. (1972) What the child knows about speech when he starts to learn to read. In J. F. Kavanagh and I. G. Mattingly, eds., *Language by ear and by eye.* Cambridge, Mass.: The MIT Press.

Schilder, P. (1935) *The image and appearance of the human body.* Psyche Monographs No. 4. London: Kegan Paul.

Schilder, P. (1944) Congenital alexia and its relation to optic perception. *Journal of Genetic Psychology* 65, 67–88.

Schonell, F. E. (1956) *Educating spastic children.* Edinburgh: Oliver and Boyd.

Schulte, C. (1967) A study of the relationship between oral language and reading achievement in second graders. Doctoral dissertation, University of Iowa.

Scriven, M. (1973) The methodology of evaluation. In B. Worthen and J. Sanders, eds., *Educational evaluation: Theory and practice.* Worthington, Ohio: Charles Jones.

Sekuler, R. W., and Houlihan, K. (1968) Discrimination of mirror-images: Choice time analysis of human adult performance. *Quarterly Journal of Experimental Psychology* 20, 204-207.

Sekuler, R. W., and Rosenblith, J. R. (1964) Discrimination of direction of line and the effect of stimulus alignment. *Psychonomic Science* 1, 143-144.

Semmes, T., Weinstein, S., Ghent, L., and Teuber, H. L. (1955) Spatial orientation in man after cerebral lesion. *Journal of Psychology* 39, 237-244.

Senf, G. M. (1969) Development of immediate memory for bisensory stimuli in normal children with learning disorders. *Developmental Psychology Monograph,* 1, 6.

Senf, G. M., and Feshbach, S. (1970) Development of bisensory memory in culturally deprived, dyslexic, and normal readers. *Journal of Educational Psychology* 61, 461-470.

Senf, G. M., and Freundl, P. C. (1971) Memory and attention factors in specific learning disabilities. *Journal of Learning Disabilities* 4, 94-106.

Senf, G. M., and Freundl, P. C. (1972) Sequential auditory and visual memory in learning disabled children. Proceedings of the Annual Convention of the American Psychological Association, 7, 511-512.

Shankweiler, D., and Liberman, A. M. (1972) Misreading: A search for causes. In J. F. Kavanagh and I. G. Mattingly, eds., *Language by ear and by eye.* Cambridge, Mass.: The MIT Press.

Shankweiler, D., and Liberman, I. Y. (1976) Exploring the relations between reading and speech. In R. M. Knights and D. J. Bakker, eds., *Neuropsychology of learning disorders: Theoretical approaches.* Baltimore: University Park Press.

Shapiro, M. B., Brierley, J., Slater, P., and Beech, H. R. (1962) Experimental studies of perceptual anomaly, VII. *Journal of Mental Science* 108, 655-668.

Shipley, T., and Jones, R. W. (1969) Initial observations on sensory interaction and the theory of dyslexia. *Journal of Communication Disorders* 2, 295-311.

Sidman, M., and Kirk, B. (1974) Letter reversals in naming, writing, and matching to sample. *Child Development* 45, 616-625.

Silberberg, N., and Feldt, L. (1968) Intellectual and perceptual correlates of reading difficulties. *Journal of School Psychology* 6, 237-245.

Silver, A. A. (1961) Diagnostic considerations in children with reading disability. *Bulletin of the Orton Society* 11, 5-12.

Silver, A. A., and Hagin, R. (1960) Specific reading disability: Delineation of the syndrome and relationship to cerebral dominance. *Comparative Psychiatry* 1, 2, 126-134.

Silver, A. A., and Hagin, R. A. (1970) Visual perception in children with reading disabilities. In F. A. Young and D. B. Lindsley, eds., *Early experience and visual information processing in perceptual and reading disorders.* Washington: National Academy of Sciences.

Simon, H. (1972) On the development of the processor. In. S. Farnham-Diggory, ed., *Information processing in children.* New York: Academic Press.

Skeffington, A. M. (1959) The role of a convex lens. *Journal of the American Optometric Association* 31, 5, 374-378.

Slosson, R. L. (1963) *Slosson Intelligence Test.* East Aurora, New York: Slosson Educational Publications.

Smith, F. (1971) *Understanding reading: A psycholinguistic analysis of reading and learning to read.* New York: Holt, Rinehart & Winston.

Smith, F. (1973) *Psycholinguistics and reading.* New York: Holt, Rinehart & Winston.

Smith, N. B. (1928) Matching ability as a factor in first grade reading. *Journal of Educational Psychology* 19, 560-571.

Sparrow, S., and Satz, P. (1970) Dyslexia, laterality and neurophsychological development. In D. J. Bakker and P. Satz, eds., *Specific reading disability: Advances in theory and method.* Rotterdam: Rotterdam University Press.

Sperling, G. (1960) The information available in brief visual presentations. *Psychological Monographs* 74, No. 20 (Whole No. 498).

Sperry, R. W. (1964) The great cerebral commissure. *Scientific American* 210, 42-52.

Spring, C. (1976) Encoding speed and memory span in dyslexic children. *The Journal of Special Education* 10, 1, 35-40.

Spring, C., and Capps, C. (1974) Encoding speed, rehearsal, and probed recall of dyslexic boys. *Journal of Educational Psychology* 66, 780-786.

Stake, R. (1967) The countenance of educational evaluation. *Teachers College Record* 68, 523-540.

Stanley, G. (1975a) Two-part stimulus integration and specific reading disability. *Perceptual and Motor Skills* 41, 873-874.

Stanley, G. (1975b) Visual memory processes in dyslexia. In D. Deutsch and J. A. Deutsch, eds., *Short-term memory.* New York: Academic Press.

Stanley, G. (1976) The processing of digits by children with specific reading disability (dyslexia). *British Journal of Educational Psychology* 46, 81-84.

Stanley, G., and Hall, R. (1973) Short-term visual information processing in dyslexics. *Child Development* 44, 841-844.

Stanley, G., and Malloy, M. (1975) Retinal and visual information storage. *Acta Psychologica* 39, 283-288.

Stanley, J., and Hopkins, K. (1972) *Educational and psychological measurement and evaluation*. Englewood Cliffs, N.J.: Prentice-Hall.

Steger, J. A., Vellutino, F. R., and Meshoulam, U. (1972) Visual-tactile and tactile-tactile paired associate learning in normal and poor readers. *Perceptual and Motor Skills* 35, 263–266.

Steiner, R., Wiener, M., and Cromer, W. (1971) Comprehension training and identification for poor and good readers. *Journal of Educational Psychology* 62, 506–513.

Steinheiser, R., and Guthrie, J. T. (1975) Reading ability and efficiency of graphemic-phonemic encoding. Unpublished manuscript.

Steinheiser, R., and Guthrie, J. T. (1974) Scanning times through prose and word strings for various targets by normal and disabled readers. *Perceptual and Motor Skills* 39, 931–938.

Sternberg, S. (1969) Memory scanning: Mental processes revealed by reaction-time experiments. *American Scientist* 57, 421–457.

Sterritt, G. M., and Rudnick, M. (1966) Auditory and visual rhythm perception in relation to reading ability in fourth-grade boys. *Perceptual and Motor Skills* 22, 859–864.

Stevenson, H. W., Parker, T., Wilkinson, A., Hegion, A., and Fish, E. (1976) Longitudinal study of individual differences in cognitive development and scholastic achievement. *Journal of Educational Psychology* 68, 377–400.

Straub, R. (1976) Discourse processing: Effects of given–new information structure on discourse memory of skilled and less-skilled readers. Master's thesis, University of Pittsburgh.

Strauss, A. A., and Lehtinen, L. E. (1947) *Psychopathology and education of the brain-injured child*. New York: Grune and Stratton.

Strickland, R. G. (1962) The language of elementary school children: Its relationship to the language of reading textbooks and the quality of reading of selected children. *Bulletin of the School of Education, Indiana University* 38 (July). Bloomington, Indiana.

Stuart, I. R. (1967) Perceptual style and reading ability: Implications for an instructional approach. *Perceptual and Motor Skills* 24, 135–138.

Stufflebeam, D. (1973) Educational evaluation and decision-making. In B. Worthen and J. Sanders, eds., *Educational evaluation: Theory and practice*. Worthington, Ohio: Charles Jones.

Sundberg, N. (1961) The practice of psychological testing in clinical services throughout the United States. *American Psychologist* 16, 79–83.

Supramaniam, S., and Audley, R. J. (1976) The role of naming difficulties in reading backwardness. Paper presented at the British Association Annual Conference, London.

Sutherland, N. S. (1957) Visual discrimination of orientation by Octopus. *British Journal of Psychology* 48, 55–71.

Symmes, J. S., and Rapoport, J. L. (1972) Unexpected reading failure. *American Journal of Orthopsychiatry* 42, 1, 82–91.

Taylor, M. M., and Creelman, C. D. (1967) PEST: Efficiency estimates on probability functions. *The Journal of the Acoustical Society of America* 41, 782–787.

Taylor, W. (1953) "Cloze procedure": A new tool for measuring readability. *Journalism Quarterly* 30, 415–453.

Teuber, H. -L. (1960) Perception. In J. Field, H. W. Magoun, and V. E. Hall, eds., *Handbook of physiology*, vol. 3. Washington, D.C.: American Physiological Society.

Thompson, L. (1966) *Reading disability*. Springfield, Ill.: Charles C. Thomas.

Thompson, M. C., and Massaro, D. W. (1973) The role of visual information and redundancy in reading. *Journal of Experimental Psychology* 98, 49–54.

Thorndike, E. L., and Lorge, I. (1944) *The teacher's word book of 30,000 words*. New York: Teacher's College, Columbia University.

Tinker, M. A. (1965) *Bases for effective reading*. Minneapolis: University of Minnesota Press.

Torgesen, J., and Goldman, T. (1977) Verbal rehearsal and short term memory in reading-disabled children. *Child Development* 48, 1, 56–60.

Treiman, R. A. (1976) Children's ability to segment speech into syllables and phonemes as related to their reading ability. Unpublished manuscript, Department of Psychology, Yale University.

Trueman, R. H. (1965) Mirror writing. *Postgraduate Medicine*, pp. 469–476. Philadelphia: University of Pennsylvania School of Medicine.

Tuddenham, R. D. (1970) Psychometricizing Piaget's *Methode Clinique*. In I. J. Athey and D. O. Rubadeau, eds., *Educational implications of Piaget's theory*. Lexington, Mass.: Ginn.

Tulving, E. (1972) Episodic and semantic memory. In E. Tulving and W. Donaldson, eds., *Organization of memory*. New York: Academic Press.

Tulving, E., and Donaldson, W. (1972) *Organization of memory*. New York: Academic Press.

Underwood, B. J. (1972) Are we overloading memory? In A. W. Melton and E. Martin, eds., *Coding processes in human memory*. Washington, D.C.: V. H. Winston.

Uzgiris, I. C., and Hunt, J. McV. (1975) *Assessment in infancy: Ordinal scales of psychological development*. Urbana: University of Illinois Press.

Vande Voort, L., and Senf, G. M. (1973) Audiovisual integration in retarded readers. *Journal of Learning Disabilities* 6, 170–179.

Vande Voort, L., Senf, G. M., and Benton, A. L. (1972) Development of audiovisual integration in normal and retarded readers. *Child Development* 44, 1260–1272.

Vellutino, F. R. (1978) Toward an understanding of dyslexia: Psychological factors in specific reading disability. In A. Benton and D. Pearl, eds., *Dyslexia: An appraisal of current knowledge.* New York: Oxford University Press.

Vellutino, F. R., Bentley, W., and Phillips, F. (1978) Inter- versus intrahemispheric learning in disabled and normal readers. *Developmental Medicine and Child Neurology* 20, 71–80.

Vellutino, F. R., and Connolly, C. (1971) The training of paraprofessionals as remedial reading assistants in an inner-city school. *The Reading Teacher* 24, 506–512.

Vellutino, F. R., DeSetto, L., and Steger, J. A. (1972) Categorical judgment and the Wepman Test of Auditory Discrimination. *Journal of Speech and Hearing Disorders* 37, 2, 252–257.

Vellutino, F. R., Harding, C. J., Phillips, F., and Steger, J. A. (1975) Differential transfer in poor and normal readers. *Journal of Genetic Psychology* 126, 3–18.

Vellutino, F. R., Pruzek, R., Steger, J. A., and Meshoulam, U. (1973) Immediate visual recall in poor and normal readers as a function of orthographic-linguistic familiarity. *Cortex* 9, 368–384.

Vellutino, F. R., Smith, H., Steger, J. A., and Kaman, M. (1975) Reading disability: Age differences and the perceptual deficit hypothesis. *Child Development* 46, 487–493.

Vellutino, F. R., Steger, J. A., DeSetto, L., and Phillips, F. (1975) Immediate and delayed recognition of visual stimuli in poor and normal readers. *Journal of Experimental Child Psychology* 19, 223–232.

Vellutino, F. R., Steger, J. A., Harding, C., and Phillips, F. (1975) Verbal vs non verbal paired-associates learning in poor and normal readers. *Neuropsychologia* 13, 75–82.

Vellutino, F. R., Steger, J. A., Kaman, M., and DeSetto, L. (1975) Visual form perception in deficient and normal readers as a function of age and orthographic linguistic familiarity. *Cortex* 11, 22–30.

Vellutino, F. R., Steger, J. A., and Kandel, G. (1972) Reading disability: An investigation of the perceptual deficit hypothesis. *Cortex* 8, 106–118.

Vellutino, F. R., Steger, B. M., Moyer, S. C., Harding, C. J., and Niles, J. A. (1977) Has the perceptual deficit hypothesis led us astray? *Journal of Learning Disabilities* 10, 6, 375–385.

Vellutino, F. R., Steger, J. A., and Pruzek, R. (1973) Inter- vs intrasensory deficit in paired associate learning in poor and normal readers. *Canadian Journal of Behavioral Science* 5, 2, 111–123.

Venezky, R. L. (1970) *The structure of English orthography.* The Hague: Mouton.

Vernon, M. D. (1971) *Reading and its difficulties.* Cambridge, England: Cambridge University Press.

Vernon, M. D. (1977) Varieties of deficiency in the reading processes. *Harvard Educational Review* 47, 396–410.

Vernon, P. E. (1965) Environmental handicaps and intellectual development. *British Journal of Educational Psychology* 35, 9–20, 117–126.

Vogel, S. A. (1974) Syntactic abilities in normal and dyslexic children. *Journal of Learning Disabilities* 7, 2, 103–109.

Vurpillot, E. (1968) The development of scanning strategies and their relation to visual differentiation. *Journal of Experimental Child Psychology* 6, 632–650.

Vygotsky, L. (1962) *Thought and language.* New York: Wiley.

Waller, T. G. (1976) Children's recognition memory for written sentences: A comparison of good and poor readers. *Child Development* 47, 90–95.

Warren, R. M. (1968) Relation of verbal transformations to other perceptual phenomena. In Conference Publication No. 42, IEE/NPL Conference on Pattern Recognition. Institute of Electrical Engineers, Teddington, England.

Warren, R. M. (1974) Auditory temporal discrimination by trained listeners. *Cognitive Psychology* 6, 237–256.

Warren, R. M., Obusek, C. J., Farmer, R. M., and Warren, R. P. (1969) Auditory sequence: Confusion of patterns other than speech and music. *Science* 164, 586–587.

Warrington, E. K. (1967) The incidence of verbal disability associated with retardation in reading. *Neuropsychologia* 5, 175–179.

Watts, A. F. (1948) *The language and mental development of children.* Boston: Heath.

Waugh, N. C., and Norman, D. A. (1965) Primary memory. *Psychological Review* 72, 89–104.

Weber, R. M. (1970) First graders' use of grammatical context in reading. In H. Levin and J. P. Williams, eds., *Basic studies in reading.* New York: Basic Books.

Wechsler, D. (1949) *Wechsler Intelligence Scale for Children.* New York: Psychological Corporation.

Wechsler, D. (1974) *Wechsler Intelligence Scale for Children–Revised.* New York: Psychological Corporation.

Wechsler, D., and Hagin, R. A. (1964) The problem of axial rotation in reading disability. *Perceptual and Motor Skills* 19, 319–326.

Weiner, J., Barnsley, R. H., and Rabinovitch, M. S. (1970) Serial order ability in good and poor readers. *Canadian Journal of Behavioral Science* 2, 116–123.

Weiner, M., and Cromer, W. (1967) Reading and reading difficulty: A conceptual analysis. *Harvard Educational Review* 37, 620–643.

Weinstein, R., and Rabinovitch, M. S. (1971) Sentence structure and retention in good and poor readers. *Journal of Educational Psychology* 62, 1, 25–30.

Wepman, J. M. (1958) *Auditory Discrimination Test.* Chicago: Language Research Associates.

Wepman, J. M. (1960) Auditory discrimination, speech, and reading. *The Elementary School Journal* 9, 325–333.

Wepman, J. M. (1961) The interrelationships of hearing, speech, and reading. *The Reading Teacher* 14, 245–247.

Werner, E. E., Simonian, K., and Smith, R. S. (1967) Reading achievement, language functioning and perceptual-motor development of 10- and 11-year-olds. *Perceptual Motor Skills* 25, 409–420.

Werner, H. (1948) *Comparative psychology of mental development.* New York: International Universities Press.

Werner, H., and Strauss, A. A. (1952) Toward a general theory of perception. *Psychological Review* 59, 4.

Wertheimer, M. (1923) Principles of perceptual organization. *Psychologische Forschung* 4, 321–350. Translated and abridged in D. D. Beardslee and M. Wertheimer, eds., *Readings in perception.* New York: Van Nostrand, 1958.

Wheeler, D. (1970) Processes in word recognition. *Cognitive Psychology* 1, 59–85.

Wickens, D. D. (1970) Encoding categories of words: An empirical approach to meaning. *Psychological Review* 77, 1, 1–15.

Wiig, E. H., Semel, M. S., and Crouse, M. B. (1973) The use of English mophology by high-risk and learning disabled children. *Journal of Learning Disabilities* 6, 457–465.

Willows, D. M. (1974) Reading between the lines: Selective attention in good and poor readers. *Child Development* 45, 408–415.

Wineman, J. H. (1971) Cognitive style and reading ability. *California Journal of Educational Research* 22, 2, 74–79.

Witkin, H. A., Dyk, R. B., Paterson, H. F., Goodenough, D. R., and Karp, S. A. (1962) *Psychological differentiation now.* New York: Wiley.

Wohlwill, J. F. (1973) *The study of behavioral development.* New York: Academic Press.

Wohlwill, J. F., and Wiener, M. (1964) Discrimination of form orientation in young children. *Child Development* 35, 1113–1125.

Wolfe, L. S. (1941) Differential factors in specific reading disability: I. Laterality of function. *The Journal of Genetic Psychology* 58, 45–56.

Woodworth, R. S. (1906) Vision and localization during eye movements. *Psychological Bulletin*

Worthen, B., and Sanders, J., eds. (1973) *Educational evaluation: Theory and practice.* Worthington, Ohio: Charles Jones.

Yeni-Komshian, G. H., Isenberg, D., and Goldberg, H. (1975) Cerebral dominance and reading disability: Left visual field deficit in poor readers. *Neuropsychologia* 13, 83–94.

Young, F. A., and Lindsley, D. B. (1970) *Early experience and visual information processing in perceptual and reading disorders.* Washington: National Academy of Sciences.

Zach, L., Kaufman, J. (1969) The effect of verbal labelling on visual motor performance. *Journal of Learning Disabilities* 2, 218–222.

Zangwill, O. L. (1962) Dyslexia in relation to cerebral dominance. In J. Money, ed., *Reading disability: Progress and research needs in dyslexia.* Baltimore: Johns Hopkins Press.

Zifcak, M. (1976) Phonological awareness and reading acquisition in first grade children. Doctoral dissertation, University of Connecticut.

Zigmond, N. (1966) Intrasensory and intersensory processes in normal and dyslexic children. Doctoral dissertation, Northwestern University.

Zinchenko, V. P. (1966) Perception as action. In volume on Perception and Action, Symposium 30, Proceedings 18th International Congress of Psychology, Moscow.

Zurif, E. B., and Carson, G. (1970) Dyslexia in relation to cerebral dominance and temporal analysis. *Neuropsychologia* 8, 351–361.

INDEX